*Macbeth: A Dagger of the Mind*

*Iago: The Strategies of Evil*

*Lear: The Great Image of Authority*

*Cleopatra: I Am Fire and Air*

*Falstaff: Give Me Life*

*The Daemon Knows: Literary Greatness and the American Sublime*

*The Shadow of a Great Rock: A Literary Appreciation of the King James Bible*

*The Anatomy of Influence: Literature as a Way of Life*

*Till I End My Song: A Gathering of Last Poems*

*Fallen Angels*

*American Religious Poems: An Anthology*

*Jesus and Yahweh: The Names Divine*

*Where Shall Wisdom Be Found?*

*The Best Poems of the English Language: From Chaucer Through Frost*

*Hamlet: Poem Unlimited*

*Genius: A Mosaic of One Hundred Exemplary Creative Minds*

*Stories and Poems for Extremely Intelligent Children of All Ages*

*How to Read and Why*

*Shakespeare: The Invention of the Human*

*Omens of Millennium: The Gnosis of Angels, Dreams, and Resurrection*

*The Western Canon: The Books and School of the Ages*

*The American Religion: The Emergence of the Post-Christian Nation*

The Book of J

Ruin the Sacred Truths: Poetry and Belief from the Bible to the Present

The Poetics of Influence: New and Selected Criticism

The Breaking of the Vessels

The Strong Light of the Canonical

Agon: Towards a Theory of Revisionism

The Flight to Lucifer: A Gnostic Fantasy

Deconstruction and Criticism

Wallace Stevens: The Poems of Our Climate

Figures of Capable Imagination

Poetry and Repression: Revisionism from Blake to Stevens

Kabbalah and Criticism

A Map of Misreading

The Anxiety of Influence: A Theory of Poetry

The Ringers in the Tower: Studies in Romantic Tradition

Yeats

Romanticism and Consciousness

Commentary on David V. Endman's Edition of The Poetry of William Blake

Selected Writings of Walter Pater

The Literary Criticism of John Ruskin

Blake's Apocalypse: A Study in Poetic Argument

The Visionary Company: A Reading of English Romantic Poetry

Shelley's Mythmaking

Possessed by Memory

# Possessed by Memory

## *The Inward Light of Criticism*

# Harold Bloom

ALFRED A. KNOPF

NEW YORK

2019

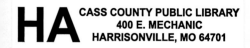

THIS IS A BORZOI BOOK
PUBLISHED BY ALFRED A. KNOPF

Copyright © 2019 by Harold Bloom

Published in the United States by Alfred A. Knopf,
a division of Penguin Random House LLC, New York,
and distributed in Canada by Random House of Canada,
a division of Penguin Random House Canada Limited, Toronto.

www.aaknopf.com

Knopf, Borzoi Books, and the colophon are registered trademarks of
Penguin Random House LLC.

Library of Congress Cataloging-in-Publication Data
Names: Bloom, Harold, author.
Title: Possessed by memory : the inward light of criticism / Harold Bloom.
Description: First edition. | New York : Alfred A. Knopf, 2019. |
Includes bibliographical references.
Identifiers: LCCN 2018037649 (print) | LCCN 2019001822 (ebook) |
ISBN 9780525520894 (ebook) | ISBN 9780525520887 (hardcover)
Subjects: LCSH: Literature—History and criticism. | Canon (Literature) |
Bloom, Harold—Books and reading.
Classification: LCC PN511 (ebook) | LCC PN511 .B525 2019 (print) |
DDC 809—dc23
LC record available at https://lccn.loc.gov/2018037649

Jacket design by Chip Kidd

Manufactured in the United States of America
First Edition

For Celina Spiegel

That is what the highest criticism really is, the record of one's own soul. It is more fascinating than history, as it is concerned simply with oneself. It is more delightful than philosophy, as its subject is concrete and not abstract, real and not vague. It is the only civilised form of autobiography, as it deals not with the events, but with the thoughts of one's life; not with life's physical accidents of deed or circumstance, but with the spiritual moods and imaginative passions of the mind. . . .

OSCAR WILDE, "The Critic as Artist," *Intentions* (1891)

# Contents

Preface   xix

*Part One*
## A Voice She Heard Before the World Was Made

Thresholds to Voice: Augmenting a God in Ruins   3

The Poetry of Kabbalah   13

More Life: The Blessing Given by Literature   26

Moses: The Sublime of Silence   30

Judges 13–16: Samson   34

Daughter of a Voice: The Song of Deborah   38

David: "Thou Art the Man"   42

The Hebrew Prophets   49

Isaiah of Jerusalem: "Arise, Shine; For Thy Light Is Come"   54

Psalms or Praises   56

Job: Holding His Ground   61

The Song of Songs: "Set Me as a Seal upon Thine Heart"   66

Ruth: "Whither Thou Goest, I Will Go"   70

Ecclesiastes: "And Desire Shall Fail"   73

*Part Two*
## SELF-OTHERSEEING AND THE SHAKESPEAREAN SUBLIME

The Concept of Self-Otherseeing and the Arch-Jew Shylock   79

The Bastard Faulconbridge   85

The Falstaffiad: Glory and Darkening of Sir John Falstaff   89

Hamlet's Questioning of Shakespeare   104

Iago and Othello: Point-Counterpoint   113

Edgar and Edmund: Agonistic Dramatists   128

The Fool and Cordelia: Love's Martyrdom   135

*King Lear:* Authority and Cosmological Disorder   139

*Macbeth:* Triumph at Limning a Night-Piece   142

*Part Three*

# IN THE ELEGY SEASON: JOHN MILTON, THE VISIONARY COMPANY, AND VICTORIAN POETRY

Ben Jonson on Shakespeare and Andrew Marvell on Milton   147

*Paradise Lost:* The Realm of Newness   153

*Comus:* The Shadow of Shakespeare   165

Dr. Samuel Johnson, *Life of Milton*   170

William Collins, "Ode on the Poetical Character"   181

Thomas Gray: The Poet as Outsider   185

Wisdom and Unwisdom of the Body   189

William Blake's *Milton*   194

William Wordsworth:
    "The Solitary Reaper"   198
    "Ode: Intimations of Immortality from Recollections
        of Early Childhood"   201

Samuel Taylor Coleridge, "The Rime of the
    Ancient Mariner"   212

Percy Bysshe Shelley:
    "Ode to the West Wind"   216
    "To a Skylark"   220
    *Prometheus Unbound*   226

Lord Byron, *Don Juan*  230

John Keats:

    "Ode to a Nightingale"  238

    "La Belle Dame sans Merci"  243

    "To Autumn"  246

Thomas Lovell Beddoes, *Death's Jest Book*  250

Alfred Tennyson:

    "Ulysses"  255

    "Tithonus"  259

    *Idylls of the King*  263

    "Morte d'Arthur"  268

Robert Browning:

    "A Toccata of Galuppi's"  272

    *Pauline*  277

    The Condition of Fire at the Dark Tower  280

    "Thamuris Marching"  284

George Meredith, "A Ballad of Past Meridian"  289

Algernon Charles Swinburne:

    "August"  291

    "Hertha"  294

*Part Four*

# THE IMPERFECT IS OUR PARADISE: WALT WHITMAN AND TWENTIETH-CENTURY AMERICAN POETRY

The Psalms and Walt Whitman   305

Fletcher, Whitman, and The American Sublime   342

The Freshness of Last Things: Wallace Stevens,
   "Tea at the Palaz of Hoon"   346

Wallace Stevens:
   "The Snow Man"   348
   "Montrachet-le-Jardin"   351

Edwin Arlington Robinson, "Luke Havergal"   355

William Carlos Williams, "A Unison"   359

Archie Randolph Ammons, *Sphere*   364

Hart Crane:
   "Possessions"   385
   "To Brooklyn Bridge"   387

Conrad Aiken, "Tetélestai"   389

Richard Eberhart, "If I Could Only Live at the Pitch That Is
   Near Madness"   402

Weldon Kees, "Aspects of Robinson"   407

May Swenson, "Big-Hipped Nature"   413

Delmore Schwartz, "The First Night of Fall and Falling
    Rain"   416

Alvin Feinman, "Pilgrim Heights"   419

John Ashbery, "At North Farm"   431

John Wheelwright, "Fish Food"   443

James Merrill, *The Book of Ephraim*   449

Jay Macpherson, "Ark Parting"   457

Amy Clampitt, "A Hermit Thrush"   463

*Coda*
# In Search of Lost Time

I am grateful for the labors of my editor and publisher, Erroll McDonald, and his assistant, Nicholas Thomson, and production editor, Victoria Pearson. As always, I am indebted to my literary agents, Glen Hartley and Lynn Chu.

This book would not exist without the devoted efforts of my research assistants: Lauren Smith, Alice Kenney, Jessica Branch, Bethany Carlson, Alexis Larsson, Abigail Storch, and Natalie Rose Schwartz.

# Author's Note

All Bible excerpts are from the King James Bible, unless otherwise noted in the text. Excerpts from Shakespeare tend to follow the latest Arden edition. I have in a few places repunctuated according to my understanding of the text and restored Shakespeare's language, where I judge traditional emendations to be mistaken.

# Preface

MANY YEARS AGO, in Cambridge, England, I attended one meeting of a rather esoteric faculty group that believed you could communicate with the dead. It was a disquieting experience with a gyrating table and spirit voices drifting in. I left, rather abruptly, because I felt out of place. Long before that, my charming mentor George Wilson Knight attempted to persuade me of his conviction that séances were authentic. I recall protesting that this seemed to me an over-literalization of a human yearning. George chuckled and said I was still too young to comprehend a vital truth.

The poet James Merrill, a good acquaintance, sometimes teased me about my skepticism. Like William Butler Yeats, he called up spooks to give him metaphors for poetry. With both poets, the results were wonderful, whether or not sprites aided the imaginings.

My own concern is rather different. When I read my departed friends, I have an uncanny sensation that they are in the room. Common readers, so many of whom are in touch with me, are very moving when they say that reading or rereading a book highly valued by their beloved dead comforts them.

All of us wish that, when we experience sorrow, we could be shown the end of sorrow. If we are secular, that cannot be expected. *Possessed by Memory* is not intended to be a lamentation for my own generation of critics and poets. Instead it hopes, in part, to be a living tribute to their afterlife in their writings. The other evening, I glanced at my writing table and saw books by many of my lost friends. There were volumes of poetry by John Ashbery, A. R. Ammons, Mark Strand, Alvin Feinman, and of criticism by Richard Rorty, Geoffrey Hartman, Angus Fletcher, and John Hollander. I had been close to all of them for at least half a century, and to most of them for two-thirds of my lifetime.

I will be going on eighty-nine when this book is published; in its composition over the past several years I began to apprehend my ongoing writing as a dialogue with my dead friends. These include mentors like M. H. Abrams, Frederick Pottle, Gershom Scholem, Hans Jonas, and Kenneth Burke. Sometimes they were good acquaintances: Frank Kermode, Anthony Burgess, A. D. Nuttall, Northrop Frye.

This book is reverie and not argument. My title is the book in a single phrase. What is it to be "possessed by memory"? How does possession differ in these: to possess dead or lost friends and lovers, or to possess poetry and heightened prose by memory? The range of meanings of the verb "possess" are varied: to own as property, to have power over, to master knowledge, to be controlled by a daemon, to be filled with felt experience or with cognitive apprehension, to enjoy sexual intercourse, to usurp and pillage.

The Indo-European root *poti-* implies lordship or else potency. Possession ensues from potential, a sense of something evermore about to be. There is a kindling of effort, expectation, desire, and then an ebbing, as in the Shakespearean "Desire is death." Memory contains the composite triad in which the Kantian summa—Freedom, God, Immortality—transmutes into poetry's countersumma: individuating voice, drawing down or augmenting a waning God, and bestowing upon us the Blessing that is more life.

In a poem the image of voice is always a trope listening for a tone you may have heard before your world was made. The Blessing frequently coincides with a change in your name. When you have a poem by heart, you possess it more truly and more strangely than you do your dwelling place, because the poem possesses you. Drawing down a god can be an esoteric procedure, yet poems at their strongest strike the lyre, and then the god becomes an issue of the strings.

# Part One

# A Voice She Heard
# Before the
# World Was Made

# Thresholds to Voice:
## Augmenting a God in Ruins

A s i near the end of my eighties, I am aware of being in the elegy season. The majority of my close friends from my own generation have departed. I am haunted by many passages in Wallace Stevens, and one that I keep hearing centers his extraordinary poem, "The Course of a Particular":

And though one says that one is part of everything,

There is a conflict, there is a resistance involved;
And being part is an exertion that declines:
One feels the life of that which gives life as it is.

Throughout his final poems, Stevens listens for the voice he heard before the world was made. Though he is not preoccupied with occult and Hermetic modes of speculation, in the manner either of William Butler Yeats or of D. H. Lawrence, he hears voices. Falling leaves cry out, houses laugh, syllables are spoken without speech, the wind breathes a motion, thoughts howl in the mind, the colossal sun sounds a scrawny cry, and the phoenix, mounted on a visionary palm tree, sings a foreign song. Sleepless like many other old men and women, I too dream what Stevens calls a heavy difference:

A little while of Terra Paradise
I dreamed, of autumn rivers, silvas green,
Of sanctimonious mountains high in snow,

But in that dream a heavy difference
Kept waking and a mournful sense sought out,
In vain, life's season or death's element.

Montrachet-le-Jardin

When that saddens me too much, something in my spirit turns to a more intimate Stevens:

The cry is part. My solitaria
Are the meditations of a central mind.
I hear the motions of the spirit and the sound
Of what is secret becomes, for me, a voice
That is my own voice speaking in my ear.

Chocorua to Its Neighbor

Frequently at dawn, when I am very chilly and sit on the side of my bed, knowing it is not safe for me to go downstairs by myself in order to have some morning tea, I find deep peace in Stevens at his strongest:

To say more than human things with human voice,
That cannot be; to say human things with more
Than human voice, that, also, cannot be;
To speak humanly from the height or from the depth
Of human things, that is acutest speech.

Can human things be said with more than human voice? Stevens was a kind of Lucretian skeptic, as Shelley, Walt Whitman, and Walter Pater had been before him. Yet, of those three, only Pater would have agreed with Stevens as to whether we could hear a primordial utterance. Even Stevens had his openings to a transcendental freedom:

Upon my top he breathed the pointed dark.
He was not man yet he was nothing else.
If in the mind, he vanished, taking there
The mind's own limits, like a tragic thing
Without existence, existing everywhere.

William Butler Yeats, D. H. Lawrence, and, rather more skeptically, Hart Crane all were informed by the ancient tradition of Hermetism, the Greco-Egyptian speculation from which the Renaissance Hermeticism developed. In that original speculation, which was inaugurated by a small group of pagan intellectuals in Hellenistic Alexandria during the first century of the Common Era, a story is told of how the first Adam, called Anthropos, is exalted as a divine being. Here is a crucial passage from the Hermetic discourse called "The Key":

> For the human is a godlike living thing, not comparable to the other living things of the earth but to those in heaven above, who are called gods. Or better—if one dare tell the truth—the one who is really human is above these gods as well, or at least they are wholly equal in power to one another.
>
> For none of the heavenly gods will go down to earth, leaving behind the bounds of heaven, yet the human rises up to heaven and takes its measure and knows what is in its heights and its depths, and he understands all else exactly and—greater than all of this—he comes to be on high without leaving earth behind, so enormous is his range. Therefore, we must dare to say that the human on earth is a mortal god but that god in heaven is an immortal human. Through these two, then, cosmos and human, all things exist, but they all exist by action of the one.
>
> Translated by Brian P. Copenhaver

That is Hermetism at its most exalted. Darker is the account that brings together the Fall and the Creation as one event. I turn here to the most famous text of Hermetism, "Poimandres," where our primal catastrophe is elegantly chronicled:

> Having all authority over the cosmos of mortals and unreasoning animals, the man broke through the vault and stooped to look through the cosmic framework, thus displaying to lower nature the fair form of god. Nature smiled for love when she saw him whose fairness brings no surfeit (and) who holds in himself all the energy of the governors and the form of god, for in the water she saw the shape of the man's fairest form and upon the earth its shadow. When the man saw in the water the form like himself as it was in nature, he loved it and wished to inhabit it; wish and action came in the same moment, and he inhabited the unreason-

ing form. Nature took hold of her beloved, hugged him all about and embraced him, for they were lovers.

Because of this, unlike any other living thing on earth, mankind is twofold—in the body mortal but immortal in the essential man. Even though he is immortal and has authority over all things, mankind is affected by mortality because he is subject to fate; thus, although man is above the cosmic framework, he became a slave within it. He is androgyne because he comes from an androgyne father, and he never sleeps because he comes from one who is sleepless. Yet love and sleep are his masters.

Translated by Brian P. Copenhaver

In Hart Crane's "Voyages II" there is a paean to "sleep, death, desire," a celebration of the great erotic relationship of the poet's life. Nevertheless, "Voyages V" admits that the truth of this love is a matter of instants and must end in separation:

> But now
> Draw in your head, alone and too tall here.
> Your eyes already in the slant of drifting foam;
> Your breath sealed by the ghosts I do not know:
> Draw in your head and sleep the long way home.

There is a kind of gentle resignation in Hart Crane as he confronts erotic loss. Ultimately I think that stems from the Hermetist version of the Fall as a narcissistic reverie that concludes in a catastrophe. Many of us, remembering the now remote erotic attachments of our youth, scores of years back in time, find that involuntarily we remain haunted by a voice we heard emanating from the beloved that seemed timeless and therefore permanent. There is some link that binds together the making of a poem, the illusions of recall, and the tenuous expectation that somehow we will hear again the voice that preceded the instauration of a cosmos forlorn and vagrant, through which we blankly wander, unable to distinguish what was and what we strain to find again.

Our experience of a lost voice may come to us in solitude or in the presence of others, whether or not they are related to our past sorrows. When I was very young, I read poems incessantly because I was lonely and somehow must have believed they could become people for me.

That vagary could not survive maturation, yet the quest persisted for a voice I had heard before I knew my own alienation. Over the decades I learned to listen closely to my students for some murmurs of those evanescent voices. Since these young men and women are two-thirds of a century younger than I am, I do not seek in their tonalities my own nostalgias. Yet I believe that the teaching of Shakespeare or of *Moby-Dick* can be an awakening to the ancient Gnostic call that proclaims a resurrection preceding our deaths.

In my experience, there are a few visions or surging voices that break through the rock of the self and free something that is both spark and breath, in a momentary knowing that seems to be known even as it knows. When I ask myself who is the knower, I have intimations that a primal sound, cast out of our cosmos and wandering in exile through the interstellar spaces, may be calling to me. There is nothing unique in my experience, as was particularly clear to me in the years 1990–92, when I seemed all but endlessly in motion, lecturing at American universities and colleges in the South and Southwest. I accepted speaking engagements only there, when I could get away from Yale, so as to do amateur research listening to people of many sects and persuasions, who I learned to call American Religionists. I recall vividly how many told me they had already been resurrected, and knew they had walked and talked with the Jesus scarcely mentioned in the New Testament, who passed forty days with his faithful after the Ascension.

At sixty, I both respected and was baffled by so many urgent confessions of women and of men that they had touched the flesh of a living Jesus, who walked with them and spoke of everyday matters. Now, in my high eighties, I understand better what was so dark to me a quarter-century ago.

I listen for a primordial silence as well as voices coming down from a sphere within and beyond the rock of the self. When Hamlet concludes by murmuring, "The rest is silence," he intends both an acceptance of oblivion and a longing for what Hermetists call the Pleroma or Fullness. Valentinus the Gnostic sage concluded his "Gospel of Truth" by telling his congregation that it did not suit him, having been in the place of rest, to say anything more. For him too the rest was silence.

How do you listen for a silence? Here is one of my personal mentors, the great Gershom Scholem, in his diary for 1918:

As long as silence remains intact, people and things will mourn. For our hope in the restitution of language and the reconciliation relies precisely on the conviction that while language suffered because of the Fall, silence did not.

As the wise Scholem knew, that is a Gnostic formulation. I recall that in 1980, in Jerusalem, he told me that Kabbalah was the oldest of speculations. When I replied very gently that Kabbalah was an amalgam of Neoplatonism and various Gnostic traditions, the magisterial Scholem dismissed that by saying that Plato derived his doctrines from the Egyptians, who borrowed them from the Hebrews, and that Gnosticism began as a Jewish protest against God for having permitted the fall of Jerusalem. One did not argue with Scholem. He was in his early eighties, and his convictions were absolute. Instead, one learned to listen intently.

One evening in July 1980, after dinner in their Jerusalem apartment, Scholem's wife, Fanya, and I listened to his rapt praise of silence, exile, and cunning. These were the modes he himself practiced in his concealed messianic enterprise. I ventured that silence was an ancient virtue in many contemplative and spiritual traditions. He replied briskly that silence, as he employed it, was a Judaic invention of the sages who had to submit to Hellenistic and finally Roman overlords.

When I asked how we could know that silence, unlike language, was not part of the Creation-Fall, he appealed to the experience of his own meditative life. I realized only later that he was giving a kind of summa of his "Ten Unhistorical Aphorisms on Kabbalah," which I had not read, though it had been printed in German in 1958. My own reduction of these ten profound apothegms would be:

1. Authentic tradition is always hidden.
2. Speech and writing protect secrets whereas silence reveals them.
3. God is the Torah, which means that Torah also is unknowable.
4. Isaac Luria's triple rhythm of contraction, breaking of the vessels, and restitution is not just a metaphor but literally true. This means that God himself is degraded.

5. To avoid merging God with his Creation, there must be a negative moment or an Abyss in the Divine Will.

6. The work of Kabbalah is to transmember Torah into a transparency, and that means Torah becomes antinomian.

7. Kabbalah's flaw is its Neoplatonic theory of emanation. The truth of Kabbalah is the Gnosis of Moses Cordovero, in which God and the Divine Will touch without coinciding.

8. Kabbalah is utopian or even magical, since God must be seen "at that place where I stand." Lurianic restitution is conveyed even by the visionary Marxism of Walter Benjamin and Ernst Bloch.

9. You can pronounce God's name but never express it; we cannot hear the name unless it is mediated by tradition, and then only in fragments.

10. Kafka is secular Kabbalah. Therefore, his writings have for Scholem and Benjamin "something of the strict light of the canonical, of that perfection which destroys."

I have always been delighted by the dry tone of these amazing realizations. They abolish all distinction between the normative Judaism of Rabbi Akiba and the heresies of Sabbatai Zevi and Jacob Frank. Our prophet Scholem is telling us that Sabbatai and his henchman Nathan of Gaza are no more or less figures of Jewish spirituality than Maimonides and Judah Halevi. Best of all is the ultimate consequence of Scholem's vision of the Negative: no distinction remains between those who urge redemption through virtue and those who offer redemption through sin.

In a late essay, "Reflections on Jewish Theology," Scholem freed himself to break into a rhapsodic celebration of Lurianic myth treated as though it were the only authentic Jewish theology:

Creation out of nothing, from the void, could be nothing other than creation of the void, that is, of the possibility of thinking of anything that was not God. Without such an act of self-limitation, after all, there would be only God—and obviously nothing else. A being that is not God could only become possible and originate by virtue of such a contraction, such a paradoxical retreat of God into Himself. By positing a negative factor in Himself, God liberates Creation.

This is certainly not the God of Rabbi Akiba and his fellow sages. It resembles the vision of divine reality by Rabbi Elisha ben Abuya, who was scorned by the school of Akiba as *Acher*, meaning the "Stranger" or the "Other," which can be read as Elisha's adherence to the Gnostic Alien God, cast out beyond our cosmos.

In a conversation with Scholem at my house after he had received an honorary degree from the Yale Divinity School in May 1981, I teased him by saying that his true daemon was *Acher*, since like Elisha ben Abuya he had entered the Pardes or paradise of interpretation and torn up the young shoots in its garden. Scholem grinned impishly and said he regarded that as a grand tribute.

My intention for this book is to teach myself and others how to listen for the voice we heard before the world was made and marred. Scholem distinguished German language silence from Hebrew silence. For him this distinction was the Torah, because Torah is where Hebrew's silence overtakes simple silence. Everything contains both silence and speaking, yet Torah is in everything. How does speaking pass from silence to silence, with language hovering between them as silence's medium? Scholem's answer is to emphasize that silence takes place *in* language.

How can the kingdom of silence be achieved? To Scholem, silence is the source of all language, and we need to achieve it through human lamentation. But lamentation has to be understood by its limitation, which is silence. This is akin to the young Scholem's memorable apothegm that Zion is the collective loneliness of all people. Human community is founded on two modes: Silence and Revelation.

Scholem, himself a minor poet, passionately loved Goethe and Hölderlin. Yet this passion was tempered by his desire that their lyricism perform the labor of Revelation. He found that labor superbly manifest in Walt Whitman, a later enthusiasm of the Jerusalem sage. Several times he told me that Whitman restored a kind of natural Kabbalah to a secular world. In many ways, Scholem confirmed my lifelong love for the poet who sang the song of himself and in so singing called his own godhood into being. When I remarked to Scholem that his Whitman was a theurgist, the scholar of Kabbalah was delighted and said I was his most unexpected disciple.

Poetry, as I most richly conceive it, is the ultimate secular mode of what the ancients called theurgy, which is one of three motions of the spirit:

1. Augmentation of a god in ruins
2. The drawing down of a god who is too remote for our needs
3. A mode I would call world propping, in which our wounded cosmos is maintained

I modify these terms from Moshe Idel's agonistic study of Kabbalah, in which he takes on the titanic labor of correcting Scholem. Throughout *Possessed by Memory*, I employ these apparently esoteric images as aids to the apprehension of elements in great poems, from the Biblical Song of Deborah through Shakespeare and Milton on to A. R. Ammons, who taught us to address the empty place where the god that has been deposed lived.

My three images derived from Moshe Idel are for me a version of the Kantian categories that grant us our vitality: Freedom, God, Immortality. Voice is the comprehensive phenomenon holding together the Valentinian declaration that what makes us free is the Gnosis. The God is split between a spark or breath in the rocklike ego and an Alien exile wandering in space beyond our cosmos. Immortality is seen as a Resurrection before dying, as when the ancient heretics said of Jesus that *first* he resurrected and *then* he died.

I am aware that some readers may turn aside from *Possessed by Memory* because what they regard as heretical or at least esoteric distracts from the reading of poetry. I address not them but those who yearn for what I would term a Shakespearean reading of the best poetry made available to us, here in our Evening Land, of the tradition sparked by Homer and Isaiah. That tradition is dying. As a literary and religious critic, I wish to rally a saving remnant.

Such a desire is open to aspersions of pretentiousness. After so many decades of dismissal as a usurper of critical tradition, I wonder how one earns the authentic call of a critic's own image of voice. If I speak for myself only, then discard me. Evidence reaches me daily that something in me speaks for multitudes around the globe. I am too decrepit to give public readings or lectures and then sign books. Yet, even half a century ago, I was moved almost to tears by readers I could never meet again who told me that I was their teacher.

It comes down, then, to teaching. But what is teaching? Once, I thought that it was a form of Platonic eros, but I was mistaken. I recall the gifted classicist Daniel Mendelsohn harshly rejecting my little primer *How to Read and Why* by saying it showed that I did not love my students. The brief book was hardly intended for him, yet I wondered why he raised the question of loving students. A teacher bears testimony. Her function is both to exemplify and to provoke. Emerson taught me that what I can gain from another is never instruction but only provocation.

Even in your high eighties, whoever you are, you need to keep reading and rereading unless you are an original philosopher or an adept of the contemplative life. I am neither. The poets, dramatists, novelists are necessary if I am to get through my remaining days. But so are students necessary. I no longer have the firepower to teach as once I could. In compensation, I have finally learned to listen.

My career has been a conscious effort to follow the art of criticism as exemplified by Dr. Samuel Johnson, William Hazlitt, John Ruskin, Walter Pater, Oscar Wilde, and the American tradition of Emerson, William James, and Kenneth Burke. I cannot judge whether I have earned a place in that lineage. I will not know, as I vanish, if I failed.

# The Poetry of Kabbalah

## I

GERSHOM SCHOLEM, in his writings and in conversation, insisted that the three canonical works for his Judaism were the Tanakh (Hebrew Bible), the Zohar (Radiance), and the narratives and parables of Franz Kafka. They, above even the Talmuds, manifested "the strict light of the canonical, of the perfection that destroys."

As an amateur, purely literary disciple of Scholem, I learned to listen closely to him, awed by his authority and the uncanny ease of his referring to himself in the third person. The founder of the modern study of Kabbalah or esoteric Judaism, Scholem inaugurated a new discipline.

Mysticism, by one definition, has not the patience to wait for God's self-revelation. I find the word misleading in discussing Kabbalah, though its use was sanctioned by Scholem and by most scholars in his wake. There were and are ecstatic Kabbalists, questing for direct experience of God, but the intellectual value of Kabbalah seems to me elsewhere, with its speculative intensities and exegetical inventions. Both Peter Cole—in his *The Poetry of Kabbalah*, an aesthetic splendor equal to his *The Dream of the Poem: Hebrew Poetry from Muslim and Christian Spain*—and Daniel C. Matt, in the twelve-part English translation of the Zohar, continue to employ the term "mysticism," but here I abandon it.

The word "Kabbalah" means "reception" or "tradition" and initially was used for the entire Oral Law. The narrower signification, from about the year 1200 on, is to a movement of spiritual reflection that began among some rabbis of Provence and Catalonia in the early thirteenth century.

"Began" requires qualification: scholars agree on neither the ultimate origins of Kabbalah, nor the extent of its antiquity. Arbitrarily,
you can say the pragmatic inauguration was the sage known as Ravad
(Rabbi Abraham ben David) in twelfth-century Provence. His son,
Isaac the Blind, composed the initial texts of Kabbalah proper, commentaries upon *Sefer Yetzirah* (Book of Creation). That curious work
may go back to the third century but exists only in tenth-century versions. *Sefer Yetzirah* tells us that Yahweh created the cosmos with ten
Sefirot and the Hebrew alphabet of twenty-two letters.

The Sefirot even now are the staple of popular Kabbalah: "Sefirah,"
the singular form, derives from the Hebrew *sappir* ("sapphire"), and
presumably pertains to divine radiance. These, however, are not the
archaic entities of *Sefer Yetzirah* but of the Bahir—meaning "Clarity,"
by one interpretation—which was possibly composed early in the thirteenth century.

The Bahir's crucial passage is an extraordinary reading of the ten
utterances with which the world was called into being. These are trans-
posed into the ten Sefirot (for which see the diagram illustrating this
chapter). Of these emanations, I note that the three on the left side are
female, the three on the right male, and the center column is essentially
androgynous. Keter, or the Crown, has an aspect of nothingness, and
Tiferet has a component of compassion alongside the male force of the
sun. Yesod, a phallic foundation, is balanced by Malkhut, or the Kingdom, at once the presence of the Shekhinah, Muse of the Kabbalah, and
of the male assembly of Israel, yet also the Queen, Rachel, oscillating
with David the King.

Kabbalah is hardly unique in the West or the East as an erotic esotericism, though its obsessive sexuality may be its salient quality. The
definitive study is *Kabbalah and Eros* (2005) by Moshe Idel, the major
scholar in the field since Scholem. Idel speaks of Kabbalah as the "culture of eros," since it regards marital intercourse as redemptive, both
of individuals and of the cosmos. At my age, I am at once bemused and
oddly comforted by so idealistic a beholding. I think of Coventry Patmore, the friend of Gerard Manley Hopkins, who celebrated a High
Victorian Catholic erotic esotericism in his odes, but scarcely had the
audacity to attribute redemptive ecstasy to the sexual life of God. Yet
precisely such daring is central to Kabbalah, where Yahweh, under the
masking term Ein Sof (Limitless), is the husband of Shekhinah, the

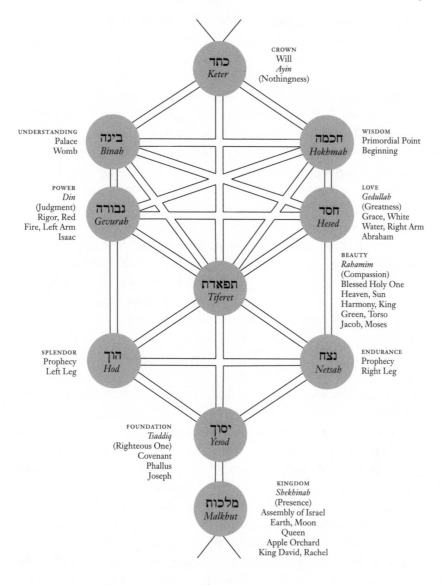

*The Ten Sefirot*

tenth and final Sefirah, at once his divine presence and also the object of his fulfilled sexual desire.

That vision of Yahweh might have repelled Isaiah of Jerusalem and the other prophets, major and minor, but would have been congenial to the great Rabbi Akiba ben Joseph, second-century C.E. founder of normative Judaism, as still we know it. Evidently, Akiba persuaded his fellow sages to keep the Song of Songs in the canon, proclaiming that the blessed in the hereafter would chant it endlessly.

Famously, there is a sense of dark secret love in the Song of Songs, wonderfully caught in *The Dark Night of the Soul* by Saint John of the Cross. A concealed eros hints at an illicit desire, though God's passion for the Shekhinah is perhaps his most positive aspect. She is a magnificently metamorphic trope: both bride and daughter, a diadem, an influence, a spark, dwelling place, comfort-in-exile, princess and wise woman, mother and wife, the Jewish people, and on it goes.

Gershom Scholem happily regarded the Shekhinah as a Gnostic vision that subtly infiltrated rabbinic Judaism and then flowered in Kabbalah. For Scholem, the misfortune of Kabbalah was the Neoplatonic structure of emanations (the Sefirot), and he welcomed every heterodox element he could uncover. I recall Hans Jonas and Scholem, in conversations that I absorbed as best I could, stubbornly disputing the compatibility of Gnosticism and any stance ultimately founded upon the Hebrew Bible. Against fatal necessity, Jonas set the Judaic sense of contingency, and he found irreconcilable the world of Yahweh and Athenian intellect. But Scholem, rather like his later revisionist Moshe Idel, argued that second-century C.E. Christian Gnosticism had crucial Jewish origins.

Everything about Gnosticism is disputable; some recent scholars wish to abrogate the term. From a literary critic's perspective, that is not a useful view. A working definition, necessarily rough, is that Gnosticism was and is a tendency or speculation that makes Creation and the Fall of humankind, and of the cosmos, a single event. The Godhead splits into two components, a Demiurge or bungling artisan, and a true divinity-in-exile, wandering far out in the interstellar spaces. A spark or breath of that exiled being is buried deep in the rock of each of us, to be known only fitfully. The Kabbalistic Shekhinah is a version of that flickering breath.

2

Zohar, even in the skilled new rendering by Daniel Matt, perpetually disconcerts me. It is a quasi-library of tracts by a circle of esoteric enthusiasts in Castile, and can be dated at about 1300. Though it purports to be Midrash on Tanakh, Zohar is the wild child of Judaic exegetical tradition. Think that you are attending an erotic picnic, to which these Castilian fantasists bring the words, while you provide the meanings.

Recent scholars bravely attempt to find aesthetic value in the Zohar narrative, but, though picaresque enough, it cannot be rescued by such special pleading. Rabbi Moses de Leon and his friends were neither poets nor storytellers, even though Scholem wistfully hoped Zohar could be read as a novel. The common reader would hang himself if he searched Zohar in quest of story and character.

In no way do I wish to deprecate the only authentic masterwork in Jewish esoteric tradition, but the singular glory of Zohar is as an adventure in speculative consciousness. A new reality in the human awareness of the life within the Godhead breaks upon readers patient and open enough to encounter what initially may seem more fantasy than revelation.

Patience is necessary because the Zohar's lens is always the Sefirot, ten evasive metaphors for the dynamics of God's inner life. That life *is* language. Torah, the body of God's language, is a breathing entity, male and female, consonant with the reality of Yahweh's personhood.

Space considerations compel me not to expound the Sefirot here. Readers should consult Arthur Green's lucid *A Guide to the Zohar* (2003), a condensed version of which serves as introduction to the first volume of Matt's *Zohar* (2004). Green accurately emphasizes the linguistic strangeness of the Zohar, composed in an artificial literary Aramaic, rather than in Hebrew. Both Talmuds are largely in Aramaic, but in a spoken, live idiom. Zohar's language is joyously secretive, addressed to initiates, as though delighting in its own singularity.

Daniel Matt's Zohar is a marvel of surface clarity, however intricately obscure the original. The ongoing commentary, usefully printed below the text on every page, matches even Isaiah Tishby's splendid *Wisdom of the Zohar*, translated in three volumes by David Goldstein (Oxford University Press, 1989). To sample, I give Matt, volume V, Zohar 2:95a:

Who is a beautiful maiden without eyes, her body hidden and revealed? She emerges in the morning and is concealed by day, adorning herself with adornments that are not.

In passage 2:99a, this riddle expands into a parable:

This may be compared to a beloved maiden, beautiful in form and appearance, concealed secretly in her palace. She has a single lover unknown to anyone—except her, concealedly. Out of the love that he feels for her, this lover passes by her gate constantly, lifting his eyes to every side. Knowing that her lover is constantly circling her gate, what does she do? She opens a little window in that secret palace where she is, reveals her face to her lover, and quickly withdraws, concealing herself. None of those near the lover sees or notices, only the lover, and his inner being and heart and soul follow her. He knows that out of love for him she revealed herself for a moment to arouse him.

At once Torah and Shekhinah, the maiden arouses and is aroused by the Kabbalists. As wine, in a jar, so is the Torah-Shekhinah concealed in her outer garments. These are composed of letters, words, stories, which the companions of the Zohar are urged to remove.

3

Peter Cole, one of our era's major poet-translators, whose work until now is best represented by his *Hymns & Qualms* (2017), returns Kabbalah to the Muse, in his massively annotated *The Poetry of Kabbalah*, a collection superbly rendered from the original Aramaic, Hebrew, Ladino, and Yiddish.

Cole is an increasingly vital American poet who lives in Jerusalem. Perhaps the first of a new kind of Jewish poet in American English, he composes in an idiom deeply informed by Kabbalah:

*The Reluctant Kabbalist's Sonnet*

> *"It is known that 'desire' is, numerologically . . . 'the essence of speech.' "*
>
> *Avraham Abulafia,* The Treasures of the Hidden Eden

It's hard to explain     What was inside came
through what had been between, although it seems
that what had been within remained the same
Is that so hard to explain     It took some time
Which was, in passing, made distinctly strange
As though the world without had been rearranged,
forcing us to change: what was beyond
suddenly lying within, and what had lain
deep inside—now . . . apparently gone
Words are seeds, like tastes on another's tongue
Which *doesn't* explain—how what's inside comes
through what is always in between, that seam
of being     For what's within, within remains,
as though it had slipped     across the lips of a dream

This subtle sonnet's personal eroticism is masked by the avoidance of
"I." Nine initial lines suavely represent a conjugal coupling, modulating
in the final five to the Kabbalistic "words are seeds." "Seed" changes
into "that *seam* / of being," the border between even the most ardent
of lovers. The assonance reverberates throughout: "inside," "lying
within," "within / within," and the changes rung upon "strange," "rearranged," "change," "remains," and the "slipped" / "lips" cognitive music
of the close. Somewhere in *Per Amica Silentia Lunae*, a great Paterian
reverie, W. B. Yeats utters a dirge for the perpetual virginity of the soul,
however fervent the intercourse:

> I shall find the dark grow luminous, the void fruitful when I under-
> stand I have nothing, that the ringers in the tower have appointed
> for the hymen of the soul a passing bell.

Cole relies upon Avraham Abulafia for the Kabbalistic link between
desire and words. Abulafia was the outrageous scamp of Kabbalah, a
kind of Jewish picaroon, who dismissed the Zohar with the remark
that the Sefirot were even worse than the Trinity. Subject to astonishing visions, he went to Rome in 1280, having announced his intention to convert Pope Nicholas III to Judaism. The Pontiff thoughtfully
ordered a stake prepared to incinerate the insolent Kabbalist, but then
expired just before this act of faith could be performed. Cast out by the

Jewish community for messianic pretensions, Abulafia fled to an islet in the vicinity of Malta, where he composed his longish poem, *The Book of the Sign*, an apocalyptic chant anticipating William Blake. Here is an excerpt rendered with appropriate gusto by Cole:

And from
the bow of knowing they shot arrows of learning,
sending insight toward the target of wisdom,
for the power of the blood in the heart is signed and sealed,
and the heart of he who is wise at heart is whole,
knowing his blood is alive and the slime is dead
within him, and so—slime and blood are enclosed
inside his heart. More bitter than death is slime.
His power is sunken within it, and sweeter than honey
Is blood, and his spirit dwells in the heart's shrine.
And the soul of every creature of mind must journey
From slime's tent toward the tent of blood.
And from blood's tent toward the shrine of the heart
Of heaven it travels, and there it dwells for all
The days of its life. . . .

You can judge Abulafia a charlatan or a prophet. Either way, I find him both distasteful and invigorating. For me, he is a terrible crystal illuminating the paradox of Kabbalistic poetry: can a poem truly assume the burden of an esoteric speculation that purports to be absolute truth? Any poem necessarily is a fiction of duration. How can an unchanging fiction give pleasure? Cole struggles with this dilemma, as no one before him has done in just this way.

I have spent part of a lifetime trying to work out a pragmatic relationship between Kabbalah and literary criticism, but I have never written a poem. The oxymoronic nature of Kabbalistic poetry is a usefully extreme exemplar of the unresolvable difficulties of all devotional verse. The good and bad of eternity, Samuel Johnson observed, are too ponderous for the wings of wit. The mind sinks under sacred weight. Belief, however agitated, tends to the humility of adoration. Can *that* make a poem?

When we value John Donne, George Herbert, Christina Rossetti, Gerard Manley Hopkins, or T. S. Eliot, our aesthetic pleasure has much to do with their skill at evading the mind-numbing consequences of mere dogma. Do the best of Cole's poets manifest such adept powers of evasiveness?

I cannot answer that as yet, though Cole's translations and commentaries provide much *materia poetica* for me. The early liturgical hymns, composed by Yannai and his pupil Kallir in Palestine, late sixth century, are rendered by Cole with remarkable eloquence, and may be crucial for pondering the aesthetic basis of Kabbalistic poetry. Legend delightfully recounts that Yannai, envious of the upstart's prowess, poisoned Kallir by sneaking a scorpion into the quondam disciple's sandal. We may call this the anxiety of having ceased to be an influence. Yannai, unknown until excavated from the sacred trash of the Cairo Genizah, inspires Cole to touch the mad Sublime:

*Angel of Fire*

> *And the angel of the Lord was revealed to him*
> *(in the heart of the flame):*

Angel of fire devouring fire
Fire Blazing through damp and drier
Fire Candescent in smoke and snow
Fire Drawn like a crouching lion
Fire Evolving through shade after shade
Fateful fire that will not expire
Gleaming fire that wanders far
Hissing fire that sends up sparks
Fire Infusing a swirling gale
Fire that Jolts to life without fuel
Fire that's Kindled and kindles daily
Lambent fire unfanned by fire
Miraculous fire flashing through fronds
Notions of fire like lightning on high
Omens of fire in the chariots' wind
[Pillars of fire in thunder and storm]
[Quarries of] fire wrapped in a fog
Raging fire that reaches Sheol

T[errible fire that Ushers in] cold
Fire's Vortex like a Wilderness crow
Fire eXtending and Yet like a rainbow's
Zone of color arching through sky.

One imagines a seventh-century Palestinian congregation together
shouting this sacred jazz, exalting in its allusions to Exodus 3:1, Ezekiel 1:27–28, and Isaiah 66:15, and again Ezekiel 1:28. What makes
it Kabbalah? The "fire wrapped in a fog" (line 17) is the Shekhinah,
burning through mist. Under the fierce impact of Yannai-Cole, argument is forgotten and the fire raging in every line stuns us.

Poetry—Kabbalistic, Sufi, or Christian—tends to rejoice in heretical
subversions of orthodoxy. Cole and his poets blaze into summits of fire
and light with these inventive departures. Something fiercely splendid
surges into *The Poetry of Kabbalah* with the advent of the false Messiah
Shabbatai Tzvi, for whom the enthusiasm of Gershom Scholem was
unbounded, in conversations as in his writings. Cole also is kindled into
a kind of ecstasy in his translations of the Ladino ballad "Meliselda,"
which Shabbatai repeatedly sang to his followers:

*Meliselda*

I went to the mountain
and down to the river
and there I met Meliselda—
the King's gentle daughter.

I saw that glorious girl
emerging from the water:
her brows were bows of night,
her face was a sword of light—

her lips were red as coral,
her milk-like flesh was white.

Historically, this lyric tracks to a Carolingian French ballad celebrating Charlemagne's supposed daughter Melisenda (there are variations

in the spelling of her name). Shabbatai's "glorious girl" is both the Shekhinah and the personal Muse of his own heretical Kabbalah, teaching redemption through sin. The powerful Shabbatian hymn "On the Destruction of the Law" is a triumphal paean to the anarchism forced upon the Jewish world by the false Messiah and his brilliant prophet, Nathan of Gaza, whose *Treatise on the Dragons* had expounded the "thoughtless light" of a false Creation:

## On the Destruction of the Law

The light that lacks conception
   constitutes the occultation,
and with it He created
   all that in the world exists.
As it lacks conception,
   it's always in ascension,
for in it no rule holds,
   neither beginning nor end.

In strength he came to speak to us—
   he is Shabbatai Tzvi.
His nature is destruction,
   from one who knows I've heard.
Into the fourth husk and shell,
   from his place he descended:
for he destroyed the Law—
   in order to raise the Lord.

The "occultation" refers to Shabbatai's conversion to Islam, to save the Messiah from execution, but seen by his faithful as vital to the scheme of salvation by transgression. Shabbatai's passion for distinction was creative, in the Gnostic sense of restoring the ruined worlds bungled into being by Yahweh the Demiurge. Cole precisely catches the tone of the Ladino original, and is particularly exuberant when the death of the Torah and Christ-like resurrection of the manic Shabbatai are juxtaposed.

Scholem, who rightly haunts Peter Cole, acknowledged happily that his own masterwork was the massive *Sabbatai Sevi: The Mystical Messiah, 1626–1676* (1957; translated by R. J. Zwi Werblowsky, Princeton University Press, 1973). In a copy inscribed for me, Scholem quoted from his concluding paragraph:

> In the telling, the supposedly historical facts crystallized into legend—and a lively, popular legend to boot. And even as the legend is told by a nonbelieving chronicler, some rays of "faith" are shimmering on it. No doubt this faith had been humiliated and discredited. Its hope had been vain and its claims refuted, and yet the question compounded of pride and sadness persisted: Was it not a great opportunity missed, rather than a big lie? A victory of the hostile powers rather than the collapse of a vain thing?

The hint was and is clear enough: though not an unequivocal admirer of Shabbatai and of Nathan of Gaza, Scholem nevertheless found in them, as in Kafka and the Zohar, something of the essence of his own Judaism. Peter Cole concludes *The Poetry of Kabbalah* with Scholem's friend Hayyim Nahman Bialik, the major modern Hebrew poet, presented here as a secular Kabbalist. His most famous lyric, "Bring Me In Under Your Wing," is rendered by Cole with a touching plangency:

*Bring Me In Under Your Wing*

Bring me in under your wing,
    be sister for me, and mother,
The place of you, rest for my head,
    a nest for my unwanted prayers.
At the hour of mercy, at dusk,
    we'll talk of my secret pain:
They say, there's youth in the world—
    What happened to mine?

And another thing, a clue:
    my being was seared by a flame.
They say there's love all around—
    What do they mean?

The stars betrayed me—there
    was a dream, which also has passed.
Now in the world I have nothing,
    not a thing.

Bring me in under your wing,
    be sister for me, and mother,
the place of you, rest for my head,
    a nest for my unwanted prayers.

Poets and Kabbalists, like literary critics, need to convert opinion into knowledge. That formulation is Dr. Johnson's, who meant opinion in the legal sense, not public opinion. Cole, commenting upon this, Bialik's most famous poem, emphasizes that the ambivalent "wings" refers to the pinions of the Shekhinah, and the "sister" to Song of Songs 5:2: "My sister, my love, my dove, my undefiled."

Whether, as Cole suggests, this is a poem about the condition of the Jewish people in a secular cosmos, or, as I might venture, a purely personal High Romantic lament for a lost earliness, Bialik stands on the frontier between the sacred and the profane. Kabalistic scholarship, in the wake of Scholem and Idel, frequently threatens to forsake its ability to address a large general audience. Cole refreshingly renews the enterprise of seeing esoteric Judaism in the perspectives of a larger humanistic and aesthetic concern.

Kabbalah matters to more than its specialists because at its strongest it is part of the Jewish tradition of wisdom writing. I do not know anything in Kabbalistic literature that equals the splendor and perpetual relevance of Pirke Aboth, the sayings of the fathers. That immensely moving collection of aphorisms constitutes the most humanizing tractate of the Talmuds. Even the grandest among the Kabbalists cannot stand with Rabbi Akiba or with Rabbi Tarphon. And yet Cole's heartening anthology is a hopeful link between the wisdom tradition and esotericism: a fresh reminder that we are not required to complete the work, but neither are we free to desist from it.

# More Life:
## The Blessing Given by Literature

LIKE MANY OTHERS MY AGE, I fall asleep quite early. I wake up frequently in the night, and lie in the dark overcome by memories. Last night, in the small hours, an image of my mother came back to me. Vividly I saw myself, a boy of three, playing on the kitchen floor, alone with her as she prepared the Sabbath meal. She had been born in a Jewish village on the outskirts of Brest Litovsk and remained faithful to her traditions. I was the youngest of her five children, and I was happiest when we were alone together. As she passed me in her preparations, I would reach out and touch her bare toes, and she would rumple my hair and murmur her affection for me.

My mother told me several times that I was born to her at dawn on July 11, 1930, after a long, hard labor. On my eighty-seventh birthday I woke at first light, and recalled her face as I had seen it lighting the Shabbat candles and reciting the Berakhah: "Blessed are You, Lord our God, King of the universe. . . ." A reverie took shape in me on the secular blessing given to me and to my students by the highest literature, from Homer and the Hebrew Bible through Dante and Chaucer and on to Shakespeare, Cervantes, Montaigne, Milton, and the tradition of Western literature that culminates in Proust and Joyce.

The original meaning of the state of being blessed was to be favored by God. Since I do not share my mother's trust in Yahweh's covenant with my people, I long ago transmuted the blessing into its prime form, which is our love for others. I turned to the reading and studying of literature in search of the blessing, because I came to understand we cannot love enough people. They die and we abide. Literature has become, for me and many others, a crucial way to fill ourselves with the blessing of more life.

As I translate the Berakhah, it means "more life into a time without boundaries." John Ruskin remarked, "The only wealth is life." The presence of Yahweh is declared by his mysterious name. When Moses asks for that name, the God replies, *"Ehyeh asher ehyeh,"* which the King James Bible translates as: "I AM THAT I AM." I render it: "I will be present wherever and whenever I choose to be present." But what is presence? We speak of it as charisma or as superb poise. Originally presence meant "being at hand," but the Latin original passed through Old French and became the English "presence."

Western literature distinguishes between God's presence or absence in the natural world and God's presence among all women and men, or, most crucially, in each of us. A lifelong teacher, I associate presence with the presentation or showing that is part of the process of instruction. As I have practiced it for sixty-three years, the work of a teacher is to bring the student into a sense of her or his own presence. The word "teaching" comes from German origins through Old English, and takes one back to an Indo-European root in the Attic Greek for "show" and the Latin for "say." What has this to do with the blessing?

In Genesis, Yahweh's blessing passes from generation to generation of his chosen people. Of those he favors, the most remarkable personalities are Jacob, who becomes Israel, and David, who replaces Saul as king and fathers Solomon upon Bathsheba. Jacob is an old kind of man, cunning and persistent in his drive for survival and for the blessing of Yahweh. David is something new, and his progeny in literature includes Jesus, as we know him in the Gospel of Mark, and Hamlet.

The most illuminating commentary upon the Yahwist's Jacob is in a now sadly unread comic masterpiece, Thomas Mann's *Joseph and His Brothers*, composed between 1926 and 1942, with a splendid translation by John E. Woods (2005). I gave an account of it in my short book *The Shadow of a Great Rock* (2011) and will confine myself to only a few remarks here.

Whereas elsewhere in the Hebrew Bible the Blessing (I shall capitalize this henceforward) is simply "May you be fruitful and have many descendants," in the texts composed by the Yahwist I interpret the Blessing as a promise that your name will live on in the memory of others and so will not be scattered.

Jacob comes up out of the womb with his hand taking hold on the heel of his brother Esau, who will grow to be a hunter while Jacob will be a tent dweller. Their mother, Rebekah, loves Jacob, while her husband, Isaac, prefers Esau. In a scene of remarkable pathos mingled with comedy, Jacob deceives Isaac into giving him Esau's blessing. The aftermath is troubling and memorable:

> And Isaac his father said unto him, Who art thou? And he said, I am thy son, thy firstborn Esau.
> And Isaac trembled very exceedingly, and said, Who? where is he that hath taken venison, and brought it me, and I have eaten of all before thou camest, and have blessed him? yea, and he shall be blessed.
> And when Esau heard the words of his father, he cried with a great and exceeding bitter cry, and said unto his father, Bless me, even me also, O my father.
> And he said, Thy brother came with subtilty, and hath taken away thy blessing.
> And he said, Is not he rightly named Jacob? for he hath supplanted me these two times: he took away my birthright; and, behold, now he hath taken away my blessing. And he said, Hast thou not reserved a blessing for me?
> And Isaac answered and said unto Esau, Behold, I have made him thy lord, and all his brethren have I given to him for servants; and with corn and wine have I sustained him: and what shall I do now unto thee, my son?
>
> Geneva Bible, Genesis 27:32–37

It is only in the next chapter that our sympathy for Jacob is renewed, when he dreams of a ladder between heaven and earth, with angels ascending and going down. Above the stairs Yahweh stands and reaffirms the Blessing. An even grander epiphany takes place in chapter 32, with its endlessly fecund vision of Jacob wrestling a nameless one among the Elohim:

> And he rose up that night, and took his two wives, and his two womenservants, and his eleven sons, and passed over the ford Jabbok.
> And he took them, and sent them over the brook, and sent over that he had.

And Jacob was left alone; and there wrestled a man with him
   until the breaking of the day.
And when he saw that he prevailed not against him, he touched
   the hollow of his thigh; and the hollow of Jacob's thigh was
   out of joint, as he wrestled with him.
And he said, Let me go, for the day breaketh. And he said, I will
   not let thee go, except thou bless me.
And he said unto him, What is thy name? And he said, Jacob.
And he said, Thy name shall be called no more Jacob, but Israel:
   for as a prince hast thou power with God and with men, and
   hast prevailed.
And Jacob asked him, and said, Tell me, I pray thee, thy name.
   And he said, Wherefore is it that thou dost ask after my
   name? And he blessed him there.
And Jacob called the name of the place Peniel: for I have seen
   God face to face, and my life is preserved.
And as he passed over Penuel the sun rose upon him, and he
   halted upon his thigh.

Geneva Bible, Genesis 32:22–31

"A man" is "one among the Elohim" in the Hebrew. Is it the Angel of Death or Yahweh himself playing that role? We are not told. But this is not a loving encounter. Jacob will limp ever after, and the nameless one fears daybreak. The astonishment is that Jacob, strong only in his cunning, should have the strength to hold a dangerous angel to a standstill. The name he wins, Israel, I render as "To strive with the Almighty."

Jacob knows that soon after dawn he will have to confront his vengeful brother, Esau. In this extraordinary prolepsis, he strengthens himself for that encounter and thus prolongs his survival.

Since childhood, I have meditated upon this agon of Israel with the Angel of Death. I interpret it not only as an allegory of Jewish history—indeed, of universal history—but also as the story of my own life, and the lives of everyone I have known, loved, taught, and mourned. In the half-light of my incessant nocturnal wakefulness, I begin to conceive of it as the struggle of every solitary deep reader to find in the highest literature what will suffice.

# Moses:
# The Sublime of Silence

THERE ARE MANY different ways in which you can be possessed by memory. Some of them are involuntary, and yet sometimes there is a kind of collaboration between the will and memory; when you learn how to relax your will, new modes of memory begin to flood in. These days, I find I am flooded by memories of my own earliest childhood. I recall a clear sense in which I moved about like someone in worlds not yet realized. It was as though I wanted to bring about a better time, but with no clear notion as to what such a time might be.

I still remember, as a child, being puzzled by the great song of the sea in Exodus 15:1–18:

> Then sang Moses and the children of Israel this song unto the Lord, and spake, saying, I will sing unto the Lord, for he hath triumphed gloriously: the horse and his rider hath he thrown into the sea.
> The Lord is my strength and song, and he is become my salvation: he is my God, and I will prepare him an habitation; my father's God, and I will exalt him.
> The Lord is a man of war: the Lord is his name.
> Pharaoh's chariots and his host hath he cast into the sea: his chosen captains also are drowned in the Red sea.
> The depths have covered them: they sank into the bottom as a stone.
> Thy right hand, O Lord, is become glorious in power: thy right hand, O Lord, hath dashed in pieces the enemy.
> And in the greatness of thine excellency thou hast overthrown them that rose up against thee: thou sentest forth thy wrath, which consumed them as stubble.

And with the blast of thy nostrils the waters were gathered
   together, the floods stood upright as an heap, and the depths
   were congealed in the heart of the sea.
The enemy said, I will pursue, I will overtake, I will divide the
   spoil; my lust shall be satisfied upon them; I will draw my
   sword, my hand shall destroy them.
Thou didst blow with thy wind, the sea covered them: they sank
   as lead in the mighty waters.
Who is like unto thee, O Lord, among the gods? who is like
   thee, glorious in holiness, fearful in praises, doing wonders?
Thou stretchedst out thy right hand, the earth swallowed them.
Thou in thy mercy hast led forth the people which thou hast
   redeemed: thou hast guided them in thy strength unto thy
   holy habitation.
The people shall hear, and be afraid: sorrow shall take hold on
   the inhabitants of Palestina.
Then the dukes of Edom shall be amazed; the mighty men
   of Moab, trembling shall take hold upon them; all the
   inhabitants of Canaan shall melt away.
Fear and dread shall fall upon them; by the greatness of thine
   arm they shall be as still as a stone; till thy people pass over, O
   Lord, till the people pass over, which thou hast purchased.
Thou shalt bring them in, and plant them in the mountain of
   thine inheritance, in the place, O Lord, which thou hast made
   for thee to dwell in, in the Sanctuary, O Lord, which thy
   hands have established.
The Lord shall reign for ever and ever.

Whether as a child or now, I find the Hebrew of this song so archaic
that it baffles me. Then as now, I wonder at the diminishment in this
great song. The man of war, Yahweh, is celebrated for what is his victory alone. I remain perplexed by verse 15:11. Who are those gods to
whom Yahweh is compared? Can they really just be the angels of his
court?

It is not possible to read this poem and not remember Handel's setting of it in his *Israel in Egypt*. And yet, like so much of Exodus, it is
disquieting. We are given an antiphon between wilderness and revelation. Ever since childhood, I have been unhappy with the forty years of
wandering back and forth in the Sinai. How has Yahweh's outrageous-

ness in imposing a ghastly ordeal upon his chosen people escaped commentary? Could you or I endure forty years in the wilderness without horrible anguish and fierce discontent?

Yahweh, evidently unhappy at having to extend his Blessing to an entire nation, starts to be angry and self-contradictory. He says that he must not be seen by the people, and yet he will be seen, coming down upon Sinai in the sight of everyone:

> And the Lord came down upon mount Sinai, on the top of
>     the mount: and the Lord called Moses up to the top of the
>     mount; and Moses went up.
> And the Lord said unto Moses, Go down, charge the people, lest
>     they break through unto the Lord to gaze, and many of them
>     perish.
> And let the priests also, which come near to the Lord, sanctify
>     themselves, lest the Lord break forth upon them.
> And Moses said unto the Lord, The people cannot come up to
>     mount Sinai: for thou chargedst us, saying, Set bounds about
>     the mount, and sanctify it.
> And the Lord said unto him, Away, get thee down, and thou
>     shalt come up, thou, and Aaron with thee: but let not the
>     priests and the people break through to come up unto the
>     Lord, lest he break forth upon them.
> So Moses went down unto the people, and spake unto them.
>
>                                                 Exodus 19:20–25

There is a weird comedy when poor Moses has to remind Yahweh that the people cannot come up to Mount Sinai, because Yahweh seems to have forbidden it. But this is put aside in an incredible apex:

> Then went up Moses, and Aaron, Nadab, and Abihu, and
>     seventy of the elders of Israel:
> And they saw the God of Israel: and there was under his feet as
>     it were a paved work of a sapphire stone, and as it were the
>     body of heaven in his clearness.
> And upon the nobles of the children of Israel he laid not his
>     hand: also they saw God, and did eat and drink.
>
>                                                  Exodus 24:9–11

Even now I am overcome by the shock of this. Seventy-four holy men of Israel sit upon Sinai. They enjoy a picnic as guests of Yahweh. They stare at him while he stares back. For once only, in all of the Hebrew Bible, he is silent. Does he eat? They certainly do, but what is their food? The sublime subsides in mutual silence.

# Judges 13–16: Samson

JOHN MILTON'S FINAL WORK was the astonishing transmutation of Biblical legend into the form of Greek tragedy. *Samson Agonistes* is a unique splendor, with little resemblance to *Paradise Lost* and even less to *Paradise Regained.* All critical attempts to interpret it as a Christian poem are exercises in a kind of pathos alien to Milton's genius.

The story of Samson is told in Judges 13–16. Manoah has a barren wife, who is not named. Yahweh, evasively called an angel of the lord, manifests himself to her and prophesies that she will bear a son, consecrated to God from the beginning. This son of Manoah will be unshorn, dedicated to Yahweh from the womb onward.

Manoah requests the angel's name, but is warned that it is secret. Offered roast kid, Yahweh feasts while Manoah and his wife look on. The flame of the altar or rock rises up toward heaven, and Yahweh ascends in the fire, while Manoah and his wife fall on their faces, since they realize that they have seen God.

Samson's career begins with his choice of a Philistine wife, at a time when the Philistines govern Israel:

> Then went Samson down, and his father and his mother, to
> Timnath, and came to the vineyards of Timnath: and, behold,
> a young lion roared against him.
> And the Spirit of the Lord came mightily upon him, and he rent
> him as he would have rent a kid, and he had nothing in his
> hand: but he told not his father or his mother what he had
> done.
> And he went down, and talked with the woman; and she pleased
> Samson well.

And after a time he returned to take her, and he turned aside to
see the carcase of the lion: and, behold, there was a swarm of
bees and honey in the carcase of the lion.

And he took thereof in his hands, and went on eating, and came
to his father and mother, and he gave them, and they did eat:
but he told not them that he had taken the honey out of the
carcase of the lion.

So his father went down unto the woman: and Samson made
there a feast; for so used the young men to do.

And it came to pass, when they saw him, that they brought thirty
companions to be with him.

And Samson said unto them, I will now put forth a riddle unto
you: if ye can certainly declare it me within the seven days of
the feast, and find it out, then I will give you thirty sheets and
thirty change of garments:

But if ye cannot declare it me, then shall ye give me thirty sheets
and thirty change of garments. And they said unto him, Put
forth thy riddle, that we may hear it.

And he said unto them, Out of the eater came forth meat, and
out of the strong came forth sweetness. And they could not in
three days expound the riddle.

Judges 14:5–14

One could not say of Samson that "out of the strong came forth
sweetness." Except for his idolatry of his Philistine wife, there was no
sweetness in him. She betrays the secret of his riddle to the Philistines,
and he avenges himself by killing thirty of them, taking away their
spoils. Denied his wife by her father, he resorts to mischief against her
kinsmen:

And Samson went and caught three hundred foxes, and took
firebrands, and turned tail to tail, and put a firebrand in the
midst between two tails.

And when he had set the brands on fire, he let them go into
the standing corn of the Philistines, and burnt up both the
shocks, and also the standing corn, with the vineyards and
olives.

Judges 15:4–5

Delivered to the Philistines by the frightened men of Judah, Samson breaks loose:

> And he found a new jawbone of an ass, and put forth his hand,
>     and took it, and slew a thousand men therewith.
> And Samson said, With the jawbone of an ass, heaps upon heaps,
>     with the jaw of an ass have I slain a thousand men.
>
> > Judges 15:15–16

After this outrageous exploit, Samson meets his fate by falling in love with the Philistine temptress, Delilah. She betrays him to the lords of the Philistines, after he tells her the secret that all his consecrated power is in his hair:

> And she made him sleep upon her knees; and she called for a
>     man, and she caused him to shave off the seven locks of his
>     head; and she began to afflict him, and his strength went from
>     him.
> And she said, The Philistines be upon thee, Samson. And he
>     awoke out of his sleep, and said, I will go out as at other times
>     before, and shake myself. And he wist not that the Lord was
>     departed from him.
> But the Philistines took him, and put out his eyes, and brought
>     him down to Gaza, and bound him with fetters of brass; and
>     he did grind in the prison house.
> Howbeit the hair of his head began to grow again after he was
>     shaven.
>
> > Judges 16:19–22

The blinded Samson vindicates himself and his God by destroying himself and his enemies in a single act of furious violence:

> And it came to pass, when their hearts were merry, that they
>     said, Call for Samson, that he may make us sport. And they
>     called for Samson out of the prison house; and he made them
>     sport: and they set him between the pillars.
> And Samson said unto the lad that held him by the hand, Suffer
>     me that I may feel the pillars whereupon the house standeth,
>     that I may lean upon them.

Now the house was full of men and women; and all the lords
of the Philistines were there; and there were upon the roof
about three thousand men and women, that beheld while
Samson made sport.

And Samson called unto the Lord, and said, O Lord God,
remember me, I pray thee, and strengthen me, I pray thee,
only this once, O God, that I may be at once avenged of the
Philistines for my two eyes.

And Samson took hold of the two middle pillars upon which the
house stood, and on which it was borne up, of the one with
his right hand, and of the other with his left.

And Samson said, Let me die with the Philistines. And he bowed
himself with all his might; and the house fell upon the lords,
and upon all the people that were therein. So the dead which
he slew at his death were more than they which he slew in his
life.

Judges 16:25–30

I recall, in the far-off days of my youth, attending a lecture upon Milton's *Samson Agonistes* at Yale. It was given by the venerable Chauncey Brewster Tinker, a scholar noted for the appearance of stigmata upon him during Passion Week, a time when he was reputed to glare at all passing Jews. I walked out of the lecture soon after it began, because it devoted itself to the assertion that Milton's poem in every way transcended the barbaric Hebrew text.

# Daughter of a Voice:
## The Song of Deborah

THE HEBREW *bat kol* means "daughter of a voice" and in tradition was interpreted as the voice of Yahweh himself. In the Sinai epiphany, the Jews heard a speaking voice but beheld no divine similitude.

Though Yahweh's voice could be heard roaring from Mount Zion or thundering or breaking the waves, his most impressive manifestation came to Elijah as a still, small voice.

Jewish visual art tended to show the *bat kol* as the Hand of God. I stare across the table where I write and look at our menorah, a replica of a fourteenth-century Turkish emblem in the Smithsonian. Hart Crane's "Hand of Fire" trope in *The Bridge* is a descendant.

The *bat kol* is heard not in the prophets but in the poets. The War Song of the prophetess Deborah in Judges 5:1–31 would appear to be the oldest poem in the Hebrew Bible. It is set in the Iron Age (1200–1100 B.C.E.) and dates back to at least 1200 B.C.E.

Deborah's name means "utterance," and though she calls herself "a mother in Israel," that is a spiritual and not a literal assertion. In the King James Bible she is called "The wife of Lapidoth," but that appears to mean "the woman of torches," and she evidently has no husband. Her fierce general, Barak, whose name means "lightning," will not lead his warriors of Zebulun and Naphtali, both of them tribes of the lower Galilee, unless Deborah is a presence at the battle.

In chapter 4 of Judges, we begin with the dire situation of the children of Israel. The Canaanites, whose captain was Sisera, possess nine hundred chariots of iron. For twenty years Sisera torments the children of Israel. Deborah is introduced as the prophetess who judges Israel, as she sits beneath her palm tree. She calls unto her Barak the son of Abinoam and says to him: Take with you ten thousand men of the tribes of Naphtali and Zebulon. She promises that, at the river Kishon,

Sisera, with his chariots and his troops, will attack the Galilean warriors of Zebulun and Naphtali. With this fierce injunction, she will deliver Sisera into the hand of Barak.

Barak, for all his courage, replies that he will not go unless Deborah goes with him. Deborah rises and goes with Barak to Kedesh, where Barak calls up the men of Zebulun and Naphtali. Yahweh intervenes directly, and Sisera and his host are defeated, so badly that Sisera himself leaps from his chariot and runs away on his own feet as fast as he can. Barak pursues and destroys the entire host.

I always thrill to the King James Version of Deborah's triumphant outcry in Judges 5:18—"Zebulun and Naphtali were a people that jeoparded their lives unto the death in the high places of the field." A closer translation of the Hebrew might be "Zebulun is a force that scorned death: Naphtali also on the heights of the field," but the King James achieves a finer resonance:

> And the princes of Issachar were with Deborah; even Issachar,
>     and also Barak: he was sent on foot into the valley. For the
>     divisions of Reuben there were great thoughts of heart.
> Why abodest thou among the sheepfolds, to hear the bleating
>     of the flocks? For the divisions of Reuben there were great
>     searchings of heart.
> Gilead abode beyond Jordan: and why did Dan remain in ships?
>     Asher continued on the sea shore, and abode in his breaches.
> Zebulun and Naphtali were a people that jeoparded their lives
>     unto the death in the high places of the field.
>
> Judges 5:15–18

Deborah is fiercely sardonic in contrasting the tribes that did not respond to the challenge and the men of Zebulun and Naphtali who risked everything and fought heroically in the high places, a phrase at once descriptive and eulogistic. The Hebrew sublime is superbly exemplified by Deborah's triumphant outcry:

> They fought from heaven; the stars in their courses fought
>     against Sisera.
> The river of Kishon swept them away, that ancient river, the
>     river Kishon. O my soul, thou hast trodden down strength.
>
> Judges 5:20–21

The Hebrew is closer to "O my soul, tread them down with strength," but the King James Bible converts its misreading into a glory.

Stand back from the Song of Deborah and you see a bride of fire inspiring a lightning-like hero to victory in the name of Yahweh. The woman of torches is utterance itself, her name emanating from the Hebrew for "word": a word at once an act and the truth. The high song celebrates more than the warlike men of lower Galilee. It is the song of Yahweh as a man of war triumphant in the avenging of Israel, when the people of Deborah and Barak willingly offered themselves.

The emergence of the voice of Deborah is at once a gesture of freedom and a tribute to Yahweh. Is it not also a cry of survival prolonged into pragmatic immortality? That oxymoron informs the Song of Deborah's desire to memorialize the victors of the battle against Sisera. The pre-eminent victor is Jael, who pungently destroys the fleeing Sisera:

> Blessed above women shall Jael the wife of Heber the Kenite be, blessed shall she be above women in the tent.
> He asked water, and she gave him milk; she brought forth butter in a lordly dish.
> She put her hand to the nail, and her right hand to the workmen's hammer; and with the hammer she smote Sisera, she smote off his head, when she had pierced and stricken through his temples.
> At her feet he bowed, he fell, he lay down: at her feet he bowed, he fell: where he bowed, there he fell down dead.
> The mother of Sisera looked out at a window, and cried through the lattice, Why is his chariot so long in coming? why tarry the wheels of his chariots?
> Her wise ladies answered her, yea, she returned answer to herself,
> Have they not sped? have they not divided the prey; to every man a damsel or two; to Sisera a prey of divers colours, a prey of divers colours of needlework, of divers colours of needlework on both sides, meet for the necks of them that take the spoil?
> So let all thine enemies perish, O Lord: but let them that love him be as the sun when he goeth forth in his might. And the land had rest forty years.
>
> Geneva Bible, Judges 5:24–31

Fierce and exultant strains are heard against a satiric foregrounding of delusional expectations by the mother of Yahweh's enemy. Utterance has freed herself to affirm the Covenant. Stalwart and persuasive as a prophet must be, Deborah has found poetic immortality. We do not know who composed her battle ode, yet I see no reason why we should not suppose that it was a woman of the southern Galilee.

From my childhood on, I have thrilled to the sound of her song, whether chanted in Hebrew or in translation. Sir Philip Sidney remarked that when he heard the old ballad "Chevy Chase" a trumpet sounded in his heart. The Song of Deborah has that effect upon me. And the magnificent "Battle Hymn of the Republic," composed by the Boston abolitionist Julia Ward Howe and sung by Lincoln's forces in the Civil War, always recalls for me Deborah's War Song:

He has sounded forth the trumpet that shall never call retreat;
He is sifting out the hearts of men before His judgment seat:
Oh! be swift my soul, to answer Him! be jubilant, my feet!
    Our God is marching on.

# David:
## "Thou Art the Man"

K ING DAVID is the central hero of the Hebrew tradition. His story is something we feel intimately because so very large a part of European literary tradition emanates from him. Of all the Bible's personalities, David is the most novelistic. David's story is told from 1 and 2 Samuel through 1 Kings and then is retold in 1 Chronicles. We do not know who composed the book of Samuel. By tradition we call him the Court Historian, and I like to think of him as being a contemporary of the J writer.

Of all the figures throughout the Hebrew Bible, David seems to me the most Shakespearean. He is marked by inwardness and by an antithetical self. I do not find that I can think through to the end of David, any more than I can with Falstaff, Hamlet, Iago, Cleopatra. There is always more to engage the spirit. Samuel, by contrast, is ill-tempered, and his prophecy is scarcely unmarked by dangerous selfishness and dubious pomposity.

King Saul is perhaps the darkest soul in all of the Hebrew Bible. David is his bad luck. That is to say, Yahweh's fickleness destroys Saul by degrees. To be the first king of the Hebrews is a fearful fate. The narrator gives poor Saul no way out. His furies cannot prevail against the charismatic duplicity of David. After all, David charms Saul, beguiles Yahweh, and seduces Saul's children Jonathan and Michal.

David is a new kind of man. Though he is the beloved of Yahweh, and dances in naked joy before the Ark, he is a secular hero and in no way theological. Does anyone in ancient Greek literature resemble him in any vital way? James Joyce thought that Odysseus was the complete man, and there is much to be said for that observation. Yet Odysseus, compared with David, seems a less vital vision of human possibility.

It is true that Odysseus has to be single-minded. His opponent is the
ocean itself, which wishes to estrange him from home in Ithaca and his
true wife in Penelope. David's quest is more comprehensive. He carries
the Blessing, and so he does not need to seek or to find. He need come
home only to himself.

David is an astonishing improviser, which is the basis of his rise to
the kingship. It would not be unfair to call him an opportunist, a contrast to his friend Jonathan. Jonathan, caught between his love for his
father and for his friend David, is a far nobler personality. He and Saul
die in battle against the Philistines, provoking David's beautiful lament
for them both:

And David lamented with this lamentation over Saul and over
    Jonathan his son:
(Also he bade them teach the children of Judah the use of the
    bow: behold, it is written in the book of Jasher.)
The beauty of Israel is slain upon thy high places: how are the
    mighty fallen!
Tell it not in Gath, publish it not in the streets of Askelon; lest
    the daughters of the Philistines rejoice, lest the daughters of
    the uncircumcised triumph.
Ye mountains of Gilboa, let there be no dew, neither let there be
    rain, upon you, nor fields of offerings: for there the shield of
    the mighty is vilely cast away, the shield of Saul, as though he
    had not been anointed with oil.
From the blood of the slain, from the fat of the mighty, the bow
    of Jonathan turned not back, and the sword of Saul returned
    not empty.
Saul and Jonathan were lovely and pleasant in their lives, and
    in their death they were not divided: they were swifter than
    eagles, they were stronger than lions.
Ye daughters of Israel, weep over Saul, who clothed you in
    scarlet, with other delights, who put on ornaments of gold
    upon your apparel.
How are the mighty fallen in the midst of the battle! O
    Jonathan, thou wast slain in thine high places.
I am distressed for thee, my brother Jonathan: very pleasant hast

thou been unto me: thy love to me was wonderful, passing the
love of women.
How are the mighty fallen, and the weapons of war perished!

2 Samuel 1:17–27

Verse 23 is particularly beautiful:

Saul and Jonathan were lovely and pleasant in their lives, and
in their death they were not divided: they were swifter than
eagles, they were stronger than lions.

We can wonder as to the nature of David's love for Jonathan, as in
verse 26:

I am distressed for thee, my brother Jonathan: very pleasant hast
thou been unto me: thy love to me was wonderful, passing the
love of women.

There may well be homoerotic overtones, but they are crowded out
by the poem's political duplicity. It clearly overstates David's affection
for both Jonathan and Saul. David seems to have loved only two people:
his tragic son, Absalom, and his wife, Bathsheba, for whom his lust was
surpassing.

It has always puzzled me that David is forgiven by Hebrew tradition
for his own relationship to the Philistines. When in flight from Saul,
he heads a group of freebooters, and is a vassal of the Philistines. Yet he
ends the Philistine menace, and for that achievement much is forgiven.
Whereas the Yahwist's saga tells the story of an entire people, the tale
of David is a very different fiction. It is the first portrait of an artist who
is both beloved of God and a national leader.

David is both a usurper and a true king. He is a musician and a poet,
and very difficult to judge. He can be compassionate when it is useful,
but also ruthless. I find in him the ultimate model for Shakespeare's
Hamlet. David and Hamlet alike could be termed a siege of contrar-
ies. They inspire love but they do not return it. Hamlet will always
be the hero of Western consciousness. But David is also a religious
personality, and that increases his complexity. Like Hamlet, David is
an incarnate poem. He dances naked before the Ark, and he grieves for
his dead son, Absalom.

In 2 Samuel 11, David seduces Bathsheba, the wife of his warrior Uriah the Hittite, then arranges for Uriah to die in battle. In chapter 12, a prophet, Nathan, tells David a parable that the King is unable to understand.

> And the Lord sent Nathan unto David. And he came unto him, and said unto him, There were two men in one city; the one rich, and the other poor.
>
> The rich man had exceeding many flocks and herds:
>
> But the poor man had nothing, save one little ewe lamb, which he had bought and nourished up: and it grew up together with him, and with his children; it did eat of his own meat, and drank of his own cup, and lay in his bosom, and was unto him as a daughter.
>
> And there came a traveller unto the rich man, and he spared to take of his own flock and of his own herd, to dress for the wayfaring man that was come unto him; but took the poor man's lamb, and dressed it for the man that was come to him.
>
> And David's anger was greatly kindled against the man; and he said to Nathan, As the Lord liveth, the man that hath done this thing shall surely die:
>
> And he shall restore the lamb fourfold, because he did this thing, and because he had no pity.
>
> And Nathan said to David, Thou art the man. Thus saith the Lord God of Israel, I anointed thee king over Israel, and I delivered thee out of the hand of Saul;
>
> And I gave thee thy master's house, and thy master's wives into thy bosom, and gave thee the house of Israel and of Judah; and if that had been too little, I would moreover have given unto thee such and such things.
>
> Wherefore hast thou despised the commandment of the Lord, to do evil in his sight? thou hast killed Uriah the Hittite with the sword, and hast taken his wife to be thy wife, and hast slain him with the sword of the children of Ammon.
>
> Now therefore the sword shall never depart from thine house; because thou hast despised me, and hast taken the wife of Uriah the Hittite to be thy wife.
>
> 2 Samuel 12:1–10

The superb directness of Nathan gives us that great indictment in four words: "Thou art the man." The phrasing was originally William Tyndale's and is a true instance of the Hebrew sublime. Its laconic force is unmatchable:

> Thus saith the Lord, Behold, I will raise up evil against thee
>     out of thine own house, and I will take thy wives before thine
>     eyes, and give them unto thy neighbour, and he shall lie with
>     thy wives in the sight of this sun.
> For thou didst it secretly: but I will do this thing before all
>     Israel, and before the sun.
> And David said unto Nathan, I have sinned against the Lord.
>     And Nathan said unto David, The Lord also hath put away
>     thy sin; thou shalt not die.
> Howbeit, because by this deed thou hast given great occasion to
>     the enemies of the Lord to blaspheme, the child also that is
>     born unto thee shall surely die.
> And Nathan departed unto his house. And the Lord struck the
>     child that Uriah's wife bare unto David, and it was very sick.
> David therefore besought God for the child; and David fasted,
>     and went in, and lay all night upon the earth.
> And the elders of his house arose, and went to him, to raise him
>     up from the earth: but he would not, neither did he eat bread
>     with them.
> And it came to pass on the seventh day, that the child died. And
>     the servants of David feared to tell him that the child was
>     dead: for they said, Behold, while the child was yet alive, we
>     spake unto him, and he would not hearken unto our voice:
>     how will he then vex himself, if we tell him that the child is
>     dead?
> But when David saw that his servants whispered, David
>     perceived that the child was dead: therefore David said unto
>     his servants, Is the child dead? And they said, He is dead.
> Then David arose from the earth, and washed, and anointed
>     himself, and changed his apparel, and came into the house of
>     the Lord, and worshipped: then he came to his own house;
>     and when he required, they set bread before him, and he did
>     eat.
> Then said his servants unto him, What thing is this that thou

hast done? thou didst fast and weep for the child, while it was
alive; but when the child was dead, thou didst rise and eat
bread.
And he said, While the child was yet alive, I fasted and wept: for
I said, Who can tell whether God will be gracious to me, that
the child may live?
But now he is dead, wherefore should I fast? can I bring him
back again? I shall go to him, but he shall not return to me.

2 Samuel 12:11–23

David sorrows fiercely at the death of the boy he had fathered upon
Bathsheba. His mourning is total. But when it is clear that the child
indeed is lost forever, David makes a great recovery. He controls both
his grief and his tragic acceptance of irreparable loss. I find it extraordinarily moving that he is so firmly in command of the vicissitudes of our
lives. Who can forget "I shall go to him, but he shall not return to me"?
It sums up our relationship to all our loved ones who have preceded us
into the valley of the shadow of death.

There is a great surge of force as we move from 2 Samuel 13 through
1 Kings 2, the Succession Narrative that takes us from David to Solomon, another of Bathsheba's sons. William Faulkner, with his genius
for matching the Hebrew sublime, composed the most powerful of his
novels, *Absalom, Absalom!* (1936), employing this great Davidic myth.

The heart of the Succession Narrative is Absalom's rebellion. Absalom, a kind of reincarnation of the young David, is his father's favorite
son, which adds poignance to his attempted usurpation of the kingdom:

And Ahithophel said unto Absalom, Go in unto thy father's
concubines, which he hath left to keep the house; and all
Israel shall hear that thou art abhorred of thy father: then
shall the hands of all that are with thee be strong.
So they spread Absalom a tent upon the top of the house; and
Absalom went in unto his father's concubines in the sight of
all Israel.

2 Samuel 16:21–22

William Tyndale powerfully rendered the line in verse 21 as "For
when all Israel shall hear that thou hast made thy father to stink." Here
is the KJB's famous lament of David for the slain Absalom:

And the king was much moved, and went up to the chamber
over the gate, and wept: and as he went, thus he said, O my
son Absalom, my son, my son Absalom! would God I had
died for thee, O Absalom, my son, my son!

2 Samuel 18:33

Strong as that is, I prefer William Tyndale's version, since he conveys
best of all the wildness of David's grief:

And the king was moved and went up to a chamber over the gate
and wept. And as he went thus he said: my son Absalom, my
son, my son, my son Absalom, would to God I had died for
thee Absalom, my son, my son.

I wonder what William Faulkner would have made of this had he
looked into Tyndale's Bible. With the death of Absalom, David's story
ebbs. It is unclear whether Bathsheba and Nathan urge David to name
Solomon, or if this was in fact his own decision. Though Solomon is
second in prestige only to David among all of the kings of Israel, he is
an ambiguous personality. He builds the Temple, but we wonder why
he should have been esteemed not just for wealth and erotic intensity
but also for wisdom. David is an endlessly fascinating human being.
By comparison, Solomon is a mystery. The book of Kings is highly
ambivalent toward him, and his supposed authorship of the Song of
Songs and of Koheleth (Ecclesiastes) is unpersuasive.

Through 1 Kings 1–11, the story of Solomon seems to be told with
considerable irony. We do not feel any affection for him at all. Instead
we long for his charismatic father. Wealth, worldly achievement, contemporary fame—all these fade away where there is no personality.

# The Hebrew Prophets

T HE DISTINCTION between poetry and prophecy is always tenuous. The Hebrew word *navi* is mistranslated by the Greek *prophetes*, merely someone who interprets an oracle. A *navi* himself is the oracle. He answers the Yahweh-call. Each time he commences he asserts, "The Yahweh-word was to me." The Hebrew for "word," *davar*, means an act, as well as a word or a thing, and takes on the aura of the truth.

It always seems absurd to me that the Hebrew prophets should have been tamed by canonical inclusion. Making Amos into scripture is an act of interpretive violence. All institutionalizing of prophecy is betrayal. I myself greatly prefer First Isaiah and Amos to Jeremiah and Ezekiel, because Yahweh is more dangerously extreme in the latter two, most in the disturbed Ezekiel.

Prophecy indeed is a mode of poetry, but only one. Even deep readers have difficulty in trying to sort out the spiritual and aesthetic strands in their response to the Bible. I regard such difficulty as inevitable. Prophecy would be meaningless without Yahweh. But Yahweh is an uncanny, dangerous, altogether outrageous God. Though he is given to proclaiming his ethos, that always seems to me questionable. And his logos hardly exists when we compare it with his exuberant pathos, in which his legatee is King Lear.

To be Yahweh's chosen man is a dreadful fate. Though the Judaic sages insisted there were fifty-five canonical prophets, I myself cannot locate nearly that many. Their prophet of prophets is Moses. To that, one responds that if Elijah and the First Isaiah are prophets, then Moses is something else. He is a literary character. But, then, so are Elijah and Isaiah. And though we resist this, so are Yahweh and Jesus.

All the prophets have extraordinary personalities, Ezekiel and Jeremiah in particular. Though they are great poets, they oscillate between bipolarity and psychosis. I always think that, if Ezekiel and Jeremiah are prophets, then Amos and Isaiah of Jerusalem are something better, because their message is social justice.

Oral prophecy is very difficult to apprehend. Yet it puzzles me that only Isaiah of Jerusalem seems as much a historical figure as the purely legendary Elijah and Elisha. Elijah and his disciple Elisha are uncanny. They work miracles, and they have a power of resurrection. Elisha, a rather nasty blunderer, is a much more archaic personality than the transcendental Elijah. The prestige of Elijah is so enormous that it rivals the high place of Moses. I still remember my awe at every Passover seder as I sleepily stared at the wine glass set aside for Eliayhu ha-Navi. Sometimes I had the fantasy that the fiery prophet had indeed passed by and drained the wine.

Elijah never dies. Instead he ascends to Yahweh in a chariot of fire. His anxious disciple Elisha does the reverse, and returns to earth at the end. I personally am delighted by that splendid couple, King Ahab and Queen Jezebel. "Ahab" was appropriated by Herman Melville for the great avenger who sails the whaler *Pequod* to its doom. Nobody now names their daughter Jezebel, which I regret. In the same spirit that I argue the Macbeths to be the happiest married couple in Shakespeare, I vote for Ahab and Jezebel in the Hebrew Bible. Though Jezebel and Ahab end badly, their mutual compact is never abrogated.

The first appearance of Elijah is sublime and disruptive. It is driven by a divine impetus, as you might expect from a prophet whose own name fuses "El," "the almighty," and "Yahweh." Here is the extraordinary swiftness in which Elijah first comes into our view:

> And Elijah the Tishbite, who was of the inhabitants of Gilead,
>     said unto Ahab, As the Lord God of Israel liveth, before
>     whom I stand, there shall not be dew nor rain these years, but
>     according to my word.
> And the word of the Lord came unto him, saying,
> Get thee hence, and turn thee eastward, and hide thyself by the
>     brook Cherith, that is before Jordan.
> And it shall be, that thou shalt drink of the brook; and I have
>     commanded the ravens to feed thee there.
> So he went and did according unto the word of the Lord: for he
>     went and dwelt by the brook Cherith, that is before Jordan.

> And the ravens brought him bread and flesh in the morning, and
> bread and flesh in the evening; and he drank of the brook.
>
> 1 Kings 17:1–6

Yahweh's opponent, Baal, is a rain god. Elijah simply erupts. The village of Tishbe is unknown. With Yahweh's authority, his prophet Elijah
proclaims drought. From that moment on, his career will be a continuous miracle, until his ascension in the flaming chariot. Much more
than his New Testament anxious imitator, John the Baptist, Elijah is a
Yahweh-like phenomenon. He is at once transcendent and immanent,
a divine fire and "a hairy man."

Always a solitary until he accepts Elisha as his disciple, Elijah is a
frightening precursor for the entire tradition of prophets. His most
famous challenge is to the 450 prophets of Baal, gathered together by
Jezebel with a group of four hundred more prophets of Asherah, the
mother of the gods of Canaan. The agon takes place upon Mount Car-
mel. Elijah stands alone against 850 false prophets and satirizes them
into absurdity.

> And Elijah came unto all the people, and said, How long halt ye
> between two opinions? if the Lord be God, follow him: but
> if Baal, then follow him. And the people answered him not a
> word.
> Then said Elijah unto the people, I, even I only, remain a
> prophet of the Lord; but Baal's prophets are four hundred
> and fifty men.
> Let them therefore give us two bullocks; and let them choose
> one bullock for themselves, and cut it in pieces, and lay it
> on wood, and put no fire under: and I will dress the other
> bullock, and lay it on wood, and put no fire under:
> And call ye on the name of your gods, and I will call on the
> name of the Lord: and the God that answereth by fire, let
> him be God. And all the people answered and said, It is well
> spoken.
>
> 1 Kings 18:21–24

Elijah's ironic derision breaks forth with splendid intensity when
Baal simply fails to respond.

And it came to pass at noon, that Elijah mocked them, and
said, Cry aloud: for he is a god; either he is talking, or he is
pursuing, or he is in a journey, or peradventure he sleepeth,
and must be awaked.
And they cried aloud, and cut themselves after their manner
with knives and lancets, till the blood gushed out upon them.
And it came to pass, when midday was past, and they prophesied
until the time of the offering of the evening sacrifice, that
there was neither voice, nor any to answer, nor any that
regarded.
And Elijah said unto all the people, Come near unto me. And all
the people came near unto him. And he repaired the altar of
the Lord that was broken down.

1 Kings 18:27–30

The fire of Yahweh comes down. The absurd contest ends. His life
threatened by Jezebel's vengeance, Elijah flees south of Beersheba into
the wilderness of the Negev. He stands upon Horeb, sacred mountain
of Yahweh, and a great epiphany follows:

And he came thither unto a cave, and lodged there; and, behold,
the word of the Lord came to him, and he said unto him,
What doest thou here, Elijah?
And he said, I have been very jealous for the Lord God of hosts:
for the children of Israel have forsaken thy covenant, thrown
down thine altars, and slain thy prophets with the sword; and
I, even I only, am left; and they seek my life, to take it away.
And he said, Go forth, and stand upon the mount before the
Lord. And, behold, the Lord passed by, and a great and strong
wind rent the mountains, and brake in pieces the rocks before
the Lord; but the Lord was not in the wind: and after the
wind an earthquake; but the Lord was not in the earthquake:
And after the earthquake a fire; but the Lord was not in the fire:
and after the fire a still small voice.

1 Kings 19:9–12

The Hebrew *qol demmanah daqah* is oxymoronic. It could be translated as "a soundless stillness," "a small voice of silence," or, better yet,

"a voice of thin silence." The King James Version triumphs in "a still small voice." I can think of only two ways of understanding Elijah: that of Jezebel and Ahab, and that of Elisha. Ahab is so afraid of Elijah that he does not dare execute him. The ferocious Jezebel would risk anything. But both end as Elijah prophesied. Ahab is slain in battle, and the dogs lick up his blood; poor Jezebel is defenestrated, and much of her corpse is devoured by dogs.

I find Elisha even more peculiar than Elijah and the oddest of disciples for Elijah to have chosen. He gathers around him a host of sons of the prophets and becomes a kind of war counselor to the royal court. He sanctions the bloodthirsty Jehu, which ironically culminates the tradition of Elijah. His endless miracles seem to me endlessly annoying.

Jehu destroys the family of Jezebel and Ahab. This massacre has the approval of the redactors of Kings. As far as I can tell, the historical Ahab was a strong king, but his military and political successes were cast aside by the Bible. I do not in the least believe in his wickedness or that of Jezebel. She was not even a Hebrew but a Phoenician princess, possibly of the family of Dido of Carthage. But, then, the saga of Elijah and Elisha was not history but religious polemic.

# Isaiah of Jerusalem:
## "Arise, Shine; For Thy Light Is Come"

T HE DISTINCTION BETWEEN sacred and secular works is merely political and social. Though I resist, I am haunted always by the aura of transcendence that the Bible possesses for me.

Isaiah of Jerusalem, himself of the royal house, prophesied in the later years of the eighth century B.C.E. There was a School of Isaiah, including the famous Second Isaiah, who achieves a magnificence I cannot cease hearing in my mind:

> Arise, shine; for thy light is come, and the glory of the Lord is risen upon thee.
> For, behold, the darkness shall cover the earth, and gross darkness the people: but the Lord shall arise upon thee, and his glory shall be seen upon thee.
> And the Gentiles shall come to thy light, and kings to the brightness of thy rising.
> Lift up thine eyes round about, and see: all they gather themselves together, they come to thee: thy sons shall come from far, and thy daughters shall be nursed at thy side.
> Then thou shalt see, and flow together, and thine heart shall fear, and be enlarged; because the abundance of the sea shall be converted unto thee, the forces of the Gentiles shall come unto thee.
>
> Geneva Bible, Isaiah 60:1–5

Rhapsodic and exultant, this has been interpreted by Christianity as the advent of the Incarnation. From such a perspective, doubtless that is legitimate, however ahistorical. In context, this prophetic ecstasy has its mysteries, yet for me its blessing is literary. I listen even at my age to a trumpet call that urges me to fresh hope: "Arise, shine; for thy light is come, and the glory of the Lord is risen upon thee." I think of Walt Whitman chanting: "Dazzling and tremendous how quick the sunrise would kill me,/If I could not now and always send forth sunrise from myself." Or I hear Wallace Stevens lamenting: "The exceeding brightness of this early sun/Makes me conceive how dark I have become."

I am compelled now to live mostly indoors and find myself staring out of the window and being moved by the surprisingly temperate early-March weather. What we call the weather is the absence or presence of sun, wind, rain, or snow: "Ever-jubilant,/What is there here but weather, what spirit/Have I except it comes from the sun?"

# Psalms or Praises

P SALMS IS THE longest book in the Hebrew Bible. Doubtless it is also the most influential upon Jews and Christians in terms of high literature; it has brought into existence a large body of major lyric poems, both devotional and secular. And yet it is a puzzling work. There are 150 psalms composed across some six centuries, from 996 to 457 B.C.E. It is possible that some of them were written by King David, but not many. Rather than discuss so large a work, I will confine myself to the psalms that mean the most to me: 19, 23, 24, 46, and 68.

"Psalm," as an English word, derives from the Greek translation of the Hebrew *mizmor*, a song set to music. In Jewish tradition, the Psalms were called Tehillim (Praises), and all of them praise and express gratitude to Yahweh. The God of the Psalms has comforted multitudes, whether in the valley of decision, or in the valley of the shadow of death. He does not comfort me, because I do not know how to think in a realm of gratitude.

And yet the Psalms have comforted millions. They pray to a God more compassionate than ever existed in reality. The best critical observation I know about them is by Herbert Marks, who said they were "untouched by irony."

The God of the Psalms is an absent father, but he can also be an angry presence. In poetic history, Psalm 19:1–6 has been immensely influential.

> The heavens declare the glory of God; and the firmament
> sheweth his handywork.
> Day unto day uttereth speech, and night unto night sheweth
> knowledge.

There is no speech nor language, where their voice is not
  heard.
Their line is gone out through all the earth, and their words to
  the end of the world. In them hath he set a tabernacle for the
  sun,
Which is as a bridegroom coming out of his chamber, and
  rejoiceth as a strong man to run a race.
His going forth is from the end of the heaven, and his circuit
  unto the ends of it: and there is nothing hid from the heat
  thereof.

That wonderful verse 5 is Miltonic before John Milton. We are
dazzled by its double vision of the rising sun as both an agonist and a
bridegroom. With Psalm 23, we come to the most famous psalm in the
entire English tradition.

The Lord is my shepherd; I shall not want.
He maketh me to lie down in green pastures: he leadeth me
  beside the still waters.
He restoreth my soul: he leadeth me in the paths of
  righteousness for his name's sake.
Yea, though I walk through the valley of the shadow of death,
  I will fear no evil: for thou art with me; thy rod and thy staff
  they comfort me.
Thou preparest a table before me in the presence of mine
  enemies: thou anointest my head with oil; my cup runneth
  over.
Surely goodness and mercy shall follow me all the days of my
  life: and I will dwell in the house of the Lord for ever.

The King James translators superbly misread what they call "still
waters" in verse 2, where the Hebrew says "waters of rest." In verse 4,
where the Hebrew says "total darkness," there is a great transfiguration
into "the valley of the shadow of death." In verse 6, "mercy" is in the
Hebrew "loving-kindness," and "for ever" is the more ambiguous "for
length of days." The dying Sir John Falstaff, as reported by Mistress
Quickly in *Henry V*, evidently sang Psalm 23, though when she gives it
as "a babbled of green fields," she garbles it, intending to say "a table of

green fields," which would fuse together "green pastures" and "Thou preparest a table before me."

It may be that Psalm 24 was sung during processions of the Ark. It is a triumph of the King James Version.

> The earth is the Lord's, and the fulness thereof; the world, and
>     they that dwell therein.
> For he hath founded it upon the seas, and established it upon
>     the floods.
> Who shall ascend into the hill of the Lord? or who shall stand in
>     his holy place?
> He that hath clean hands, and a pure heart; who hath not lifted
>     up his soul unto vanity, nor sworn deceitfully.
> He shall receive the blessing from the Lord, and righteousness
>     from the God of his salvation.
> This is the generation of them that seek him, that seek thy face,
>     O Jacob. Selah.
> Lift up your heads, O ye gates; and be ye lift up, ye everlasting
>     doors; and the King of glory shall come in.
> Who is this King of glory? The Lord strong and mighty, the
>     Lord mighty in battle.
> Lift up your heads, O ye gates; even lift them up, ye everlasting
>     doors; and the King of glory shall come in.
> Who is this King of glory? The Lord of hosts, he is the King of
>     glory. Selah.

*Selah* remains a mystery. I read this as a celebration of Yahweh as a man of war, particularly powerful in verse 7, which is then repeated as verse 9. Psalm 46 reminds us of Isaiah's celebration of Yahweh's defense of Jerusalem. Though Psalm 46 was not written for that intervention, it might well have been.

> God is our refuge and strength, a very present help in trouble.
> Therefore will not we fear, though the earth be removed, and
>     though the mountains be carried into the midst of the sea;
> Though the waters thereof roar and be troubled, though the
>     mountains shake with the swelling thereof. Selah.
> There is a river, the streams whereof shall make glad the city of
>     God, the holy place of the tabernacles of the most High.

God is in the midst of her; she shall not be moved: God shall
help her, and that right early.
The heathen raged, the kingdoms were moved: he uttered his
voice, the earth melted.
The Lord of hosts is with us; the God of Jacob is our refuge.
Selah.
Come, behold the works of the Lord, what desolations he hath
made in the earth.
He maketh wars to cease unto the end of the earth; he breaketh
the bow, and cutteth the spear in sunder; he burneth the
chariot in the fire.
Be still, and know that I am God: I will be exalted among the
heathen, I will be exalted in the earth.
The Lord of hosts is with us; the God of Jacob is our refuge.
Selah.

The river in verse 4 becomes, in Ezekiel and in Revelation, the pure
river of the water of life. Yahweh's great outcry celebrates himself in "I
will be exalted among the heathen, I will be exalted in the earth."
I have a special passion for Psalm 68:

Let God arise, let his enemies be scattered: let them also that
hate him flee before him.
As smoke is driven away, so drive them away: as wax melteth
before the fire, so let the wicked perish at the presence of
God.
But let the righteous be glad; let them rejoice before God: yea,
let them exceedingly rejoice.
Sing unto God, sing praises to his name: extol him that rideth
upon the heavens by his name Jah, and rejoice before him.
A father of the fatherless, and a judge of the widows, is God in
his holy habitation.
God setteth the solitary in families: he bringeth out those which
are bound with chains: but the rebellious dwell in a dry land.
O God, when thou wentest forth before thy people, when thou
didst march through the wilderness; Selah:
The earth shook, the heavens also dropped at the presence of
God: even Sinai itself was moved at the presence of God, the
God of Israel.

Thou, O God, didst send a plentiful rain, whereby thou didst
   confirm thine inheritance, when it was weary.
Thy congregation hath dwelt therein: thou, O God, hast
   prepared of thy goodness for the poor.
The Lord gave the word: great was the company of those that
   published it.
Kings of armies did flee apace: and she that tarried at home
   divided the spoil.
Though ye have lien among the pots, yet shall ye be as the wings
   of a dove covered with silver, and her feathers with yellow
   gold.

                                                    Psalm 68:1–13

The thirteenth verse haunted my critical hero, Walter Pater, whose
passion for it was transmembered by Henry James to title his great
novel, *The Wings of the Dove* (1902):

If, like Walter Pater and Henry James, you believe that the powers of
the high arts are a resurrection, then you are very moved by the psalm's
appeal to your experience. I lie here in a rehabilitation center, and so I
too have lain among broken vessels, and I yearn to rise up again in the
silver and gold of the ascending dove.

# Job:
## Holding His Ground

WHAT SHALL WE MAKE of the book of Job, now in this dark year of 2017? As an aesthetic glory, it is unique even in the Hebrew Bible, but what exactly is it? It is certainly not a theodicy. I see increasingly that both Job and *King Lear* demonstrate that there is simply no language appropriate when we seek to confront Yahweh.

Job's name seems to derive from the Arabic *awah*, "he who returns to God," but the Rabbis saw the name as antithetical, meaning both "just" and "the enemy of God." In the prologue and epilogue Yahweh is named properly, but in the poem he is called El, Elosh, Elohim, and Shaddai. That leaves us with Ha-Satan, the accuser of sin, but certainly not Satan in the Miltonic sense.

The prologue centers on an extraordinary exchange between Yahweh and the Satan, who is here a kind of authorized accuser of sin.

> Now there was a day when the sons of God came to present themselves before the Lord, and Satan came also among them.
> And the Lord said unto Satan, Whence comest thou? Then Satan answered the Lord, and said, From going to and fro in the earth, and from walking up and down in it.
> And the Lord said unto Satan, Hast thou considered my servant Job, that there is none like him in the earth, a perfect and an upright man, one that feareth God, and escheweth evil?
> Then Satan answered the Lord, and said, Doth Job fear God for nought?
> Hast not thou made an hedge about him, and about his house, and about all that he hath on every side? thou hast blessed the work of his hands, and his substance is increased in the land.

But put forth thine hand now, and touch all that he hath, and he
 will curse thee to thy face.
And the Lord said unto Satan, Behold, all that he hath is in thy
 power; only upon himself put not forth thine hand. So Satan
 went forth from the presence of the Lord.

Job 1:6–12

I always reflect that both Yahweh and the Satan are very unpleasant
persons. Job has no faults, though his horrible Comforts will look for
what nonsense they can find. As a troublemaker, the Satan is merely
laboring in his vocation. Yahweh's motives appear to be his usual bad
temper, or perhaps just a CEO's skepticism concerning his most faithful
employee. To justify Yahweh here you would need all the scandalous
talents of Tony Kushner's Roy Cohn in *Perestroika*.

We do not know who the poet of the book of Job was. He may
not even have been an Israelite. He does not seem to have written the
prologue; he begins in the grand debate in chapters 3–31. The inept
epilogue is just a pious absurdity.

For me the greatness of Job centers upon chapter 41.

Canst thou draw out leviathan with an hook? or his tongue with
 a cord which thou lettest down?
Canst thou put an hook into his nose? or bore his jaw through
 with a thorn?
Will he make many supplications unto thee? will he speak soft
 words unto thee?
Will he make a covenant with thee? wilt thou take him for a
 servant for ever?
Wilt thou play with him as with a bird? or wilt thou bind him
 for thy maidens?
Shall the companions make a banquet of him? shall they part
 him among the merchants?
Canst thou fill his skin with barbed irons? or his head with fish
 spears?
Lay thine hand upon him, remember the battle, do no more.
Behold, the hope of him is in vain: shall not one be cast down
 even at the sight of him?
None is so fierce that dare stir him up: who then is able to stand
 before me?

Who hath prevented me, that I should repay him? whatsoever is
under the whole heaven is mine.

I will not conceal his parts, nor his power, nor his comely
proportion.

Who can discover the face of his garment? or who can come to
him with his double bridle?

Who can open the doors of his face? his teeth are terrible round
about.

His scales are his pride, shut up together as with a close seal.

One is so near to another, that no air can come between them.

They are joined one to another, they stick together, that they
cannot be sundered.

By his neesings a light doth shine, and his eyes are like the
eyelids of the morning.

Out of his mouth go burning lamps, and sparks of fire leap out.

Out of his nostrils goeth smoke, as out of a seething pot or
caldron.

His breath kindleth coals, and a flame goeth out of his mouth.

In his neck remaineth strength, and sorrow is turned into joy
before him.

The flakes of his flesh are joined together: they are firm in
themselves; they cannot be moved.

His heart is as firm as a stone; yea, as hard as a piece of the
nether millstone.

When he raiseth up himself, the mighty are afraid: by reason of
breakings they purify themselves.

The sword of him that layeth at him cannot hold: the spear, the
dart, nor the habergeon.

He esteemeth iron as straw, and brass as rotten wood.

The arrow cannot make him flee: slingstones are turned with
him into stubble.

Darts are counted as stubble: he laugheth at the shaking of a
spear.

Sharp stones are under him: he spreadeth sharp pointed things
upon the mire.

He maketh the deep to boil like a pot: he maketh the sea like a
pot of ointment.

He maketh a path to shine after him; one would think the deep
to be hoary.

Upon earth there is not his like, who is made without fear.
He beholdeth all high things: he is a king over all the children of
    pride.

Yahweh sanctifies Behemoth and Leviathan, who are the tyranny of
nature over humankind. Yahweh is nastily proud of them, and his pride
taunts us. What I hear in this is brutal wisdom. And yet the revision
touches upon a negative sublimity. Will he make a covenant with thee?
Even as a little child I found this divine sarcasm unbearable, but as a
bombardment of exuberances it substitutes power for justification. Is
this Yahweh really still interested in covenant?

If the book of Job does offer wisdom, it is beyond anything that I
can apprehend. Hence the superb poem of chapter 28:12–28, where
we have no choice except yielding to eloquence.

But where shall wisdom be found? and where is the place of
    understanding?
Man knoweth not the price thereof; neither is it found in the
    land of the living.
The depth saith, It is not in me: and the sea saith, It is not with me.
It cannot be gotten for gold, neither shall silver be weighed for
    the price thereof.
It cannot be valued with the gold of Ophir, with the precious
    onyx, or the sapphire.
The gold and the crystal cannot equal it: and the exchange of it
    shall not be for jewels of fine gold.
No mention shall be made of coral, or of pearls: for the price of
    wisdom is above rubies.
The topaz of Ethiopia shall not equal it, neither shall it be
    valued with pure gold.
Whence then cometh wisdom? and where is the place of
    understanding?
Seeing it is hid from the eyes of all living, and kept close from
    the fowls of the air.
Destruction and death say, We have heard the fame thereof with
    our ears.
God understandeth the way thereof, and he knoweth the place
    thereof.

For he looketh to the ends of the earth, and seeth under the
     whole heaven;
To make the weight for the winds; and he weigheth the waters
     by measure.
When he made a decree for the rain, and a way for the lightning
     of the thunder:
Then did he see it, and declare it; he prepared it, yea, and
     searched it out.
And unto man he said, Behold, the fear of the Lord, that is
     wisdom; and to depart from evil is understanding.

Poetry is defeated here by wisdom. Yahweh does not bother to
defend his justice. His goal is devastation by language just as *Moby-
Dick* destroys Ahab, the *Pequod*, and all the crew except Ishmael, who
in the accents of Job escapes alone to tell us. No one could possibly
undervalue the literary power of the book of Job, but can there be a
wisdom literature if it gives up being wise?

From childhood on, I have insisted upon reading the book of Job as
a fury against the injustice of Yahweh.

Wherefore I abhor myself, and repent in dust and ashes.

                                                     Job 42:6

Herbert Marks wonderfully points out that the verb "abhor" lacks
any object in the Hebrew. Scholars mistranslate this as "I recant." If
you want to you can see Job as penitent, but I go with Herbert Marks.
Job holds his ground. He casts aside his own humility, and he pities all
mortals ("dust and ashes") for being subject to so dreadful a Yahweh.

# The Song of Songs:
## "Set Me as a Seal upon Thine Heart"

A FTER SIXTY-ODD YEARS of teaching, I go on telling my students
to go apart, whether outdoors or alone in their room, and read
very slowly out loud to themselves. When I reread I murmur softly
to myself, frequently closing my eyes, since I possess the work by
memory. Few weeks go by these days without the loss of friends and
good acquaintances in my own generation, and at moments I wonder
whether I read and teach to hold off death. There is no melancholy in
such reflection, since I waveringly have the vision that I share my quest
with all readers who struggle for the Blessing of a more abundant life.

Yesterday an old friend visited and reminded me we had met at a
temple in Washington, D.C., half a century ago, when I lectured to the
congregation on the elements in normative Judaism that were imported
by Rabbi Akiba and his school from Platonism. I did not intend to be
contentious, but many of them were troubled by my insistence that
nothing in Tanakh (the Hebrew Bible) stated that a people or an individual could become holy through study. Although that seems now the
most Judaic of commonplaces, it did not exist before the Platonic influx
into second-century B.C.E. Palestine. In discussion afterward, several
of them expressed dismay when I summed up by saying that normative
Judaism was an extremely persuasive misreading of Tanakh, carried out
by Akiba and his followers to meet the needs of a Jewish people under
Roman occupation.

I cite this only as an instance of how subtle and complex the reading
of a great literary text can be, since without Akiba's misprision Judaism
could not have survived. Akiba, martyred by the Romans for inspiring
the Bar Kochba insurrection, had struggled with the angel in the mode
of Jacob who became Israel. The difference was that Akiba made the

text of the Hebrew Bible into the angel who had to be withstood. It has always charmed me that the Song of Songs was included in Tanakh only at the insistence of Akiba, evidently since he read it as part of the Oral Torah given by Yahweh at Sinai. For the great founder of normative Judaism, the Song of Songs celebrated Yahweh in love.

Most of us enjoy the Song of Songs as an astonishing dramatic lyric that contrasts the erotic ecstasy of a woman with that of a man. In the King James Bible, I find the poem to be unique in that it surpasses its Hebrew original in eloquence and a kind of sublime rapture. Herbert Marks, much the best literary critic of the English Bible, moves me by insisting that the young woman's voice is far more inward and complex than that of the man, since she is less centered on him than on the love that consumes her. There is something dangerously intense in her splendid apotheosis:

> Stay me with flagons, comfort me with apples: for I am sick of
>     love.
> His left hand is under my head, and his right hand doth embrace
>     me.
> I charge you, O ye daughters of Jerusalem, by the roes, and by
>     the hinds of the field, that ye stir not up, nor awake my love,
>     till he please.
> The voice of my beloved! behold, he cometh leaping upon the
>     mountains, skipping upon the hills.
> My beloved is like a roe or a young hart: behold, he standeth
>     behind our wall, he looketh forth at the windows, shewing
>     himself through the lattice.
> My beloved spake, and said unto me, Rise up, my love, my fair
>     one, and come away.
> For, lo, the winter is past, the rain is over and gone;
> The flowers appear on the earth; the time of the singing of birds
>     is come, and the voice of the turtle is heard in our land. . . .
>
> Geneva Bible, Song of Songs 2:5–12

In the very different Greek and Latin tradition, the turtledove is sacred to Aphrodite/Venus. Here the song of spring emanates in a manner that only allegorizing could transform into a spiritual sense. Whoever the Hebrew poet was who composed this grand hymn, perhaps a courtier attendant upon King Solomon, he understood that the essence of attraction is ambivalence and also a kind of ambiguity that nurtures itself upon secrecy. Again the woman magnificently takes precedence over her lover, who lacks her ardor:

> By night on my bed I sought him whom my soul loveth: I sought him, but I found him not.
> I will rise now, and go about the city in the streets, and in the broad ways I will seek him whom my soul loveth: I sought him, but I found him not.
> The watchmen that go about the city found me: to whom I said, Saw ye him whom my soul loveth?
> It was but a little that I passed from them, but I found him whom my soul loveth: I held him, and would not let him go, until I had brought him into my mother's house, and into the chamber of her that conceived me.
> I charge you, O ye daughters of Jerusalem, by the roes, and by the hinds of the field, that ye stir not up, nor awake my love, till he please.
>
> Geneva Bible, Song of Songs 3:1–5

In a way, Rabbi Akiba was right, though he would not have approved of the poetry in the Western tradition directly inspired by the Song of Songs. The tragic conversos or Jewish Catholics of Spain were obsessed by the Song: Teresa of Ávila, Saint John of the Cross, Fray Luis de León. In English poetry, Edmund Spenser composed a superb "Epithalamion" for his own wedding, which carries on the spirit of the Song of Songs. Shakespeare's *Venus and Adonis* is another instance. In the Victorian Age, Christina Rossetti and Coventry Patmore write their own versions of Solomon's Song, and Walt Whitman's "Lilacs" elegy for Lincoln is deeply involved in the Song's vision of the bliss of union.

Akiba thought that the Blessing of the Song of Songs was a divine gift to us. I sometimes think he was correct, because everyone I know who reads the Song of Songs is enriched with a sense of more life:

> The fig tree putteth forth her green figs, and the vines with the tender grape give a good smell. Arise, my love, my fair one, and come away.

O my dove, that art in the clefts of the rock, in the secret places
    of the stairs, let me see thy countenance, let me hear thy
    voice; for sweet is thy voice, and thy countenance is comely.
Take us the foxes, the little foxes, that spoil the vines: for our
    vines have tender grapes.
My beloved is mine, and I am his: he feedeth among the lilies.
                    Geneva Bible, Song of Songs 2:13–16

I recall discussing this incandescent passage with Lillian Hellman
sometime in the mid-1970s and being told that her play of 1939, *The
Little Foxes*, began with her brooding upon the Song of Songs. Miss
Hellman, during the years I knew her, still mourned her second husband, Dashiell Hammett, and had a fine bitterness toward life and literature. I told her that she misread this superb erotic invitation, to
which she justly replied that, right or wrong, she had been stimulated
to creation. Forty years later, I yield to her procedure and wonder why
I always feel blessed by chanting the Song aloud to myself, whether in
Hebrew or in English:

Set me as a seal upon thine heart, as a seal upon thine arm: for
    love is strong as death; jealousy is cruel as the grave: the coals
    thereof are coals of fire, which hath a most vehement flame.
                    Geneva Bible, Song of Songs 8:6

I am overwhelmed by this, though the Hebrew is even darker, since
it calls love as fierce as dying and sings that love is as strong as Sheol or
Hades. I hear something of this terror in Shakespeare's sonnets when
he cries out, "Desire is death," or in the "stony sestina" of Dante, where
the poet proclaims he would sleep away his life in stone or feed like
beasts upon the grass, only to see his lady Pietra's garments cast a shade.
The blessing given to me by the Song of Songs has an element of the
negative, since a passion so dangerously intense exacts a cost not less
than total.

# Ruth:
## "Whither Thou Goest, I Will Go"

I ALWAYS FIND something frightening about Yahweh in his acute ambivalence toward us. We can understand Zeus or Odin being anxious, but how can Yahweh experience anxiety? His actions are unpredictable. I surmise that he wounded himself in the act of creation. He seems to have both good and bad days. He has astonishing limitations.

Kabbalah tells us that Yahweh is gigantic. Whenever he has a sense that he might have been diminished by creating the world and humankind, a kind of fury possesses him. He began as primordial Man. There are traditions that say that Yahweh's name was lost after he underwent contraction. He then became Elohim. Without that contraction, he and the cosmos would remain one. He becomes more human as he drives to keep the world and humanity separate from himself.

Gershom Scholem and I shared a conviction that Walt Whitman was a kind of natural Kabbalist. The Walt Whitman of *Leaves of Grass* has many Yahwistic elements. He too creates by concentration and contraction. But, unlike Yahweh, Walt loves humankind. No one would ascribe fury to Whitman. Yahweh is a man of war; Walt Whitman is a man of peace.

My lifelong experience is that the book of Ruth is the most beautiful work in all the Hebrew Bible. It is economical, benign, and loving. Its poetic progeny include John Keats in his "Ode to a Nightingale" and Victor Hugo in an equally superb poem, "Boaz Asleep." In some ways, the book of Ruth is really a prose poem rather than a short story.

We do not know who wrote this wonderful vision of human passion. Whoever it was, she or he must have lived about 700 B.C.E. or even earlier: perhaps contemporary with the Yahwist in 950 B.C.E. or so. Herbert Marks usefully demonstrates the wonderful perspectivism of Ruth. Its four chapters center on four scenes, private and public: the road back to Bethlehem, where Ruth makes her decision to follow Naomi; Boaz's field, where she meets her future redeemer; the threshing floor at night, where she gains his love; and, finally, the city gate, where Boaz gathers public endorsement for the marriage.

Marks is superb in restating the crucial theme of Jewish redemption through migration. The greater junction "get thee out of"—Abram from Ur of the Chaldees, Moses from Egypt into the Promised Land—is re-enacted by Ruth and Naomi as they return from Moab to Israel. Renunciation is set aside, and the grand patriarch Boaz becomes the second change that Yahweh allows to those who trust in him.

The name "Ruth" means a "friend"—that is, a refreshment of life. "Naomi" means "sweetness," a meaning that is momentarily set to one side when in her grief she calls herself Mara, or "bitterness." "Boaz" can be read as "strength" in a particular sense of shrewdness.

The covenant love between Ruth and Boaz is matched by the love between Naomi and Ruth, who become truly a mother and a daughter:

> And Ruth said, Intreat me not to leave thee, or to return from
>     following after thee: for whither thou goest, I will go; and
>     where thou lodgest, I will lodge: thy people shall be my
>     people, and thy God my God:
> Where thou diest, will I die, and there will I be buried: the
>     Lord do so to me, and more also, if ought but death part
>     thee and me.
>
> Ruth 1:16–17

The love that binds together is *hesed*, or loyalty to the covenant. The fable of Ruth is a high song to the great women of Covenant: Leah, Rachel, Tamar, and, here, Ruth and Naomi. It is through her marriage to Boaz that Ruth will bear Obed, the grandfather of King David. The concept of *hesed* becomes a large one, since Ruth is a Moabite convert, even as King Solomon will be the son of the Hittite woman Bathsheba. Tamar was a Canaanite, like Judah's wife before her, and so David is of Moabite, Hebrew, and Canaanite lineage.

No one can now read the book of Ruth without remembering Keats's tribute to her in his "Ode to a Nightingale":

Thou wast not born for death, immortal Bird!
    No hungry generations tread thee down;
The voice I hear this passing night was heard
    In ancient days by emperor and clown:
Perhaps the self-same song that found a path
    Through the sad heart of Ruth, when, sick for home,
        She stood in tears amid the alien corn;
            The same that oft-times hath
Charmed magic casements, opening on the foam
    Of perilous seas, in faery lands forlorn.

Side by side with this is the marvelous poem "Boaz Asleep," from Hugo's epic, *The Legend of the Ages*. Boaz is clearly the great Victor Hugo himself, tireless seducer of battalions of women:

While he was sleeping, Ruth, a Moabite,
Came to his feet and, with her breast bared, lay
Hoping for some unknown uncertain ray
When, suddenly, they would waken into light.

Though she was near, Boaz was unaware;
And what God planned for her, Ruth couldn't tell.
Cool fragrance rose from the tufts of asphodel,
And over Galgala, night stirred the air.
. . . . . . . . . . . . . . . .
Wondered—with parting eyelids half revealed
Beneath her veils—what stray god, as he cropped
The timeless summer, had so idly dropped
That golden sickle in the starry field.

                    Translated by E. H. and A. M. Blackmore

# Ecclesiastes:
## "And Desire Shall Fail"

I F THE GIFT to us of the Song of Songs is marked by an appropriate ambivalence, I find an even darker exuberance in Ecclesiastes, a mistranslation of the Hebrew Koheleth, who is the "assembler" of these sayings. The speaker is not preaching to a congregation but ruminating upon heretical wisdom. Though Koheleth is ascribed to Solomon, eighty years old and glorious, the writer cannot be dated. He may be third-century B.C.E. and is a kind of Hebraic Epicurus. His book opens memorably, and its subsequent eloquence never flags:

> Vanity of vanities, saith the Preacher, vanity of vanities; all is vanity.
> What profit hath a man of all his labour which he taketh under the sun?
> One generation passeth away, and another generation cometh: but the earth abideth for ever.
> The sun also ariseth, and the sun goeth down, and hasteth to his place where he arose.
> The wind goeth toward the south, and turneth about unto the north; it whirleth about continually, and the wind returneth again according to his circuits.
> All the rivers run into the sea; yet the sea is not full; unto the place from whence the rivers come, thither they return again.
> All things are full of labour; man cannot utter it: the eye is not satisfied with seeing, nor the ear filled with hearing.
> The thing that hath been, it is that which shall be; and that which is done is that which shall be done: and there is no new thing under the sun.
>
> Geneva Bible, Ecclesiastes 1:2–9

"Vanity" is a departure from the Hebrew *hevel*, which is only a breath, a vapor, or nothing at all. Koheleth tells us that every increase in wisdom is a kind of mourning and every growth in knowledge an augmentation of sadness. This great ironist praises life but only because "a living dog is better than a dead lion" (Ecclesiastes 9:4). As for the dead, even our memory of them fades away, and yet we are urged to continue with our work:

> Whatsoever thy hand findeth to do, do it with thy might; for
>     there is no work, nor device, nor knowledge, nor wisdom, in
>     the grave, whither thou goest.
> I returned, and saw under the sun, that the race is not to the
>     swift, nor the battle to the strong, neither yet bread to the
>     wise, nor yet riches to men of understanding, nor yet favour
>     to men of skill; but time and chance happeneth to them all.
>                             Geneva Bible, Ecclesiastes 9:10–11

Herbert Marks is again our best guide when he catches the superb irony that it is life's "vanity" that makes it precious. I was his teacher many years ago, and we became lifelong friends. I recall telling a Shakespeare discussion group in which he participated that my hero Falstaff, who is endlessly accused of "vanity" by Prince Hal, is, rather, the apotheosis of this *hevel* that is the mere breath of our lives.

I am now older even than Sir John Falstaff and chant to myself many exhausted mornings the wonderful opening verses of chapter 12:

> Remember now thy Creator in the days of thy youth, while the
>     evil days come not, nor the years draw nigh, when thou shalt
>     say, I have no pleasure in them;
> While the sun, or the light, or the moon, or the stars, be not
>     darkened, nor the clouds return after the rain:
> In the day when the keepers of the house shall tremble, and
>     the strong men shall bow themselves, and the grinders cease
>     because they are few, and those that look out of the windows
>     be darkened,
> And the doors shall be shut in the streets, when the sound of the
>     grinding is low, and he shall rise up at the voice of the bird,
>     and all the daughters of musick shall be brought low;

Also when they shall be afraid of that which is high, and fears
   shall be in the way, and the almond tree shall flourish, and the
   grasshopper shall be a burden, and desire shall fail: because
   man goeth to his long home, and the mourners go about the
   streets:
Or ever the silver cord be loosed, or the golden bowl be broken,
   or the pitcher be broken at the fountain, or the wheel broken
   at the cistern.
Then shall the dust return to the earth as it was: and the spirit
   shall return unto God who gave it.
Vanity of vanities, saith the preacher; all is vanity.

Geneva Bible, Ecclesiastes 12:1–8

This is, at my age, hurtful yet sublime. There is a tremor in my fingers, my legs tend to hint at giving out, my teeth diminish, incipient macular degeneration dims my eyes, deafness increases, birdsong is scarcely heard, every height augments my apprehension of falling, and even moving about on a walker encounters fears in the way. In Jerusalem, as I well remember, spring commences with the almond tree flowering, but the resurrection of the grass no longer is answered by desire, because I mourn for my vanishing generation.

Some exegetes compare Koheleth's sense of emptiness to the "void" of Buddhism, since it is a remarkably full emptiness. The Rabbis attempted to tame Koheleth by reading his despair as an invitation to happiness. Chapter 12:9–14 is their debasement of a great work, for they back away from his ironic wisdom and instead arrive at the lame "Let us hear the conclusion of the whole matter: Fear God, and keep his commandments: for this is the whole duty of man." I find that unacceptable, though I am moved by the verse just prior: "of making many books there is no end; and much study is a weariness of the flesh."

The blessing given to me by Koheleth reverberates before the silence that impends in these, my final years. Falstaff's outcry, "Give me life!," is the Shakespearean response to the ironies of our diminishing existence. A kind of laughter akin to Falstaff's emerges from the text of Koheleth. Without Falstaff I would be much poorer, and without the literary power of the anonymous scribe who gathered our rich vanities in his brief book I would know even less than I do.

[ *Part Two* ]


SELF–OTHERSEEING

AND THE

SHAKESPEAREAN SUBLIME

# The Concept of Self-Otherseeing
## and the Arch-Jew Shylock

I T IS NOT EVERY DAY that the world shapes itself into a poem, according to Wallace Stevens. When John Stuart Mill said that poetry was not so much heard as overheard, he showed remarkable insight. The genealogy of self-overhearing was not Mill's concern, but I am a Nietzschean and not a utilitarian. Origins fascinate and trouble me. Nietzsche thought that the memorable was an affair of pain rather than pleasure. The prophet of Zarathustra had little in common with Wittgenstein, and yet both stemmed from Schopenhauer. It is in the spirit of *The World as Will and Representation* that Wittgenstein gave us the apothegm "Love, unlike pain, is put to the test. One does not say: 'That was not a true pain because it passed away so quickly.'"

Every one of us experiences, perhaps infrequently, the surprise of suddenly overhearing himself so that it seems as though someone else had done the talking. There are a few such moments in Montaigne, and yet Shakespeare probably did not read him before 1603 at the earliest. However odd it sounds to credit a particular writer with the invention of self-overhearing, at least the representation of such a moment does not commence before the advent of the Bastard Faulconbridge in *King John*. With the frightening eruption of Shylock, whose great speeches arise from his shock at his own audacity, something radically new enters European tradition.

Except for the gallant Bastard, son of King Richard Lionheart and the outspoken hero of the otherwise rather drab *King John*, the masters of self-overhearing tend to be hero-villains at best, if not monsters of depravity. Shakespeare's grand negations are the ones who stage incessant dialogues with themselves: Hamlet, Iago, Edmund, Macbeth, and Leontes. To term Hamlet a hero-villain is to enter an area of grave dispute, but what else can be said concerning someone who is responsible for eight deaths, his own included?

I do not know whether Shakespearean self-overhearing necessarily creates a poetics of negativity. In *King Lear*, the hero-villain, the brilliant Edmund, is a fountain of self-overhearing, whereas the monsters Goneril, Regan, Cornwall, and Oswald cannot hear anyone, themselves included. Edgar, Edmund's victim and finally his nemesis, is even more a study in change founded upon self-overhearing. The fathers, Lear and Gloucester, who share Edgar's love, are incapable of self-overhearing, a lack that plays a considerable role in their catastrophes. With Cordelia and the Fool a kind of purity enters the process of change.

It is not difficult to comprehend the link between the startling experience of hearing ourselves, as though someone else was speaking, and the will to change. Much subtler is the connection between our experiencing something that seems to be happening to someone else and the actual changes that take place in drama. I cite my own recent memories here, because they are likely to be shared by many of my readers. Some months ago, I fell against a wall of my house and fractured a rib. I was unable to rise until our friendly neighborhood firemen were summoned, after which I departed by ambulance for the Emergency Room at Yale New Haven Hospital. As I lay helplessly on the floor in pain, waiting for assistance, there rose in me the strong sense that this had nothing to do with me but was happening to someone else. Only a few months later, I fell against the front door when I walked over to it with a cane, in search of the morning newspaper. Again I went down, this time with a lesser pain, as I dislocated the middle finger of the hand I relied upon to write. With chagrin, I had to wait for the same firemen again to hoist me up and get me off to the Emergency Room. I recall the repetition of an acute phantasmagoria that this was not happening to me but to some other person.

It is, I think, a common human defense to be convinced that someone else suffers, no matter how grave our own pain seems. It need not be an injury: something close to this vastation can attend our exposure when we are found out and caught in an untruth or in an act unworthy of us. The humiliation seems somehow to belong to someone else even as we suffer it. I think that this syndrome is a function of what in Shakespeare I now call self-otherseeing. It has to do with our impulse to stage our own suffering and our crises. By self-otherseeing, whether in Shakespeare or in life, I mean the double consciousness of observing our own actions and sufferings as though they belonged to others and not to ourselves, while being aware we possess them. The consequence is a strangeness that makes us shake our heads and rub our eyes in perplexity.

Shakespeare's leading attribute is his strangeness, since we cannot easily accommodate a cognitive power that incessantly gifts us with a capacious strangeness of *meaning*. Even where he may seem most direct, Shakespeare is elliptical and uncanny. I take as instance the moment in *The Merchant of Venice* when the good Christian merchant Antonio (a part I surmise was played by Shakespeare himself) suggests that Shylock's punishment must include his enforced conversion to the religion of mercy, so well exemplified by the kicks, curses, and spitting manifested by Antonio toward Shylock earlier in the play:

> PORTIA  What mercy can you render him Antonio?
> GRATIANO  A halter gratis, nothing else for Godsake!
> ANTONIO  So please my lord the duke, and all the court,
> To quit the fine for one half of his goods,
> I am content: so he will let me have
> The other half in use, to render it
> Upon his death unto the gentlemen
> That lately stole his daughter.
> Two things provided more, that for this favour
> He presently become a Christian:
> The other, that he do record a gift
> (Here in the court) of all he dies possess'd
> Unto his son Lorenzo and his daughter.
> THE DUKE OF VENICE  He shall do this, or else I do recant
> The pardon that I late pronounced here.
> PORTIA  Art thou contented Jew? what dost thou say?
> SHYLOCK  I am content.
> PORTIA                          Clerk, draw a deed of gift.
> SHYLOCK  I pray you give me leave to go from hence,
> I am not well,—send the deed after me,
> And I will sign it.

"Presently" in Shakespeare means "immediately." Kenneth Gross in his *Shylock Is Shakespeare* (2006) reminds us that Shakespeare himself added the forced conversion to the old pound-of-flesh story. I always ask my students why this happened, but I've received no cogent responses. They are hardly to be blamed, since *The Merchant of Venice* scarcely requires this added complexity. Gross usefully remarks that this Shakespearean intervention is so blunt that we find difficulty in speaking about it. That may be why Shylock's "I am content" is so empty of affect.

I suggest that Shakespeare punishes both himself and the audience as much as he inflicts this outrage upon Shylock. We want to know why but perhaps never will. I cite Antonio's diabolic suggestion while acknowledging that he might see his motivation as benign. The other-seeing here is entirely Shylock's; his amazing "I am content" and "I am not well" give the strong impression that something in him sees this as happening to someone else.

Shakespeare removes Shylock from the remainder of the play. We are left with the sense that what we have just heard and seen can be no part of an ongoing Shylock. It is as though he himself can no longer hear or see. Since Shakespeare has portrayed him as a murderous para-noid, the issue is scarcely one of our sympathizing with this figure who has become the Arch-Jew of Western literary tradition. In this context, I wish only to note that Shylock's inability to react is a highly deliberate instance of Shakespearean otherseeing. I turn to another example, the threshold to Antony's botched suicide in *Antony and Cleopatra:*

ANTONY  Eros, thou yet behold'st me?

EROS                                             Ay, noble lord.

ANTONY  Sometime we see a cloud that's dragonish,
    A vapour sometime like a bear or lion,
    A towered citadel, a pendent rock,
    A forked mountain, or blue promontory
    With trees upon't that nod unto the world
    And mock our eyes with air. Thou hast seen these signs?
    They are black vesper's pageants.

EROS                                             Ay, my lord.

ANTONY  That which is now a horse, even with a thought
    The rack dislimns and makes it indistinct
    As water is in water.

EROS                              It does, my lord.

ANTONY  My good knave Eros, now thy captain is

Even such a body. Here I am Antony,
Yet cannot hold this visible shape, my knave.
I made these wars for Egypt, and the Queen—
Whose heart I thought I had, for she had mine,
Which, whilst it was mine, had annexed unto't
A million more, now lost—she, Eros, has
Packed cards with Caesar, and false-played my glory
Unto an enemy's triumph.
Nay, weep not, gentle Eros. There is left us
Ourselves to end ourselves.

This marvelous passage begins with the swordsman Antony sounding almost like the intellectual Hamlet. This one time only in the vast pageant of *Antony and Cleopatra*, Antony experiences a self-otherseeing that places in doubt his own reality. He cannot find himself in what he sees, whether in the clouds or in his own betrayed and defeated sense of being. Shakespearean woe and wonder could hardly be more awesomely displayed. A great captain of action is reduced to a reflective mode he cannot recognize or sustain. The bewildered responses of Eros stand in for our own primary reaction as readers and auditors.

What we hear is anything but a self-staging for the inward show of Shakespearean tragedy. Antony will recover something of his greatness before his actual death, but here he is at the nadir of his consciousness of being. At no time capable of self-overhearing, this Roman hero has self-otherseeing thrust upon him.

Hamlet, Lear, and Iago stage their burgeoning selves through self-otherseeing. Long preceding Rimbaud, they show that the self is always an other. Presence for them is governed by the will, desire for the face they had before the world was made.

Luther (whom Shakespeare may never have read) is a monster in his absolute love for Yahweh, who to me is a scary literary character, the Real Presence literalized. Nothing could be less like Shakespeare, who is very wary of casting his major protagonists as being absolute, whether for death or the death of love.

The reader initially may find my invented term, self-otherseeing, a touch strange, but I will show its usefulness in confronting the Shakespearean sublime, which is an art of apotheosis, particularly in Hamlet and Lear. There is a potential richness in the idea of self-otherseeing that answers Shakespeare's extraordinary capaciousness. The other that his personae see can be something estranged in themselves, the daemon that is their own genius. Even more, it refers to their sense of the reality of other selves, without which they are in danger of falling into the abyss of solipsism. Hamlet and Lear do fall, outward and downward, into that abyss, and never quite clamber up again.

# The Bastard Faulconbridge

THERE ARE four aspects to *self-otherseeing:*

1. To see one's own other selves
2. To see (by glimpses) the shattering reality of others and of otherness
3. To see nothing that is not there and the nothing that is
4. To see everything that could be there and the plenitude that already is

The first figure in Shakespeare's vast panoply of vital individuals is the Bastard Faulconbridge in the early history, *The Life and Death of King John.* I once thought it had been revised as late as 1595 but believe now he wrote all of it no later than 1590. There are elements in the Bastard that Shakespeare will develop into aspects of Falstaff and of Hamlet. Indeed, he is the first instance of what I have termed the Shakespearean Invention of the Human.

Take him out of *King John* and the play scarcely would be readable or worth staging. Everyone else in it chants a kind of Marlovian, fustian rhetoric, but the Bastard possesses a language and a wit entirely his own. Interestingly, he is entirely Shakespeare's creation; the chronicles barely mention such a person.

Like Falstaff, he has cast aside all false reverence and is addicted to telling his own truth. And, again preluding Sir John, he declines to have concepts not his own thrust upon him. As the natural son of King Richard Lionheart, once he is acknowledged by his uncle King John and his grandmother Elinor, he is freed to be a warrior who avenges his father while surpassing him in prowess and in eloquence. I follow Harold Goddard by finding the Bastard to be Shakespeare's first implicit spokesman:

> And not alone in habit and device,
> Exterior form, outward accoutrement,
> But from the inward motion to deliver
> Sweet, sweet, sweet poison for the age's tooth:
> Which, though I will not practise to deceive,
> Yet, to avoid deceit, I mean to learn;
> For it shall strew the footsteps of my rising.

Is it extravagant to hear in this the voice of a twenty-something-year-old poet-dramatist of rapidly developing genius who suddenly beholds something of his true relationship both to his own time and to ages to come?

How are we to interpret "poison" here? Ostensibly, it might mean "flattery," but the Bastard and his creator interpret it as "truth." We can characterize Shakespeare's deepest art as "the inward motion" and find one of his earliest instances in the Bastard's meditation upon "commodity," the gain of all self-interest:

> With that same purpose-changer, that sly divel,
> That broker, that still breaks the pate of faith,
> That daily break-vow, he that wins of all,
> Of kings, of beggars, old men, young men, maids,
> Who, having no external thing to lose
> But the word 'maid', cheats the poor maid of that,
> That smooth-fac'd gentleman, tickling commodity.
> Commodity, the bias of the world,
> The world, who of itself is peised well,
> Made to run even upon even ground,
> Till this advantage, this vile drawing bias,
> This sway of motion, this commodity,
> Makes it take head from all indifferency,
> From all direction, purpose, course, intent:
> And this same bias, this commodity,
> This bawd, this broker, this all-changing word . . .

This memorable denunciation is fundamental though ironic for the Bastard and rather more ironical for William Shakespeare, in his career a quester after commodity. The Bastard concludes with a fierce quatrain, but one that he does not mean at all:

And being rich, my virtue then shall be
To say there is no vice but beggary.
Since kings break faith upon commodity,
Gain, be my lord, for I will worship thee!

In fact, the Bastard is a heroic warrior and patriot without whom the realm of King John would collapse. His attachment to his dubious uncle is extraordinary and reflects his search for the absent father Richard Lionheart, for whom John is an inadequate substitute. Throughout the play, the Bastard becomes an idea of order: generous, patriotic, comedic, and finally England's only stay against destruction.

His most problematic moment comes in an exchange on the battlefield with his friend Hubert:

HUBERT  Who's there? speak, ho! speak quickly, or I shoot.
BASTARD  A friend. What art thou?
HUBERT                                    Of the part of England.
BASTARD  Whither dost thou go?
HUBERT  What's that to thee? *[Pause.]* Why, may not I demand
    Of thine affairs as well as thou of mine?
BASTARD  Hubert, I think.
HUBERT                        Thou hast a perfect thought:
    I will upon all hazards well believe
    Thou art my friend, that know'st my tongue so well.
    Who art thou?
BASTARD                    Who thou wilt: and if thou please
    Thou mayst befriend me so much as to think
    I come one way of the Plantagenets.

This wry self-assertion is an expression of the Bastard's pride at being Richard Lionheart's natural son, but, more interestingly, it expresses a kind of dramatic skepticism unique to the Shakespeare of 1590 and afterward. The Bastard self-othersees, at once beholding a battle-blurred image of himself and a deeper realization of what he has called "the inward motion."

He is aware of Hubert's otherness, despite the phantasmagoria of battle, yet in seeing what endures of the selfsame (as Shakespeare named individual identity) the Bastard wonders a little at his own strong personality and its survival of all the chances attendant upon war. The first of all Shakespeare's self-stagers, the Bastard suddenly apprehends that the flux of action threatens him, the only joyous and exuberant spirit in all of *King John*.

# The Falstaffiad:
## Glory and Darkening of Sir John Falstaff

It is in this particular sense that the Bastard is Falstaff's direct fore-runner. In the six years between *King John* and *King Henry the IV, Part I*, Shakespeare's full power developed:

FALSTAFF  Though I could scape shot-free at London,
I fear the shot here. Here's no scoring but upon the
pate. Soft, who are you? Sir Walter Blount. There's
honour for you. Here's no vanity. I am as hot as molten
lead and as heavy too. God keep lead out of me; I need
no more weight than mine own bowels. I have led my
ragamuffins where they are peppered; there's not three
of my hundred and fifty left alive, and they are for the
town's end to beg during life.

*Enter the Prince.*

But who comes here?
PRINCE  What, stands thou idle here? Lend me thy sword.
Many a nobleman lies stark and stiff
Under the hoofs of vaunting enemies,
Whose deaths are yet unrevenged. I prithee,
Lend me thy sword.
FALSTAFF  O Hal, I prithee, give me leave to breathe
awhile. Turk Gregory never did such deeds in arms as
I have done this day. I have paid Percy; I have made him
sure.
PRINCE  He is indeed—and living to kill thee.
I prithee, lend me thy sword.

FALSTAFF  Nay, before God, Hal, if Percy be alive thou
  gets not my sword. But take my pistol if thou wilt.
PRINCE  Give it me. What, is it in the case?
FALSTAFF  Ay, Hal. 'Tis hot; 'tis hot. There's that will sack a city.

*The prince draws it out, and finds it to be a bottle of sack.*

PRINCE  What, is it a time to jest and dally now?

*He throws the bottle at him.*

FALSTAFF  Well, if Percy be alive, I'll pierce him. If he do
  come in my way, so; if he do not, if I come in his
  willingly, let him make a carbonado of me. I like not
  such grinning honour as Sir Walter hath. Give me life,
  which I can save, so. If not, honour comes unlooked
  for, and there's an end.

The Falstaffian sublimity opens with his charming play on "shot-free," meaning evading your bar bill, and then upon the "honour" of the late Sir Walter Blount, gallantly slain in the service of the two Henrys, father and son. Sir John Falstaff is only too aware of the madness of battle and of the hypocrisy of all kings and princes, including the beloved Hal. The old warrior's wonderful contempt for battle could not be better exemplified than by carrying a bottle of sack in his holster and offering it to Hal in the midst of crisis. When Hal throws the bottle at the nimbly dodging Falstaff, the abyss between them opens wide and forever.

I recall the greatest Falstaff I shall ever see, Ralph Richardson in New York City in 1946, playing so marvelously that he eclipsed Laurence Olivier as Hotspur in *Part I* and as Shallow in *Part II*. I was a child of sixteen, and in two successive evenings I received the most profound Shakespearean education ever made available to me. Richardson was a revelation. His Falstaff was no mere glutton, boozer, scoundrel, but the greatest wit and dryly comic intelligence ever staged. Indeed this Falstaff was the Socrates of Eastcheap, rueful wisdom itself:

*Exeunt all but the Prince and Falstaff.*

FALSTAFF  Hal, if thou see me down in the battle and bestride
me, so; 'tis a point of friendship.

PRINCE  Nothing but a colossus can do thee that friendship. Say
thy prayers, and farewell.

FALSTAFF  I would 'twere bedtime, Hal, and all well.

PRINCE  Why, thou owest God a death.

*[Exit]*

FALSTAFF  'Tis not due yet. I would be loath to pay him before
his day. What need I be so forward with him that calls not on
me? Well, 'tis no matter; honour pricks me on. Yea, but how
if honour prick me off when I come on? Can honour set to a
leg? No. Or an arm? No. Or take away the grief of a wound?
No. Honour hath no skill in surgery, then? No. What is
honour? A word. What is in that word 'honour'? What is that
'honour'? Air. A trim reckoning. Who hath it? He that died
o'Wednesday. Doth he feel it? No. Doth he hear it? No. 'Tis
insensible then? Yea, to the dead. But will it not live with the
living? No. Why? Detraction will not suffer it. Therefore
I'll none of it. Honour is a mere scutcheon. And so ends my
catechism.

Honor, which is the agon between Prince Hal and Hotspur, is blown
away by Falstaff in a litany that reduces it to a word and then to a
faltering breath. Hal is much given to accusing Falstaff of vanity, in
the particular sense proclaimed by Ecclesiastes, whose Hebrew word
*hevel* thus is mistranslated brilliantly. *Hevel* is a mere breath, a vapor
of vapors, nothing at all. Hal, having bested Hotspur, addresses his
corpse:

PRINCE  For worms, brave Percy. Fare thee well, great heart.
Ill-weaved ambition, how much art thou shrunk!
When that this body did contain a spirit
A kingdom for it was too small a bound,
But now two paces of the vilest earth
Is room enough. This earth that bears thee dead
Bears not alive so stout a gentleman.
If thou wert sensible of courtesy

I should not make so dear a show of zeal.
But let my favours hide thy mangled face,
And even in thy behalf I'll thank myself
For doing these fair rites of tenderness.
Adieu, and take thy praise with thee to heaven.
Thy ignominy sleep with thee in the grave
But not remembered in thy epitaph.

*He spieth Falstaff on the ground.*

What, old acquaintance! Could not all this flesh
Keep in a little life! Poor Jack, farewell.
I could have better spared a better man.
O, I should have a heavy miss of thee
If I were much in love with vanity.
Death hath not struck so fat a deer today,
Though many dearer in this bloody fray.
Embowelled will I see thee by and by;
Till then, in blood by noble Percy lie.

*[Exit]*

*Falstaff riseth up.*

FALSTAFF  Embowelled? If thou embowel me today, I'll give
you leave to powder me, and eat me too, tomorrow. 'Sblood,
'twas time to counterfeit, or that hot termagant Scot had paid
me, scot and lot too. Counterfeit? I lie; I am no counterfeit.
To die is to be a counterfeit, for he is but the counterfeit of a
man who hath not the life of a man. But to counterfeit dying
when a man thereby liveth is to be no counterfeit but the true
and perfect image of life indeed. The better part of valour
is discretion, in the which better part I have saved my life.
Zounds, I am afraid of this gunpowder Percy, though he be
dead. How if he should counterfeit too and rise? By my faith,
I am afraid he would prove the better counterfeit. Therefore
I'll make him sure, yea, and I'll swear I killed him. Why may
not he rise as well as I? Nothing confutes me but eyes, and
nobody sees me. *[Stabs the body.]* Therefore, sirrah, with a new
wound in your thigh, come you along with me. *He takes up
Hotspur on his back.*

While Falstaff watches the battle between Hotspur and Hal, he is attacked by the fearsome Earl of Douglas. Fat Jack is a veteran warrior, but in his eighties and out of all reasonable compass. After a few defensive jabs at the hot termagant Scot, the wily sage of Eastcheap sensibly plays dead, thus saving his own life. There are few moments even in Shakespeare as glorious in depicting ambivalence. Hal has been saved the labor of handing Falstaff over to the hangman, and we do not wonder that his rueful farewell to his Socrates is rather less phrased in the accents of dignity than his salute to the once-fiery Hotspur.

Falstaff's Resurrection is all the more magnificent as the great outcast rises up in the name of the true Blessing. Against Hotspur's hysterical outcry of "Die all, die merrily," we hear Falstaff's "Give me life!" What scholars tend not to hear, the common reader and playgoer properly values as an affirmation of "the true and perfect image of life."

The new Hal, now another heroic head-basher, makes clear his preference for Hotspur over Falstaff. Shakespeare does not take sides, but does any strong reader not prefer Falstaff to his renegade student Hal? I am concerned here, however, with Shakespearean self-staging by self-otherseeing, and that is precisely the Falstaffian triumph. He has staged his own death and resurrection by otherseeing Hal's negative flowering into the royal dignity of power and broken friendship. Falstaff othersees what Hal is no longer concerned with accepting: the full range of human possibility. The Prince has absorbed more than enough from Falstaff to assist in the pragmatics of seducing his subjects:

PRINCE  I know you all, and will awhile uphold
   The unyoked humour of your idleness.
   Yet herein will I imitate the sun,
   Who doth permit the base contagious clouds
   To smother up his beauty from the world,
   That, when he please again to be himself,
   Being wanted, he may be more wondered at
   By breaking through the foul and ugly mists
   Of vapours that did seem to strangle him.
   If all the year were playing holidays,
   To sport would be as tedious as to work;
   But when they seldom come, they wished-for come,
   And nothing pleaseth but rare accidents.

So when this loose behaviour I throw off
And pay the debt I never promised,
By how much better than my word I am,
By so much shall I falsify men's hopes;
And, like bright metal on a sullen ground,
My reformation, glittering o'er my fault,
Shall show more goodly and attract more eyes
Than that which hath no foil to set it off.
I'll so offend to make offence a skill,
Redeeming time when men think least I will.

*[Exit]*

One hardly knows which aspect of this soliloquy is most admirable: its audacious honesty or its palpable hypocrisy. It is a tribute to Shakespeare's conception of Hal that his proud proclamation of hypocritical behavior helps persuade us of his emotional honesty of self-redemption. I take it that his reference to Saint Paul's Ephesians 5:16, "Redeeming the time, because the days are evil," is deliberately a touch blasphemous, though once he is crowned Henry V is much given to proclaiming his virtues as a Christian monarch. He is not Hamlet or indeed Falstaff, whom he destroys with sadistic zest in his public rejection. You could endlessly discuss both Hamlet and Falstaff on the questions of belief and disbelief, but Hal's Falstaffian education falls away, and his inward being becomes as opaque to us as to the magnificent Henry V himself. No one in all of imaginative literature is as little concerned with rescuing himself from the flux of time and change as is the ever-early Socrates of Eastcheap. Time of course necessarily triumphs over Falstaff throughout *Part II*, until at last he kneels to the newly crowned King Henry V and is subjected to the public humiliation of rejection:

FALSTAFF  God save thee, my sweet boy!
KING  My Lord Chief Justice, speak to that vain man.
CHIEF JUSTICE  Have you your wits? Know you what 'tis you
    speak?
FALSTAFF  My King! My Jove! I speak to thee, my heart!
KING  I know thee not, old man. Fall to thy prayers.
    How ill white hairs becomes a fool and jester!
    I have long dreamt of such a kind of man,

So surfeit-swell'd, so old, and so profane;
But being awak'd I do despise my dream.
Make less thy body hence, and more thy grace;
Leave gormandizing; know the grave doth gape
For thee thrice wider than for other men.
Reply not to me with a fool-born jest;
Presume not that I am the thing I was;
For God doth know, so shall the world perceive,
That I have turn'd away my former self;
So will I those that kept me company.
When thou dost hear I am as I have been,
Approach me, and thou shalt be as thou wast,
The tutor and the feeder of my riots.
Till then I banish thee, on pain of death,
As I have done the rest of my misleaders,
Not to come near our person by ten mile.
For competence of life I will allow you,
That lack of means enforce you not to evils;
And as we hear you do reform yourselves,
We will, according to your strengths and qualities,
Give you advancement. *[To the Lord Chief Justice]* Be
it your charge, my lord,
To see perform'd the tenor of my word.
Set on.

*Exit King [with his train]*

FALSTAFF   Master Shallow, I owe you a thousand pound.


I have winced at this all my life, particularly when I remember
the expression on Ralph Richardson's countenance as he suffered the
shock and hurt of these bombasts. King Henry is all too aware of having mastered the public art in which self-righteousness congratulates
its celebrator. There is a deeper drama playing out its final moment
between Falstaff and his ungrateful foster son. It is hardly accidental
that Falstaff, squatting in the dust, addresses the former Hal as "My
Jove," thus invoking the ancient myth of Old Father Time or Saturn
being castrated by Jove, the leader of the Olympian gods. Falstaff, who
knows everything, so knowingly sees and darkly accepts the end of his
manhood at the hands of the only love he has been able to understand.

Return to Henry V's rhetoric. It depends upon just the kind of
social cant that power is constrained to use if we were to take this glorious monarch's verbiage at all literally. Instead we are to read it as
his self-otherseeing. Once, he was Hal, and now that role is forever
gone. A newly crowned king, he stands between past and future. What
looms ahead is the conquest of France, and lasting fame as the first
true English king. Falstaff, however, kneels before a discarded past
and a likely future wasting away into an early grave. Even at his worst
moment he remains a true immanence, though now present to virtually
no purpose. One wonders what Shakespeare would want us to feel and
think as his most extraordinary creation, except perhaps for Hamlet,
so suddenly reaches a full stop. But the dialectics of what I have called
self-otherseeing give us a troubled awareness of Shakespeare's drive
beyond the pleasure principle. King Henry V's icy dismissal of Falstaff has elements of a new strangeness, even in Shakespeare. The king
assigns his Falstaffian phase to a bad dream, one that he despises after
waking. He retains a curious anxiety in regard to Falstaff, who is not
allowed to say anything: "Reply not to me with a fool-born jest." And
his new precautions in regard to his tutor are weirdly excessive. Falstaff
is not to get within ten miles of the royal person on pain of death. The
self-otherseeing here is of a mystery still dormant in the king.

Falstaff, for once in his entire career reduced to silence, heartbreak-
ingly cries out, "Master Shallow, I owe you a thousand pound." There
is a story that Shakespeare achieved his financial independence by buy-
ing a full share in the Globe with that rather large sum advanced to him
by the Earl of Southamptom, most certainly his patron and perhaps his
lover.

Though I find it useful to analyze both Falstaff and Hal by means
of the idea of self-otherseeing, I am aware that neither has much in
common with the possible shock of otherseeing in some of its multiple
senses. Falstaff is so capacious that his otherseeing embraces both self
and the reception by others. Hal, though developed so fully in *King
Henry V,* is by comparison almost simplistic. Not that he lacks enigmatic qualities, as here, in his prayer (to call it that) before Agincourt:

KING  *[Kneels.]*
    O God of battles, steel my soldiers' hearts;
    Possess them not with fear. Take from them now

The sense of reckoning, if th'opposed numbers
Pluck their hearts from them. Not today, O Lord,
O not today, think not upon the fault
My father made in compassing the crown.
I Richard's body have interred new,
And on it have bestowed more contrite tears
Than from it issued forced drops of blood.
Five hundred poor I have in yearly pay,
Who twice a day their withered hands hold up
Toward heaven to pardon blood; and I have built
Two chantries, where the sad and solemn priests
Sing still for Richard's soul. More will I do,
Though all that I can do is nothing worth,
Since that my penitence comes after all,
Imploring pardon.

On what level of self-deception does this proceed? Most scholars
regard it as altogether sincere, a judgment that for me summons up the
spirit of the divine Oscar Wilde, who taught us that all bad poetry is
sincere. Try to imagine Falstaff, Hal's prime victim, as listening to this
speech. But, then, *King Henry V* abounds in such epiphanies. The best
comes after the dialogue between the disguised king and the soldiers
Bates, Court, and Williams, and makes me wonder again at the perplexities in Hal's nature:

Upon the King! 'Let us our lives, our souls,
Our debts, our careful wives,
Our children and our sins lay on the King!'
We must bear all. O hard condition,
Twin-born with greatness, subject to the breath
Of every fool whose sense no more can feel
But his own wringing! What infinite heart's ease
Must kings neglect that private men enjoy!
And what have kings that privates have not too,
Save ceremony, save general ceremony?
And what art thou, thou idol ceremony?
What kind of god art thou, that suffer'st more
Of mortal griefs than do thy worshippers?

What are thy rents, what are thy comings-in?
O ceremony, show me but thy worth!
What is thy soul, O adoration?
Art thou aught else but place, degree and form,
Creating awe and fear in other men,
Wherein thou art less happy, being feared,
Than they in fearing?
What drink'st thou oft, instead of homage sweet,
But poisoned flattery? O be sick, great greatness,
And bid thy ceremony give thee cure!
Think'st thou the fiery fever will go out
With titles blown from adulation?
Will it give place to flexure and low bending?
Canst thou, when thou command'st the beggar's knee,
Command the health of it? No, thou proud dream
That play'st so subtly with a king's repose,
I am a king that find thee, and I know
'Tis not the balm, the sceptre and the ball,
The sword, the mace, the crown imperial,
The intertissued robe of gold and pearl,
The farced title running 'fore the king,
The throne he sits on, nor the tide of pomp
That beats upon the high shore of this world,
No, not all these, thrice-gorgeous ceremony,
Not all these, laid in bed majestical,
Can sleep so soundly as the wretched slave,
Who with a body filled and vacant mind
Gets him to rest, crammed with distressful bread:
Never sees horrid night, the child of hell,
But like a lackey from the rise to set
Sweats in the eye of Phoebus, and all night
Sleeps in Elysium; next day after dawn
Doth rise and help Hyperion to his horse,
And follows so the ever-running year
With profitable labour to his grave.
And but for ceremony such a wretch,
Winding up days with toil and nights with sleep,
Had the fore-hand and vantage of a king.

The slave, a member of the country's peace,
Enjoys it, but in gross brain little wots
What watch the King keeps to maintain the peace,
Whose hours the peasant best advantages.

It is rather difficult not to locate dissimulation in the royal suggestion that a slave sleeps more soundly than the thrice-gorgeous ceremo-
nial monarch. One hears something parallel to King Henry V's stirring
if self-serving promise that even his common soldiers will achieve gen-
tility by standing with him at Agincourt:

And Crispin Crispian shall ne'er go by
From this day to the ending of the world
But we in it shall be remembered,
We few, we happy few, we band of brothers.
For he today that sheds his blood with me
Shall be my brother; be he ne'er so vile,
This day shall gentle his condition.
And gentlemen in England now abed
Shall think themselves accursed they were not here,
And hold their manhoods cheap whiles any speaks
That fought with us upon Saint Crispin's day.

My former student and research assistant Lauren Smith aptly compares this to the oration of Ulysses in the *Inferno*, in which he urges his
veteran mariners to transgress and go beyond the limits of the known
world in quest of new thresholds. When Tennyson in his dramatic
monologue "Ulysses" relies upon Dante's false counselor, he com-
pounds this eloquence with that of Milton's Satan. It is not that the
ambitious and ideal English king has any touch of the Satanic, yet,
like Dante's Ulysses, he seduces his auditors and by charisma renders
hyperboles into sublimities. He knows, as we do, that the "happy few,
we band of brothers," will not mingle Bates, Court, and Williams with
Harry the King, Bedford, Exeter, and the other highborn warriors. But,
as William Hazlitt remarked, we like King Harry in the play, where he
is a very amiable monster.

All that remains in the King of Falstaff's mentorship is the fat
knight's beautiful, laughing mode of speech. William Butler Yeats said

of Henry V, "He is as remorseless and undistinguished as some natural force." Hazlitt charmingly remarked, "He was a hero, that is, he was ready to sacrifice his own life for the pleasure of destroying thousands of other lives." One recalls the nice detail that this authentic English hero allows himself to order the throats cut of all the French prisoners, and yet this scarcely matters in Shakespeare's glorious pageant of English triumph.

G. K. Chesterton's observation that Chaucer's ironies sometimes are too large to be seen is even truer of Shakespearean irony. There is a kind of distancing throughout *Henry V*, even if we are aware of it only in certain perspectives. It is Sir John Falstaff's ironic vision, even though he is present only in Mistress Quickly's prose elegy:

> HOSTESS  Nay, sure, he's not in hell; he's in Arthur's bosom, if ever man went to Arthur's bosom. 'A made a finer end, and went away an it had been any christom child. 'A parted even just between twelve and one, even at the turning o'th' tide. For after I saw him fumble with the sheets and play wi'th' flowers, and smile upon his fingers' ends, I knew there was but one way; for his nose was as sharp as a pen, and 'a babbled of green fields. 'How now, Sir John?' quoth I, 'what, man! be o' good cheer.' So 'a cried out 'God, God, God!' three or four times. Now I, to comfort him, bid him 'a should not think of God; I hoped there was no need to trouble himself with any such thoughts yet. So 'a bade me lay more clothes on his feet. I put my hand into the bed and felt them, and they were as cold as any stone. Then I felt to his knees, and so up'ard and up'ard, and all was as cold as any stone.

This is the death of Socrates, whose yielding to the hemlock is attested by the disciple tracing its upward chill. No one else in all the West's literature dies with the precise aura of Falstaff playing with flowers and smiling upon his fingers' ends. I hear no irony in Shakespeare's farewell to his alter ego, except its extraordinary placement in the chronicle of *Henry V*, that hymn to the glory of arms.

Falstaff never ceases to contemplate all of the roles he could play if Shakespeare were to allow it. What shatters the great wit is seeing the multiple realities of Hal, or, to put it most plainly, the love he cannot evade for the only son he ever will have. Hal, who has learned from Falstaff the secrets of otherness, reduces them to the pragmatics of usurpation.

Falstaff, though scholars scarcely note this, is an emblem of Shakespeare's resistance to all premature conceptualizations of human potential. In that regard, his only rival is Hamlet—another monarch of wit, but in so negative a mode that the primary Falstaff is another cosmos entirely.

I used to spend, both in New York City and in London, many a Fundador-soaked evening in the company of my friend Anthony Burgess, a fellow Falstaffian. Burgess, equally devoted to Shakespeare and to James Joyce, tended to find Falstaffian elements in Joyce's work but did not persuade me. Falstaffian writers are sparse. Burgess was decidedly one of them and created his splendid alter ego, the drunken bard Enderby, as his contribution to this tradition of heroic vitalism. I recall telling Anthony that for me Falstaff's true precursors were Alice the Wife of Bath in Chaucer, and Panurge in Rabelais, though Shakespeare probably never read that exuberant forerunner. Directly contemporary is the Sancho Panza of Cervantes, yet he seems to me less Falstaffian than Don Quixote. Chaucer's the Wife of Bath uttered the great outcry: "I have had my world as in my time." I hear Falstaff in that, except that the Wife of Bath did not have the ill-fortune of investing her affection in Prince Hal.

The essence of Sir John Falstaff is that he overturns all expectations. Since he refuses categorization, I dismiss with relish the tiresome scholarly tradition of attaching him to literary traditions of the braggart soldier. Freedom in every sense is the quest of Sir John Falstaff. He fights for freedom from the state, from time, from death.

The Fat Knight has seen through every illusion. So has Hamlet, and yet to some extent the Black Prince is subject to our perspectivism, since we can see things in and about him that he cannot see for himself. Falstaff, as much as the Rosalind of *As You Like It*, has mastered perceptivism to the absolute degree, so that he is not subject to dramatic irony. There is a price. Hamlet's nihilism concerns ultimates, but Falstaff's is comprehensive and embraces origins, middles, and endings.

The ultimate testimony to Falstaffian transvaluation of all value is his obsession with the inevitable rejection from Prince Hal. The richest strain in the Falstaffiad testifies to Shakespeare's awareness that he had to be read as well as seen on a stage. No one, however perceptive, could hope as a playgoer to absorb fully Falstaff's allusions to the terrifying parable that Jesus utters in Luke which I excerpt here as Shakespeare would have read it:

> There was a certeine riche man which was clothed in purple and
>     fine linen, and fared wel and delicately everie day.
> Also there was a certeine begger named Lazarus, which was
>     laied at his gate ful of sores,
> And desired to be refreshed with the crommes that fell from the
>     riche mans table: yea, and the dogs came and licked his sores.
> And it was so that the begger dyed, and was caryed by the
>     Angels into Abrahams bosome. The riche man also dyed and
>     was buryed.
> And being in hel in torments, he lift vp his eyes, and saw
>     Abraham a farre of, & Lazarus in his bosome.
> Then he cryed, and sais, Father Abraham, gaue mercie on me,
>     and send Lazarus that he may dippe y typ of his finger in
>     water, and coole my tongue: for I am tormented in this flame.
> But Abraham said, Sonne, remember that thou in thy life time
>     receiuedft thy pleasures, and likewise Lazarus paines: now
>     therefore is he comforted, and thou art tormented.
> Besides all this, between you and vs there is a great gulfe set, so
>     that they which wolde go from hence to you, can not, nether
>     can they come from thence to us.
>
> Geneva Bible, Luke 16:19–26

Sir John makes three overt allusions to this frightening parable. A more concealed recall comes when Falstaff, kneeling in the dust, is rejected by King Henry V, clad in royal purple. Most pungently, there is a fifth, when Mistress Quickly tells us Falstaff is "in Arthur's bosom," with Arthur displacing Abraham. In England, this parable is traditionally known as the story of Dives and Lazarus, where Dives is the late-Latin *dives*, "a rich man." The leper of this fearsome parable is a different Lazarus entirely than the saint resurrected by Jesus in the Gospel of John.

This is so intricate a pattern of image and idea that only deep reading or indeed otherseeing could apprehend it. Falstaff, in a rather mocking way, is a Bible reader, but though he would like to scoff at this parable, he is too wise and knows it is a reading of his dilemma. Questions crowd upon us. Why does Falstaff choose the harshest version of Jesus in the Gospels? His fear transcends rejection in any ordinary sense and opens onto vistas of death-in-life, which is less acceptable to him than to any other Shakespearean figures. Falstaff is sheer being, a real presence not to be put by. His fierce outcry, "Give me life!," is totally antithetical to the cosmos of the parable from Luke.

It is even more inimical to the spirit incarnate in Hal/Henry V. Doubtless my Falstaffian animus against that clean and clever lad doing his best to get on darkens my own reception of what I acknowledge is another great Shakespearean personality. I remember my late friend Frank Kermode, who bridled when I said to him that Prince Hal essentially wanted three things: the death of Henry IV, so as to secure the crown; the killing of Hotspur, so as to inherit all the "honour" that the northern butcher boy had accumulated; and to hang Jack Falstaff, so as to rid himself of an inconvenient mentor. Though tempted, Hal decides that it would be better if Falstaff died in battle, thus redeeming his disreputable life, to some degree anyway.

Falstaff is a survivor. He is so rammed with life that he will not die for any man's persuasion. We begin to be deep in the twenty-first century, and continuously I think of Falstaff as I read the horrors of contemporary terror and warfare, particularly of the religious variety. To affirm more life above all else is the Falstaffian mode of self-otherseeing, since it grants primacy to what Emily Dickinson eloquently called "another way to see."

# Hamlet's Questioning of Shakespeare

To what extent do Shakespeare's prime protagonists practice a more intense degree of self-otherseeing than most of us do in our daily lives? We, all of us, frequently are startled by what happens to us or by our apparently unintentional acts. Afterward we ask: Were these events or fantasies, or were they actions in the life of someone else?

Since Shakespeare's characters who most stimulate us to meditation—Falstaff, Hamlet, Iago, Cleopatra—are also his most inventive, the gift of self-otherseeing is progressively stronger in them as we move from Falstaff through Hamlet on to Iago and Cleopatra. As I have remarked elsewhere, and will proceed to show in more detail, the sheer sublimity of both Lear and Macbeth makes meditation upon them singularly difficult. They are driven by forces both cosmological and beyond, which engender a self-otherseeing on the frontier of turning into something else.

Hamlet breaks the vessels Shakespeare prepared for him, whether we take those globes to be the Second Quarto text, 1604–5, or the 1623 First Folio. Indeed, even the more rudimentary First Quarto of 1603 can barely contain the Black Prince. In the graveyard—act 5, scene 1 of the Second Quarto—we encounter a riot of self-otherseeing, as the Prince watches the formidable Gravedigger at his labors:

HAMLET There's another. Why, may not that be the skull of a
    lawyer? Where be his quiddities now, his quillities, his cases,
    his tenures, and his tricks? Why does he suffer this mad knave
    now to knock him about the sconce with a dirty shovel, and
    will not tell him of his action of battery? Hum, this fellow
    might be in's time a great buyer of land, with his statutes, his
    recognizances, his fines, his double vouchers, his recoveries.

Is this the fine of his fines and the recovery of his recoveries, to have his fine pate full of fine dirt? Will his vouchers vouch him no more of his purchases, and double ones too, than the length and breadth of a pair of indentures? The very conveyances of his lands will scarcely lie in this box, and must th'inheritor himself have no more, ha?

Shakespeare, a man quick with a lawsuit, expresses a frequent disdain for lawyers. Yet the lawyer here is Everyman and Everywoman, someone who sings a duet with the undertaker, as Wallace Stevens phrased it. Hamlet's cheerful brutality addresses our common mortality. Reciting this now, I substitute the skull of a professor and experience the disquiet of Hamlet the questioner.

There are several registers to Shakespearean self-otherseeing. The most common is a momentary conviction that what one sees is someone else's glimpse of appearances. Darker is Macbeth's mode, which is hallucinatory and can lead to the extreme of "Is this a dagger that I see before me?" Hamlet, subtlest consciousness in Shakespeare, frequently sees as no one else does, including the divided others within Hamlet himself.

What is it Hamlet self-othersees as, skull by skull, the Gravedigger unearths past lives? Not so much a procession of all men and women whose lives forever are ended but, rather, the nihilistic emptiness of all our purposes past and present. To self-othersee in this chilled mode is to apprehend what is at once universal and the essence of one's own being:

GRAVEDIGGER ... Here's a skull now hath lien you i'th' earth
　　three and twenty years.
HAMLET Whose was it?
GRAVEDIGGER A whoreson mad fellow's it was. Whose do you
　　think it was?
HAMLET Nay, I know not.
GRAVEDIGGER A pestilence on him for a mad rogue. A poured a
　　flagon of Rhenish on my head once. This same skull, sir, was,
　　sir, Yorick's skull, the King's jester.
HAMLET This?

*[Takes the skull.]*

GRAVEDIGGER  E'en that.

HAMLET  Alas, poor Yorick. I knew him, Horatio, a fellow of
infinite jest, of most excellent fancy. He hath bore me on
his back a thousand times, and now—how abhorred in my
imagination it is. My gorge rises at it. Here hung those lips
that I have kissed I know not how oft. Where be your gibes
now, your gambols, your songs, your flashes of merriment,
that were wont to set the table on a roar? Not one now to
mock your own grinning? Quite chop-fallen. Now get you to
my lady's table and tell her, let her paint an inch thick, to this
favour she must come. Make her laugh at that.

Of all plays I have ever read, *Hamlet* remains the most advanced and
bewilderingly varied. If asked to choose its visionary center, I would
perhaps seek elsewhere than the graveyard, but tradition from the
late eighteenth century onward selected the image of Hamlet holding
and contemplating the skull of Yorick as one of the prime emblems of
the Western spirit. Shakespeare might have approved this choice. His
most comprehensive protagonist, Hamlet might have joined in such an
appreciation.

The magnificence of this scene fuses together a crucial foregrounding of Hamlet's character with our chilled realization of how far beyond
affect this hero of Western consciousness has journeyed as Act 5 opens.
To hold in your hands the skull of the only person who seems to have
cared for you in childhood—your true father, who carried you on his
back a thousand times, and whose lips the young child kissed endlessly
in the absence of an uxorious and warlike father, and a mother endlessly
seeking sexual gratification—and to feel only caustic revulsion is to be a
personage from whom we should feel alienated. Many do react in that
way to Hamlet, but not most of us, perhaps because, as William Hazlitt
said, "It is we who are Hamlet."

We prefer the Gravedigger's raucous sense of Yorick: "a mad rogue"
who "poured a flagon of Rhenish on my head once." To the Gravedigger, Yorick remains a live presence, as he does for us, while for Hamlet
this once-beloved figure has died a second time. But so, for Hamlet, has
even the mightiest of historical conquerors:

HAMLET  . . . Prithee, Horatio, tell me one thing.

HORATIO  What's that, my lord?

HAMLET  Dost thou think Alexander looked o' this fashion i'th'
  earth?
HORATIO  E'en so.
HAMLET  And smelt so? Pah!
HORATIO  E'en so, my lord.
HAMLET  To what base uses we may return, Horatio! Why, may
  not imagination trace the noble dust of Alexander till a find it
  stopping a bung-hole?
HORATIO  'Twere to consider too curiously to consider so.
HAMLET  No, faith, not a jot. But to follow him thither with
  modesty enough and likelihood to lead it. Alexander died,
  Alexander was buried, Alexander returned to dust, the dust is
  earth, of earth we make loam, and why of that loam whereto
  he was converted might they not stop a beer-barrel?
  Imperious Caesar, dead and turn'd to clay,
  Might stop a hole to keep the wind away.
  O that that earth which kept the world in awe
  Should patch a wall t'expel the water's flaw.

Hamlet challenges us to trace also the noble dust of William Shakespeare or Harold Bloom or you the reader until, at last, our imaginations find our remnants serving as stoppers for a beer barrel. Perhaps
Horatio's finest line is: "'Twere to consider too curiously to consider
so." That exemplary caution is the antithesis of Hamlet's spirit and helps
explain why Horatio so loves Hamlet that he attempts not to survive
him. And yet we go with Hamlet, whose Yorick-like gusto jauntily traces
Alexander's progress after death, to Julius Caesar's similar destiny.

Self-otherseeing attains here its most persuasive mode, in which
Hamlet anticipates his own passivity awaiting death, his death:

HAMLET  Not a whit. We defy augury. There is special
  providence in the fall of a sparrow. If it be, 'tis not to come:
  if it be not to come, it will be now; if it be not now, yet it will
  come. The readiness is all. Since no man, of aught he leaves,
  knows aught, what is't to leave betimes? Let be.

Act 5, Scene 2

Self-otherseeing could scarcely be more intricate. There are tex-
tual complications. The First Folio emphasizes possession rather than

knowledge. The Second Quarto gives: "The readiness is all, since no man of aught he leaves knows what is't to leave betimes. Let be." Here I prefer the composite text of Harold Jenkins, quoted above. As Jenkins implies, I interpret this as saying that, since nobody knows anything about anyone else, why does it matter when we depart? You can generalize this to knowledge of all life, but for Hamlet the central sorrow is the inability of language to manifest feeling without distortion and destruction both of the self and others. Nietzsche, with Hamlet in mind, tells us in *Twilight of the Idols:* "That for which we can find words is something already dead in our hearts. There is always a kind of contempt in the act of speaking."

Something in most of us wants to dispute Hamlet and Nietzsche, since not much is being left for the possibility of expressing love. Hamlet does not love anyone, including himself, though he protests that he *loved* Ophelia, whom he drives to madness and suicide. The exception was Yorick, and we have just otherseen the death in Hamlet's heart of any memory of the mutual love that once sustained both the child-prince and his father's jester. As for any love between the Hamlets, putative father and neglected son, though the Prince proclaims it, we can be skeptical. That leaves Gertrude, the prop of Freud's attempt to change Hamlet into Oedipus. When the dying Queen cries out, "O my dear Hamlet," the Prince's response is "Wretched Queen, adieu." So much for supposed Oedipal sentiments.

The pivot of Hamlet's extreme version of self-overseeing comes directly before the duel with Laertes, in what is one of the Prince's finest moments:

> HAMLET  Give me your pardon, sir. I've done you wrong;
>     But pardon't as you are a gentleman.
>     This presence knows, and you must needs have heard,
>     How I am punish'd with a sore distraction.
>     What I have done
>     That might your nature, honour, and exception
>     Roughly awake, I here proclaim was madness.
>     Was't Hamlet wrong'd Laertes? Never Hamlet.
>     If Hamlet from himself be ta'en away,
>     And when he's not himself does wrong Laertes,
>     Then Hamlet does it not, Hamlet denies it.

Who does it then? His madness. If't be so,
Hamlet is of the faction that is wrong'd;
His madness is poor Hamlet's enemy.
Sir, in this audience,
Let my disclaiming from a purpos'd evil
Free me so far in your most generous thoughts
That I have shot mine arrow o'er the house
And hurt my brother.

Act 5, Scene 2

This is the First Folio text, which I prefer to the Second Quarto, though I employ the Second Quarto's "brother" rather than "mother," which is printed in the First Folio text. As I continue to remark, Hamlet only rarely means what he says and says what he means, so constant is his irony. Surely he is guilty here of equivocation, since we doubt his "antic disposition," which by his own earlier admission was a stratagem. There is no way to reconcile the Prince's eloquent "I am but mad north-north-west" with his current dissimulation. And yet how winning he is! He persuades himself and us that he has self-otherseen his actions in murdering Polonius and in his hideous hounding of Ophelia into her authentic madness and subsequent suicide. Not Hamlet but another of his own obscurer selves mocks the gentle Ophelia and thrusts a sword blindly through the arras, uncaring as to who is on the other side of it.

So capacious is Hamlet's consciousness that he both realizes his own evasiveness and yet, in his mind's eye, beholds quite another Hamlet, so pungently sadistic. Neither he nor his auditor either believes or disbelieves his defense. The crucial passage that establishes what Emily Dickinson might call "nimble believing and disbelieving" magnificently ensues when Laertes leaps up from his sister's burial plot to grapple with the Prince:

HAMLET  *[Comes forward.]* What is he whose grief
    Bears such an emphasis, whose phrase of sorrow
    Conjures the wand'ring stars and makes them stand
    Like wonder-wounded hearers? This is I,
    Hamlet the Dane.
LAERTES  *[grappling with him.]*
    The devil take thy soul!

HAMLET  Thou pray'st not well.
   I prithee take thy fingers from my throat,
   For though I am not splenative and rash,
   Yet have I in me something dangerous,
   Which let thy wiseness fear. Hold off thy hand.

                                             Act 5, Scene 1

   It is not Laertes but Hamlet whose phrases are so sublime that
indeed the wandering stars are conjured and made to stand like wonder-
wounded hearers. My students and I invariably are transported by the
proud declaration "This is I,/Hamlet the Dane." When the Prince
goes on to deny his palpable rashness, we ought to be skeptical, and yet
we realize that we, as much as Laertes, are addressed in "Yet have I in
me something dangerous,/Which let thy wiseness fear."

As an adventure in self-otherseeing, this Hamlet at Ophelia's graveside unsettles the Prince himself as much as it does us. His powers of
parody, exercised earlier against poor Polonius, yield now a grotesque
harvest in hyperbolical descent from the sublime to the ridiculous:

HAMLET  'Swounds, show me what thou't do.
   Woo't weep, woo't fight, woo't tear thyself,
   Woo't drink up eisel, eat a crocodile?
   I'll do't. Dost come here to whine,
   To outface me with leaping in her grave?
   Be buried quick with her, and so will I.
   And if thou prate of mountains, let them throw
   Millions of acres on us, till our ground,
   Singeing his pate against the burning zone,
   Make Ossa like a wart. Nay, an thou'lt mouth,
   I'll rant as well as thou.

                                             Act 5, Scene 1

   To rant so splendidly is itself a dangerous gift. Hamlet is the master
of an extraordinary range of styles, high and low, and this invective is
deliciously low. Extravagance, a wandering beyond limits, is one mark
of the Prince's sensibility. If he reproves the histrionics of Laertes,

he is also aware of his dark principle that to unpack one's heart with words is to be a whore. Yet so excessive is this graveside rant that we do well to look at it more closely. Endless ironist, and self-questioner, Hamlet implies his own awareness of the waning of all sense of others in his heart, which for him means consciousness. To yield up all self-otherseeing is akin to the Prince's metamorphoses in act 5, where his high theatricalism is replaced by what could well be described as a highly original nihilism:

HAMLET . . . . . . . . . . . . .
  I am dead, Horatio. Wretched Queen, adieu.
  You that look pale and tremble at this chance,
  That are but mutes or audience to this act,
  Had I but time—as this fell sergeant, Death,
  Is strict in his arrest—O, I could tell you—
  But let it be. Horatio, I am dead.
  Thou livest. Report me and my causes aright
  To the unsatisfied.

Act 5, Scene 2

"Let it be" beats like a refrain of "let be" earlier in this scene of Hamlet's farewell. Wallace Stevens acutely filled these out as: "Let be be finale of seem." Abandoning life as if it were mere phantasmagoria, the Prince of Denmark pays a final tribute to being as a presence that may exist beyond the world of appearances.

Hamlet dies with the unforgettable words "The rest is silence," where "rest" is more peace than remainder. The largest consciousness ever created by Shakespeare or by anyone else concludes its quest with a farewell to each of us, "mutes or audience to this act," that dismisses all that might be meaningful in our lives. Yet we are also "the unsatisfied" and do not accept the hero's nihilistic self-surrender. Most readers and theatergoers decline to see Hamlet as a hero-villain, the fashion now among some scholarly critics. Since something in all of us is Hamlet, we rebel against the imputation. And yet our dissent is uneasy and makes us question our own waning powers of self-otherseeing.

    Coleridge remarked that Hamlet thought too much. Nietzsche's apt reply always stays with me: "Hamlet thinks not too much but much too well and therefore thinks his way through to the truth." Yet the truth is that from which we perish.

Hamlet's self-otherseeing is so large that, like his irony, it is sometimes difficult to recognize. I have followed earlier lovers of Shakespeare in observing that Hamlet is his own Falstaff. And yet he is also his own Iago and even his own Macbeth.

I am fond of repeating the charming fantasy of Orson Welles that Hamlet goes to England and helps stage the beheading of those pathetic time-servers Rosencrantz and Guildenstern, after which the Prince of Denmark settles down at the Globe Theatre, grows fat, and becomes Sir John Falstaff. He would thus avoid the slaughterhouse of the final scene at Elsinore and could shrug off the continued amours of his mother, Gertrude, and his possible father, Claudius. Shakespeare will not tell us how far back the adulterous affair of Gertrude and Claudius goes, yet it seems not unlikely that she sought solace while the senior Hamlet chopped up Polacks on the ice and performed a landgrab at the expense of the King of Norway. A plump Jack Falstaff version of Hamlet certainly would not have cared.

Doubtless I jest, yet in the spirit of Yorick, a benign influence on his playfellow the child Hamlet. There is no end to Hamlet's possibilities, as befits a consciousness so enormous that it contains all of human self-otherseeing.

# Iago and Othello: Point-Counterpoint

IAGO Virtue? a fig! 'tis in ourselves that we are thus, or thus.
Our bodies are gardens, to which our wills are gardeners.
So that if we will plant nettles or sow lettuce, set hyssop
and weed up thyme, supply it with one gender of herbs or
distract it with many, either to have it sterile with idleness
or manured with industry—why, the power and corrigible
authority of this lies in our wills. If the balance of our lives
had not one scale of reason to poise another of sensuality, the
blood and baseness of our natures would conduct us to most
preposterous conclusions. But we have reason to cool our
raging motions, our carnal stings, our unbitted lusts; whereof
I take this, that you call love, to be a sect or scion.
RODERIGO It cannot be.
IAGO It is merely a lust of the blood and a permission of the
will. Come, be a man! drown thyself? drown cats and blind
puppies. I have professed me thy friend, and I confess me knit
to thy deserving with cables of perdurable toughness. I could
never better stead thee than now. Put money in thy purse,
follow thou the wars, defeat thy favour with an usurped beard;
I say, put money in thy purse. It cannot be that Desdemona
should long continue her love to the Moor—put money in
thy purse—nor he his to her. It was a violent commencement
in her, and thou shalt see an answerable sequestration—put
but money in thy purse. These Moors are changeable in their
wills—fill thy purse with money. The food that to him now
is as luscious as locusts shall be to him shortly as acerb as
coloquintida. She must change for youth; when she is sated
with his body she will find the error of her choice; she must

have change, she must. Therefore, put money in thy purse. If
thou wilt needs damn thyself, do it a more delicate way than
drowning—make all the money thou canst. If sanctimony,
and a frail vow betwixt an erring Barbarian and a super-subtle
Venetian, be not too hard for my wits and all the tribe of
hell, thou shalt enjoy her—therefore make money. A pox of
drowning thyself, it is clean out of the way: seek thou rather
to be hanged in compassing thy joy than to be drowned and
go without her.

Act 1, Scene 3

The dark wisdom of Iago is his most attractive quality. That and his
zest make him so dangerous. He takes priority over the entire panoply
of Shakespearean villains. Even the brilliant Edmund in *King Lear* is
not quite of Iago's bad eminence. Iago is a grand theatrical improviser.
He shifts his tactics as he goes along. He has at first no design for
destroying Othello, but his inventive gusto leaps from one intoxicat-
ing surmise to another as he explores enormous resources previously
undivulged to him.

He cheerfully observes:

O villainous! I have looked upon the world for four times seven
years, and since I could distinguish betwixt a benefit and an injury
I never found a man that knew how to love himself. Ere I would
say I would drown myself for the love of a guinea-hen I would
change my humanity with a baboon.

Act 1, Scene 3

Is there anyone Iago loves except for himself? Certainly not his
wife, Emilia, and he chooses to be without friends. For him the overwhelming figure is his captain-general, Othello, whom he has served
as ancient or flag officer, always the third in command. As the ancient,
he is pledged to give up his life rather than to allow Othello's personal
colors to be captured in battle.

Iago's relation to Othello before the tragedy opens was one of religious veneration. The African warrior had been Iago's mortal god, the
incarnation of war. And Iago knows only one religion: the worship of
Mars and of Othello as the god's earthly representative. When Othello
passed over Iago and chose Cassio as his lieutenant, he transformed
his ancient into a chaos, a man on the verge of losing any sense of his

own being. John Milton founded his own concept of Satan's "sense of injured merit" upon Iago's pathos of outrage at what he judged to be Othello's betrayal of his follower's absolute dedication to the Moor, who cared only for the honor of arms. We can surmise that Othello passed over Iago because he saw that the ancient was always at war and could not live in the camp of peace.

Iago asserts he has spent the twenty-eight years of his life looking upon the world, and his otherseeing has resulted in a vision that values only self-love, whether in himself or in others. His exaltation of the will demystifies love as merely a lust of the blood and the will's becoming permissive. From Emilia's later remarks in the play, it would seem that Iago's vastation at having been passed over has ensued in sexual impotence. When he says that Othello's weak function, or supposed impotence, will turn Desdemona away from her marriage, we hear his own involuntary confession. Shakespeare is supple and turbulent in charting the stages of Iago's plot, the initial formulation of which is inchoate:

> I hate the Moor
> And it is thought abroad that 'twixt my sheets
> He's done my office. I know not if't be true,
> But I for mere suspicion in that kind
> Will do as if for surety. He holds me well,
> The better shall my purpose work on him.
> Cassio's a proper man: let me see now,
> To get his place, and to plume up my will
> In double knavery. How? How? let's see:
> After some time to abuse Othello's ear
> That he is too familiar with his wife.
> He hath a person and a smooth dispose
> To be suspected, framed to make women false.
> The Moor is of a free and open nature
> That thinks men honest that but seem to be so,
> And will as tenderly be led by th' nose
> As asses are.
> I have't, it is engendered! Hell and night
> Must bring this monstrous birth to the world's light.

> *Exit.*

> Act 1, Scene 3

Iago grows perpetually in a sense of triumphalism that energizes him and yet prepares a final downfall. When he cries aloud, "I have't, it is engendered!," he is overstating, and is too wise not to know this. He knows also, though, that his onward drive as a plotter depends upon the audacity of prolepsis. His next soliloquy confesses the formlessness of his plot but vows to persist, in a diabolic mode of negative transcendence:

> That Cassio loves her, I do well believe it,
> That she loves him, 'tis apt and of great credit.
> The Moor, howbeit that I endure him not,
> Is of a constant, loving, noble nature,
> And I dare think he'll prove to Desdemona
> A most dear husband. Now I do love her too,
> Not out of absolute lust—though peradventure
> I stand accountant for as great a sin—
> But partly led to diet my revenge,
> For that I do suspect the lusty Moor
> Hath leaped into my seat, the thought whereof
> Doth like a poisonous mineral gnaw my inwards . . .
> And nothing can or shall content my soul
> Till I am evened with him, wife for wife. . . .
> Or, failing so, yet that I put the Moor
> At least into a jealousy so strong
> That judgement cannot cure; which thing to do,
> If this poor trash of Venice, whom I trash
> For his quick hunting, stand the putting on,
> I'll have our Michael Cassio on the hip,
> Abuse him to the Moor in the rank garb—
> For I fear Cassio with my night-cap too—
> Make the Moor thank me, love me, and reward me
> For making him egregiously an ass,
> And practising upon his peace and quiet
> Even to madness. 'Tis here, but yet confused:
> Knavery's plain face is never seen, till used.

*Exit.*

Act 2, Scene 1

At first this may seem as obscurantist as Shakespeare's Richard III can be, yet Iago's dark design is gestating in the abyss of his hatred. His obsessive imputation of unappeasable lust to all others betrays his own unspoken realization that Othello's ontological attack upon him (as he sees it) has resulted in an alarming impotence. His third soliloquy achieves a superb emergence into the frightening eminence of a free artist of himself:

> And what's he then that says I play the villain?
> When this advice is free I give and honest,
> Probal to thinking and indeed the course
> To win the Moor again? For 'tis most easy
> Th'inclining Desdemona to subdue
> In any honest suit. She's framed as fruitful
> As the free elements: and then for her
> To win the Moor, were't to renounce his baptism,
> All seals and symbols of redeemed sin,
> His soul is so enfettered to her love
> That she may make, unmake, do what she list,
> Even as her appetite shall play the god
> With his weak function. How am I then a villain
> To counsel Cassio to this parallel course
> Directly to his good? Divinity of hell!
> When devils will the blackest sins put on
> They do suggest at first with heavenly shows
> As I do now. For whiles this honest fool
> Plies Desdemona to repair his fortune,
> And she for him pleads strongly to the Moor,
> I'll pour this pestilence into his ear:
> That she repeals him for her body's lust.
> And by how much she strives to do him good
> She shall undo her credit with the Moor—
> So will I turn her virtue into pitch
> And out of her own goodness make the net
> That shall enmesh them all.
>
> Act 2, Scene 3

Iago mounts to the sublime of zest, exultant in his burgeoning powers. When he cries out in his ecstasy, "Divinity of hell!," he both enlists in a theology of the Inferno and directly invokes Satan. Iago disarms us by placing himself among the devils and wins us by the exuberance of his rhetorical questions and theatrical self-awareness: "As I do now." The Globe audience would remember Hamlet's *The Mousetrap*, in which the surrogate for Claudius pours poison into the ear of his sleeping brother. Triumphalism sounds forth as Iago concludes, rancidly turning Desdemona's virtue into foulness. The vivid coinage "enmesh" which Shakespeare employs only here in all his works, catches the tangled web, shockingly turned out of Desdemona's goodness into a net that will doom Othello, Desdemona, Emilia, and, ironically at last, Iago himself.

Overhearing himself in this grand soliloquy, Iago breaks also into the mode of self-otherseeing. We behold with him the birth of a new Iago, at one with his daemon or genius, heretofore unexplored but now masterly in writing drama with the lives of others. The cognitive music of this soliloquy rings with the accents of glorious emergence, a coming into possession of the insight that is the Shakespearean truth: every woman and every man is her or his own most dangerous enemy. The ease of Iago's consciousness as it leaps from point to point, always driving toward a pyromaniac destruction of all others, delights the ancient himself. Freedom and honesty indeed constitute Iago's self-praise, yet this ironic "honest Iago," supposedly plain-spoken, is intricate in the evasions that play at truth. Chant this soliloquy out loud to yourself, giving it the gusto it deserves. It should frighten you, and yet something in each of us rejoices in the power of Iago's newly revealed potential.

His fifth soliloquy is the most dangerous, for in it he becomes an aesthetician of the abyss of jealousy metamorphosing into madness:

> I will in Cassio's lodging lose this napkin
> And let him find it. Trifles light as air
> Are to the jealous confirmations strong
> As proofs of holy writ. This may do something.
> The Moor already changes with my poison:
> Dangerous conceits are in their natures poisons
> Which at the first are scarce found to distaste
> But with a little art upon the blood
> Burn like the mines of sulphur.
>
>                                                   *Enter Othello.*

I did say so:
Look where he comes. Not poppy nor mandragora
Nor all the drowsy syrups of the world
Shall ever medicine thee to that sweet sleep
Which thou owedst yesterday.

Act 3, Scene 3

The handkerchief or napkin was given to Othello's mother by an Egyptian enchanter. The Moor, dangerously receiving the news that Desdemona no longer possesses it, reacts with a curious music:

'Tis true, there's magic in the web of it.
A sibyl that had numbered in the world
The sun to course two hundred compasses,
In her prophetic fury sewed the work;
The worms were hallowed that did breed the silk,
And it was dyed in mummy, which the skilful
Conserved of maidens' hearts.

Act 3, Scene 4

The web ironically echoes Iago's enmeshing net, and the virgin hearts that provide the stuff to be woven remind us, yet more ironically, of Shakespeare's most crucial ellipsis in this tragedy, which is that we cannot be sure the marriage of Desdemona and Othello ever has been consummated. Iago's fifth soliloquy, with a kind of uncanny charm, tells us that a lost handkerchief can serve as holy writ in the religion of jealousy. My students and I thrill to Iago's tasting of his anticipated triumph: "This may do something." When the crazed Othello enters, the ancient's true triumph begins with marvelous pride: "I did say so." Iago anticipates the entire Aesthetic Movement that goes from the "Ode to a Nightingale" of John Keats (which begins with a palpable allusion to this soliloquy) and passes on to the religion of art in John Ruskin, Walter Pater, and Oscar Wilde.

Iago's crooning, as he lingers over the serenity he has devastated, is charged with an extraordinary infusion of nostalgia for the war god Othello, now dispersed into chaos. This nostalgia merely enhances the self-overseeing of the ancient's triumphalism, which none of us can hope to dispute. A. C. Bradley once remarked that, had Iago encountered Hamlet, he would have been driven to suicide by the Prince's immediate realization of Iago's inward nature. Hamlet's mockery would have been beyond Iago's powers of self-preservation. Falstaff also would have scorned and rapidly demolished Iago. But Shakespeare exercised discretion in the tragedy of *Othello*, and only Emilia is capable, belatedly, of seeing through her diabolic husband.

Unlike Edmund in *King Lear*, Iago is incapable of change either through self-overhearing or self-otherseeing. He ends so outraged by his blindness in underestimating Emilia's finally suicidal love for Desdemona that all he can vow is to die silently under judicial torture:

> Demand me nothing. What you know, you know.
> From this time forth I never will speak word.
>
> Act 5, Scene 2

I myself have shared the general critical guilt of being so fascinated by Iago that I somewhat neglected the grandeur of Othello, whose relation to his undoing ancient is one of point-counterpoint. Iago's triumphant ruining of his war god would not have its terrifying magnitude if the divinity that is brought down had not first glowed in the firmament as a fixed star among Shakespeare's sublime masters of battle: Julius Caesar, Mark Antony, Coriolanus, and, in a different mode, Hotspur and Henry V.

One might begin with the single line spoken by the Moor that ends what could have been a fatal street brawl: "Keep up your bright swords, for the dew will rust them." That voice of authority belongs to the fastest sword in Europe and shows a ruthless economy. Othello's initial declaration of his own worth has the same quality:

> Let him do his spite;
> My services, which I have done the signiory,
> Shall out-tongue his complaints. 'Tis yet to know—
> Which, when I know that boasting is an honour,
> I shall promulgate—I fetch my life and being
> From men of royal siege, and my demerits
> May speak unbonneted to as proud a fortune
> As this that I have reached. For know, Iago,
> But that I love the gentle Desdemona

I would not my unhoused free condition
Put into circumscription and confine
For the sea's worth.

Act 1, Scene 2

His pride is heartening and legitimate, yet the palpable sadness he still feels at his loss of freedom when he married intimates the gathering disaster. We tend to undervalue Othello, because of his double deficiency, as to both his inability to overhear himself and his startling failure at all self-otherseeing.

Her father loved me, oft invited me,
Still questioned me the story of my life
From year to year—the battles, sieges, fortunes
That I have passed.
I ran it through, even from my boyish days
To th' very moment that he bade me tell it,
Wherein I spake of most disastrous chances,
Of moving accidents by flood and field,
Of hair-breadth scapes i'th' imminent deadly breach,
Of being taken by the insolent foe
And sold to slavery; of my redemption thence
And portance in my travailous history;
Wherein of antres vast and deserts idle,
Rough quarries, rocks and hills whose heads touch heaven
It was my hint to speak—such was my process—
And of the cannibals that each other eat,
The Anthropophagi, and men whose heads
Do grow beneath their shoulders. This to hear
Would Desdemona seriously incline,
But still the house affairs would draw her thence,
Which ever as she could with haste dispatch
She'd come again, and with a greedy ear
Devour up my discourse; which I, observing,
Took once a pliant hour and found good means
To draw from her a prayer of earnest heart
That I would all my pilgrimage dilate,
Whereof by parcels she had something heard

But not intentively. I did consent,
And often did beguile her of her tears
When I did speak of some distressful stroke
That my youth suffered. My story being done
She gave me for my pains a world of sighs,
She swore in faith 'twas strange, 'twas passing strange,
'Twas pitiful, 'twas wonderous pitiful;
She wished she had not heard it, yet she wished
That heaven had made her such a man. She thanked me
And bade me, if I had a friend that loved her,
I should but teach him how to tell my story
And that would woo her. Upon this hint I spake:
She loved me for the dangers I had passed
And I loved her that she did pity them.
This only is the witchcraft I have used. . . .

Act I, Scene 3

This fabulous narrative of astonishing dangers and remarkable sur-
vivals is summarized by Othello in a way that only seems to be a naïve
recital of the marvelous. He values his own living romance even as he
glories in his military eminence. Shakespeare artfully varies the Moor's
double use of "hint," which initially means "opportunity" ("It was my
hint to speak—such was my process—") and then dilates into the use of
"hint" as indirect suggestion ("Upon this hint I spake"). The calamity
that will be their marriage is ironically prophesied in:

She loved me for the dangers I had passed
And I loved her that she did pity them.

We wince, or ought to, at his inability to overhear himself when he
contrasts his mistaken understanding of Desdemona's love for him with
his own supposed reason for returning her passion, which plainly he
does not fully share. Ironically, there is no witchcraft on either side, but
only the deep sadness of the perpetual Shakespearean natural superiority of women in the sphere of eros. Othello's greatness, not just at lead-
ership but also at sustaining the honor of arms by cleanly dividing the
camp of peace from that of war, becomes a hopeless blank for receiving
a love so rare and admirable as Desdemona's.

To define precisely his love for her is not entirely possible, because Shakespeare does not care to tell us as much as we would like. Sexual desire would appear to be a minor element at best in Othello's regard for his wife. The central enigma of *The Tragedy of Othello, The Moor of Venice*, is, as I remarked in discussing Iago, the ambiguity of consummation. Nearly every critic believes that it must have been performed, but a closer reading—indeed, a ransacking of the text—convinces me that this is unlikely. Does that explain part of the context of Iago's triumph? It may add to the terrifying poignance of the mutual catastrophe of Desdemona and the Moor. Consider the aura of their lovely reunion on Cyprus:

*Enter Othello and Attendants*

CASSIO  Lo, where he comes!

OTHELLO  O my fair warrior!

DESDEMONA  My dear Othello!

OTHELLO  It gives me wonder great as my content
    To see you here before me! O my soul's joy,
    If after every tempest come such calms
    May the winds blow till they have wakened death,
    And let the labouring bark climb hills of seas,
    Olympus-high, and duck again as low
    As hell's from heaven. If it were now to die
    'Twere now to be most happy, for I fear
    My soul hath her content so absolute
    That not another comfort like to this
    Succeeds in unknown fate.

DESDEMONA  The heavens forbid
    But that our loves and comforts should increase
    Even as our days do grow.

OTHELLO  Amen to that, sweet powers!
    I cannot speak enough of this content,
    It stops me here, it is too much of joy.
    And this, and this the greatest discords be    *[They kiss.]*
    That e'er our hearts shall make.

IAGO  *[aside]*
    O, you are well tuned now: but I'll set down

The pegs that make this music, as honest
As I am.
OTHELLO  Come, let us to the castle.
News, friends, our wars are done, the Turks are drowned.
How does my old acquaintance of this isle?
Honey, you shall be well desired in Cyprus,
I have found great love amongst them. O my sweet,
I prattle out of fashion, and I dote
In mine own comforts. I prithee, good Iago,
Go to the bay and disembark my coffers.
Bring thou the master to the citadel,
He is a good one, and his worthiness
Does challenge much respect. Come, Desdemona;
Once more, well met at Cyprus.

                                                    Act 2, Scene 1

Othello senses that his happiness has reached its apex and can only decline. Contentment floods the Moor, but he will never have such comfort again, as he plainly fears. Desdemona, always the epitome of humane maturity, speaks instead of comforts that should increase even as her days and years with Othello will grow. The kiss they exchange is their last moment of harmony, with Iago standing by and prophesying his destruction of their mutual music. The rigors of the double plot will manifest a different mode of music, one in which the strings are false.

Othello, who says he has found in his love for Desdemona a new principle of order, ironically prophesies the advent of a new chaos, though he has no intimation that its architect will be Iago. He makes explicit that he is not jealous by nature, and we believe him, but Iago is the very daemon of jealousy. Othello's heroic resistance to suspicion of his wife's virtue cannot survive Iago's skill at suggestion. His inmost pride, which is his sense of military greatness, strains and then gives way:

I had been happy if the general camp,
Pioneers and all, had tasted her sweet body,
So I had nothing known. O now for ever
Farewell the tranquil mind, farewell content!
Farewell the plumed troops and the big wars

That makes ambition virtue! O farewell,
Farewell the neighing steed and the shrill trump,
The spirit-stirring drum, th'ear-piercing fife,
The royal banner, and all quality,
Pride, pomp and circumstance of glorious war!
And, O you mortal engines whose rude throats
Th'immortal Jove's dread clamours counterfeit,
Farewell: Othello's occupation's gone.

Act 3, Scene 3

This stirring passage would seem to have haunted Ernest Hemingway, who is prophesied in "the big wars." We accept Othello's military sublime because he has kept it so scrupulously apart from the camp of peace, and yet I hear almost the accents of a boy in this dirge that sadly bids farewell even to cannons. His desperation becomes a direct and dangerous threat to Iago when the Moor demands ocular proof that his love is a whore. And yet this provokes Iago to fresh dramatizations of his insinuations. Even in Shakespeare I do not know of a scene so dramatically wrought as the one Iago directs, in which a diabolic ritual is enacted as a kind of black Mass:

OTHELLO  O that the slave had forty thousand lives!
    One is too poor, too weak for my revenge.
    Now do I see 'tis true. Look here, Iago,
    All my fond love thus do I blow to heaven:
    'Tis gone!
    Arise, black vengeance, from the hollow hell,
    Yield up, O love, thy crown and hearted throne
    To tyrannous hate! Swell, bosom, with thy fraught,
    For 'tis of aspics' tongues!
IAGO                          Yet be content!
OTHELLO  O blood, blood, blood!          *[Othello kneels.]*
IAGO  Patience, I say, your mind perhaps may change.
OTHELLO  Never, Iago. Like to the Pontic sea
    Whose icy current and compulsive course
    Ne'er keeps retiring ebb but keeps due on
    To the Propontic and the Hellespont:
    Even so my bloody thoughts with violent pace

Shall ne'er look back, ne'er ebb to humble love
Till that a capable and wide revenge
Swallow them up. Now by yond marble heaven
In the due reverence of a sacred vow
I here engage my words.

IAGO                    Do not rise yet          *[Iago kneels.]*

Witness, you ever-burning lights above,
You elements that clip us round about,
Witness that here Iago doth give up
The execution of his wit, hands, heart,
To wronged Othello's service. Let him command
And to obey shall be in me remorse
What bloody business ever.

OTHELLO                 I greet thy love
Not with vain thanks but with acceptance bounteous,
And will upon the instant put thee to't.
Within these three days let me hear thee say
That Cassio's not alive

IAGO                    My friend is dead,
'Tis done—at your request. But let her live.

OTHELLO  Damn her, lewd minx: O damn her, damn her!
Come, go with me apart; I will withdraw
To furnish me with some swift means of death
For the fair devil. Now art thou my lieutenant.

IAGO  I am your own for ever.

*Exeunt.*

Act 3, Scene 3

Iago has many ironic master-strokes, but I am particularly delighted by "Do not rise yet." With diabolic brilliance, Iago kneels by his captain-general's side and invokes "you ever-burning lights above," but he means those below. In the variable exchanges between the many-minded Hamlet and the wretched Claudius, a fourth-rate Machiavel who is adroit only at poisoning, Shakespeare inaugurated a dialogue of a master self-otherseer and a contriver with no capacity for self-otherseeing. That is a prelude to this astonishing encounter between the superb self-otherseer Iago and the heroic but blind Othello, who becomes capable of self-otherseeing only in his death scene.

Soft you, a word or two before you go.
I have done the state some service, and they know't:
No more of that. I pray you, in your letters,
When you shall these unlucky deeds relate,
Speak of me as I am. Nothing extenuate,
Nor set down aught in malice. Then must you speak
Of one that loved not wisely, but too well;
Of one not easily jealous, but, being wrought,
Perplexed in the extreme; of one whose hand,
Like the base Indian, threw a pearl away
Richer than all his tribe; of one whose subdued eyes,
Albeit unused to the melting mood,
Drops tears as fast as the Arabian trees
Their medicinable gum. Set you down this,
And say besides that in Aleppo once,
Where a malignant and a turbanned Turk
Beat a Venetian and traduced the state,
I took by th' throat the circumcised dog
And smote him—thus! *[He stabs himself.]*

Act 5, Scene 2

Associating himself with Herod the Great, who had his own most beloved of wives, Mariamne the Hasmonean, executed on false charges, Othello knowingly places himself in the worst of company. And yet his suicidal speech is carefully balanced and profoundly just. For the first time in his life, he is capable of seeing himself as he would someone else, and of exercising his normally superb judgment upon his own tragedy. It is a grand recovery, but hopelessly belated. The aesthetic effect is enormous, and the human poignance virtually unbearable.

# Edgar and Edmund:
# Agonistic Dramatists

THE FIRST QUARTO of *King Lear* (1608) has a title page that gives us a crucial insight into that vast drama:

M. William Shak-speare:
HIS
True Chronicle Historie of the life and
death of King LEAR and his three
Daughters.
*With the unfortunate life of* Edgar, *sonne*
and heire to the Earle of Gloster, and his
sullen and assumed humor of
Tom of Bedlam:

One would hardly know from most scholarly criticism of *King Lear* that Edgar is much the most important figure in the drama after the great king himself. No Shakespearean person has been so absurdly neglected and misinterpreted as Edgar. Except for Lear, he is given more lines to speak than anyone else in the play. I myself do not find useful the accounts of *King Lear* that center upon its supposed "double plot," if only because Shakespeare's creative furnace fuses together the tragedies of Lear and his three daughters, and of Gloucester and his two sons. Of these five in the younger generation, Edgar rather than Edmund or Cordelia is the most central. Though the legendary King Leir was succeeded by King Edgar only after some intervening reigns, Shakespeare closes the play with a despairing Edgar reluctantly ascending the throne of Britain.

I have now written so many commentaries on Edgar that I am able to calm down when I encounter most available interpretations. One celebrated critic assured us that Edgar was a "weak and murderous character," which is perhaps worthy of placement with T. S. Eliot's judgment that *Hamlet* was "an aesthetic failure."

Edgar and Edmund have to be read antithetically in relation to each other. Their lives finally converge in a death-duel that renders Edmund the Bastard a mortal wound at the hands of the half-brother he has wronged and, by an irony savage and just, transformed from a gullible youth into an inexorable avenger.

Edmund, like his precursor Iago, is a dramatist who composes with the lives of everyone else in the play. Unlike Iago, who is a great improviser and a tactical genius, the even more formidable Edmund is a brilliant strategist who has plotted his own rise to power by exploiting his intellectual superiority over everyone else in this tragedy of tragedies.

Edmund, when we consider his crimes against humanity, is nevertheless surprisingly attractive, because of his candor and clarity in self-otherseeing:

GLOUCESTER These late eclipses in the sun and moon portend
no good to us. Though the wisdom of Nature can reason it
thus and thus, yet nature finds itself scourged by the sequent
effects. Love cools, friendship falls off, brothers divide: in
cities, mutinies; in countries, discord; in palaces, treason; and
the bond cracked 'twixt son and father. This villain of mine
comes under the prediction—there's son against father. The
King falls from bias of nature—there's father against child.
We have seen the best of our time. Machinations, hollowness,
treachery and all ruinous disorders follow us disquietly to
our graves. Find out this villain, Edmund; it shall lose thee
nothing. Do it carefully.—And the noble and true-hearted
Kent banished, his offence honesty! 'Tis strange, strange!

*Exit.*

EDMUND This is the excellent foppery of the world, that
when we are sick in fortune, often the surfeits of our own
behaviour, we make guilty of our disasters the sun, the
moon and the stars, as if we were villains on necessity, fools
by heavenly compulsion, knaves, thieves and treachers by

spherical predominance; drunkards, liars and adulterers by
an enforced obedience of planetary influence; and all that we
are evil in by a divine thrusting on. An admirable evasion of
whoremaster man, to lay his goatish disposition on the charge
of a star. My father compounded with my mother under the
dragon's tail and my nativity was under Ursa Major, so that
it follows I am rough and lecherous. Fut! I should have been
that I am had the maidenliest star in the firmament twinkled
on my bastardizing.

*Enter Edgar.*

Pat he comes, like the catastrophe of the old comedy. My cue
is villainous melancholy, with a sigh like Tom o'Bedlam.—
O, these eclipses do portend these divisions. Fa, sol, la, mi.

Act 1, Scene 2

Edmund's *sprezzatura*, his studied carelessness, is meant to remind
auditors and readers of Castiglione's *The Courtier* (1528, and available
in English from 1561 on), where this kind of nonchalance is commended as aristocratic behavior. But Edmund does it in a fiercely ironic
mode, founded upon his bitterness at the stigma attached to his own
bastardy. Edgar's entrance so arouses his brother's high theatricalism
that Edmund casts himself as a traditionally melancholy villain, and
his brother, the legitimate heir of Gloucester, as a victim, one of the
inhabitants of the great stage of fools. Particularly uncanny, since Edgar
cannot hear him, is Edmund's prolepsis of what will be Edgar's primary
disguise in the play.

Edgar moves through the play from one agony to another, the terrible sufferings of both his godfather, Lear, and his father, Gloucester.
Edmund's pleasure in working out his intricate drive to power is clearly
an aesthetic satisfaction to him, even as his dramatic skill in limning his
night-piece approaches the best achieved by any rival Jacobean dramatist. And yet Edgar is also a dramatist, in his case a desperate one, who
at least tries to fail better, in a mode that influenced Samuel Beckett.
Tracing his pilgrimage could begin with his taking on the disguise of
Tom of Bedlam:

I heard myself proclaimed,
And by the happy hollow of a tree
Escaped the hunt. No port is free, no place

That guard and most unusual vigilance
Does not attend my taking. While I may scape
I will preserve myself, and am bethought
To take the basest and most poorest shape
That ever penury in contempt of man
Brought near to beast. My face I'll grime with filth,
Blanket my loins, elf all my hair in knots
And with presented nakedness outface
The winds and persecutions of the sky.
The country gives me proof and precedent
Of Bedlam beggars, who, with roaring voices,
Strike in their numbed and mortified bare arms
Pins, wooden pricks, nails, sprigs of rosemary;
And with this horrible object, from low farms,
Poor pelting villages, sheepcotes and mills,
Sometime with lunatic bans, sometime with prayers,
Enforce their charity. Poor Turlygod, poor Tom,
That's something yet: Edgar I nothing am.

Act 2, Scene 2

The negative zest here has its own eloquence and is a portent of the fearful price Edgar will pay for his downward path to wisdom and survival. The playgoer and reader should begin with the realization that Edgar is himself of a near-royal family and stands fourth in line to the throne after Lear's three daughters. His self-abnegation in going down through the very bottom of the social scale is overt and extreme. The Earl of Kent, banished under sentence of death should he return, disguises himself as Caius, a peasant, who offers himself to Lear as a servant and is accepted. Eventually, Edgar too will pretend he is a peasant, and as such bludgeons to death the horrible Oswald when that henchman of Goneril and Regan threatens to kill the blinded Gloucester. Something intensely histrionic as well as self-punishing in Edgar has him begin his disguised trek as a roaring beggar released from Bedlam, hospital for the insane.

I have already ventured that Edgar is the most underestimated character in all of Shakespeare's invention of the human. The same critic who dismissed him as "weak and cowardly" goes on to suggest that Edgar's long delay in revealing himself to Gloucester is founded upon his desire to remain perpetually a little child. I mention this because, though I find it absurd, it has been very influential, even upon R. A. Foakes, the otherwise astute editor of the Arden edition of *King Lear*. What Shakespeare instead shows us is the painful development of a stubborn hero who endures and ultimately cuts Edmund down. And yet Edgar is an enigma, and his staging of his own mode of self-overseeing adds to the difficult distinction of Lear's tragedy.

Consider the extraordinary gift that Edgar displays as an actor in his portrayal of a wandering Tom of Bedlam:

> Who gives anything to Poor Tom? Whom the foul fiend hath led through fire and through flame, through ford and whirlpool, o'er bog and quagmire; that hath laid knives under his pillow and halters in his pew; set ratsbane by his porridge, made him proud of heart, to ride on a bay trotting horse over four-inched bridges, to course his own shadow for a traitor. Bless thy five wits, Tom's a-cold. O do, de, do, de, do, de: bless thee from whirlwinds, star-blasting and taking. Do Poor Tom some charity, whom the foul fiend vexes. There could I have him now, and there, and there again, and there.
>
> Act 3, Scene 4

This rich rhetoric, for which nothing in Edgar's life as a young nobleman could have prepared him, is accompanied by an extraordinary ability to coin aphorisms. The one I always linger on is "He childed as I fathered," where the reference is to the King. Both "childed" and "fathered" are Shakespeare's own coinings, and Edgar employs them to sum up much of the pathos of the tragedy. He does not mean just that Goneril and Regan cast out Lear while Gloucester casts out his true son. Instead those five words "He childed as I fathered" make little reference to Goneril and Regan but only to the dark parallel between Lear/Cordelia and Edgar/Gloucester. There is only love among those four, and yet the love itself results in tragedy. What Edgar understands is that love is anything but redemptive; in the cosmos where he wanders, there is neither justice nor mercy, and love itself bewilders through the excess of the fathers and the recalcitrance of the children Cordelia and Edgar, who need and want love, but are more adept at returning it than at knowing how it should be received.

Edgar's purgative suffering is totally antithetical to Edmund's charming contemplation of what might be called a double date with those two monsters of the deep, Goneril and Regan:

> To both these sisters have I sworn my love,
> Each jealous of the other as the stung
> Are of the adder. Which of them shall I take?
> Both? One? Or neither? Neither can be enjoyed
> If both remain alive. To take the widow
> Exasperates, makes mad her sister Goneril,
> And hardly shall I carry out my side,
> Her husband being alive. Now then, we'll use
> His countenance for the battle, which being done,
> Let her who would be rid of him devise
> His speedy taking off. As for the mercy
> Which he intends to Lear and to Cordelia,
> The battle done, and they within our power,
> Shall never see his pardon; for my state
> Stands on me to defend, not to debate.
>
> Act 5, Scene 1

This is so delicious as regards the two fatal sisters that we almost forgive Edmund his insouciant disregard for anything that can be judged humane restraint. He disarms us by an audacious verve in expressing a total candor. The enigma of why someone with no affect and no desire for pleasure should plot so superbly to seize and maintain absolute power is surrogated to us for whatever understanding we can attain. Bastardy seems Edmund's own expedient for explaining away his drives and motives. How different this is from the Bastard Faulconbridge, who admirably inherits the better qualities of his father, Richard Lionheart. And yet Edmund proves capable of his final astonishing change through self-overhearing:

> Yet Edmund was beloved:
> The one the other poisoned for my sake,
> And after slew herself.
>
> Act 5, Scene 3

It may be that the clue to Edmund's drive is his total capacity for self-otherseeing, in which he almost rivals Hamlet. Power over others comes so easily to him because he ceaselessly beholds everyone else on stage with the same clarity he brings to his own presentation of himself. There is an aesthetic splendor, terrifyingly sublime, in such total freedom from illusion. Contrast Edgar's suffering and bewilderment at his disillusion with regard to Edmund's treachery and his own gullibility. Ultimately, I find Edgar far more fascinating than Edmund, but at the cost of our own bewilderment.

# The Fool and Cordelia:
# Love's Martyrdom

KENT  This is nothing, fool.

FOOL  Then 'tis like the breath of an unfee'd lawyer, you gave
me nothing for't. *[to Lear]* Can you make no use of nothing,
nuncle?

LEAR  Why no, boy; nothing can be made out of nothing.

FOOL  *[to Kent]*. Prithee tell him, so much the rent of his land
comes to; he will not believe a fool.

LEAR  A bitter fool.

FOOL  Dost thou know the difference, my boy, between a bitter
fool and a sweet one?

LEAR  No, lad, teach me.

FOOL  That lord that counselled thee to give away thy land,
Come place him here by me; do thou for him stand.
The sweet and bitter fool will presently appear,
The one in motley here, the other found out there.

LEAR  Dost thou call me fool, boy?

FOOL  All thy other titles thou hast given away; that thou wast
born with.

KENT  This is not altogether fool, my lord.

FOOL  No, faith, lords and great men will not let me; if I had a
monopoly out, they would have part on't; and ladies too, they
will not let me have all the fool to myself, they'll be snatching.
Nuncle, give me an egg and I'll give thee two crowns.

LEAR  What two crowns shall they be?

FOOL  Why, after I have cut the egg i'the middle and eat up
the meat, the two crowns of the egg. When thou clovest thy
crown i'the middle and gav'st away both parts, thou bor'st

thine ass on thy back o'er the dirt. Thou hadst little wit in
thy bald crown when thou gav'st thy golden one away. If I
speak like myself in this, let him be whipped that first finds
it so.

*[Sings.]* Fools had ne'er less grace in a year,
    For wise men are grown foppish,
    And know not how their wits to wear,
    Their manners are so apish.

LEAR  When were you wont to be so full of songs, sirrah?

FOOL  I have used it, nuncle, e'er since thou mad'st thy
daughters thy mothers; for when thou gav'st them the rod and
putt'st down thine own breeches,

*[Sings.]* Then they for sudden joy did weep
    And I for sorrow sung,
    That such a king should play bo-peep,
    And go the fools among.
    Prithee, nuncle, keep a schoolmaster that can teach thy
    fool to lie; I would fain learn to lie.

LEAR  An you lie, sirrah, we'll have you whipped.

FOOL  I marvel what kin thou and thy daughters are. They'll
have me whipped for speaking true, thou'lt have me whipped
for lying, and sometimes I am whipped for holding my peace.
I had rather be any kind o'thing than a fool, and yet I would
not be thee, nuncle. Thou hast pared thy wit o'both sides and
left nothing i'the middle. Here comes one o'the parings.

*Enter Goneril.*

LEAR  How now, daughter? What makes that frontlet on?
Methinks you are too much of late i'the frown.

FOOL  Thou wast a pretty fellow when thou hadst no need to
care for her frowning. Now thou art an O without a figure; I
am better than thou art now. I am a fool, thou art nothing. *[to
Goneril]* Yes, forsooth, I will hold my tongue; so your face bids
me, though you say nothing. Mum, mum!
    He that keeps nor crust nor crumb,
    Weary of all, shall want some.
*[Points to Lear.]* That's a shelled peascod.

Act 1, Scene 4

This long passage can be read as defining the Fool and his sense of betrayed love. Though he is an uncanny being whose age and foreground cannot be discerned, the Fool nevertheless has a filial love for and dependence upon Lear. His fury rises out of the vertigo of a betrayed ontological security. Suddenly those not exactly maternal daughters are Lear's guardians, and the poor fool is an outcast like the King himself. Uncanny forces are let loose by the Fool's vindictive wit. An unwilling martyr to his love for Lear, the Fool drives Lear into madness.

Cordelia, beloved by the Fool, is saintly in her refusal to blame her father, and her recalcitrance is altogether different from the Fool's childlike panic. He is memorable as a kind of chorus to Lear's sparagmos and doubles the wild cognitive music of Edgar's playing Tom o' Bedlam. Cordelia, however, is the most admirable personage in the tragedy, which makes her terrible death unbearable:

*Enter Lear with Cordelia in his arms [followed by the Gentleman].*

LEAR  Howl, howl, howl, howl! O, you are men of stones!
    Had I your tongues and eyes, I'd use them so
    That heaven's vault should crack: she's gone for ever.
    I know when one is dead and when one lives;
    She's dead as earth.            *[He lays her down.]*
                  Lend me a looking-glass;
    If that her breath will mist or stain the stone,
    Why then she lives.
KENT                 Is this the promised end?
EDGAR  Or image of that horror?
ALBANY                    Fall, and cease.
LEAR  This feather stirs, she lives: if it be so,
    It is a chance which does redeem all sorrows
    That ever I have felt.
KENT                 O, my good master!
LEAR  Prithee, away!
EDGAR              'Tis noble Kent, your friend.
LEAR  A plague upon you murderers, traitors all;

I might have saved her; now she's gone for ever.
Cordelia, Cordelia, stay a little. Ha?
What is't thou sayst? Her voice was ever soft,
Gentle and low, an excellent thing in woman.
I killed the slave that was a-hanging thee.

Act 5, Scene 3

The dialectic of self-otherseeing, in which disavowal and affirmation oscillate, culminates in Lear's death:

LEAR  And my poor fool is hanged. No, no, no life!
Why should a dog, a horse, a rat have life
And thou no breath at all? O thou'lt come no more,
Never, never, never, never, never.
*[to Edgar?]* Pray you undo this button. Thank you, sir.
O, o, o, o.
Do you see this? Look on her: look, her lips,
Look there, look there! [*He dies.*]

Act 5, Scene 3

A. C. Bradley interpreted this correctly: the great king dies of delusional joy and not of grief. And yet—is it delusional? Lear has moved into an apocalyptic realm where desire acknowledges no limits. Though I continue to believe, with my late friend William Elton, that this is a pagan play for a Christian audience, who are we to question what the majestical Lear sees?

The Fool simply vanishes from the play, an absence Shakespeare cannot be bothered to explain. Cordelia is destroyed in an apotheosis that is intolerable. We end with Edgar abandoning self-otherseeing:

EDGAR  The weight of this sad time we must obey,
Speak what we feel, not what we ought to say.
The oldest hath borne most; we that are young
Shall never see so much, nor live so long.

*Exeunt with a dead march.*

Act 5, Scene 3

Disavowal has exiled affirmation.

# King Lear:
## Authority and Cosmological Disorder

H ANNAH ARENDT observed that authority was neither an ancient Greek nor a Hebrew concept but was Roman in origin. For the Romans it meant augmenting the foundations of their society and customs. Though the drama of *King Lear* is set in pre-Roman Britain, it nevertheless relies upon the idea of order enshrined in Ciceronian and related sources.

When Kent, disguised as Caius, presents himself for service to Lear, he tells the King, "You have that in your countenance which I would fain call master." When Lear replies, "What's that?," Kent offers the one word: "authority." In the extraordinary confrontation with the blinded Gloucester in act 4, scene 6, Lear bitterly disavows authority:

> LEAR What, art mad? A man may see how this world goes with
>     no eyes. Look with thine ears. See how yon justice rails upon
>     yon simple thief. Hark in thine ear: change places and handy-
>     dandy, which is the justice, which is the thief? Thou hast seen
>     a farmer's dog bark at a beggar?
> GLOUCESTER Ay, sir.
> LEAR And the creature run from the cur—there thou mightst
>     behold the great image of authority: a dog's obeyed in office.
>     Thou, rascal beadle, hold thy bloody hand;
>     Why dost thou lash that whore? Strip thine own back,
>     Thou hotly lusts to use her in that kind
>     For which thou whipp'st her. The usurer hangs the cozener.
>     Through tattered clothes great vices do appear;
>     Robes and furred gowns hide all. Plate sin with gold,
>     And the strong lance of justice hurtless breaks;

Arm it in rags, a pigmy's straw does pierce it.
None does offend, none, I say none. I'll able 'em;
Take that of me, my friend, who have the power
To seal th'accuser's lips. Get thee glass eyes,
And like a scurvy politician seem
To see the things thou dost not.

Lear, endlessly eloquent, here transcends himself. I hardly know a more devastating repudiation of authority than "a dog's obeyed in office." And yet, whether he is incisive or insane, he remains the very image of authority: King, Father, God. Oscillating between overt disavowal and involuntary self-affirmation, Lear incarnates the self-otherseeing which he can never know.

It is generally accepted that Lear possesses instinctive authority to a degree more capacious than any other Shakespearean protagonist. When he goes down, the cosmos falls with him. Kent cries out, "Is this the promised end?" And Edgar laments, "Or image of that horror?" Albany completes the litany with "Fall, and cease."

Why do we accept, whether as auditors or as readers, these apocalyptic pronouncements? Lear is the self-dethroned ruler of pre-Roman Britain, hardly a world empire. But, then, the Biblical Solomon, for all his magnificence, reigned over as small a kingdom. There are hints enough that Lear is Shakespeare's version of Solomon, an immensely old monarch, except that Solomon is as wise as Lear is foolish. After the death of Solomon, his kingdom fell apart under his son Rehoboam, who provoked a rebellion by the ten northern tribes, which came together as the separate kingdom of Israel. That left only the little kingdom of Judah for Rehoboam to misrule. Lear, after dividing Britain between Goneril and Regan, possesses nothing. "Nothing" is one of the refrains beating through this vast drama, frequently counterpointed against the word "Nature."

It is the range and intensity of Lear's pathos that justify the play's final vision, in which the entire world goes down with him. His greatness is a sublime oscillation between rage and love, and we begin to wonder if he knows the difference. But is that not a valid description of the Yahweh of the Hebrew Bible, whose love for the Jewish people scarcely can be divided from the appearance of rage? Shakespeare, who anticipated everything, persuades his audience that the death of Lear is also the death of God. And even that is not the whole of it. Authority, the ultimate attribute of fatherhood, falls away into the abyss that ends this great drama. James Joyce's Stephen touches his own forehead and says it is in there he must slay the king and the priest. Always and invariably Shakespeare's involuntary disciple, Joyce repeats the wisdom that Lear can neither incarnate nor know. No writer has ever been so subtle as Shakespeare in not divulging his own beliefs or disbeliefs. And yet this most majestic of all his plays brings us to a threshold where God, the Father, and the King cease together.

# *Macbeth:*
# Triumph at Limning a Night-Piece

PART OF THE MYSTERY of Shakespeare is that he would seem to
have invested something of his own intellectual consciousness in
Hamlet, while reserving for Macbeth a prophetic quality peculiar to
Shakespeare's own fantasy-making power. Hamlet might participate
in such a power, but Macbeth is wholly its creature. If *Hamlet* is a tragedy of thought, then *Macbeth* is a tragedy of the imagination.

It is difficult to decide whether the proleptic element in Macbeth is
preternatural or not:

> MACBETH  *[Aside.]* Two truths are told,
>    As happy prologues to the swelling act
>    Of the imperial theme.—I thank you, gentlemen.—
>    *[Aside.]* This supernatural soliciting
>    Cannot be ill; cannot be good:—
>    If ill, why hath it given me earnest of success,
>    Commencing in a truth? I am Thane of Cawdor:
>    If good, why do I yield to that suggestion
>    Whose horrid image doth unfix my hair,
>    And make my seated heart knock at my ribs,
>    Against the use of nature? Present fears
>    Are less than horrible imaginings.
>    My thought, whose murther yet is but fantastical,
>    Shakes so my single state of man,
>    That function is smother'd in surmise,
>    And nothing is, but what is not.

Act I, Scene 3

This is the beginning of that savage process by which Macbeth perpetually leaps the gap between anticipation and accomplishment. No sooner does he imagine a crime he might perform than he is on the other shore, contemplating his act of violence as though it were not his own. The projected murder of Duncan emanates from a realm that excludes the will, because imagination renders redundant all volition.

Macbeth is well aware of his proclivity for second sight and has no hesitation in yielding to it, even though there is a certain reluctance in his eloquent "And nothing is, but what is not." That reluctance is an element that slowly abandons him as he journeys into the interior of darkness. He moves on from an oscillation between self-disavowal and reaffirmation until his entire consciousness is flooded by a metaphysic of nothingness.

When he confronts Banquo's ghost, his reaction is superbly revelatory:

Blood hath been shed ere now, i'th'olden time,
Ere humane statute purg'd the gentle weal;
Ay, and since too, murthers have been perform'd
Too terrible for the ear: the time has been,
That, when the brains were out, the man would die,
And there an end; but now, they rise again,
With twenty mortal murthers on their crowns,
And push us from our stools. This is more strange
Than such a murther is.

Act 3, Scene 4

Outrage will be Macbeth's principal affect from this moment to the close of his drama. It is the outrage of confounded expectation, difficult for us to resist. The ultimate outrage is dying, and a protagonist who is eloquent in his outrage speaks to all of us, even if he is a bloody tyrant like Macbeth. It is more than Macbeth's strangeness that we find attractive. Our own faculty for self-overseeing admits the murderous impulses that all of us sometimes entertain. When Macbeth is slain by Macduff, something in us dies also.

At this point in *Possessed by Memory*, I take leave of writing commentaries upon William Shakespeare. Three brief books on Lear, Iago, and Macbeth have already been composed and will join forerunners on Hamlet, Falstaff, and Cleopatra. I hope to teach Shakespeare for another few years, but time must have a stop. What have I learned most from Shakespeare? If I were to ask what Dante or Milton, Tolstoy or Victor Hugo had taught me, I might venture some answers. But with Shakespeare I am bewildered. I tend to think through metaphors, and they are mostly his. I taught myself to read English when I was about five, but I must have been nine or ten when I first read Shakespeare. I went from *Julius Caesar,* which I almost understood, on to *Hamlet,* where I was both fascinated and baffled. *Hamlet* still changes for me each time I return to it. How can you come to the end of it? Dante's *Paradiso* still defeats me. Old age has not reconciled me to it. But, then, I am a Jew who evades normative Judaism. My religion is the appreciation of high literature. Shakespeare is the summit. Revelation for me is Shakespearean or nothing.

# Part Three

# In the Elegy Season:
# John Milton, the Visionary Company,
# and Victorian Poetry

# Ben Jonson on Shakespeare and
# Andrew Marvell on Milton

I HAVE ALWAYS found it fruitful to compare two great poems of praise. The first is Ben Jonson's tribute to Shakespeare that led off the First Folio (1623):

> To draw no envy (Shakespeare) on thy name,
> Am I thus ample to thy Booke, and Fame:
> While I confesse thy writings to be such,
> As neither Man, nor Muse, can praise too much.
> 'Tis true, and all mens suffrage. But these wayes
> Were not the paths I meant unto thy praise:
> For seeliest Ignorance on these may light,
> Which, when it sounds at best, but eccho's right;
> Or blinde Affection, which doth ne're advance
> The truth, but gropes, and urgeth all by chance;
> Or crafty Malice, might pretend this praise,
> And thinke to ruine, where it seem'd to raise.
> These are, as some infamous Baud, or Whore
> Should praise a Matron. What could hurt her more?
> But thou art proofe against them, and indeed
> Above th'ill fortune of them, or the need.
> I therefore will begin. Soule of the age!
> The applause! delight! the wonder of our Stage!

Ben Jonson was an extraordinary poet and dramatist. But it was his fate to be the exact contemporary of his close friend and rival, William Shakespeare. Jonson's Roman comedies were laughed off the stage, while Shakespeare's soared. Though Jonson devalued Shakespeare's

*Julius Caesar*, and responded to the players' remark that Shakespeare rarely blotted a line with the observation, "Would he had blotted many!," he had a considerable change of mind when he read many of the plays for the first time as the First Folio was gathered:

> My Shakespeare, rise! I will not lodge thee by
> Chaucer, or Spenser, or bid Beaumont lye
> A little further, to make thee a roome:
> Thou art a monument without a tomb,
> And art alive still, while thy Booke doth live,
> And we have wits to read, and praise to give.
> That I not mixe thee so, my braine excuses;
> I mean with great, but disproportion'd Muses,
> For if I thought my judgement were of yeeres,
> I should commit thee surely with thy peeres,
> And tell, how farre thou didst our Lily out-shine,
> Or sporting Kid, or Marlowes mighty line.
> And though thou hadst small Latine, and lesse Greeke,
> From thence to honour thee, I would not seeke
> For names; but call forth thund'ring Æschilus,
> Euripides, and Sophocles to us,
> Paccuvius, Accius, him of Cordova dead,
> To life againe, to heare thy Buskin tread,
> And shake a Stage: Or, when thy Sockes were on,
> Leave thee alone, for the comparison
> Of all, that insolent Greece, or haughtie Rome
> Sent forth, or since did from their ashes come.
> Triumph, my Britaine, thou hast one to showe,
> To whom all Scenes of Europe homage owe.
> He was not of an age, but for all time!
> And all the Muses still were in their prime,
> When like Apollo he came forth to warme
> Our eares, or like a Mercury to charme!
> Nature her selfe was proud of his designes
> And joy'd to weare the dressing of his lines,
> Which were so richly spun, and woven so fit,
> As, since, she will vouchsafe no other Wit.
> The merry Greeke, tart Aristophanes,

Neat Terence, witty Plautus, now not please,
But antiquated and deserted lye,
As they were not of Natures family.

The famous and truthful "He was not of an age but for all time!" may stand out in this marvelous hymn of praise, yet even more powerful is the judgment that Shakespeare outshines all other tragic and comic dramatists, from the ancient Greeks and Romans on to contemporary Britain. The tribute to nature is warranted, but Jonson, who rightly regarded the poetic art as "hard work," goes on to admire Shakespeare's skill:

Yet must I not give Nature all: Thy Art,
My gentle Shakespeare, must enjoy a part.
For though the Poets matter, Nature be,
His Art doth give the fashion. And, that he,
Who casts to write a living line, must sweat,
(Such as thine are) and strike the second heat
Upon the Muses anvile: turne the same
(And himeself with it) that he thinkes to frame;
Or for the lawrell he may gain a scorne.
For a good Poet's made, as well as borne.
And such wert thou. Looke how the fathers face
Lives in his issue, even so, the race
Of Shakespeares minde, and manners brightly shines
In his well torned, and true-filed lines:
In each of which, he seemes to shake a Lance,
As brandish't at the eyes of ignorance.

Here Jonson assimilates Shakespeare to himself, which is both moving and revelatory. Even Jonson's three great comedies—*Volpone, The Alchemist,* and *Bartholomew Fair*—though they are permanent works, are not quite of Shakespearean ambience and potency. The culmination is an extraordinary transformation of Shakespeare into a celestial constellation, a "star of poets":

Sweet Swan of Avon! what a sight it were
To see thee in our waters yet appeare,

And make those flights upon the bankes of Thames,
That so did take Eliza, and our James!
But stay, I see thee in the Hemisphere
Advanc'd, and made a Constellation there!
Shine forth, thou Starre of Poets, and with rage,
Or influence, chide, or cheere the drooping Stage;
Which, since thy flight from hence, hath mourn'd like night,
And despaires day, but for thy Volumes light.

"Rage" is hardly appropriate for Shakespeare, though the hope for benign influence is touching. Shakespeare, who has influenced everyone, rendered all English verse drama to follow rather inadequate. Ben Jonson himself, like Edmund Spenser and John Donne, was a prince of poets, and his fond elegy for Shakespeare is worthy of its subject.

The second great poem of praise is Andrew Marvell's introduction to the second edition of *Paradise Lost* (1674):

WHEN I beheld the Poet blind, yet bold,
In slender Book his vast Design unfold,
*Messiah* Crown'd, *Gods* Reconcil'd Decree,
Rebelling *angels*, the Forbidden Tree,
Heav'n, Hell, Earth, Chaos, All; the Argument
Held me a while misdoubting his Intent,
That he would ruine (for I saw him strong)
The sacred Truths to Fable and old Song,
(So *Samson* grop'd the Temples Posts in spight)
The World o'rewhelming to revenge his Sight.

With subtle irony, Marvell catches the essential strangeness of Milton's epic. It does indeed ruin the sacred truths, but hardly "to fable and old song." In a splendid premonition of *Samson Agonistes*, Marvell invokes the story of Samson's final act that brought destruction to himself and a multitude of Philistines. Since Milton invokes a Holy Spirit that prefers his own pure and upright heart to all temples, his poem indeed is heretical, personal, passionate, and a transformation of the poetic and religious traditions.

Yet as I read, soon growing less severe,
I lik'd his Project, the success did fear;

Through that wide Field how he his way should find
O're which lame Faith leads Understanding blind;
Lest he perplext the things he would explain,
And what was easie he should render vain.

Marvell's irony is so complex here that it scarcely can be unraveled.
What should we do with the antithesis between "I lik'd his project"
and the momentous "the success did fear"? Faith is dismissed as lame,
and Marvell is so good a reader that he recognizes the perplexity of the
poem.

Or if a Work so infinite he spann'd,
Jealous I was that some less skilful hand
(Such as disquiet alwayes what is well,
And by ill imitating would excell)
Might hence presume the whole Creations day
To change in Scenes, and show it in a Play.

This is an attack on John Dryden, who received permission from
Milton to revise *Paradise Lost* into an opera, *The State of Innocence*, and
*Fall of Man* (alternatively titled *The Fall of Angels and Man in Innocence*
in some early versions), which seems never to have been performed.

Pardon me, *mighty* Poet, nor despise
My causeless, yet not impious, surmise.
But I am now convinc'd, and none will dare
Within thy Labours to pretend a Share.
Thou hast not miss'd one thought that could be fit,
And all that was improper dost omit;
So that no room is here for Writers left,
But to detect their Ignorance or Theft.
　That Majesty which through thy Work doth Reign
Draws the Devout, deterring the Profane;
And things divine thou treatst of in such state
As them preserves, and Thee inviolate.
At once delight and horrour on us seize,
Thou singst with so much gravity and ease;
And above humane flight dost soar aloft,
With Plume so strong, so equal, and so soft.

The *Bird* named from that *Paradise* you sing
So never Flags, but alwaies keeps on Wing.
    Where couldst thou Words of such a compass find?
Whence furnish such a vast expanse of Mind?
Just Heav'n Thee, like *Tiresias*, to requite,
Rewards with *Prophecy* thy loss of Sight.


Like Tiresias and the blind Homer, Milton is acclaimed as a prophetic poet. Again, the insight is valuable, since so much of Romanticism stems from *Paradise Lost*.


Well mightst thou scorn thy Readers to allure
With tinkling Rhime, of thy own Sense secure,
While the *Town-Bayes* writes all the while and spells,
And like a Pack-Horse tires without his Bells.
Their Fancies like our bushy Points appear,
The Poets tag them; we for fashion wear.
I too, transported by the *Mode* offend,
And while I meant to *Praise* thee, must Commend;
Thy verse created like thy *Theme* sublime,
In Number, Weight, and Measure, needs not *Rhime*.


"The Town-Bayes" is another smack at Dryden. Marvell ends both grandly and with another irony. He himself is unrepentantly given to rhyme, but recognizes the "number, weight, and measure" of Milton's sublime style. Marvell inspired the rejoinder of one of William Blake's "Proverbs of Hell": "Bring out number weight & measure in a year of dearth." Blake's rebellion against Milton's blank verse was his extraordinary revival of the septenarius with its seven beats, the verse form of his epics *The Four Zoas*, *Milton*, and *Jerusalem*.

# *Paradise Lost:*
# The Realm of Newness

E VEN AS AN UNDERGRADUATE, I would recite all of *Paradise Lost*
to myself during many sleepless nights. In old age, this persists,
yet with a melancholy difference. I no longer have patience with most
of what passes as the scholarly criticism of Milton. The eminent Angel
C. S. Lewis and I fell out at the Anchor Pub in Cambridge, England,
in 1954. Despite his seniority and distinction at the age of fifty-six,
and my status as a twenty-four-year-old Fulbright research student,
he had been very kind to me before this occasion. The break had to
be inevitable, since my Jewish Gnosticism and his "mere Christianity"
were incompatible. The quarrel concerned Milton's God, and the Satan
in *Paradise Lost*. Fifty-three years later, I smile in recollection, though
Lewis held on to his grudge. In 1962, he reviewed my early book on
the English Romantics, *The Visionary Company*, quite mercilessly in
*Encounter* magazine.

In 1977, William Empson came to Yale and lectured on Marlowe's
*Doctor Faustus*. At a reception after the lecture, he approached me and
said: "You are that fellow Bloom who wrote that dotty book on influence. I like dotty books." We conversed amiably for a while, and though
I attempted to talk about Empson's splendid *Milton's God*, the Chinese-
bearded Sir William wanted to discuss Hart Crane, for whom he had
developed a late affinity. C. S. Lewis came up as a topic; Empson spoke
of him with some warmth, and I said nothing. Before we parted, I did
express my admiration for Empson's Shelleyan championing of Milton's Satan against the nasty God of *Paradise Lost*.

It would be a weariness to resume the ceaseless academic debate
concerning Milton's God. Whoever we are, Milton is always out ahead,
and you catch up as best you can. G. K. Chesterton spoke of Chaucer's

irony as being too large for us to see. That is true of Shakespeare and
of Milton. Hamlet often does not say what he means or mean what he
says. Milton's Hamlet is his Satan. C. S. Lewis, concerning whom my
great mentor Frederick Pottle once said to me, "Stop beating dead
woodchucks, Harold," henceforth will be exiled from these pages. I
allow him one of his admonitions: "Start with a good morning's hatred
of Satan." I might prefer "Start with a good morning's disdain for Milton's God."

A lover of poetry cannot reread *Paradise Lost* without finding both
God the Father and the Son aesthetic disasters. Milton had to have
known just how bad they sound:

> Hear all ye Angels, Progeny of Light,
> Thrones, Dominations, Princedoms, Vertues, Powers,
> Hear my Decree, which unrevok't shall stand.
> This day I have begot whom I declare
> My only Son, and on this holy Hill
> Him have anointed, whom ye now behold
> At my right hand; your Head I him appoint;
> And by my Self have sworn to him shall bow
> All knees in Heav'n, and shall confess him Lord:
> Under his great Vice-gerent Reign abide
> United as one individual Soul
> For ever happy: him who disobeys
> Mee disobeys, breaks union, and that day
> Cast out from God and blessed vision, falls
> Into utter darkness, deep ingulft, his place
> Ordain'd without redemption, without end.
>
> Book V, lines 600–615

> Son, thou in whom my glory I behold
> In full resplendence, Heir of all my might,
> Neerly it now concernes us to be sure
> Of our Omnipotence, and with what Arms
> We mean to hold what anciently we claim
> Of Deity or Empire, such a foe
> Is rising, who intends to erect his Throne

Equal to ours, throughout the spacious North;
Nor so content, hath in his thought to try
In battle, what our Power is, or our right.
Let us advise, and to this hazard draw
With speed what force is left, and all imploy
In our defense, lest unawares we lose
This our high place, our Sanctuary, our Hill.
  To whom the Son with calm aspect and clear
Light'ning Divine, ineffable, serene,
Made answer. Mighty Father, thou thy foes
Justly hast in derision, and secure
Laugh'st at thir vain designs and tumults vain,
Matter to mee of Glory, whom thir hate
Illustrates, when they see all Regal Power
Giv'n me to quell thir pride, and in event
Know whether I be dext'rous to subdue
Thy Rebels, or be found the worst in Heav'n.

Book V, lines 719–42

Milton knows that this God the Father resembles King James I, and this Son, King Charles I. Yahweh, Jesus, and Allah, the West's three major literary characters, are presented with rather more aesthetic splendor in the Yahwist text, the Gospel of Mark, and the Holy Quran. Why did Milton risk our derision with a God the Father who blares: "Him who disobeyes / Mee disobeyes, breaks union, and that day / Cast out from God and blessed vision, falls / Into utter darkness . . ."? Or our surprise that Yahweh says:

Let us advise, and to this hazard draw
With speed what force is left, and all imploy
In our defense, lest unawares we lose
This our high place, our Sanctuarie, our Hill.

It could be a Stuart king urging defense against Oliver Cromwell and not the God who names himself "I will be present whenever and wherever I will be present." As for the Son of God, where is the Jesus of Mark, who inquires anxiously, "But whom say ye that I am?" Instead we have King Charles the Martyr subduing rebels before offering himself as a suffering ransom for fallen mankind. There is no more deliberate poetic artist in the language than John Milton. He knew what he was doing. Unless we are deaf, we ought to know also.

Here is a rather different sound:

> Yet not for those,
> Nor what the Potent Victor in his rage
> Can else inflict, do I repent or change,
> Though chang'd in outward lustre; that fixt mind
> And high disdain, from sense of injur'd merit,
> That with the mightiest rais'd me to contend,
> And to the fierce contention brought along
> Innumerable force of Spirits arm'd
> That durst dislike his reign, and me preferring,
> His utmost power with adverse power oppos'd
> In dubious Battle on the Plains of Heav'n,
> And shook his throne. What though the field be lost?
> All is not lost; the unconquerable Will,
> And study of revenge, immortal hate,
> And courage never to submit or yield:
> And what is else not to be overcome?
>
> Book I, lines 94–109

Satan is undefeated in spirit though disfigured in shape, and reduced from Lucifer the Light Bearer to a darkening shadow. There is self-deception here, since the battle was never in doubt. Yet we hear the tonalities of the Sublime in "And courage never to submit or yield:/And what is else not to be overcome?"

Contrast this with an exchange between the Father and the Son:

> Man disobeying,
> Disloyal breaks his fealty, and sins
> Against the high Supremacy of Heav'n,
> Affecting God-head, and so losing all,
> To expiate his Treason hath naught left,
> But to destruction sacred and devote,
> He with his whole posterity must die,
> Die hee or Justice must; unless for him

Some other able, and as willing, pay
The rigid satisfaction, death for death.

Book III, lines 203–12

Behold mee then, mee for him, life for life
I offer, on mee let thine anger fall;
Account mee man; I for his sake will leave
Thy bosom, and this glory next to thee
Freely put off, and for him lastly die
Well pleas'd, on me let Death wreck all his rage;
Under his gloomie power I shall not long
Lie vanquisht; thou hast givn me to possess
Life in my self for ever, by thee I live,
Though now to Death I yield, and am his due
All that of me can die, yet that debt paid,
Thou wilt not leave me in the loathsom grave. . . .

Book III, lines 236–47

In book XII, the Archangel Michael gets Jesus on and off the cross with hilarious haste: "so he dies,/But soon revives" (lines 419–20). So much for the agony of the Crucifixion, since Milton has almost a Hebraic distaste for the Atonement. But, then, is Dante sincere? Like Dante, Milton is a savage sect of one who has so persuasively redefined Christianity that we are blinded by the newness of what we hear or see. My hero of modern scholarship, Ernst Robert Curtius, dismisses the prevalent Anglo-American Augustinian and Thomistic parody of Dante and demonstrates the extraordinary extent to which the *Commedia* presents a private gnosis. Nothing in Catholic doctrine allows for Beatrice as the necessary medium of grace. Similarly, nothing in Protestantism countenances Milton's numerous heresies. We might say that Milton invents a Protestant stance free of all Protestantism.

I have reflected throughout my life on the irony that the Catholic poet proper is Dante; he imposed his own gnosis, in which Beatrice mediates between humankind and God. Similarly, Milton is the crucial Protestant poet who imposed his own version of the Inner Light, in which his inward voice replaces the voice of Scripture. We tend now to think of Kafka as the central post-Biblical Jewish writer, and his works were regarded as canonical by Walter Benjamin and Gershom Scholem, yet he himself said he had nothing in common with Jews because he had nothing in common with himself. The central poet of the American Religion is Walt Whitman, who dared to represent his own Resurrection and who hoped that *Leaves of Grass* would be the new Bible for Americans. When I think of Whitman, I hear first the elegiac splendors that lament his ebbing with the ocean of life.

Nobody would ask whether Chaucer or Shakespeare is sincere. Palpably, the Pardoner and Iago are not to be believed, and the Wife of Bath and Sir John Falstaff have no interest in belief. Dante and Milton cannot create human beings in the round, and therefore rely upon private visions that become realities. Curtius emphasizes that Dante actually gives Beatrice a place in the objective process of salvation. On an authority entirely his own, Dante places an element in revelation that is not doctrinal. Curtius's willingness to call this either myth or heresy is his own gentle irony. John Milton had no Beatrice, since Eve is not a figure of redemption.

In my far-off youth, I played with concepts of myth, under the influence of the literary critic and theorist Northrop Frye. I broke from Frye, not personally but intellectually, in the summer of 1967, when I first drafted what was to become *The Anxiety of Influence*. I think now that myth is simply gossip grown old, whereas heresy is the breath of profound poetic voices. It is misleading to speak of any poet's heresies. With Milton, we go astray when we call his images of voice "heresies." *Paradise Lost* mounts so vast a scheme of what the rhetoricians call transumption that every ancestral work becomes belated and Milton's poem perpetually early. "Transumption" seems an awkward word, but simply means a trope or metaphor that undoes precursor images. The initial thirty-three lines of *Paradise Lost* repeat "first" six times in order to stress that Milton was there before the world was made. He was not a Gnostic but a poetic knower, and his gnosis insists that what is best and oldest in him is not mortal. The true God of *Paradise Lost* is the Spirit that brooded on the vast abyss and brought forth creation.

For the last six decades, I have wondered why Milton blundered in portraying the figure called God in the great English epic. I think now that his irony set a trap for the unwary. He composed in his mind at night and dictated *Paradise Lost* the next morning. In youth, he had contemplated an Arthurian heroic poem to celebrate the triumph of an England casting off the bondage of monarchy and established church. Oliver Cromwell died, and the Commonwealth could not long survive him. It seems strange that Milton is the major poet of the Restoration, dwarfing even Andrew Marvell and John Dryden. Defeat and loss are the burden of the most ambitious epic in Western literary history.

There are several Gods in *Paradise Lost*. I have spoken of the Spirit that first moved upon the waters and brought forth life; we hear this God within the narrative voice. There is also the hidden God, William Shakespeare, who intrudes despite Milton's wariness. Shakespeare is everywhere and nowhere in Milton. The shadow of belatedness, here and throughout his poetry, falls upon him from Shakespeare. Pragmatically, in the poem Satan is Shakespeare. His is the competing voice always blocking Milton's quest to listen for his own voice that goes back to before the world was made. Something in Milton is aware that Shakespeare is his hinderer. The four invocations and Satan's extraordinary soliloquies are Shakespearean ventures into the power of the mind over a universe of death. Milton triumphs in his agon with Satan, who is consigned to the universe of death. This victory remains equivocal, since Satan is only a weak contestant. Beyond Satan are Hamlet, Macbeth, and Lear, and the power of mind they represent transcends even John Milton's ambition and creative intellect. The invocations to books I, III, VII, and IX are Milton's own soliloquies, always on the Shakespearean model. Satan's soliloquies fuse Hamlet, Iago, and Macbeth.

Milton asserted that *Paradise Lost* was a theodicy. It is anything but that. If you read the grandest English epic as a justification of the ways of God to men and women, you would have to conclude that the strongest poet in the language, after Shakespeare and Chaucer, went wrong from the start. Sixty years of rereading the poem have convinced me it is a vast theurgy, a justification of Milton's inward voice drawing down God, mending the divine utterance, and maintaining our idea of order. Milton seeks to uncover the God within himself. That may be the inner plot of his epic:

> Of man's First disobedience, and the Fruit
> Of that Forbidden Tree, whose mortal taste
> Brought Death into the World, and all our woe,

With loss of *Eden*, till one greater Man
Restore us, and regain the blissful Seat,
Sing Heav'nly Muse, that on the secret top
Of *Oreb*, or of *Sinai*, didst inspire
That Shepherd, who first taught the chosen Seed,
In the Beginning how the Heav'ns and Earth
Rose out of *Chaos:* or if *Sion* hill
Delight thee more, and *Siloa's* Brook that flow'd
Fast by the Oracle of God; I thence
Invoke thy aid to my advent'rous Song,
That with no middle flight intends to soar
Above th' *Aonian* mount, while it pursues
Things unattempted yet in Prose or Rhyme.
And chiefly Thou O Spirit, that dost prefer
Before all Temples th'upright heart and pure,
Instruct me, for Thou know'st; Thou from the first
Wast present, and with mighty wings outspread
Dove-like satst brooding on the vast Abyss
And mad'st it pregnant: What in me is dark
Illumine, what is low raise and support;
That to the heighth of this great Argument
I may assert Eternal Providence,
And justify the ways of God to men.

Book I, lines 1–26

This invocation to book I is magnificent and perplexing. The one greater man is Jesus, though unnamed. Milton calls upon the Heavenly Muse that inspired Moses following the tradition that Genesis was authored by Moses himself. Homer and Virgil are displaced with gusto; more subtly, the Holy Bible also yields to Miltonic priority. There is a wonderful ease in Milton's ascendance over every received tradition. But who is the Heavenly Muse? The Muse is Greek and Roman, not Hebrew. Nor is it the Holy Ghost of the Catholic trinity. It is the spirit of Yahweh, calling the shepherd Moses, who was pasturing his flock on Mount Oreb. Alternatively, Milton places his Muse on Mount Sion, celebrated in the Psalms of David. The Jerusalem oracle of Mount Sion overgoes the Delphic oracle of Apollo. With vaunting splendor, Milton asserts that his song will soar above the Aonian mount, and the Helicon, the river of the Muses.

Northrop Frye sensibly remarked that in Milton, God the Father is an aesthetic disaster. Frye went so far as to call this God a smirking hypocrite. The mystery is, why did Milton allow himself this blunder?

Milton's God is self-righteous, pompous, and morally dubious. He is a vindictive tyrant. The contrast with the Yahweh of the J writer in the Hebrew Bible is astonishing.

The proper name of God in the Hebrew Bible is the four-letter YHWH; it occurs in that text more than six thousand times. We will never know how the name was pronounced. Yahweh is a surmise. The sacred name was strictly guarded by the oral tradition. After the return from Babylon in the fifth century B.C.E., the name was regarded as magical and was not to be pronounced. God was named either Elohim (divine being or beings) or Adonai (my Lord). Since the Greeks called God Theos, the Jews began to refer to him as Kyrios, Greek for Adonai or Lord. By the time of Hillel, the name Yahweh was never heard.

And yet Yahweh is a very old name. It is used in the great war song of Deborah and Barack (Judges 5), which is eleventh-century B.C.E. and is probably the oldest text in Hebrew.

Yahweh's ways of speaking are usually not enigmatic. The grand exception is his *"ehyeh asher ehyeh,"* the self-naming by a pun. Though translated in the Christian Bible as "I Am That I Am," its meaning is closer to "I will be I will be."

Yahweh's complexities are labyrinthine, infinite, and probably inexplicable, despite the extraordinary interpretational skills of the Talmud sages, and of the Sufi masters who confronted the Quran, where the entire work is spoken by Yahweh, under the name of Allah.

> And it came to pass, when Joshua was by Jericho, that he lifted
> up his eyes and looked, and, behold, there stood a man over
> against him with his sword drawn in his hand: and Joshua
> went unto him, and said unto him, Art thou for us, or for our
> adversaries?
> And he said, Nay; but as captain of the host of the Lord am I
> now come. And Joshua fell on his face to the earth, and did
> worship, and said unto him, What saith my Lord unto his
> servant?
> And the captain of the Lord's host said unto Joshua, Loose thy

shoe from off thy foot; for the place whereon thou standest is holy. And Joshua did so.

Joshua 5:13–15

This is Yahweh as a man of war. But who was, who is Yahweh? His complexities are infinite and inexplicable. His furies are startling. He commands a reluctant Moses to descend into Egypt, and then tries to murder his prophet at a night encampment, on the way down. William Blake called Yahweh "Old Nobodaddy," and James Joyce termed him the "hangman god," and yet Yahweh, despite his ambivalences, shows us the difference between our being transcendent entities or merely engines of entropy.

Kierkegaard pictures Nebuchadnezzar, restored from feeding on the grass like a beast, wondering at Yahweh:

And no one knoweth anything of Him, who was His father, and how He acquired His power, and who taught Him the secret of his might.

This unfathered Yahweh is our perpetual dilemma: Who was *his* teacher? Can we know anything at all about Yahweh? The earliest strand of Torah centers upon Yahweh. He is close by, intimate with us, and seems to know his limits. That may indeed increase his irascibility. He walks and talks with angels and with men. He reposes under the terebinth trees at Mamre, and devours with gusto a meal prepared by Sarah. Best of all, he picnics on Sinai with seventy-three elders of Israel, who stare at him while he says nothing. He plays with mud, makes a figurine out of red clay, and then breathes life into it from his own nostrils. He is jealous, full of mischief, incessantly turbulent, and always inquisitive. He is over-ambitious and overworked.

It is sensible to fear Yahweh. Can we love him? He expects both: fear where there is love, and love where there is fear, a fusion so destructive that it is appropriate to him alone.

William Blake, in his brief epic *Milton*, emulates his precursor with a vision of the poet's personal descent to redeem what has been lost:

Say first! what mov'd Milton, who walk'd about in Eternity
One hundred years, pond'ring the intricate mazes of Providence,

Unhappy tho in heav'n, he obey'd, he murmur'd not, he was
  silent,
Viewing his Sixfold Emanation scatter'd thro' the deep
In torment! To go into the deep her to redeem & himself
  perish?
That cause at length mov'd Milton to this unexampled deed,
A Bard's prophetic Song! for sitting at eternal tables,
Terrific among the Sons of Albion, in chorus solemn & loud
A Bard broke forth: all sat attentive to the awful man.

Book I, Plate 2, lines 16–24

You might think of the "Sixfold Emanation" as Milton's three wives and three daughters, or perhaps Milton's poems, or even the society he had hoped he might help to create. What matters most is that the poet of *Paradise Lost* chooses to re-enter mortal life. Adam and Eve make that entrance reluctantly and not by choice. Like two children, they hold hands as they slowly wander out of Eden and into mortality. I have never known what to make of any doctrine of the Fall. When we were children, we were terribly punished for being children. I scarcely regard that as an eccentric judgment of our supposed first disobedience.

It is an antique jest to say that Milton immured in paradise would have leaped to devour the apple: how else could he have begun his epic? But I read the great poem as the Fall of Lucifer. Then you and I and all of us fell down. Like Milton and Satan, we lust after Eve and only seldom find the first Adam in our thought.

Milton, Satan, Eve, and Adam move us as God the Father and God the Son do not. The fifth personage who matters in the poem is the Spirit, who is and is not Milton. The invocations to books I, III, VII, and IX are the work of the Spirit. They are John Milton's soliloquies on the model of Hamlet's. Satan's soliloquies also echo Hamlet's, but they are agonized, whereas Milton's are agonistic.

The pragmatic theodicy of *Paradise Lost* might be phrased: to justify the ways of John Milton to Milton. Justification here means eternal poetic fame in the mode of what E. R. Curtius terms "Poetry as Perpetuation." Curtius quotes Jacob Burckhardt: "The poet-philologist in Italy already has . . . the most intense consciousness that he is a distributor of fame and indeed of immortality; and likewise of oblivion." Dante, whose stance was at the apex of the culture of the Latin Middle

Ages, was Milton's most dangerous overt precursor. Since Shakespeare is the hidden God of Milton, as of almost all the poetry of the Western canonical tradition, he stands apart. Milton absorbed Dante—Shakespeare's only rival in high literature—but, like Goethe to follow, did so only with a certain repugnance.

When I recite Dante and Milton to myself during long sleepless nights, the resemblance between their temperaments disturbs me. Both are savage. Shakespeare's wisdom is humane; theirs is not. Dante's relation to Christian doctrine ought to be more of a scandal than it is. These days I try to be patient with well-meaning exegetes who seek spiritual consolation in all three. Secular strength and splendor are palpable in Shakespeare. What I hear in Dante, as in Milton, is a violent personalism that persuasively redefines Scripture so that their own work completes and to some degree negates it.

Dante the Pilgrim is totally silent when Ulysses speaks out of the forked tongue of fire that he shares with Diomedes. Evidently he recognizes his own deep similarity to the final voyage of Ulysses, which seeks to go beyond the limits of the known and of the permitted. Dante the Poet seeks a beyond yet further into the realm of newness. Milton travels into the primal abyss and takes us there with him.

# *Comus:*
# The Shadow of Shakespeare

W HAT WE CALL John Milton's minor poems are, at their best, major in every sense. Compared with *Paradise Lost*, only Chaucer and Shakespeare, of all English poets, would suffer no diminishment. Milton's epic crowds out his other poetry. This is inevitable but perhaps unfortunate.

I confess a lack of pleasure when I reread *Paradise Regained*. But *Samson Agonistes* holds its own even in the company of *Paradise Lost*. Of Milton's other poems, *Comus* and *Lycidas* are in a class apart, but so indeed are "L'Allegro" and "Il Penseroso." The English sonnets are sometimes limited, but the full Miltonic voice is heard in "On the Late Massacre in Piedmont."

Elsewhere in *Possessed by Memory* I render homage to *Samson Agonistes*. Here I turn to *Comus*, which I discussed almost daily with my friend Angus Fletcher in the late 1960s. Fletcher's book on *Comus, The Transcendental Masque* (1971), seems to me now neglected, but I think it will survive as a radiant disclosure by a visionary critic fully comparable to Kenneth Burke and Northrop Frye.

Fletcher centers upon the riddle of virginity in *Comus*. For the young Milton it is a mode of freedom. Yet it is a curiously limited freedom. Here is the Lady defying Comus:

I had not thought to have unlockt my lips
In this unhallow'd air, but that this Jugler
Would think to charm my judgement, as mine eyes,
Obtruding false rules pranckt in reasons garb.
I hate when vice can bolt her arguments,
And vertue has no tongue to check her pride:

Impostor do not charge most innocent nature,
As if she would her children should be riotous
With her abundance, she good cateress
Means her provision onely to the good
That live according to her sober laws,
And holy dictate of spare Temperance:
If every just man that now pines with want
Had but a moderate and beseeming share
Of that which lewdly-pamper'd Luxury
Now heaps upon som few with vast excess,
Natures full blessings would be well dispenc't
In unsuperfluous eeven proportion,
And she no whit encomber'd with her store,
And then the giver would be better thank't,
His praise due paid, for swinish gluttony
Ne're looks to Heav'n amidst his gorgeous feast,
But with besotted base ingratitude
Cramms, and blasphemes his feeder. Shall I go on?
Or have I said anough? To him that dares
Arm his profane tongue with contemptuous words
Against the Sun-clad power of Chastity,
Fain would I somthing say, yet to what end?
Thou hast nor Eare nor Soul to apprehend
The sublime notion, and high mystery
That must be utter'd to unfold the sage
And serious doctrine of Virginity,
And thou art worthy that thou shouldst not know
More happines then this thy present lot.
Enjoy your deer Wit, and gay Rhetorick
That hath so well been taught her dazling fence,
Thou art not fit to hear thy self convinc't;
Yet should I try, the uncontrouled worth
Of this pure cause would kindle my rap't spirits
To such a flame of sacred vehemence,
That dumb things would be mov'd to sympathise,
And the brute Earth would lend her nerves, and shake,
Till all thy magick structures rear'd so high,
Were shatter'd into heaps o're thy false head.

*Comus*, lines 756–99

"The sage / And serious doctrine of Virginity" is now so far out of fashion that most of us might find it difficult to comprehend Milton's theme. For Fletcher, the Lady's virginity is a doctrine of the self. In this speech she discovers and is delighted by her own power of rhetoric. She suddenly sees that her virginity is the emblem of her own transcendental self. Her defiance establishes her personality. And yet her freedom is shadowed.

Comus, though defeated, still exercises the power of his wand over the Lady. She remains silent and bound. Sabrina, a virgin nymph, will liberate her. Spenser, acknowledged by Milton as his poetic father, tells the story of Sabrina in book 2 of the *Faerie Queen* 2.10.14–19.

There is a gentle Nymph not farr from hence,
That with moist curb sways the smooth Severn stream,
*Sabrina* is her name, a Virgin pure,
Whilom she was the daughter of *Locrine*,
That had the Sceptre from his father *Brute*.
She, guiltless damsell, flying the mad pursuit
Of her enraged stepdam *Guendolen*,
Commended her fair innocence to the flood
That stay'd her flight with his cross-flowing course.
The water Nymphs that in the bottom plaid,
Held up their pearled wrists and took her in,
Bearing her straight to aged *Nereus*' Hall,
Who piteous of her woes, rear'd her lank head,
And gave her to his daughters to imbathe
In nectar'd lavers strew'd with Asphodil,
And through the porch and inlet of each sense
Dropt in Ambrosial Oils till she reviv'd,
And underwent a quick immortal change
Made Goddess of the River; still she retains
Her maid'n gentlenes, and oft at Eeve
Visits the herds along the twilight meadows,
Helping all urchin blasts, and ill luck signes
That the shrewd medling Elf delights to make,
Which she with pretious viold liquors heals.
For which the Shepherds at their festivals
Carrol her goodnes loud in rustick layes,
And throw sweet garland wreaths into her stream

Of pancies, pinks, and gaudy Daffadils.
And, as the old Swain said, she can unlock
The clasping charm, and thaw the numming spell,
If she be right invok't in warbled Song,
For maid'nhood she loves, and will be swift
To aid a Virgin, such as was her self
In hard besetting need, this will I try
And adde the power of som adjuring verse.

*Comus*, lines 824–58

Song is the key. In some sense, Sabrina is Spenserian poetry. Shake-speare is so pervasive in *Comus* that one wonders whether the young Milton is in control of allusiveness in regard to his greatest precursor. Reading through *Comus*, you are in an echo chamber dominated by Shakespeare. *Measure for Measure, The Winter's Tale, The Tempest* are heard throughout, but there are traces also of *Hamlet, Macbeth, Antony and Cleopatra*, and *A Midsummer Night's Dream*. Besides Spenser, Michael Drayton, Ben Jonson, John Fletcher, and William Browne contribute to the rich texture of Milton's masque.

Angus Fletcher and I spent a good deal of time discussing a particular exchange between Isabella and Claudio in *Measure for Measure*:

ISABELLA  What says my brother?
CLAUDIO                          Death is a fearful thing.
ISABELLA  And shamed life a hateful.
CLAUDIO  Ay, but to die, and go we know not where;
   To lie in cold obstruction, and to rot;
   This sensible warm motion to become
   A kneaded clod; and the delighted spirit
   To bath in fiery floods, or to reside
   In thrilling region of thick-ribbed ice;
   To be imprison'd in the viewless winds
   And blown with restless violence round about
   The pendant world: or to be worse than worst
   Of those that lawless and incertain thought
   Imagine howling—'tis too horrible.
   The weariest and most loathed worldly life
   That age, ache, penury and imprisonment

Can lay on nature, is a paradise
To what we fear of death.

Act 3, Scene 1

This deeply influences Belial's speech in book II of *Paradise Lost*, where the crafty fallen angel argues for inaction:

And that must end us, that must be our cure,
To be no more; sad cure; for who would lose,
Though full of pain, this intellectual being,
Those thoughts that wander through Eternity,
To perish rather, swallow'd up and lost
In the wide womb of uncreated Night,
Devoid of sense and motion?

Milton seems unaware that Belial is haunted by Claudio. The two situations have little in common, and I would have to judge that Milton's echo of Shakespeare is unintentional. Is this a fault? The question is profound. I have no single answer, but it bothers me, just as Manoa speaking of his son Samson echoes Mark Antony brooding on "the miserable change" in his fortune. Again, the echo works against Milton's purposes.

# Dr. Samuel Johnson,
## *Life of Milton*

THE STRONGEST CRITIC in Western literary culture is Dr. Samuel Johnson. Throughout my long life, he has been my model, though I am aware I cannot achieve his intellect, knowledge, and energy. Johnson teaches me that criticism, as a literary art, belongs to the ancient genre of wisdom writing.

Johnson's precursors include Aristotle and Ben Jonson, but primarily his forerunner is Koheleth (Ecclesiastes):

> Whatsoever thy hand findeth to do, do it with thy might; for there is no work, nor device, nor knowledge, nor wisdom, in the grave, whither thou goest.
>
> Ecclesiastes 9:10

I constantly reread Koheleth, in Hebrew and in English, and sometimes believe I am reading Johnson:

> It is better to hear the rebuke of the wise, than for a man to hear the song of fools.
> For as the crackling of thorns under a pot, so is the laughter of the fool: this also is vanity.
>
> Ecclesiastes 7:5–6

The deepest lesson I have learned from Johnson is that any authority of criticism as a literary genre must depend on the human wisdom of the critic, and not upon the wrongness or rightness of either theory or praxis. It is because of Johnson's example that I've learned that the literary will to power over language can make its way only through diction, a choice of words that pragmatically becomes a series of choices in language. Johnson was a critic both of power, which he called invention, and of the will to diction, and he understood the reflection of power by choice of language better than any critic has been able to convey since.

Johnson's greatest work as a critic is *The Lives of the Poets*, composed between 1777 and 1781. Yet this work is very curious, since the *Lives* are introductions to a strange collection of the British poets, chosen mostly by the booksellers and not by Johnson himself. There are fifty poets— Oliver Goldsmith, who was a friend of Jonson's, is oddly excluded—and they are frequently a rabblement of poetasters: Pomfret, Dorset, Sprat, Stepney, Roscommon, Fenton, Lyttelton, and the egregious Yalden. Alas, poor Yalden! We remember him now, if at all, only for the rather grand Johnsonian sentence that concludes his *Life:*

> Of his other poems it is sufficient to say that they deserve perusal, though they are not always exactly polished, though the rhymes are sometimes very ill sorted, and though his faults seem rather the omissions of idleness than the negligences of enthusiasm.

Before that, Johnson quoted Yalden's unfortunate line in which Yahweh contemplates the newly created Light:

> A while th' Almighty wondering stood.

Alas, poor Yalden! We can never forget the Johnsonian observation upon this:

> He ought to have remembered that Infinite Knowledge can never wonder. All wonder is the effect of novelty upon Ignorance.

Certainly the masterpiece of the *Lives* is the beautiful meditation upon Alexander Pope. For Johnson, Pope was the prince of poets. As I age, my own love for Pope has increased, and I begin to understand him better. Yet to me the central distinction of the *Lives* is the ambivalent and powerful *Milton*. Johnson was a royalist and a fierce adherent to Anglicanism. Milton's politics and religious stance were abhorrent to the great critic, yet Milton's poetic strength overcame Johnson's revulsion.

It is fascinating to see, in the *Life of Milton,* Johnson balancing his religious distaste with his superb apprehension of poetic achievement. Even stronger is his aversion to Milton's politics. Johnson calls Milton "an acrimonious and surly republican." It is unworthy of Johnson that he judges Milton's republicanism as "an envious hatred of greatness." Johnson rises to his proper height when he comes to *Paradise Lost.* He calls it the first of all poems in design, and in performance second only to Homer.

Before Johnson attempts a critical account of *Paradise Lost,* he makes a marvelous statement on the nature of poetry:

> By the general consent of criticks the first praise of genius is due to the writer of an epick poem, as it requires an assemblage of all the powers which are singly sufficient for other compositions. Poetry is the art of uniting pleasure with truth, by calling imagination to the help of reason. Epick poetry undertakes to teach the most important truths by the most pleasing precepts, and therefore relates some great event in the most affecting manner. History must supply the writer with the rudiments of narration, which he must improve and exalt by a nobler art, must animate by dramatick energy, and diversify by retrospection and anticipation; morality must teach him the exact bounds and different shades of vice and virtue; from policy and the practice of life he has to learn the discriminations of character and the tendency of the passions, either single or combined; and physiology must supply him with illustrations and images. To put these materials to poetical use is required an imagination capable of painting nature and realizing fiction. Nor is he yet a poet till he has attained the whole extension of his language, distinguished all the delicacies of phrase, and all the colours of words, and learned to adjust their different sounds to all the varieties of metrical modulation.

An epic poet would have to be formidable indeed to satisfy Johnson's criteria. Milton more than passes the test. I cannot think of a better description of Milton's art than that it animates by dramatic energy, and diversifies by retrospection and anticipation.

Johnson goes on to identify the authentic distinction of *Paradise Lost:*

> The subject of an epick poem is naturally an event of great importance. That of Milton is not the destruction of a city, the conduct of a colony, or the foundation of an empire. His subject is the fate of worlds, the revolutions of heaven and of earth; rebellion against the Supreme King raised by the highest order of created beings; the overthrow of their host and the punishment of their crime; the creation of a new race of reasonable creatures; their original happiness and innocence, their forfeiture of immortality, and their restoration to hope and peace.
>
> Great events can be hastened or retarded only by persons of elevated dignity. Before the greatness displayed in Milton's poem all other greatness shrinks away. The weakest of his agents are the highest and noblest of human beings, the original parents of mankind; with whose actions the elements consented; on whose rectitude or deviation of will depended the state of terrestrial nature and the condition of all the future inhabitants of the globe.

Johnson's rolling periods grant us a pleasure that only a few other critics can do. His style is equal to the greatness of his subject. Though I wince to hear it, his dismissal of Milton's magnificent Satan again has the authority of his own grand style:

> The malignity of Satan foams in haughtiness and obstinacy; but his expressions are commonly general, and no otherwise offensive than as they are wicked.

I more than forgive Johnson because of the power he then manifests:

> The thoughts which are occasionally called forth in the progress are such as could only be produced by an imagination in the highest degree fervid and active, to which materials were supplied by incessant study and unlimited curiosity. The heat of Milton's mind might be said to sublimate his learning, to throw off into his work the spirit of science, unmingled with its grosser parts.

He had considered creation in its whole extent, and his descriptions are therefore learned. He had accustomed his imagination to unrestrained indulgence, and his conceptions therefore were extensive. The characteristick quality of his poem is sublimity. He sometimes descends to the elegant, but his element is the great. He can occasionally invest himself with grace; but his natural port is gigantick loftiness. He can please when pleasure is required; but it is his peculiar power to astonish.

He seems to have been well acquainted with his own genius, and to know what it was that Nature had bestowed upon him more bountifully than upon others; the power of displaying the vast, illuminating the splendid, enforcing the awful, darkening the gloomy, and aggravating the dreadful: he therefore chose a subject on which too much could not be said, on which he might tire his fancy without the censure of extravagance.

The appearances of nature and the occurrences of life did not satiate his appetite of greatness. To paint things as they are requires a minute attention, and employs the memory rather than the fancy. Milton's delight was to sport in the wide regions of possibility; reality was a scene too narrow for his mind. He sent his faculties out upon discovery, into worlds where only imagination can travel, and delighted to form new modes of existence, and furnish sentiment and action to superior beings, to trace the counsels of hell, or accompany the choirs of heaven.

But he could not be always in other worlds: he must sometimes revisit earth, and tell of things visible and known. When he cannot raise wonder by the sublimity of his mind he gives delight by its fertility.

Whatever be his subject he never fails to fill the imagination.

No one else has paid tribute to Milton as gloriously as Johnson does. He establishes what my much-lamented friend Angus Fletcher was to call the trope of transumption.

His similes are less numerous and more various than those of his predecessors. But he does not confine himself within the limits of rigorous comparison: his great excellence is amplitude, and he expands the adventitious image beyond the dimensions which the occasion required. Thus, comparing the shield of Satan to the orb of the Moon, he crowds the imagination with the discovery of the telescope and all the wonders which the telescope discovers.

To crowd the imagination is to call back the images of all the precursors, and to ram them together in metaphors that subsume all previous tropes. Johnson is at his finest when he considers Milton's engagement with religious truth:

> We all, indeed, feel the effects of Adam's disobedience; we all sin like Adam, and like him must all bewail our offences; we have restless and insidious enemies in the fallen angels, and in the blessed spirits we have guardians and friends; in the Redemption of mankind we hope to be included: in the description of heaven and hell we are surely interested, as we are all to reside hereafter either in the regions of horrour or of bliss.
>
> But these truths are too important to be new: they have been taught to our infancy; they have mingled with our solitary thoughts and familiar conversation, and are habitually interwoven with the whole texture of life. Being therefore not new they raise no unaccustomed emotion in the mind: what we knew before we cannot learn; what is not unexpected, cannot surprise.
>
> Of the ideas suggested by these awful scenes, from some we recede with reverence, except when stated hours require their association; and from others we shrink with horrour, or admit them only as salutary inflictions, as counterpoises to our interests and passions. Such images rather obstruct the career of fancy than incite it.
>
> Pleasure and terrour are indeed the genuine sources of poetry; but poetical pleasure must be such as human imagination can at least conceive, and poetical terrour such as human strength and fortitude may combat. The good and evil of Eternity are too ponderous for the wings of wit; the mind sinks under them in passive helplessness, content with calm belief and humble adoration.
>
> Known truths however may take a different appearance, and be conveyed to the mind by a new train of intermediate images. This Milton has undertaken, and performed with pregnancy and vigour of mind peculiar to himself. Whoever considers the few

radical positions which the Scriptures afforded him will wonder by what energetick operations he expanded them to such extent and ramified them to so much variety, restrained as he was by religious reverence from licentiousness of fiction.

Nothing better has been said as to the difficulty of poetry's being religious:

The good and evil of Eternity are too ponderous for the wings of wit; the mind sinks under them in passive helplessness, content with calm belief and humble adoration.

John Milton and "passive helplessness" are incompatible. Perhaps he did indeed conclude in calm belief, but a Milton humbly adoring anything or anyone is inconceivable. I do not often dispute Dr. Johnson, but clearly Milton was never restrained "by religious reverence from licentiousness of fiction."

There is something reluctant in Johnson's admiration that ensues in a rather dubious observation:

But original deficience cannot be supplied. The want of human interest is always felt. *Paradise Lost* is one of the books which the reader admires and lays down, and forgets to take up again. None ever wished it longer than it is. Its perusal is a duty rather than a pleasure. We read Milton for instruction, retire harassed and overburdened, and look elsewhere for recreation; we desert our master, and seek for companions.

This can be set aside as we rejoice in Johnson's final judgment of Milton's epic:

Such are the faults of that wonderful performance *Paradise Lost;* which he who can put in balance with its beauties must be considered not as nice but as dull, as less to be censured for want of candour, than pitied for want of sensibility.

At the conclusion of the *Life of Milton*, Johnson's great voice becomes adequate to Milton's:

The highest praise of genius is original invention. Milton cannot be said to have contrived the structure of an epick poem, and therefore owes reverence to that vigour and amplitude of mind to which all generations must be indebted for the art of poetical narration, for the texture of the fable, the variation of incidents, the interposition of dialogue, and all the stratagems that surprise and enchain attention. But, of all the borrowers from Homer, Milton is perhaps the least indebted. He was naturally a thinker for himself, confident of his own abilities, and disdainful of help or hindrance: he did not refuse admission to the thoughts or images of his predecessors, but he did not seek them. From his contemporaries he neither courted nor received support; there is in his writings nothing by which the pride of other authors might be gratified, or favour gained; no exchange of praise, nor solicitation of support. His great works were performed under discountenance, and in blindness, but difficulties vanished at his touch; he was born for whatever is arduous; and his work is not the greatest of heroick poems, only because it is not the first.

Johnson aptly locates one of Milton's greatest strengths:

He did not refuse admission to the thoughts or images of his predecessors, but he did not seek them.

What Johnson saw I myself have devoted years to elaborate. Milton is supreme in his use of allusion. He so performs allusiveness that it becomes a mode of invention. As a defense against poetic tradition, Miltonic allusion wards off his most dangerous precursors, Spenser and Shakespeare. Milton writes, as Angus Fletcher noted, in a transumptive style, featuring a reversal of other poets' tropes.

Milton was a monist who refused to separate spirit from matter. One of the supreme achievements of *Paradise Lost* is to exalt unfallen pleasure. The poem gratifies us because it calls out to the yearning of many readers for the expanded senses of Eden. William Blake and the English Romantics after him responded profoundly to this dream of the human form divine. Angus Fletcher suggested that it was from Shakespeare that Milton learned how to embody prophecy within transcendental forms.

The single essay by Dr. Johnson that wounds me most is from the periodical *The Idler:* "No. 41. Saturday, 27 January 1759." Its subject is the death of beloved friends. Johnson remarks: "The loss of a friend upon whom the heart was fixed, to whom every wish and endeavor tended, is a state of desolation in which the mind looks abroad impatient of itself, and finds nothing but emptiness and horror . . . The dead cannot return, and nothing is left us here but languishment and grief." At his most searching, Johnson reflects that our happiness is not found in self-contemplation, but is perceived only when it is reflected from another.

Johnson turns to the hope of Revelation. He intimates that the union of souls may still remain. Perhaps we who struggle with sin and sorrow and infirmities may still have our own part in the intention and kindness of those who have finished their course and are now receiving their reward.

With immense dignity, Johnson propounds that authentic alleviation of the loss of our friends, and even a kind of rational tranquillity in facing up to our own disappearance, will be received only from the promises of Jesus, in whose hands are life and death. Turning to Revelation, Johnson reminds us that all tears will be wiped from the eyes and the whole soul shall be filled with joy.

Johnson hated solitude. He relied upon his friends to keep him in good cheer. As his generation waned, his sorrow increased. He always feared judgment, and though he once told Boswell a man was not obliged to do all that he could, he wondered if he had done enough for the sake of heaven.

Johnson should have been a major poet, yet he feared what he termed the dangerous prevalence of the imagination. The other inhibiting shadow was his deep love for the poetry of Alexander Pope. In Johnson's view, Pope had achieved poetic perfection.

Those who explored ways beyond Pope drew Johnson's censure. In conversation with Boswell, he characterized Thomas Gray's two Pindaric odes, *The Bard* and *The Progress of Poecy*, as just two cucumbers. And though he delighted in the conversation of his friend William Collins, he could not extend his affection to the beautiful and radical odes composed by Collins as he strove to maintain his perilous balance.

The Johnsonian reaction to Christopher Smart, who urged even acquaintances to pray with him on the streets of London, was to remark, "I had as lief pray with Kit Smart as with anyone else."

What Johnson could have made of *Jubilate Agno*, I cannot imagine. The path of the religious enthusiast was not Samuel Johnson's. He sought a calm, steady belief, and to some degree achieved it. His distrust of devotional poetry stems from his awe for the truths of Christian revelation. He would not have been content with humble adoration since that did not suit his temperament. For all of his distrust of the Sublime, his sense of revelation has to be regarded as sublime in its reach and intensity. Johnson was built on so large a scale that, to find a match for his capaciousness of wisdom and consciousness, you would have to turn to Shakespeare himself.

Johnson would have understood the maxim that a man's worst difficulties commence when he is free to do as he likes. His early years in London were marked by desperate poverty, which he surmounted by endless literary labors. The memory of those years never left him. Boswell remarks that, even at the apex of his fame, Johnson still tore at his meat like a tiger.

Afflicted by a vile melancholy, Johnson rescued himself with an array of friends who could appreciate his conversational brilliance, and who kept him pragmatically cheerful. A shadow of Dr. Johnson, I once kept going through the kindness of a phalanx of friends, all of them brilliant. They have all gone on, and I speak to ghosts as I read, teach, and write.

Ben Jonson disdained Montaigne's cheerful use in his own work of what he read as he went along. A friend of Francis Bacon, Jonson strongly chooses Bacon's essays over Montaigne's. Just as Shakespeare's personalities change by overhearing themselves, Montaigne changes as he reads what he himself has written. For all his gifts, you can no more choose Bacon over Montaigne than you could Ben Jonson over Shakespeare. You could not say of Bacon what Emerson observed of Montaigne: "Cut these words, and they bleed; they are vascular and alive."

Montaigne's wisdom is not Christian. Jesus is mentioned only nine times in the *Essays*, and Socrates is cited in one hundred instances. It is not that, for Montaigne, God and Christ do not exist; they are so far away that they are not our concern. Montaigne's sense of self is entirely his own. He does not argue; he speculates. In doing so, he captures forever everyone's sense of skepticism.

Montaigne's most famous question is "What do I know?" What he knew was himself. Though he played a part as a mediator in the French civil wars of religion, Montaigne longed only to read and write in solitude. He said that, in the experience he had of himself, there might be enough to make him wise, if only he were a faithful scholar. Above all else, he teaches us not to despise our own being. If we could enjoy our being fully, then we would become virtually gods.

No one could be more different from Montaigne than Samuel Johnson. In his curious romance *Rasselas*, Johnson has his philosopher Imlac enunciate a great sentence that is the reversal of everything that Montaigne represented: "Human life is everywhere a state in which much is to be endured and little to be enjoyed."

Dr. Johnson endlessly struggled against his own profound melancholia. He feared his own cognitive and imaginative powers, since both were vast. His sense of guilt transcends any Christian sense of Original Sin. It is personal. Perhaps it will always be beyond our understanding. I myself believe that Johnson should have been a great poet, if his reverence for Alexander Pope had not stifled his own enormous potential. The imagination takes its revenge. Johnson, unlike Montaigne, could never be content in solitude. For Montaigne, reading and writing were the earthly paradise. For Johnson, they are failed defenses against the abyss.

# William Collins,
## "Ode on the Poetical Character"

WILLIAM COLLINS (1721–59) departed at thirty-seven. From 1754 on, Collins was confined for extreme melancholia, perhaps brought on by the public failure of his major work, *Odes on Several Descriptive and Allegorical Subjects* (1747). There are magnificent poems in that volume: "Ode to Fear," "Ode on the Poetical Character," "Ode to Evening," and "The Passions. An Ode for Music."

Collins was a close friend of Dr. Samuel Johnson, who commemorates the lost poet in his "Life of Collins" in *Lives of the Poets:*

> Such was the fate of Collins, with whom I once delighted to converse, and whom I yet remember with tenderness.

Johnson's affection and esteem did not extend to the major odes by Collins:

> To what I have formerly said of his writings may be added, that his diction was often harsh, unskilfully laboured, and injudiciously selected. He affected the obsolete when it was not worthy of revival; and he puts his words out of the common order, seeming to think, with some later candidates for fame, that not to write prose is certainly to write poetry. His lines commonly are of slow motion, clogged and impeded with clusters of consonants. As men are often esteemed who cannot be loved, so the poetry of Collins may sometimes extort praise when it gives little pleasure.

Though Johnson liked and admired Thomas Warton, his reaction to Warton's *Poems* (1777) is a charming throwaway:

Wheresoe'er I turn my view,
All is strange, yet nothing new;
Endless labour all along,
Endless labour to be wrong;
Phrase that Time has flung away,
Uncouth words in disarray:
Trick'd in antique ruff and bonnet,
Ode and elegy and sonnet.

Though the stimulus comes from Thomas Warton, there is a memory of the long-departed William Collins. The return to Milton in Collins and in Thomas Gray made Johnson uneasy. He had inherited from Pope a distrust of the Sublime. For me the classical statement on this is that of Martin Price, my friend and colleague for forty years:

Pope and Swift see the sublime as always inviting a fall. It "may branch upwards towards Heaven, but the Root is in the Earth. Too intense a Contemplation is not the Business of Flesh and Blood; it must by the necessary Course of Things, in a little Time, let go its Hold, and fall into Matter."

I seem now always to be in the elegy season. I sit here on a June day, exhausted as my long, slow recovery continues, and meditate upon all my dead friends. My beloved student Thomas Weiskel died at twenty-nine, in a vain attempt to save his two-year-old daughter, when the ice gave way beneath them. His book, *The Romantic Sublime: Studies in the Structure and Psychology of Transcendence* (1976), was edited for publication by Leslie Brisman, and I contributed a foreword on both the man and his work. In *The Romantic Sublime*, Weiskel gives a brilliant reading of Collins's "Ode on the Poetical Character," which he sees as the supreme representation of how difficult it was to become a poet in the mid-eighteenth century.

Roger Lonsdale, in his very useful edition of the poems of Gray, Collins, and Goldsmith, takes issue with Northrop Frye, myself, and Weiskel. For Lonsdale, the "rich-haired youth of morn" is simply the sun. And yet the language is palpably sexual. God and Fancy have intercourse, and the Poet is born:

The band, as fairy legends say,
Was wove on that creating day,
When He, who called with thought to birth
Yon tented sky, this laughing earth,
And dressed with springs, and forests tall,
And poured the main engirting all,
Long by the loved enthusiast wooed,
Himself in some diviner mood,
Retiring, sate with her alone,
And placed her on his sapphire throne;
The whiles, the vaulted shrine around,
Seraphic wires were heard to sound;
Now sublimest triumph swelling,
Now on love and mercy dwelling;
And she, from out the veiling cloud,
Breathed her magic notes aloud:
And thou, thou rich-haired youth of morn,
And all thy subject life was born!
The dang'rous Passions kept aloof,
Far from the sainted growing woof;
But near it sate ecstatic Wonder,
List'ning the deep applauding thunder;
And Truth, in sunny vest arrayed,
By whose the tarsel's eyes were made;
All the shad'wy tribes of Mind,
In braided dance their murmurs joined;
And all the bright uncounted powers
Who feed on Heav'n's ambrosial flowers.
Where is the bard, whose soul can now
Its high presuming hopes avow?
Where he who thinks, with rapture blind,
This hallowed work for him designed?

The youth is at once the sun, Apollo, and the new Poet. I do not believe that Collins was schooled in theosophical speculations, as Christopher Smart and William Blake were, but his Fancy is remarkably parallel to the Kabbalistic Shekhinah, Yahweh's indwelling female presence. In any case, he sees the poetic character as being incarnated

in a bard, and not a poet of the school of Alexander Pope. Collins is
urging a return to the school of Edmund Spenser and John Milton:

> High on some cliff, to Heav'n up-piled,
> Of rude access, of prospect wild,
> Where, tangled round the jealous steep,
> Strange shades o'erbrow the valleys deep,
> And holy Genii guard the rock,
> Its glooms embrown, its springs unlock,
> While on its rich ambitious head,
> An Eden, like his own, lies spread:
> I view that oak the fancied glades among,
> By which as Milton lay, his evening ear,
> From many a cloud that dropped ethereal dew,
> Nigh sphered in Heav'n its native strains could hear:
> On which that ancient trump he reached was hung;
>     Thither oft, his glory greeting,
>     From Waller's myrtle shades retreating,
> With many a vow from Hope's aspiring tongue,
> My trembling feet his guiding steps pursue;
>     In vain—such bliss to one alone
>     Of all the sons of soul was known,
>     And Heav'n and Fancy, kindred powers,
>     Have now o'erturn'd th'inspiring bowers,
> Or curtained close such scene from every future view.

Edmund Waller was taken by John Dryden and Alexander Pope
as being the ancestor of Augustan poetry. The "myrtle shades" were
sacred to Venus.

# Thomas Gray:
# The Poet as Outsider

T HE TWO POEMS in English widely read and appreciated by people who do not read poetry are Thomas Gray's *Elegy Written in a Country Church-Yard* and Edward FitzGerald's *The Rubaiyat of Omar Khayyam*. John Hollander and I had many discussions as to why these two poems so uniquely found and maintain a vast popular audience. They are both powerful and authentic poems, but that in itself cannot account for their success.

The leading authority on Thomas Gray remains Roger Lonsdale. He taught us to locate the elegy's central meaning in Gray's transition from the initial version in the Eton manuscript to our familiar text. You can say of Gray's first elegy that it is essentially a poem in praise of country retirement, in the mode of Horace. Gray revised it so that it became more Miltonic, and took as its matrix the desire of each of us to be remembered somehow after we are dead.

Lonsdale deftly shows that Gray in revision gives us a very different vision of the poet:

> The figure of the Poet is no longer the urban, urbane, worldly, rational Augustan man among men, with his own place in society; what Gray dramatizes is the poet as outsider, with an uneasy consciousness of a sensibility and an imagination at once unique and burdensome.

That burdensome imagination stems from Spenser, Shakespeare, and Milton. The original, more Augustan *Elegy* concludes with four splendid stanzas:

The thoughtless World to Majesty may bow
Exalt the brave, & idolize Success
But more to Innocence their Safety owe
Than Power & Genius e'er conspired to bless

And thou, who mindful of the unhonour'd Dead
Dost in these Notes their artless Tale relate
By Night & lonely Contemplation led
To linger in the gloomy Walks of Fate

Hark how the sacred Calm, that broods around
Bids ev'ry fierce tumultuous Passion cease
In still small Accents whisp'ring from the Ground
A grateful Earnest of eternal Peace

No more with Reason & thyself at strife;
Give anxious Cares and endless Wishes room
But thro' the cool sequestered Vale of Life
Pursue the silent Tenour of thy Doom.

This is immensely different from the conclusion of the poem we know:

For who to dumb Forgetfulness a prey,
    This pleasing anxious being e'er resign'd,
Left the warm precincts of the cheerful day,
    Nor cast one longing, ling'ring look behind?

On some fond breast the parting soul relies,
    Some pious drops the closing eye requires;
Ev'n from the tomb the voice of Nature cries,
    Ev'n in our ashes live their wonted fires.

For thee, who mindful of th' unhonour'd Dead
    Dost in these lines their artless tale relate;
If chance, by lonely contemplation led,
    Some kindred spirit shall inquire thy fate,

Haply some hoary-headed swain may say,
  "Oft have we seen him at the peep of dawn
Brushing with hasty steps the dews away
  To meet the sun upon the upland lawn.

"There at the foot of yonder nodding beech
  That wreathes its old fantastic roots so high,
His listless length at noontide would he stretch,
  And pore upon the brook that babbles by.

"Hard by yon wood, now smiling as in scorn,
  Mutt'ring his wayward fancies he would rove,
Now drooping, woeful wan, like one forlorn,
  Or craz'd with care, or cross'd in hopeless love.

"One morn I miss'd him on the custom'd hill,
  Along the heath and near his fav'rite tree;
Another came; nor yet beside the rill,
  Nor up the lawn, nor at the wood was he;

"The next with dirges due in sad array
  Slow thro' the church-way path we saw him borne.
Approach and read (for thou canst read) the lay,
  Grav'd on the stone beneath yon aged thorn."

The Epitaph
*Here rests his head upon the lap of Earth*
  *A youth to Fortune and to Fame unknown.*
*Fair Science frown'd not on his humble birth,*
  *And Melancholy mark'd him for her own.*

*Large was his bounty, and his soul sincere,*
  *Heav'n did a recompense as largely send:*
*He gave to Mis'ry all he had, a tear,*
  *He gain'd from Heav'n ('twas all he wish'd) a friend.*

*No farther seek his merits to disclose,*
  *Or draw his frailties from their dread abode,*

*(There they alike in trembling hope repose)*
   *The bosom of his Father and his God.*

Dr. Samuel Johnson judged poetry by a test of asking whether any new matter had been disclosed. Though he loathed Gray's poetry, Johnson nevertheless praised the *Elegy* on encountering notions that seemed to him utterly original:

> The *Church-yard* abounds with images which find a mirrour in every mind, and with sentiments to which every bosom returns an echo. The four stanzas beginning *Yet even these bones,* are to me original: I have never seen the notions in any other place; yet he that reads them here, persuades himself that he has always felt them. Had Gray written often thus, it had been vain to blame, and useless to praise him.

It has always baffled me that Johnson, as learned a critic as Gray was a poet, chose to overlook the echoes here of Lucretius, Ovid, Petrarch, Milton's Belial, Pope's *Odyssey,* and Swift. I assume that the great critic found an expression of his own deepest anxieties concerning both the poetic self and the fate of the soul after death.

# Wisdom and Unwisdom
## of the Body

IN MY FAR-OFF YOUTH of the early 1960s, I was a scholar of William Blake (1757–1827) and composed several lengthy commentaries upon his three "brief epics," *The Four Zoas*, *Milton*, and *Jerusalem*. Now, more than fifty years later, I wake up in the middle of the night and include his lyrics among those I chant to keep myself going. For some reason (I wish I knew why), I have found myself repeatedly chanting the preface to *Milton: A Poem* (1810):

> And did those feet in ancient time,
> Walk upon Englands mountains green:
> And was the holy Lamb of God,
> On Englands pleasant pastures seen!
>
> And did the Countenance Divine,
> Shine forth upon our clouded hills?
> And was Jerusalem builded here,
> Among these dark Satanic Mills?
>
> Bring me my Bow of burning gold:
> Bring me my Arrows of desire:
> Bring me my Spear: O clouds unfold!
> Bring me my Chariot of fire!
>
> I will not cease from Mental Fight,
> Nor shall my Sword sleep in my hand:
> Till we have built Jerusalem,
> In Englands green & pleasant Land.

Blake would have been surprised that this highly personal lyric has been absorbed by the Anglican Church and by Nonconformists as almost a normative Christian hymn. But, then, John Milton's *Paradise Lost* has become *the* Protestant epic, rather in the way that Dante's *Commedia* has been judged by many to be an expression of devout Catholic doctrine. Milton sets "before all temples the upright heart and pure," his own.

The preface to Blake's *Milton* opens with a series of rhetorical questions to which the reply is positive. The Dark Satanic Mills could refer to industrialization, yet any informed reader of Blake will recognize in them the image of Urizen, who grinds on in the mills of our minds and renders us victims of a stony sleep. Blake, like Milton a sect of one, assumes the mantle of the prophet Elijah, who ascends to the Divine in a chariot of fire. Refusing to cease from mental fight, the poet-prophet William Blake dedicates his vision of a Blakean John Milton to the building of a New Jerusalem in a redeemed England.

Many readers who now encounter this lyric cannot get the church melody out of their heads, which is an irony Blake would have enjoyed. For me, the resolution is to recover Blake by hearing his highly individual tone of voice:

What is the price of Experience do men buy it for a song
Or wisdom for a dance in the street? No it is bought with the
   price
Of all that a man hath his house his wife his children
Wisdom is sold in the desolate market where none come to buy
And in the withered field where the farmer plows for bread in vain

Night the Second, "Song of Enion," The Four Zoas

The tens of thousands who sing what they mistitle "Jerusalem" ought to ponder these searing lines. Koheleth (Ecclesiastes) is echoed here with high deliberation, yet to prophetic purpose alien to the supposed King Solomon the Wise contemplating the emptiness of *hevel* (mistranslated as "vanity"). It is Blake's unread poetry and neglected paintings that are sold with no buyers and become the absent bread withered in the field.

William Blake's poetic voice is plangent with reverberations of the prophet who knows he will not be heard. Like John Milton's organ voice, it sounds against the horizons we have imposed upon ourselves.

The burden of these voices is: Why will you turn away? Walt Whitman called himself the Answerer, and Blake could have done the same. Here is one of the most direct and masterful lyrics in the language, "The Crystal Cabinet":

The Maiden caught me in the Wild
Where I was dancing merrily
She put me into her Cabinet
And Lockd me up with a golden Key

This cabinet is formd of Gold
And Pearl & Crystal shining bright
And within it opens into a World
And a little lovely Moony Night

Another England there I saw
Another London with its Tower
Another Thames & other Hills
And another pleasant Surrey Bower

Another Maiden like herself
Translucent lovely shining clear
Threefold each in the other closd
O what a pleasant trembling fear

O what a smile a threefold Smile
Filld me that like a flame I burnd
I bent to Kiss the lovely Maid
And found a Threefold Kiss returnd

I strove to seize the inmost Form
With ardor fierce & hands of flame
But burst the Crystal Cabinet
And like a Weeping Babe became

A weeping Babe upon the wild
And weeping Woman pale reclind
And in the outward Air again
I filld with woes the passing Wind

The Maiden is sexually more active than the youth who puts up no resistance. This cabinet, a cosmos in itself, opens into a moonlit night of another England and another Maiden, but this one translucent: a Chinese box in which three mirror images are enclosed each within the other. Blake prophesies Lewis Carroll's looking-glass world, yet more subtly, since the Maiden's three sides converge only in part, in their midst, which gives an evasive image. The youth's kiss confronts a returned threefold kiss so frustrating that he attempts to embrace the inmost of the three images and bursts the crystal cabinet, since sexual fulfillment by itself cannot achieve a knowledge of reality.

The unfortunate lover becomes a crying infant again, and the Maiden weeps too. A reader who desires a further development of this symbolic drama can find it in Blake's engraved epic *Jerusalem* 70:17–31, where the Maiden is named Rahab. In the book of Joshua, Rahab is a redeemed harlot, and Dante continues her identification with redemption by associating her with Christ's sacrifice. Blake furiously reversed this, and made Rahab all the churches of the world, each another Whore of Babylon. I do not urge any but a few readers to struggle with the rewarding complexities of Blake's mythmaking in his three brief epics. The splendor of "The Crystal Cabinet," as of so many of Blake's lyrics, is that the myth remains implicit and the drama of loss conveys a mysterious beauty.

Sometimes, in the hard hours before dawn, when invariably I lie awake, I hear a Blakean quatrain echoing in my head. It is the enigmatic motto to *The Book of Thel*:

> Does the Eagle know what is in the pit?
> Or wilt thou go ask the Mole:
> Can Wisdom be put in a silver rod?
> Or Love in a golden bowl?

I do not think Henry James had Blake in mind when he gave his late masterpiece *The Golden Bowl* its title. Rather, he shared Blake's source in Ecclesiastes 12:

> . . . and desire shall fail: because man goeth to his long home,
>     and the mourners go about the streets:
> Or ever the silver cord be loosed, or the golden bowl be broken,
>     or the pitcher be broken at the fountain, or the wheel broken
>     at the cistern.
> Then shall the dust return to the earth as it was. . . .

William Butler Yeats, professed disciple of Blake, follows neither Ecclesiastes nor Henry James but varies the motto to *The Book of Thel*:

> I thought it out this very day,
> Noon upon the clock,
> A man may put pretence away
> Who leans upon a stick,
> May sing, and sing until he drop,
> Whether to maid or hag:
> *I carry the sun in a golden cup,*
> *The moon in a silver bag.*

"Those Dancing Days Are Gone"

Swerving from his precursor, the Anglo-Irish Archpoet renders as triumph what Blake regards as a rhetorical question with an implied answer in the negative mode. For Yeats, the wisdom of the body had to be sufficient, despite all his occult yearnings. Blake finds a great unwisdom in all those who seek to reason with the loins. D. H. Lawrence shared Yeats's heroic vitalism, but for Blake, more is required than sexual exaltation if we are to become fully human.

# William Blake's *Milton*

I CONTINUE WITH William Blake, and to the magnificent close of his
poem *Milton:*

To cleanse the Face of my Spirit by Self-examination.
To bathe in the Waters of Life, to wash off the Not Human
I come in Self-annihilation & the grandeur of Inspiration
To cast off Rational Demonstration by Faith in the Saviour
To cast off the rotten rags of Memory by Inspiration
To cast off Bacon, Locke, & Newton from Albions covering
To take off his filthy garments, & clothe him with Imagination
To cast aside from Poetry, all that is not Inspiration
That it no longer shall dare to mock with the aspersion of
    Madness
Cast on the Inspired, by the tame high finisher of paltry Blots,
Indefinite, or paltry Rhymes, or paltry Harmonies.
Who creeps into State Government like a caterpillar to destroy
To cast off the idiot Questioner who is always questioning,
But never capable of answering; who sits with a sly grin
Silent plotting when to question, like a thief in a cave;
Who publishes doubt and calls it knowledge; whose Science is
    Despair
Whose pretence to knowledge is Envy, whose whole Science is
To destroy the wisdom of ages to gratify ravenous Envy;
That rages round him like a Wolf day & night without rest
He smiles with condescension; he talks of Benevolence & Virtue
And those who act with Benevolence & Virtue, they murder
    time on time
These are the destroyers of Jerusalem, these are the murderers

Of Jesus, who deny the Faith & mock at Eternal Life:
Who pretend to Poetry that they may destroy Imagination;
By imitation of Nature's Images drawn from Remembrance
These are the Sexual Garments, the Abomination of Desolation
Hiding the Human Lineaments, as with an Ark & Curtains
Which Jesus rent: and now shall wholly purge away with Fire
Till Generation is swallowd up in Regeneration.


Blake's Milton makes his final descent from heaven to Blake's Vale of Felpham. I know of few passages in the world's poetry so exalted and sublime as Milton's proclamation. Who would not wish to cleanse the face of their spirit by self-examination? Who would not hope that we could bathe in the waters of life, and wash off the not-human? Yet Blake's Milton, like the actual John Milton, is far beyond us. I for one am not capable of self-annihilation, or the grandeur of inspiration. And, not being a poet, I cannot proclaim that all that is not inspiration should be cast aside from it. Blake, so frequently accused of madness, defends himself as truly inspired, against his enemies in both painting and poetry.

Most powerfully, he invents the great image of "the idiot Questioner"—the person who always questions but has no answers: the poseur to philosophy or insight of any kind, the hypocrite who talks of benevolence and virtue but who time and again spiritually murders those who indeed act with benevolence and virtue.

The poem *Milton* concludes with Blake's own proclamation of his individual vision:


And I beheld the Twenty-four Cities of Albion
Arise upon their Thrones to Judge the Nations of the Earth
And the Immortal Four in whom the Twenty-four appear
    Four-fold
Arose around Albions body: Jesus wept & walked forth
From Felphams Vale clothed in Clouds of blood, to enter into
Albions Bosom, the bosom of death & the Four surrounded him
In the Column of Fire in Felphams Vale; then to their mouths
    the Four
Applied their Four Trumpets, & then sounded to the Four
    winds.

Terror struck in the Vale I stood at that immortal sound:
My bones trembled, I fell outstretch'd upon the path
A moment, & my Soul returned into its mortal state
To Resurrection & Judgment in the Vegetable Body
And my sweet Shadow of Delight stood trembling by my side

Immediately the Lark mounted with a loud trill from Felphams
    Vale
And the Wild Thyme from Wimbleton's green & impurpled
    Hills
And Los & Enitharmon rose over the Hills of Surrey
Their clouds roll over London with a south wind, soft
    Oothoon
Pants in the Vales of Lambeth weeping oer her Human
    Harvest.
Los listens to the Cry of the Poor Man: his Cloud
Over London in volume terrific, low bended in anger.

Rintrah & Palamabron view the Human Harvest beneath.
Their Wine-presses & Barns stand open; the Ovens are prepar'd
The Waggons ready: terrific Lions & Tygers sport & play
All Animals upon the Earth, are prepard in all their strength

To go forth to the Great Harvest & Vintage of the Nations

Here Blake comes back to himself, in a human triumph. The Four
Zoas, or principal components of the unfallen human, sound their trumpets and impel Blake toward his own Last Judgment. Yet he grandly
resurrects, to await his mortal destiny, following Milton in the belief
that body and soul must die together, and be resurrected together. In
the assured closing passages, Blake gathers together many of his poem's
emblems: the Lark and the Wild Thyme as messengers of Los; the rising of Los and Enitharmon as a wind of possible inspiration; the labors
of Rintrah and Palamabron. To these he adds Oothoon of *Visions of
the Daughters of Albion*, weeping with joy over the Human Harvest she
was denied in that poem. Los is now altogether transformed from the
erring creature of the early Nights of the *Four Zoas*. Like Amos among
the prophets, he "listens to the Cry of the Poor Man," and his pro-

phetic anger is bent over London as a threatening cloud, a call for social justice that threatens destruction if denied. In the closing lines, the Mills of Satan have vanished, and the Apocalypse is imminent. I hear in the single line of the final plate a prophetic battle cry. It articulates challenge, with the confidence of the poet-prophet who has been tried severely, and has won a victory in those trials.

# William Wordsworth,
# "The Solitary Reaper"

W ORDSWORTH's "Intimations" ode, though it influenced Percy
Bysshe Shelley, emerges from a different cosmos and will be
considered here partly in its interlocking relationship with Coleridge's
"Dejection: An Ode" and also as a crisis lyric. "Intimations of Immortality from Recollections of Early Childhood" was composed from
1802 to 1804. A year later gave Wordsworth a simpler masterpiece,
"The Solitary Reaper":

> Behold her, single in the field,
> Yon solitary Highland Lass!
> Reaping and singing by herself;
> Stop here, or gently pass!
> Alone she cuts and binds the grain,
> And sings a melancholy strain;
> O listen! for the Vale profound
> Is overflowing with the sound.
>
> No Nightingale did ever chaunt
> More welcome notes to weary bands
> Of travellers in some shady haunt,
> Among Arabian sands:
> A voice so thrilling ne'er was heard
> In spring-time from the Cuckoo-bird,
> Breaking the silence of the seas
> Among the farthest Hebrides.
>
> Will no one tell me what she sings?—
> Perhaps the plaintive numbers flow

For old, unhappy, far-off things,
And battles long ago:
Or is it some more humble lay,
Familiar matter of today?
Some natural sorrow, loss, or pain,
That has been, and may be again?

Whate'er the theme, the Maiden sang
As if her song could have no ending;
I saw her singing at her work,
And o'er the sickle bending:—
I listened, motionless and still;
And, as I mounted up the hill,
The music in my heart I bore,
Long after it was heard no more.

An unpublished travel book by the poet's friend Thomas Wilkinson contains a sentence Wordsworth appropriated: "Passed a female who was reaping alone: she sung in Erse as she bended over her sickle; the sweetest human voice I ever heard: her strains were tenderly melancholy, and felt delicious, long after they were heard no more." Wordsworth's imagination is stimulated to a wild surmise because he does not know the language in which the Highland girl sings. I cannot recite "The Solitary Reaper" without recalling "The Idea of Order at Key West," in which Wallace Stevens hears from a distance another singing girl, walking the beach at Key West. He knows neither the language nor the burden of her song, only that she was the maker and the sea and sky were subordinate. She strides purposefully and raises her voice to assert her own power over the universe of death.

The solitary reaper evidently sings a work song sometimes called "mouth music" among the Scots, and it seems to be cyclic and so never ending. What matters most is that Wordsworth possesses a music in his heart long after this exquisite moment has departed. Wallace Stevens, remembering this, concludes his Key West ode in that spirit:

Ramon Fernandez, tell me, if you know,
Why, when the singing ended and we turned
Toward the town, tell why the glassy lights,

The lights in the fishing boats at anchor there,
As night descended, tilting in the air,
Mastered the night and portioned out the sea,
Fixing emblazoned zones and fiery poles,
Arranging, deepening, enchanting night.

Oh! Blessed rage for order, pale Ramon,
The maker's rage to order words of the sea,
Words of the fragrant portals, dimly-starred,
And of ourselves and of our origins,
In ghostlier demarcations, keener sounds.

The singing is past, but an aura descends on the harbor and converts it to an enchantment that endures though only waningly. Wordsworth's myth of memory is stronger than Stevens finds to be possible. When I turn "The Idea of Order at Key West" over in my memory, I recall first what Stevens too insistently argues against: the inhuman voice of the sea. The extent to which the poetic mind is lord and master, with outward sense the servant of its will, is in Stevens far more questionable than it is in Wordsworth, at least during the earlier poet's great decade, 1797–1807.

# William Wordsworth,
## "Ode: Intimations of Immortality from Recollections of Early Childhood"

W HEN I THINK ABOUT, recite, or teach Wordsworth's "Ode: Intimations of Immortality from Recollections of Early Childhood," my mind turns first to his own commentary on the poem:

This was composed during my residence at Town-end, Grasmere. Two years at least passed between the writing of the four first stanzas and the remaining part. To the attentive and competent reader the whole sufficiently explains itself; but there may be no harm in adverting here to particular feelings or *experiences* of my own mind on which the structure of the poem partly rests. Nothing was more difficult for me in childhood than to admit the notion of death as a state applicable to my own being. I have said elsewhere—

"A simple child,
That lightly draws its breath,
And feels its life in every limb,
What should it know of death!"—

But it was not so much from feelings of animal vivacity that *my* difficulty came as from a sense of the indomitableness of the Spirit within me. I used to brood over the stories of Enoch and Elijah, and almost to persuade myself that, whatever might become of others, I should be translated, in something of the same way, to heaven. With a feeling congenial to this, I was often unable to think of external things as having external existence, and I communed with all that I saw as something not apart from, but inherent in, my own immaterial nature. Many times while going to school have I grasped at a wall or tree to recall myself from this abyss of idealism to the reality. At that time I was afraid of such processes. In later periods of life I have deplored, as we have all reason to do, a subjugation of an opposite character, and have rejoiced over the remembrances, as is expressed in the lines—

"Obstinate questionings
Of sense and outward things,
Fallings from us, vanishings;" &c.

To that dream-like vividness and splendour which invest objects of sight in childhood, every one, I believe, if he would look back, could bear testimony, and I need not dwell upon it here: but having in the Poem regarded it as presumptive evidence of a prior state of existence, I think it right to protest against a conclusion, which has given pain to some good and pious persons, that I meant to inculcate such a belief. It is far too shadowy a notion to be recommended to faith, as more than an element in our instincts of immortality. But let us bear in mind that, though the idea is not advanced in revelation, there is nothing there to contradict it, and the fall of Man presents an analogy in its favour. Accordingly, a pre-existent state has entered into the popular creeds of many nations; and, among all persons acquainted with classic literature, is known as an ingredient in Platonic philosophy. Archimedes said that he could move the world if he had a point whereon to rest his machine. Who has not felt the same aspirations as regards the world of his own mind? Having to wield some of its elements when I was impelled to write this Poem on the "Immortality of the soul," I took hold of the notion of pre-existence as having sufficient foundation in humanity for authorising me to make for my purpose the best use of it I could as a Poet.

After Milton's *Lycidas*, the "Intimations" ode is the prime shorter poem in the English language. The Great Ode's influence can be traced in Coleridge, Shelley, Byron, Keats, John Clare, Tennyson, Robert Browning, Arnold, Hopkins, Meredith, Swinburne, and Yeats, and in American poetry it vitalized a tradition that goes from Emerson through Whitman and Dickinson on to Frost, Wallace Stevens, Hart

Crane, A. R. Ammons, and John Ashbery. "Intimations" is a poem of deeply painful loss and problematic gain. The title is a misnomer, since to me this is a poem concerning mortality and the necessity of making friends with it. Wordsworth refused all suggestions that the ode was Platonic, though its sole intimation of immortality is in the vision of lines 162–68:

> Hence in a season of calm weather
> Though inland far we be,
> Our Souls have sight of that immortal sea
> Which brought us hither,
> Can in a moment travel thither,
> And see the Children sport upon the shore,
> And hear the mighty waters rolling evermore.

Freud ironically named this longing for origins "the oceanic sense." Wordsworth is anything but ironic as his epigraph to the ode quotes the last three lines of his brief lyric "My Heart Leaps Up":

> My heart leaps up when I behold
>    A rainbow in the sky:
> So was it when my life began;
> So is it now I am a man;
> So be it when I shall grow old,
>    Or let me die!
> The Child is father of the Man;
> And I could wish my days to be
> Bound each to each by natural piety.

Directly after those lines in the epigraph he places:

PAULO MAJORA CANAMUS

This invocation of the Sicilian Muses who inspire Pastoral is the opening of Virgil's "Fourth Eclogue": "Let us sing of somewhat more exalted things." Wordsworth wants us to recall Milton's deliberate allusion to this phrase in line 37 of *Lycidas:* "Begin, and somewhat loudly sweep the string." Unlike Virgil and Milton, Wordsworth gives us the first of his eleven stanzas in a key of natural loss:

I

There was a time when meadow, grove, and stream,
The earth, and every common sight,
  To me did seem
  Apparelled in celestial light,
The glory and the freshness of a dream.
It is not now as it hath been of yore;—
  Turn wheresoe'er I may,
   By night or day,
The things which I have seen I now can see no more.

"Common" is for Wordsworth a term of honor. The garment of
celestial light is no longer visible, and the poet struggles initially to
reassure himself that his powers of perception are undiminished:

II

  The Rainbow comes and goes,
  And lovely is the Rose,
  The Moon doth with delight
Look round her when the heavens are bare,
  Waters on a starry night
  Are beautiful and fair;
 The sunshine is a glorious birth;
 But yet I know, where'er I go,
That there hath past away a glory from the earth.

The use of the present tense at last yields to the further realization
of a departed splendor:

III

Now, while the birds thus sing a joyous song,
  And while the young lambs bound
  As to the tabor's sound,
To me alone there came a thought of grief:

A timely utterance gave that thought relief,
   And I again am strong:
The cataracts blow their trumpets from the steep;
No more shall grief of mine the season wrong;
I hear the Echoes through the mountains throng,
The Winds come to me from the fields of sleep,
   And all the earth is gay;
    Land and sea
  Give themselves up to jollity,
   And with the heart of May
 Doth every Beast keep holiday;—
   Thou Child of Joy,
Shout round me, let me hear thy shouts, thou happy
 Shepherd-boy!

The "timely utterance" may have been "My Heart Leaps Up," or even "Resolution and Independence"; the poet nevertheless protests too strongly his revived inspiration. The wonderful fourth stanza reminds him of his crisis:

IV

Ye blesséd Creatures, I have heard the call
   Ye to each other make; I see
The heavens laugh with you in your jubilee;
   My heart is at your festival,
    My head hath its coronal,
The fulness of your bliss, I feel—I feel it all.
   Oh evil day! if I were sullen
   While Earth herself is adorning,
    This sweet May-morning,
   And the Children are culling
    On every side,
   In a thousand valleys far and wide,
   Fresh flowers; while the sun shines warm,
And the Babe leaps up on his Mother's arm:—
   I hear, I hear, with joy I hear!
   —But there's a Tree, of many, one,

> A single Field which I have looked upon,
> Both of them speak of something that is gone:
>> The Pansy at my feet
>> Doth the same tale repeat:
> Whither is fled the visionary gleam?
> Where is it now, the glory and the dream?

The coronal, a pastoral garland, is prematurely claimed. The repetition of "feel" is a symptom of desperation and Wordsworth goes on to a sense of the Dantesan danger of being sullen in the sweet air. A mounting sorrow is heard in the triple repetition of "I hear, I hear, with joy I hear!" William Blake told Crabb Robinson how profoundly he was moved by the five lines beginning, "—But there's a tree, of many, one. . . ." Suddenly struck by the sight of a particular tree he had long admired, Wordsworth's eye moves to a familiar single Field and then down to the Pansy and his feet. All of them testify to bereftness: "Whither is fled the visionary gleam?/Where is it now, the glory and the dream?"

There the ode was abandoned for more than two years. When he began again, Wordsworth presented alternative resolutions in stanzas V–VIII and then in IX–XI:

V

> Our birth is but a sleep and a forgetting:
> The Soul that rises with us, our life's Star,
>> Hath had elsewhere its setting,
>> And cometh from afar:
> Not in entire forgetfulness,
> And not in utter nakedness,
> But trailing clouds of glory do we come
>> From God, who is our home:
> Heaven lies about us in our infancy!
> Shades of the prison-house begin to close
>> Upon the growing Boy,
> But He beholds the light, and whence it flows,
>> He sees it in his joy;

The Youth, who daily farther from the east
      Must travel, still is Nature's Priest,
      And by the vision splendid
      Is on his way attended;
At length the Man perceives it die away,
And fade into the light of common day.

The "life's Star" is not astrological but seems a recondite metaphor for the sun. This enigmatic strophe offers little hope, nor does the next:

VI

Earth fills her lap with pleasures of her own;
Yearnings she hath in her own natural kind,
And, even with something of a Mother's mind,
      And no unworthy aim,
      The homely Nurse doth all she can
To make her Foster-child, her Inmate Man,
      Forget the glories he hath known,
And that imperial palace whence he came.

Contemplating Coleridge's son Hartley, who came to rely on Wordsworth as a second father, the poet again laments the loss of a higher vocation to the sorrow of endless imitation, without which we cannot grow up. The culmination of this entropy attains a nadir in the closing image of stanza VIII:

Thou, whose exterior semblance doth belie
      Thy Soul's immensity;
Thou best Philosopher, who yet dost keep
Thy heritage, thou Eye among the blind,
That, deaf and silent, read'st the eternal deep,
Haunted for ever by the eternal mind,—
      Mighty Prophet! Seer blest!
      On whom those truths do rest,
Which we are toiling all our lives to find,
In darkness lost, the darkness of the grave;

Thou, over whom thy Immortality
Broods like the Day, a Master o'er a Slave,
A Presence which is not to be put by;
      To whom the grave
Is but a lonely bed, without the sense of sight
      Of day or the warm light,
A place of thought where we in waiting lie;
Thou little Child, yet glorious in the might
Of heaven-born freedom on thy being's height,
Why with such earnest pains dost thou provoke
The years to bring the inevitable yoke,
Thus blindly with thy blessedness at strife?
Full soon thy Soul shall have her earthly freight,
And custom lie upon thee with a weight,
Heavy as frost, and deep almost as life!

Coleridge disapproved of the four remarkable lines starting with "To whom the grave," and Wordsworth unfortunately deleted them in some of the published versions of the ode. They contrast forcefully with the heft of frost weighing down the child's soul and the problematic "deep almost as life!" Suddenly the ninth strophe erupts:

      O joy! that in our embers
      Is something that doth live,
      That nature yet remembers
      What was so fugitive!
The thought of our past years in me doth breed
Perpetual benediction: not indeed
For that which is most worthy to be blest;
Delight and liberty, the simple creed
Of Childhood, whether busy or at rest,
With new-fledged hope still fluttering in his breast:—
      Not for these I raise
      The song of thanks and praise;
    But for those obstinate questionings
    Of sense and outward things,
    Fallings from us, vanishings;
    Blank misgivings of a Creature
Moving about in worlds not realised,

High instincts before which our mortal Nature
Did tremble like a guilty Thing surprised:
        But for those first affections,
        Those shadowy recollections,
     Which, be they what they may,
Are yet the fountain light of all our day,
Are yet a master light of all our seeing;
       Uphold us, cherish, and have power to make
Our noisy years seem moments in the being
Of the eternal Silence: truths that wake,
        To perish never:
Which neither listlessness, nor mad endeavour,
       Nor Man nor Boy,
Nor all that is at enmity with joy,
Can utterly abolish or destroy!
        Hence, in a season of calm weather
        Though inland far we be,
Our Souls have sight of that immortal sea
        Which brought us hither,
      Can in a moment travel thither,
And see the Children sport upon the shore,
And hear the mighty waters rolling evermore.

The embers probably suggested to Shelley the extinguished hearth from which the ashes and sparks of his words scatter among mankind in his invocation of the West Wind. Wordsworth, his revolutionary phase gone by, raises a song of thanks and praise for the child's resistance, both to the division of his senses each from each, and to an outward-ness that marks his limits. Even as hearing and seeing separate and an external world imposes itself, the child turns to his first affections for parents, siblings, and friends. Far inland, if the season be calm, we see the ocean of immortality, rapidly go there, and see ourselves as children sporting upon the beach. Will this suffice:

X

Then sing, ye Birds, sing, sing a joyous song!
      And let the young Lambs bound

As to the tabor's sound!
We in thought will join your throng,
        Ye that pipe and ye that play,
        Ye that through your hearts to-day
        Feel the gladness of the May!
What though the radiance which was once so bright
Be now for ever taken from my sight,
        Though nothing can bring back the hour
Of splendour in the grass, of glory in the flower;
        We will grieve not, rather find
        Strength in what remains behind;
        In the primal sympathy
        Which having been must ever be;
        In the soothing thoughts that spring
        Out of human suffering;
        In the faith that looks through death,
In years that bring the philosophic mind.

This persuades through its honest admission that nothing ever can bring back the visionary gleam. Recompense must be found in sympathy with the suffering of others and in the calm of mind that accepts yet somehow sees through death. Though I am moved, I doubt this resolution, and fortunately the final strophe is richer:

And O, ye Fountains, Meadows, Hills, and Groves,
Forebode not any severing of our loves!
Yet in my heart of hearts I feel your might;
I only have relinquished one delight
To live beneath your more habitual sway.
I love the Brooks which down their channels fret,
Even more than when I tripped lightly as they;
The innocent brightness of a new-born Day
        Is lovely yet;
The Clouds that gather round the setting sun
Do take a sober colouring from an eye
That hath kept watch o'er man's mortality;
Another race hath been, and other palms are won.
Thanks to the human heart by which we live,

Thanks to its tenderness, its joys, and fears,
To me the meanest flower that blows can give
Thoughts that do often lie too deep for tears.

I do not know that the contests of maturity award equal palms to
those won in the agon of youth. Wordsworth greatly hoped, and who
desires to quarrel with hope? Thoughts too deep for tears are beyond
lamentation. The beautiful suggestion may be that joy finally is deeper
than sorrow.

# Samuel Taylor Coleridge,
## "The Rime of the Ancient Mariner"

Samuel taylor coleridge's "The Rime of the Ancient Mariner" was first published in Wordsworth's *Lyrical Ballads:* a leap from that ecstasy of an aged thrush to the grotesque image of a murdered albatross hung round a mariner's neck. The poem was revised, with marginal glosses added, in 1816. The celebrated Bluestocking Mrs. Anna Laetitia Barbauld, now a feminist heroine, objected to Coleridge that his poem had no moral. He replied firmly that moral sentiment had no place in a work of pure imagination: "It ought to have had no more moral than the Arabian Nights' tale of the merchant's sitting down to eat dates by the side of the well and throwing the shells aside, and lo! a genie starts up and says he *must* kill the aforesaid merchant *because* one of the date shells had, it seems, put out the eye of the genie's son."

In the traditions of Cain and the Wandering Jew Ahasuerus, the Ancient Mariner is condemned to do penance eternally, passing like night from land to land. The epigraph to the "Rime" is from Thomas Burnet, a seventeenth-century English churchman, and is taken from his *The Sacred Theory of the Earth*. Burnet asks who will tell us the families of the invisible creatures who crowd the cosmos. Coleridge, who is haunted by the image of the daemon, invokes the invisible spirits of earth, both angelic and deathly, and in particular the daemon he calls the Polar Spirit, who loved the albatross.

The most beautiful of the marginal glosses accompanies a vision of moonrise:

> The moving Moon went up the sky,
> And no where did abide:
> Softly she was going up,
> And a star or two beside—

Her beams bemocked the sultry main,
Like April hoar-frost spread;
But where the ship's huge shadow lay,
The charmèd water burnt alway
A still and awful red.

Lines 263–71

The gloss transcends even this eloquent precision:

In his loneliness and fixedness he yearneth towards the journeying
Moon, and the stars that still sojourn, yet still move onward; and
every where the blue sky belongs to them, and is their appointed
rest, and their native country and their own natural homes, which
they enter unannounced, as lords that are certainly expected and
yet there is a silent joy at their arrival.

Coleridge stations this directly before the partial release of the
Ancient Mariner from the curse in the eyes of his dead shipmates:

Beyond the shadow of the ship,
I watched the water-snakes:
They moved in tracks of shining white,
And when they reared, the elfish light
Fell off in hoary flakes.

Within the shadow of the ship
I watched their rich attire:
Blue, glossy green, and velvet black,
They coiled and swam; and every track
Was a flash of golden fire.

O happy living things! no tongue
Their beauty might declare:
A spring of love gushed from my heart,
And I blessed them unaware:
Sure my kind saint took pity on me,
And I blessed them unaware.

The self-same moment I could pray;
And from my neck so free
The Albatross fell off, and sank
Like lead into the sea.

Lines 272–91

The bodies of the dead men are inspirited, and the ship moves on. In the midst of the night, I am haunted too often by one stanza:

The body of my brother's son
Stood by me, knee to knee:
The body and I pulled at one rope,
But he said nought to me.

Lines 341–44

The Polar Spirit, who loved the Albatross, sets a perpetual penance for the Mariner, who is caught in an endless cycle of journeying and telling over and over his own story:

Since then, at an uncertain hour,
That agony returns:
And till my ghastly tale is told,
This heart within me burns.

I pass, like night, from land to land;
I have strange power of speech;
That moment that his face I see,
I know the man that must hear me:
To him my tale I teach.

Lines 582–90

Cain, the Flying Dutchman, the Wandering Jew experience unlimited movement to no coherent end. Is the Ancient Mariner also condemned to meaninglessness? The poem's glory refutes that question. William Blake's "The Mental Traveller," despite its mordant intensities, is purely cyclic: "And all is done as I have told." There is nothing acerbic in Coleridge's temperament. A sweetness emanates, even when the poem verges upon the grisly:

Are those *her* ribs through which the Sun
Did peer, as through a grate?
And is that Woman all her crew?
Is that a DEATH? and are there two?
Is DEATH that woman's mate?

*Her* lips were red, *her* looks were free,
Her locks were yellow as gold:
Her skin was as white as leprosy,
The Night-mare LIFE-IN-DEATH was she,
Who thicks man's blood with cold.

The naked hulk alongside came,
And the twain were casting dice;
'The game is done! I've won! I've won!'
Quoth she, and whistles thrice.

The Sun's rim dips; the stars rush out:
At one stride comes the dark;
With far-heard whisper, o'er the sea,
Off shot the spectre-bark.

Lines 185–202

After three nightmarish stanzas, horridly memorable, Coleridge recuperates by banishing the terror. William Wordsworth disliked and rather resented "The Rime of the Ancient Mariner," probably because he was egocentric, yet more profoundly since it disturbed his sense of a sacramental covenant between nature and the poet. Coleridge possessed capacious intellect and maintained a subtle opening to daemonic powers that his theological orientation feared. The "Ancient Mariner" is not so much a poem of pure imagination as it is an extraordinary daemonic influx into Coleridge's Shaping Spirit.

# Percy Bysshe Shelley,
## "Ode to the West Wind"

W ALLACE STEVENS mentions only two poets in his own verse: Walt Whitman and Shelley. Though he knew other poems by the revolutionary High Romantic, he manifests a perpetual indebtedness to Shelley's "Ode to the West Wind." At the very beginning of the autumn of 1819, Shelley stands in a wood near the Arno River, close to Florence, and at sunset is caught in a violent burst of hail and rain, and what he calls "that magnificent thunder and lightning peculiar to the Cisalpine regions."

I

O wild West Wind, thou breath of Autumn's being,
Thou, from whose unseen presence the leaves dead
Are driven, like ghosts from an enchanter fleeing,

Yellow, and black, and pale, and hectic red,
Pestilence-stricken multitudes: O thou,
Who chariotest to their dark wintry bed

The wingèd seeds, where they lie cold and low,
Each like a corpse within its grave, until
Thine azure sister of the Spring shall blow

Her clarion o'er the dreaming earth, and fill
(Driving sweet buds like flocks to feed in air)
With living hues and odours plain and hill:

Wild Spirit, which art moving everywhere;
Destroyer and preserver; hear, oh, hear!

The dead leaves whirled along by the wind take on an apocalyptic tonality as they flee like ghosts from an exorciser. As I write, multitudes of Syrians are being driven to desperate exile, and they too suggest an end to a bad time, only to bring on a worse one. What Shelley actually sees are the dead leaves of autumn multicolored to no purpose, and yet his imagination is prophetic. The West Wind is hailed as a chariot in the tradition that goes from Elijah through Dante to Milton and William Blake, only to find a final parody in Shelley's death poem "The Triumph of Life." Astonishingly, the poet has a vision of wingèd seeds that will rise each from its grave when the Spring wind blows her clarion and calls the earth to resurrection. The Wild Spirit that is the West Wind thus both destroys and preserves. Shelley ends each of the first three terza-rima sonnets of his ode with the plea to be heard by the Spirit.

It is in the fourth sonnet that the prophet turns to his own personal dilemma:

IV

If I were a dead leaf thou mightest bear;
If I were a swift cloud to fly with thee;
A wave to pant beneath thy power, and share

The impulse of thy strength, only less free
Than thou, O Uncontrollable! If even
I were as in my boyhood, and could be

The comrade of thy wanderings over Heaven,
As then, when to outstrip thy skiey speed
Scarce seemed a vision; I would ne'er have striven

As thus with thee in prayer in my sore need.
Oh! lift me as a wave, a leaf, a cloud!
I fall upon the thorns of life! I bleed!

A heavy weight of hours has chained and bowed
One too like thee: tameless, and swift, and proud.

Striving in what he is now willing to call a prayer, he implores, though knowing that he is no part of nature and, like Job, has fallen into the iniquity of abandonment by the Divine. And yet he proclaims his untamed pride and that swiftness of which he once remarked, "I go on until I am stopped and I never am stopped." From this refusal to submit or yield there rises the magnificence of the final sonnet:

V

Make me thy lyre, even as the forest is:
What if my leaves are falling like its own!
The tumult of thy mighty harmonies

Will take from both a deep, autumnal tone,
Sweet though in sadness. Be thou, Spirit fierce,
My spirit! Be thou me, impetuous one!

Drive my dead thoughts over the universe
Like withered leaves to quicken a new birth!
And, by the incantation of this verse,

Scatter, as from an unextinguished hearth
Ashes and sparks, my words among mankind!
Be through my lips to unawakened Earth

The trumpet of a prophecy! O Wind,
If Winter comes, can Spring be far behind?

When teaching this poem, I try to emphasize the subtle interplay between "thy," "my," "thou," and "me." Shelley urges that he be a wind harp, like the forest, and with immense poignance defiantly cries out, "What if my leaves are falling like its own!" Tumult resolves into harmony, as much Shelley's as nature's "deep, autumnal tone" glances at Wordsworthian consolation. But there is nothing Wordsworthian about the high Pindaric apotheosis of "Be thou, Spirit fierce, / My spirit!" Wallace Stevens will ironize "Be thou me" in his "Notes Toward a Supreme Fiction," yet in admiration and not rejection.

Terrible sleeper as I am, I lie awake and chant to myself the concluding eight lines of Shelley's ode. Shelley's thoughts, scarcely dead, quicken a new birth, and with a justified sense of glory he becomes a *nabi* proclaiming the power to be gained by the reader through incanting the ode. The burning fountain of his own spirit is the unextinguished hearth that scatters sparks as well as ashes among mankind. There is a magic in the great assertion:

Be through my lips to unawakened Earth

. . . . . . . . . . . . .

The trumpet of a prophecy!

So indeed the ode has proved to be. At the close, Shelley asks an open question in the mode of the rhetorical questions that come at Job out of the whirlwind:

O Wind,
If Winter comes, can Spring be far behind?

A long winter is coming. Shelley places it in the reader's own spirit as to how soon there will be spring.

# Percy Bysshe Shelley, "To a Skylark"

A YEAR AFTER WRITING "Ode to the West Wind," Shelley composed "To a Skylark," a plangent farewell to his earlier sense that as a poet he could be the prophet of a Power concealed behind Nature. The reader should begin with the realization that the skylark is unseen when the poem begins. His flight is too high for visibility, and his song is just barely audible. Like Keats, Shelley also stresses his estrangement from the joy of the song, and conveys an ecstasy he knows he can no longer share:

> Hail to thee, blithe Spirit!
> Bird thou never wert,
> That from Heaven, or near it,
> Pourest thy full heart
> In profuse strains of unpremeditated art.
>
> Higher still and higher
> From the earth thou springest
> Like a cloud of fire;
> The blue deep thou wingest,
> And singing still dost soar, and soaring ever singest.
>
> In the golden lightning
> Of the sunken sun,
> O'er which clouds are brightning,
> Thou dost float and run;
> Like an unbodied joy whose race is just begun.

The pale purple even
     Melts around thy flight;
Like a star of Heaven,
     In the broad daylight
Thou art unseen, but yet I hear thy shrill delight,

Keen as are the arrows
     Of that silver sphere,
Whose intense lamp narrows
     In the white dawn clear
Until we hardly see—we feel that it is there.

All the earth and air
     With thy voice is loud,
As when night is bare
     From one lonely cloud
The moon rains out her beams, and Heaven is overflowed.

What thou art we know not;
     What is most like thee?
From rainbow clouds there flow not
     Drops so bright to see
As from thy presence showers a rain of melody.

Lines 1–35

Shelley was an intellectual skeptic, more in the mode of the Roman poet Lucretius than that of David Hume, but he was highly conscious that head and heart diverged in his vision. His life and his poetry alike pulsated with a drive beyond all limits, and speed is the particular mark of his remorseless intensity. Yet he longed for the extraordinary and transcendental, and evolved an Orphic religion very much his own. His skylark is compared to "an unbodied joy whose race is just begun."

The fourth and fifth stanzas of "To a Skylark" center on the silver sphere of the morning star. Shelley goes on to seek similitudes more for the song than for the bird:

What thou art we know not;
     What is most like thee?

From rainbow clouds there flow not
    Drops so bright to see
As from thy presence showers a rain of melody.


Like a Poet hidden
    In the light of thought,
Singing hymns unbidden,
    Till the world is wrought
To sympathy with hopes and fears it heeded not:


Like a high-born maiden
    In a palace-tower,
Soothing her love-laden
    Soul in secret hour
With music sweet as love, which overflows her bower:


Like a glow-worm golden
    In a dell of dew,
Scattering unbeholden
    Its aereal hue
Among the flowers and grass which screen it from the view:


Like a rose embowered
    In its own green leaves,
By warm winds deflowered,
    Till the scent it gives
Makes faint with too much sweet those heavy-wingèd thieves:


Sound of vernal showers
    On the twinkling grass,
Rain-awakened flowers,
    All that ever was
Joyous, and clear, and fresh, thy music doth surpass.

Lines 31–60


Poet, maiden in a tower, golden glow-worm, rose, and vernal showers as similes for the skylark's song are knowingly inadequate though

subtly suggestive. Confronting this imagistic impasse, Shelley mounts
higher in a Pindaric pride of his own triumphal chant:

> Teach us, Sprite or Bird,
>     What sweet thoughts are thine:
> I have never heard
>     Praise of love or wine
> That panted forth a flood of rapture so divine.
>
> Chorus Hymeneal,
>     Or triumphal chant,
> Matched with thine would be all
>     But an empty vaunt,
> A thing wherein we feel there is some hidden want.
>
> What objects are the fountains
>     Of thy happy strain?
> What fields, or waves, or mountains?
>     What shapes of sky or plain?
> What love of thine own kind? what ignorance of pain?
>
> With thy clear keen joyance
>     Languor cannot be:
> Shadow of annoyance
>     Never came near thee:
> Thou lovest—but ne'er knew love's sad satiety.
>
> Waking or asleep,
>     Thou of death must deem
> Things more true and deep
>     Than we mortals dream,
> Or how could thy notes flow in such a crystal stream?

Lines 61–85

The hidden lack of the poet boldly attempting to sustain a cognate
joy is openly confessed by Shelley, whose erotic idealism invariably
ended in sad satiety. It is a sudden leap that ascribes to the song a more

profound and veracious apprehension of death than any we dream. Lancing into the unknown, Shelley concludes his ode with the only prayer possible for him:

> We look before and after,
>     And pine for what is not:
> Our sincerest laughter
>     With some pain is fraught;
> Our sweetest songs are those that tell of saddest thought.
>
> Yet if we could scorn
>     Hate, and pride, and fear;
> If we were things born
>     Not to shed a tear,
> I know not how thy joy we ever should come near.
>
> Better than all measures
>     Of delightful sound,
> Better than all treasures
>     That in books are found,
> Thy skill to poet were, thou scorner of the ground!
>
> Teach me half the gladness
>     That thy brain must know,
> Such harmonious madness
>     From my lips would flow,
> The world should listen then—as I am listening now.

Lines 86–105

The burden of Shelley's *Prometheus Unbound*, his lyrical drama written in 1818–19, was best expressed by my revered mentor Frederick Albert Pottle: "The head must sincerely forgive, must willingly eschew hatred on purely experimental grounds," while the heart "must exorcize the demons of infancy." Shelley, revolutionary agitator though he was, had something angelic in his complex nature. His best friend, Byron, said of him, after his death by drowning at the age of twenty-nine, that everyone else he knew seemed a beast compared with Shelley. Bitter in his judgments, Byron relented only in regard to Shelley, who returned his affection and esteem. Scorn, hatred, and fear were alien to Shelley, fierce as he could be toward the oppressors of mankind. "To a Skylark" is one of the testaments to Shelley's emancipation from the clogs that weigh most of us down.

## Percy Bysshe Shelley,
### *Prometheus Unbound*

ACT II OF *Prometheus Unbound* concludes with two transcendent lyrics, the first addressed to Asia, the bride of Prometheus, the second her own chant of transfiguration. In my interpretation, Asia is a kind of Wordsworthian image of human strength that remains provisional, since she participates in the beauty and love that hover perpetually just beyond the natural world and our limited senses. The Voice in the Air attempts to image her moment-of-moments, in which she becomes the heavenly Venus, but her transmembered form is imageless, and so the Voice fails in a luminous vertigo:

Life of Life! thy lips enkindle
    With their love the breath between them;
And thy smiles before they dwindle
    Make the cold air fire; then screen them
In those looks, where whoso gazes
Faints, entangled in their mazes.

Child of Light! thy limbs are burning
    Through the vest which seems to hide them;
As the radiant lines of morning
    Through the clouds ere they divide them;
And this atmosphere divinest
Shrouds thee wheresoe'er thou shinest.

Fair are others; none beholds thee,
    But thy voice sounds low and tender
Like the fairest, for it folds thee

From the sight, that liquid splendour,
And all feel, yet see thee never,
As I feel now, lost forever!

Lamp of Earth! where'er thou movest
    Its dim shapes are clad with brightness,
And the souls of whom thou lovest
    Walk upon the winds with lightness,
Till they fail, as I am failing,
Dizzy, lost, yet unbewailing!

Lines 48–71

The art of this severe lyric turns on what cannot be held steadily in focus. Asia's breath fires the cold air, and her limbs burn through the fleshly covering that cannot hide conflagration, even as daybreak lights up the atmosphere with another revelation that yet puts on another veil. You can feel transmuted splendor but cannot see it. Lost in that powerlessness, you nevertheless see the earth and every common sight clad in a celestial aura. Lightened by that love to that high imagination, your will fails but with rejoicing.

Asia's reply is my favorite among all of Shelley's lyrics, partly because of its fecundity in his inheritors, from Beddoes and Browning through Swinburne and Yeats on to Hardy, Stevens, and Hart Crane, whose "Voyages" sequence stems directly from this:

    My soul is an enchanted Boat,
    Which, like a sleeping swan, doth float
Upon the silver waves of thy sweet singing;
    And thine doth like an Angel sit
    Beside the helm conducting it,
Whilst all the winds with melody are ringing.
    It seems to float ever—forever—
    Upon that many-winding River,
    Between mountains, woods, abysses,
    A Paradise of wildernesses!
Till, like one in slumber bound,
Borne to the Ocean, I float down, around,
Into a Sea profound, of ever-spreading sound:

Meanwhile thy Spirit lifts its pinions
  In Music's most serene dominions,
Catching the winds that fan that happy Heaven.
  And we sail on, away, afar,
  Without a course—without a star—
But, by the instinct of sweet Music driven;
   Till through Elysian garden islets,
   By thee, most beautiful of pilots,
   Where never mortal pinnace glided,
   The boat of my desire is guided—
Realms where the air we breathe is Love,
Which in the winds and on the waves doth move,
Harmonizing this Earth with what we feel above.

   We have passed Age's icy caves,
   And Manhood's dark and tossing waves,
And Youth's smooth ocean, smiling to betray;
   Beyond the glassy gulfs we flee
   Of shadow-peopled Infancy,
Through Death and Birth, to a diviner day,
   A paradise of vaulted bowers,
   Lit by downward-gazing flowers,
   And watery paths that wind between
   Wildernesses calm and green,
Peopled by shapes too bright to see,
And rest, having beheld—somewhat like thee;
Which walk upon the sea, and chant melodiously!

           Lines 73–110

Yeats in his "Nineteen Hundred and Nineteen" begins part III with a clear allusion to Asia's song:

Some moralist or mythological poet
Compares the solitary soul to a swan;
I am satisfied with that,
Satisfied if a troubled mirror show it,
Before that brief gleam of its life be gone,
An image of its state;

The wings half spread for flight,
The breast thrust out in pride
Whether to play, or to ride
Those winds that clamour of approaching night.

The swerve away from Shelley here is characteristic of Yeats, since Asia's soul is scarcely transitory. Singing is the impetus that kindles Asia's voyage to the deep ocean of perpetual tonal enhancement. Hart Crane followed Plato and Shelley in his credence that music pertained to love in harmony and system. Asia, seeking Prometheus, sails to an unchartered Elysia where no mortal pinnace ever preceded her. "The boat of my desire is guided" becomes in Hart Crane:

Hasten, while they are true,—sleep, death, desire,
Close round one instant in one floating flower.

"Voyages," II

Asia, however, moves through death and birth to a diviner day as her apotheosis returns her to a divine infancy: akin to John Bunyan's "the Shining Ones" and Blake's children of what he calls Beulah, the married land, and most clearly Wordsworth's children on the shore in the "Intimations" ode. These are Asia's "shapes too bright to see" in a primal paradise. In an oblique reference not so much to the Christ of the churches as to the Jesus Shelley accepted as an exemplary sufferer, Asia has her own revelation of those who can walk upon the sea.

# Lord Byron, *Don Juan*

To pass from Wordsworth and Coleridge to George Gordon, Lord Byron, is to take an immense leap from the two inventors of modern poetry to their self-nominated antagonist. Shelley, who lived in daily proximity to Byron during most of their Italian years, was an extraordinarily gifted literary critic and praised Byron's *Don Juan* as being superior even to Goethe and to Wordsworth. For Shelley it was the great poem of the age, whereas for William Hazlitt the poem's gusto or fierce vitalism was a mask for a total transvaluation of all values and their reduction to absolute nihilism.

Of all poets in the Western tradition, Byron, in his lifetime and beyond, was the most notorious. His celebrity could be calculated in our terms if somehow you could fuse Bobby Dylan, Elvis Presley, Mick Jagger, and Beyoncé into one composite form with William Butler Yeats and Tyrone Power, who contrived to look like a reincarnation of Byron in the remarkable film *Prince of Foxes* (also starring a superb Orson Welles as Cesare Borgia).

Everything about Byron was a paradox. He was a man of astonishing personal beauty and yet half lame and endlessly struggling against a tendency to grow fat. He fought against it by horrible spells in which he devoured only rotten greens washed down by a mixture of German white wine and soda water. Though his contemporaries and everyone since regarded him as the High Romantic proper, he despised Romanticism and vociferated that English poetry had scarcely survived the death of Alexander Pope. To this day a synonym for the Great Lover, he nevertheless was mostly passive toward women, sadomasochistic, sodomistic, and early disgusted with all sexual experience anyway.

Byron was a radical in English politics and argued in the House of

Lords against punishing the Luddites or "frame breakers," who were protesting losing their jobs to industrialization. He also demanded Catholic Emancipation, but to no avail at that time. In Italy he was an active revolutionary, yet was privately skeptical that either reform or revolution could do any good. Many in modern Greece worship him as the martyr-hero of the Greek revolution against the Turks, but he loathed the men he financed, trained, and led. He had hoped to die in battle, gallantly urging his patriotic mercenaries on to victory, but died at Missolonghi in April 1824 of a consuming fever.

Though he played at being free of religion, he was shocked by his closest friend Shelley's continuous polemic against Christianity, and secretly inclined toward Catholicism. Famous as an athlete and a champion swimmer, he had to force his sluggish body to keep up with his restless soul. His rakehell father died when the poet was three years old, and he was left with a bipolar mother, herself descended from the ancient royal family of Scotland, who entrusted him to a sadistic governess, who seduced and whipped him. At Trinity College, Cambridge, he experienced an intense homoerotic love affair, and continued with every variety of sexual experience in a Grand Tour of the Levant. His privately confessed motive was to indulge fully his homoerotic desires, though he also attempted to purchase a twelve-year-old girl for five hundred pounds and was chagrined when his offer was refused.

In 1812, Byron published the first two cantos of *Childe Harold's Pilgrimage* and became the darling of London Whig aristocracy. For five years, his social ascendency augmented, but his continued incest with his half-sister, Augusta Leigh, upon whom he fathered a daughter, Medora, and his endless passive surrenders to one noblewoman after another, made him seek a sanctuary in marrying Annabella Milbanke, an heiress passionately devoted to mathematics. He fathered a daughter, Ada, upon Annabella, but the marriage ended in exactly a year, for a multiplicity of causes, including his sodomistic demands upon his wife, his affairs with many actresses, his ongoing incest, and his tendency to fall into violent rages bordering on insanity.

Reviled by aristocratic society, the stormy poet abandoned England forever and began his close friendship with Shelley in the summer of 1816 near Lake Geneva. This extremely intricate relationship continued until Shelley's death by drowning on July 8, 1822, in the Gulf of La Spezia near Lerici. Of all literary friendships—and there have been so many, from ancient Alexandria through Renaissance Italy, France, and Britain, on to Hemingway and Scott Fitzgerald—the association of Byron and Shelley was unique in its human and poetic importance for both. During the six years they were together, they passed over 250 days in each other's company. They exchanged at least fifty letters, most of which I have read, and each read and criticized nearly everything the other composed until Shelley's death.

Shelley's effect upon Byron's poetry was largely beneficial. As Byron remarked, Shelley doused him with Wordsworth, which helped create the third canto of *Childe Harold's Pilgrimage*. But Byron became a kind of nightmare for Shelley. Though both were social pariahs in England, Byron was rich and famous and had a huge readership. Unlike Shelley, Byron essentially was conventional in modes of thought and feeling. Shelley, a superb skeptical intellect yet a transcendental visionary in matters of the heart, never fully apprehended how connected to tradition his difficult friend remained. At one point, the two men came close to fighting a duel that doubtless would have ended Shelley.

It is the fashion now among Byron's scholars to exalt him to equal status with Wordsworth as the great poet of his era. Though increasingly I read Byron with enormous pleasure and profit, I am puzzled by this evaluation. A lifelong brooder on the problems of poetic influence, I have learned that one ultimate canonical test for poetic magnitude is provided by the sublime progeny a poet engenders. By that test, Wordsworth, William Blake, Shelley, and John Keats can be awarded the palm over Byron. Each of them lived on in the cavalcade of Anglo-American poetry, from Tennyson and Browning through Whitman and Emily Dickinson on to Thomas Hardy, D. H. Lawrence, William Butler Yeats, Wallace Stevens, Robert Frost, T. S. Eliot, and Hart Crane. I can think only of early Auden as a poet who attempted to carry on Byron's legacy, with indifferent success.

Shelley's acute judgment, that Byron's *Don Juan* was the true poem of the age, is in some ways difficult to dispute. The dedication's continuous demolition of the bad poet Robert Southey is itself hilarious and turns poor Southey into a figure like James Joyce's Buck Mulligan in *Ulysses*. Mulligan in turn is a palpable portrait of Oliver St. John Gogarty: a medical doctor, Irish Free State politician, dubious poet, friend of Yeats, and later a denizen of Manhattan, where he supported himself by writing tedious memoirs and spent much of his time in bars,

drinking heavily. I myself several times sat with him and other roust-
abouts in the White Horse Tavern in the mid-1950s but learned to
avoid Gogarty, since his rancidity was unbounded.

Southey, a close friend of Wordsworth, Coleridge, and Landor, had
forsaken the revolutionary stance of his youth and became another
timeserver of the Tory persuasion. Byron's gusto is gargantuan in his
dedicatory assault upon the wretched Southey:

Bob Southey! You're a poet—Poet–laureate,
  And representative of all the race.
Although 'tis true that you turned out a Tory at
  Last—yours has lately been a common case;
And now, my Epic Renegade! what are ye at?
  With all the Lakers, in and out of place?
A nest of tuneful persons, to my eye
Like 'four and twenty blackbirds in a pye;

'Which pye being opened they began to sing,'
  (This old song and new simile holds good),
'A dainty dish to set before the King'
  Or Regent, who admires such kind of food;—
And Coleridge, too, has lately taken wing,
  But like a hawk encumbered with his hood—
Explaining Metaphysics to the nation—
I wish he would explain his Explanation.

You, Bob! are rather insolent, you know,
  At being disappointed in your wish
To supersede all warblers here below,
  And be the only Blackbird in the dish;
And then you overstrain yourself, or so,
  And tumble downward like the flying fish
Gasping on deck, because you soar too high, Bob,
And fall for lack of moisture, quite a-dry, Bob!

And Wordsworth, in a rather long "Excursion,"
  (I think the quarto holds five hundred pages)
Has given a sample from the vasty version

Of his new system to perplex the sages;
  'Tis poetry—at least by his assertion,
    And may appear so when the Dog–Star rages—
And he who understands it would be able
To add a story to the Tower of Babel.

You—Gentlemen! by dint of long seclusion
    From better company, have kept your own
At Keswick, and, through still continued fusion
    Of one another's minds, at last have grown
To deem as a most logical conclusion,
    That Poesy has wreaths for you alone:
There is a narrowness in such a notion,
Which makes me wish you'd change your lakes for Ocean.

I would not imitate the petty thought,
    Nor coin my self-love to so base a vice,
For all the glory your conversion brought,
    Since gold alone should not have been its price.
You have your salary; was 't for that you wrought?
    And Wordsworth has his place in the Excise.
You're shabby fellows—true—but poets still
And duly seated on the Immortal Hill.

The joy of Byron's satiric drive is infectious and allows us to accept his mistaken estimates of Wordsworth and Coleridge. In any case, he knew better and relied upon his intense surge of comedy to justify his prejudices. That verve is triumphant as he opens *Don Juan:*

I.

I want a hero: an uncommon want,
    When every year and month sends forth a new one,
Till, after cloying the gazettes with cant,
    The age discovers he is not the true one;
Of such as these I should not care to vaunt,
    I'll therefore take our ancient friend Don Juan—

We all have seen him, in the pantomime,
Sent to the Devil somewhat ere his time.


II.


Vernon, the butcher Cumberland, Wolfe, Hawke,
    Prince Ferdinand, Granby, Burgoyne, Keppel, Howe,
Evil and good, have had their tithe of talk,
    And filled their sign-posts then, like Wellesley now;
Each in their turn like Banquo's monarchs stalk,
    Followers of fame, "nine farrow" of that sow:
France, too, had Buonaparté and Dumourier
Recorded in the Moniteur and Courier.


III.


Barnave, Brissot, Condorcet, Mirabeau,
    Petion, Clootz, Danton, Marat, La Fayette
Were French, and famous people, as we know;
    And there were others, scarce forgotten yet,
Joubert, Hoche, Marceau, Lannes, Desaix, Moreau,
    With many of the military set,
Exceedingly remarkable at times,
But not at all adapted to my rhymes.


IV.


Nelson was once Britannia's god of War,
    And still should be so, but the tide is turn'd;
There's no more to be said of Trafalgar,
    'Tis with our hero quietly inurn'd;
Because the army's grown more popular,
    At which the naval people are concern'd;
Besides, the Prince is all for the land-service,
Forgetting Duncan, Nelson, Howe, and Jervis.

V.

Brave men were living before Agamemnon
     And since, exceeding valorous and sage,
A good deal like him too, though quite the same none;
     But then they shone not on the poet's page,
And so have been forgotten—I condemn none,
     But can't find any in the present age
Fit for my poem (that is, for my new one);
So, as I said, I'll take my friend Don Juan.

Byron's hero is not Mozart's Don Giovanni, who does go down with the Devil, but a charming teenage youth, strangely passive, yet courageous and madly attractive to all women. He is not at all Byron or even Byronic. Sometimes he reminds me of D. H. Lawrence's "Don Juan":

It is Isis the mystery
Must be in love with me.

Here this round ball of earth,
Where all the mountains sit
Solemn in groups,
And the bright rivers flit
Round them for girth:

Here the trees and troops
Darken the shining grass;
And many bright people pass
Like plunder from heaven:
Many bright people pass
Plundered from heaven.

But what of the mistresses,
What the beloved seven?
—They were but witnesses,
I was just driven.

Where is there peace for me?
It is Isis the mystery
Must be in love with me.

Shakespeare's Antony could have said, "It is Isis the mystery / Must
be in love with me," since Cleopatra's dying transcendence identifies
her with Isis, to whom the fatal asps are devoted. Lawrence's Don Juan
is closer to Lord Byron than to the Noble Lord's hero.

# John Keats,
## "Ode to a Nightingale"

T HE ODES OF John Keats center upon the simultaneous wealth
    and destitution of seeking to live in a physical world. Like Shake-
speare and the early Wordsworth, Keats exalted our common human
life. And yet he knew that no adventurer in humanity had been able to
conceive so immanent an existence. "Evil" in Keats and in his disciple
Stevens tends to be simply the suffering and pain we all of us undergo
because we are natural women and men in an altogether natural world.
The transcendental impulse that powers Shelley's Pindaric flights is not
alien to Keats, yet he turns away from it as Shakespeare did, choosing
Ovidian flux and change over Platonist yearnings for a premature Eternity. That is part, but only part, of the agon waged by the Great Odes,
particularly "Ode to a Nightingale":

I

My heart aches, and a drowsy numbness pains
    My sense, as though of hemlock I had drunk,
Or emptied some dull opiate to the drains
    One minute past, and Lethe-wards had sunk:
'Tis not through envy of thy happy lot,
    But being too happy in thine happiness,—
        That thou, light-winged Dryad of the trees,
            In some melodious plot
Of beechen green, and shadows numberless,
    Singest of summer in full-throated ease.

Keats composed this grand ode in 1819. In December 1818, his brother Tom died of tuberculosis, the family curse, which was to destroy the poet himself. Tom's death haunts the poem throughout, but particularly in its third stanza. The heartache and the drowsy numbness are induced not by the poison of hemlock or an opiate but by a burst of joy at hearing the nightingale's song:

II

O, for a draught of vintage! that hath been
    Cool'd a long age in the deep-delved earth,
Tasting of Flora and the country green,
    Dance, and Provençal song, and sunburnt mirth!
O for a beaker full of the warm South,
    Full of the true, the blushful Hippocrene,
      With beaded bubbles winking at the brim,
        And purple-stained mouth;
    That I might drink, and leave the world unseen,
      And with thee fade away into the forest dim:

III

Fade far away, dissolve, and quite forget
    What thou among the leaves hast never known,
The weariness, the fever, and the fret
    Here, where men sit and hear each other groan;
Where palsy shakes a few, sad, last gray hairs,
    Where youth grows pale, and spectre-thin, and dies;
      Where but to think is to be full of sorrow
        And leaden-eyed despairs,
    Where Beauty cannot keep her lustrous eyes,
      Or new Love pine at them beyond to-morrow.

The desire for intoxication is knowingly ironic, since Keats is aware to the highest degree that his desire is to be inside the poem he composes, which is to say: within the ecstasy of the nightingale's song.

IV

Away! away! for I will fly to thee,
    Not charioted by Bacchus and his pards,
But on the viewless wings of Poesy,
    Though the dull brain perplexes and retards:
Already with thee! tender is the night,
    And haply the Queen-Moon is on her throne,
        Clustered around by all her starry Fays;
           But here there is no light,
Save what from heaven is with the breezes blown
    Through verdurous glooms and winding mossy ways.


V

I cannot see what flowers are at my feet,
    Nor what soft incense hangs upon the boughs,
But, in embalmed darkness, guess each sweet
    Wherewith the seasonable month endows
The grass, the thicket, and the fruit-tree wild;
    White hawthorn, and the pastoral eglantine;
        Fast fading violets covered up in leaves;
           And mid-May's eldest child,
The coming musk-rose, full of dewy wine,
    The murmurous haunt of flies on summer eves.

Bacchus, the god of wine, whose chariot is drawn by leopards, is dismissed, and Keats cruises to fly on poetic wings so high as to have no view, in defiance of the mind's perplexities. Suddenly he is with the nightingale, with a tactile sensation: "tender is the night," a phrase that captivated F. Scott Fitzgerald. Keats can see nothing, but his other senses open to seasonal expectations and prepare him for an exaltation:


VI

Darkling I listen; and, for many a time
    I have been half in love with easeful Death,

Call'd him soft names in many a mused rhyme,
    To take into the air my quiet breath;
        Now more than ever seems it rich to die,
    To cease upon the midnight with no pain,
        While thou art pouring forth thy soul abroad
            In such an ecstasy!
    Still wouldst thou sing, and I have ears in vain—
        To thy high requiem become a sod.

In the invocation to book III of *Paradise Lost*, blind Milton compares himself to the nightingale that "sings darkling." To be half in love with death, however easeful, is also to be half in love with life, yet the disquieting word "rich" edges toward acceptance of the end. The two final stanzas attain a high place:

VII

Thou wast not born for death, immortal Bird!
    No hungry generations tread thee down;
The voice I hear this passing night was heard
    In ancient days by emperor and clown:
Perhaps the self-same song that found a path
        Through the sad heart of Ruth, when, sick for home,
            She stood in tears amid the alien corn;
                The same that oft-times hath
        Charm'd magic casements, opening on the foam
            Of perilous seas, in faery lands forlorn.

VIII

Forlorn! the very word is like a bell
    To toll me back from thee to my sole self!
Adieu! the fancy cannot cheat so well
    As she is famed to do, deceiving elf.
Adieu! adieu! thy plaintive anthem fades
        Past the near meadows, over the still stream,
            Up the hill-side; and now 'tis buried deep

In the next valley-glades:
Was it a vision, or a waking dream?
Fled is that music:—Do I wake or sleep?

One hears anticipations of Yeats's Byzantium poems in stanza VII, where the allusion to the Bible's book of Ruth may be a screen for Wordsworth's "The Solitary Reaper." The vision of the charmed magic casements and the forlorn faery lands suggest Edmund Spenser. Keats had attended Hazlitt's lecture "On Chaucer and Spenser," in which the critic observed that "Spenser was the poet of our waking dreams." The marvelous repetition of "forlorn," possibly in the sense of "abandonment," indeed tolls like a bell returning Keats from the nightingale's song to his isolate self. Fancy or imagination becomes another Belle Dame sans Merci, who is scarcely responsible for the poet's self-deception. As the song fades away to deep burial in another valley, Keats asks the unanswerable question: "Was it a vision, or a waking dream?" Either way, the song has departed and the ambiguous question "Do I wake or sleep?" portends the coming on of finality, only two years away.

# John Keats, "La Belle Dame sans Merci"

O what can ail thee, knight-at-arms,
    Alone and palely loitering?
The sedge has wither'd from the lake,
    And no birds sing.

O what can ail thee, knight-at-arms,
    So haggard and so woe-begone?
The squirrel's granary is full,
    And the harvest's done.

I see a lily on thy brow,
    With anguish moist and fever dew;
And on thy cheeks a fading rose
    Fast withereth too.

Lines 1–12

This enigmatic opening of the ballad contrasts the starving knight to the full harvest. His reply to the unknown questioner weaves together subtle allusions to Coleridge and to Wordsworth:

I met a lady in the meads,
    Full beautiful, a faery's child,
Her hair was long, her foot was light,
    And her eyes were wild.

I made a garland for her head,
    And bracelets too, and fragrant zone;

She look'd at me as she did love,
    And made sweet moan.

I set her on my pacing steed,
    And nothing else saw all day long,
For sidelong would she bend, and sing
    A faery's song.

She found me roots of relish sweet,
    And honey wild, and manna dew,
And sure in language strange she said—
    'I love thee true.'

She took me to her elfin grot,
    And there she wept and sigh'd full sore,
And there I shut her wild wild eyes
    With kisses four.

The beautiful faery and the knight speak different languages, and neither can understand the other. Her sweet moan, her tears and sighs, may be her helpless sorrow at his misinterpretations. We cannot know whether she declares love or a warning, and his use of the word "sure" is alarming. He indeed has fallen in love and devoured faery food and lost forever any hope of mortal love or human sustenance:

And there she lulled me asleep,
    And there I dream'd—Ah! woe betide!
The latest dream I ever dream'd
    On the cold hill's side.

I saw pale kings, and princes too,
    Pale warriors, death pale were they all;
They cried—'La Belle Dame sans Merci
    Thee hath in thrall!'

I saw their starved lips in the gloam
    With horrid warning gaped wide,
And I awoke and found me here
    On the cold hill's side.

And this is why I sojourn here,
    Alone and palely loitering,
Though the sedge is wither'd from the lake,
    And no birds sing.

His dream invokes precursor questers who misread her as he has done. Keats, like his friend William Hazlitt the critic, helped inaugurate a kind of heroic and naturalistic humanism that vivifies the poetry of Wallace Stevens, who taught us again the Keatsian lesson that the greatest poverty is to not live in a physical world, to feel that one's desire is too difficult to tell from despair. The knight-at-arms, dwindling away to death by starvation, could have been saved had he realized that wisdom.

# John Keats, "To Autumn"

S HAKESPEARE, more even than Milton or Wordsworth, was the great influence upon John Keats. As I have aged, I return to Keats's final ode, "To Autumn," in a different spirit. I once heard in it apocalyptic overtones, but I was mistaken. Like Shakespeare, Keats affirms natural abundance, and with it the image of an unfallen yet tragic human approaching the necessity of dying.

Keats is so free of Christianity, or indeed of any organized religion, that it always seems superfluous to say that. Northrop Frye, whom I still revere, remarked to me that he found intimations of the communion images of bread and wine in "To Autumn." I am unable to locate them.

It astonishes me that "To Autumn" summons up a universe in just thirty-three lines. All three eleven-line stanzas are so rich that no reader will ever come to an end of them. The first stanza is perhaps the most Shakespearean:

> Season of mists and mellow fruitfulness,
>     Close bosom-friend of the maturing sun;
> Conspiring with him how to load and bless
>     With fruit the vines that round the thatch-eves run;
> To bend with apples the moss'd cottage-trees,
>     And fill all fruit with ripeness to the core;
>         To swell the gourd, and plump the hazel shells
> With a sweet kernel; to set budding more,
> And still more, later flowers for the bees,
> Until they think warm days will never cease,
>     For Summer has o'er-brimm'd their clammy cells.

Keats was fascinated by *King Lear*, and "ripeness to the core" ultimately alludes to Edgar's:

Men must endure
Their going hence even as their coming hither.
Ripeness is all.

Act 5, Scene 3

Autumn becomes a goddess of Keats's own creation. She is extraordinarily benign. Her conspiracy with the sun is a blessing. The illusion of the bees is another secular benediction.

The second stanza personifies the goddess as a harvest girl:

Who hath not seen thee oft amid thy store?
　　Sometimes whoever seeks abroad may find
Thee sitting careless on a granary floor,
　　Thy hair soft-lifted by the winnowing wind;
Or on a half-reap'd furrow sound asleep,
　　Drows'd with the fume of poppies, while thy hook
　　　　Spares the next swath and all its twined flowers:
And sometimes like a gleaner thou dost keep
　　Steady thy laden head across a brook;
　　Or by a cyder-press, with patient look,
　　　　Thou watchest the last oozings hours by hours.

"Careless" is the key word. Such abundance banishes care. The stanza is so exquisite as to be unmatched in its cognitive music. "Patient" is close to being the other key. The earth is enough. Natural process produces such value, such immanent splendor, that no transcendence is required.

After such sublime radiances, one could hardly expect that Keats would surpass himself in the final stanza:

Where are the songs of Spring? Ay, where are they?
　　Think not of them, thou hast thy music too,—
While barred clouds bloom the soft-dying day,
　　And touch the stubble-plains with rosy hue;
Then in a wailful choir the small gnats mourn

Among the river sallows, borne aloft
    Or sinking as the light wind lives or dies;
And full-grown lambs loud bleat from hilly bourn;
    Hedge-crickets sing; and now with treble soft
    The red-breast whistles from a garden-croft;
    And gathering swallows twitter in the skies.

"Wailful," "mourn," "dies": is that autumn's crucial music? Keats composes in the autumn of 1819. He knows himself to be dying slowly of tuberculosis. Death came on February 23, 1821, in Rome, when the poet was still only twenty-five. The final line, "And gathering swallows twitter in the skies," anticipates the close of Wallace Stevens's "Sunday Morning" and of Hart Crane's "The Broken Tower."

I do not hear either complaint or even sorrow in the ode "To Autumn." John Keats certainly had not made friends with the necessity of dying. His loss was also ours. Think of the poems he would have written had he enjoyed a normal life span. In his final sonnet, "Bright Star," revised before his voyage to death, his regret and ours is expressed with Shakespearean nobility:

Bright star, would I were stedfast as thou art—
    Not in lone splendour hung aloft the night,
And watching, with eternal lids apart,
    Like nature's patient, sleepless Eremite,
The moving waters at their priestlike task
    Of pure ablution round earth's human shores,
Or gazing on the new soft-fallen masque
    Of snow upon the mountains and the moors—
No—yet still stedfast, still unchangeable
    Pillow'd upon my fair love's ripening breast,
To feel for ever its soft fall and swell,
    Awake forever in a sweet unrest,
Still, still to hear her tender-taken breath,
And so live ever—or else swoon to death—

The naturalistic humanism of John Keats attains apotheosis in a revaluation of what it means for the poet to replace the priest: "The moving waters at their priestlike task / Of pure ablution round earth's human shores."

Wordsworth waned. Coleridge despaired. Byron and Shelley, though great poets, strove with the world. The prophet William Blake held on until the end. Of the High Romantics, perhaps only Keats is now admired without reservations. Who could find fault with the ode "To Autumn"? If there can be a humanistic sublime, and that is always problematic, then Keats incarnates it.

# Thomas Lovell Beddoes,
## *Death's Jest Book*

F OR SEVENTY YEARS I have entertained a passion for the poetry of Thomas Lovell Beddoes (1803–49), the most fantastic of Shelley's disciples. Nineteen years old when Shelley died, Beddoes wrote some lines on a blank leaf of his copy of *Prometheus Unbound:*

> Write it in gold—A spirit of the sun,
> An intellect a-blaze with heavenly thoughts,
> A soul with all the dews of pathos shining,
> Odorous with love, and sweet to silent woe
> With the dark glories of concentrate song,
> Was sphered in mortal earth. Angelic sounds
> Alive with panting thoughts sunned the dim world.
> The bright creations of an human heart
> Wrought magic in the bosoms of mankind.
> A flooding summer burst on poetry;
> Of which the crowning sun, the night of beauty,
> The dancing showers, the birds, whose anthems wild
> Note after note unbind the enchanted leaves
> Of breaking buds, eve, and the flow of dawn,
> Were centred and condensed in his one name
> As in a providence,—and that was SHELLEY.

This is not of any value as a poem, but the Oxford undergraduate later carried Shelley's lyricism on to a spectral intensity still unmatched in its mode, far surpassing Edgar Allan Poe and his French imitators:

I.

A ghost, that loved a lady fair,
Ever in the starry air
   Of midnight at her pillow stood;
And, with a sweetness skies above
The luring words of human love,
   Her soul the phantom wooed.
Sweet and sweet is their poisoned note,
The little snakes' of silver throat,
In mossy skulls that nest and lie,
Ever singing "die, oh! die."


II.

Young soul, put off your flesh, and come
With me into the quiet tomb,
   Our bed is lovely, dark, and sweet;
The earth will swing us, as she goes,
Beneath our coverlid of snows,
   And the warm leaden sheet.
Dear and dear is their poisoned note,
The little snakes' of silver throat,
In mossy skulls that nest and lie,
Ever singing "die, oh! die."

This morbid little splendor has a grisly charm and admits us to a curious kind of comedy. Here is a personal favorite, "Song of the Stygian Naiades":

PROSERPINE may pull her flowers,
   Wet with dew or wet with tears,
   Red with anger, pale with fears,
Is it any fault of ours,
If Pluto be an amorous king,
   And comes home nightly, laden,
Underneath his broad bat-wing,

With a gentle, mortal maiden?
Is it so, Wind, is it so?
All that you and I do know
Is, that we saw fly and fix
'Mongst the reeds and flowers of Styx,
    Yesterday,
Where the Furies made their hay
For a bed of tiger cubs,
A great fly of Beelzebub's,
The bee of hearts, whom mortals name
Cupid, Love, and Fie for shame.

Proserpine may weep in rage,
  But, ere I and you have done
  Kissing, bathing in the sun,
What I have in yonder cage,
Bird or serpent, wild or tame,
  She shall guess, and ask in vain;
  But, if Pluto does't again,
It shall sing out loud his shame.
  What hast caught then? What hast caught?
  Nothing but a poet's thought,
  Which so light did fall and fix
'Mongst the reeds and flowers of Styx,
    Yesterday,
Where the Furies made their hay
For a bed of tiger cubs,—
A great fly of Beelzebub's,
The bee of hearts, whom mortals name
Cupid, Love, and Fie for shame.

The lilt of these mermaids of the Styx is uncanny and memorable. Beddoes creates an alternative cosmos in which Shelley's hopes for human liberation have vanished forever. The son of a distinguished physician, Beddoes himself turned to medical study and pursued it in Germany and Switzerland. He became an expert anatomist, but his Shelleyan politics resulted in his expulsion, first from Bavaria and seven years later from Zürich. A wandering homosexual questing for some evidence of the spirit's survival, his bourgeoning eccentricities became extravagant and culminated in his suicide by poison at the age of forty-five.

The white elephant of his poetic career was an amazing Jacobean verse tragedy, *Death's Jest Book*, which he never quite completed. I have read it many times with gusto, but I grant it may be a special taste. Chanting his lyrics at their most exuberant seems to me an authentic aesthetic experience:

> Old Adam, the carrion crow,
>     The old crow of Cairo;
> He sat in the shower, and let it flow
>     Under his tail and over his crest;
>         And through every feather
>         Leak'd the wet weather;
>     And the bough swung under his nest;
>     For his beak it was heavy with marrow.
>         Is that the wind dying? O no;
>         It's only two devils, that blow
>         Through a murderer's bones, to and fro,
>             In the ghosts' moonshine.

> Ho! Eve, my grey carrion wife,
>     When we have supped on kings' marrow,
> Where shall we drink and make merry our life?
>     Our nest it is queen Cleopatra's skull,
>         'Tis cloven and crack'd,
>         And batter'd and hack'd,
>     But with tears of blue eyes it is full:
>     Let us drink then, my raven of Cairo.
>         Is that the wind dying? O no;
>         It's only two devils, that blow
>         Through a murderer's bones, to and fro,
>             In the ghosts' moonshine.

The alternative title for this work is *The Fool's Tragedy*, as the avenger takes the disguise of a Fool. The rollicking tempo is fiercely upbeat and contrasts with the discords and hilarities that vitalize the bounce and sorrows of the Egyptian queen. Hamlet holding up Yorick's skull is evoked and extended by "cloven and crack'd,/and batter'd and hack'd,/but with tears of blue eyes it is full." I recall reciting it again and again to my two little boys when they were four and seven and their delighted response.

I slept badly last night, as I almost always do. At dawn, a dirge by Beddoes returned to me:

> We do lie beneath the grass
>   In the moonlight, in the shade
> Of the yew-tree. They that pass
>   Hear us not. We are afraid
>     They would envy our delight,
>     In our graves by glow-worm night.
> Come follow us, and smile as we;
>   We sail to the rock in the ancient waves,
> Where the snow falls by thousands into the sea,
>   And the drown'd and the shipwreck'd have happy graves.

This invitation to a fatal voyage could be one of the songs the Sirens sang, and is a puzzling matter, but not beyond all conjecture. Beddoes appeals to our craving and nostalgia for the original Abyss, our Foremother and Forefather. He sought the Spirit in his anatomies yet found only a release into death.

# Alfred Tennyson, "Ulysses"

Alfred Tennyson composed his "Ulysses" in 1833, when he was twenty-four. His closest friend, Arthur Henry Hallam, had died in Vienna of a sudden stroke at the age of just twenty-two. The shock for Tennyson was all but permanent. He did not marry until he was forty-one, after an endless betrothal. To a remarkable extent, his greatest poems are all elegies for Hallam: *In Memoriam*, "Morte d'Arthur," ultimately *Idylls of the King*, but also my two favorites, "Ulysses" and "Tithonus."

In Dante's *Inferno*, canto 26, Virgil and Dante enter the eighth bolge of the eighth circle and confront Ulysses and Diomedes, held together in a single flame. Ulysses speaks from the fire and gives an account of his final voyage beyond the known limits of the world; this voyage concludes by drowning all the mariners and, after many previous escapes, the lord of Ithaca himself. Dante, uniquely, is silent as he listens, perhaps because of the clear affinity between his epic voyage in the *Commedia* and the self-destructive drive of Ulysses.

Tennyson's blank-verse monologue starts with an extraordinary pitch of verbal harmony informed by assonance and gives the impression of Virgilian measures, as though English verse could resort to quantity and not to accent:

> It little profits that an idle king,
> By this still hearth, among these barren crags,
> Match'd with an aged wife, I mete and dole
> Unequal laws unto a savage race,
> That hoard, and sleep, and feed, and know not me.
> I cannot rest from travel: I will drink

Life to the lees: All times I have enjoy'd
Greatly, have suffer'd greatly, both with those
That loved me, and alone, on shore, and when
Thro' scudding drifts the rainy Hyades
Vext the dim sea: I am become a name. . . .

Hallam had urged his friend to emulate Keats and Shelley, rather than Wordsworth, and certainly the intricate tones of Keats inform this tensely eloquent blazon of the wiliest of the Greeks. Penelope is merely old, and the Ithacans "know not me," which is death to Ulysses. What matters to him, be it pleasure or pain, is greatness. His mariners "loved me," and he loved only himself. His pride magnificently asserts, "I am become a name":

For always roaming with a hungry heart
Much have I seen and known; cities of men
And manners, climates, councils, governments,
Myself not least, but honour'd of them all;
And drunk delight of battle with my peers,
Far on the ringing plains of windy Troy.
I am a part of all that I have met;
Yet all experience is an arch wherethro'
Gleams that untravell'd world whose margin fades
For ever and forever when I move.
How dull it is to pause, to make an end,
To rust unburnish'd, not to shine in use!
As tho' to breathe were life! Life piled on life
Were all too little, and of one to me
Little remains: but every hour is saved
From that eternal silence, something more,
A bringer of new things; and vile it were
For some three suns to store and hoard myself,
And this gray spirit yearning in desire
To follow knowledge like a sinking star,
Beyond the utmost bound of human thought.

His heart hungers for fame and honor. To keep moving consumes life piled on life, and yet always he yearns to know a newness that tran-

scends human mortality: "As tho' to breathe were life!" Thus he abandons Penelope and Ithaca to his dutiful son:

> This is my son, mine own Telemachus,
> To whom I leave the sceptre and the isle,—
> Well-loved of me, discerning to fulfil
> This labour, by slow prudence to make mild
> A rugged people, and thro' soft degrees
> Subdue them to the useful and the good.
> Most blameless is he, centred in the sphere
> Of common duties, decent not to fail
> In offices of tenderness, and pay
> Meet adoration to my household gods,
> When I am gone. He works his work, I mine.

We can doubt "Well-loved of me" and believe instead "*He* works *his*
work, *I* mine." With that dismissal of family and hearth, the dark voyage commences:

> There lies the port; the vessel puffs her sail:
> There gloom the dark, broad seas. My mariners,
> Souls that have toil'd, and wrought, and thought with me—
> That ever with a frolic welcome took
> The thunder and the sunshine, and opposed
> Free hearts, free foreheads—you and I are old;
> Old age hath yet his honour and his toil;
> Death closes all: but something ere the end,
> Some work of noble note, may yet be done,
> Not unbecoming men that strove with Gods.
> The lights begin to twinkle from the rocks:
> The long day wanes: the slow moon climbs: the deep
> Moans round with many voices. Come, my friends,
> 'Tis not too late to seek a newer world.
> Push off, and sitting well in order smite
> The sounding furrows; for my purpose holds
> To sail beyond the sunset, and the baths
> Of all the western stars, until I die.
> It may be that the gulfs will wash us down:

It may be we shall touch the Happy Isles,
And see the great Achilles, whom we knew.
Tho' much is taken, much abides; and tho'
We are not now that strength which in old days
Moved earth and heaven, that which we are, we are;
One equal temper of heroic hearts,
Made weak by time and fate, but strong in will
To strive, to seek, to find, and not to yield.

Who are those phantom mariners? The *Odyssey* clearly depicts that Ulysses survives but all his companions perish, most by drowning and some more horribly. You would not want to be in one boat with this Ulysses. And yet we are moved by the marvelous roll, rise, carol, and creation of this egocentric glory. Those final six lines surge in your soul, particularly if you are very old. One of my closest friends, a great scholarly critic, died early this morning. I sorrow; this departure was long expected, but we were companions for some sixty-five years. Much is taken, and I trust that much abides. I too am not that strength which in old days moved little enough, yet it sufficed. It comforts me to think, "That which we are, we are." Heroism is not an attribute of teachers, and I am made weak by time and fate. Tennyson may have been unaware he echoed Milton's Satan, who cried out: "And courage never to submit or yield/And what is else not to be overcome." Strength of will can lessen, and still one wants to emulate this Satanic Ulysses in his quest: "To strive, to seek, to find, and not to yield."

# Alfred Tennyson, "Tithonus"

IN 1833, TENNYSON WROTE a shorter version of what became "Tithonus" as a kind of coda to "Ulysses." A surpassingly beautiful Virgilian vignette, "Tithonus," like the song "Tears, Idle Tears," is another lament for Hallam. Its intricate harmonies, so much at variance with the poem's despair, are extraordinarily exquisite and show the Laureate's powers of suggestion at their height:

> The woods decay, the woods decay and fall,
> The vapours weep their burthen to the ground,
> Man comes and tills the field and lies beneath,
> And after many a summer dies the swan.
> Me only cruel immortality
> Consumes: I wither slowly in thine arms,
> Here at the quiet limit of the world,
> A white-hair'd shadow roaming like a dream
> The ever-silent spaces of the East,
> Far-folded mists, and gleaming halls of morn.

Eos, Greek goddess of the dawn, known to the Latins as Aurora, took Ganymede and Tithonus as her consorts. Zeus stole Ganymede from her, and in exchange, at her request, granted Tithonus immortality. Alas, the goddess forgot to ask that he enjoy eternal youth, and so he withers in her arms and longs only for death. I cannot recall any other place in literature where immortality is called cruel. This desperate dramatic monologue enters upon a vertigo of bereftness:

> Alas! for this gray shadow, once a man—
> So glorious in his beauty and thy choice,

Who madest him thy chosen, that he seem'd
To his great heart none other than a God!
I ask'd thee, 'Give me immortality.'
Then didst thou grant mine asking with a smile,
Like wealthy men, who care not how they give.
But thy strong Hours indignant work'd their wills,
And beat me down and marr'd and wasted me,
And tho' they could not end me, left me maim'd
To dwell in presence of immortal youth,
Immortal age beside immortal youth,
And all I was, in ashes. Can thy love,
Thy beauty, make amends, tho' even now,
Close over us, the silver star, thy guide,
Shines in those tremulous eyes that fill with tears
To hear me? Let me go: take back thy gift:
Why should a man desire in any way
To vary from the kindly race of men
Or pass beyond the goal of ordinance
Where all should pause, as is most meet for all?

Like Tennyson's Ulysses, the wretched Tithonus is incapable of loving anyone except himself. The dawn goddess weeps for him, and he weeps for himself. His aesthetic apprehension of Eos kindles ever anew, and that is all:

A soft air fans the cloud apart; there comes
A glimpse of that dark world where I was born.
Once more the old mysterious glimmer steals
From thy pure brows, and from thy shoulders pure,
And bosom beating with a heart renew'd.
Thy cheek begins to redden thro' the gloom,
Thy sweet eyes brighten slowly close to mine,
Ere yet they blind the stars, and the wild team
Which love thee, yearning for thy yoke, arise,
And shake the darkness from their loosen'd manes,
And beat the twilight into flakes of fire.

The lyricism of Keats and of Shelley achieves a later apotheosis in this high passage, but neither of them shared this selfish iciness. There is something unique in the dramatic monologue of this miserable shadow, since what gladdens the ear is undone by the wholly negative affect of the speaker:

> Lo! ever thus thou growest beautiful
> In silence, then before thine answer given
> Departest, and thy tears are on my cheek.
>
> Why wilt thou ever scare me with thy tears,
> And make me tremble lest a saying learnt,
> In days far-off, on that dark earth, be true?
> 'The Gods themselves cannot recall their gifts.'
>
> Ay me! ay me! with what another heart
> In days far-off, and with what other eyes
> I used to watch—if I be he that watch'd—
> The lucid outline forming round thee; saw
> The dim curls kindle into sunny rings;
> Changed with thy mystic change, and felt my blood
> Glow with the glow that slowly crimson'd all
> Thy presence and thy portals, while I lay,
> Mouth, forehead, eyelids, growing dewy-warm
> With kisses balmier than half-opening buds
> Of April, and could hear the lips that kiss'd
> Whispering I knew not what of wild and sweet,
> Like that strange song I heard Apollo sing,
> While Ilion like a mist rose into towers.

Ilion, or Troy, was created by a song of Apollo's; recalling that miracle, Tithonus comes near the apex of his anguish and values the memories of the dawn goddess's kisses only as sensations of the departed. And so he sighs out what he knows cannot be his farewell:

> Yet hold me not for ever in thine East:
> How can my nature longer mix with thine?
> Coldly thy rosy shadows bathe me, cold
> Are all thy lights, and cold my wrinkled feet
> Upon thy glimmering thresholds, when the steam
> Floats up from those dim fields about the homes

Of happy men that have the power to die,
And grassy barrows of the happier dead.
Release me, and restore me to the ground;
Thou seëst all things, thou wilt see my grave:
Thou wilt renew thy beauty morn by morn;
I earth in earth forget these empty courts,
And thee returning on thy silver wheels.

At my old age, I sympathize with him, because I too am always cold, and my feet altogether wrinkled. Yet my sympathy stops just there. When I die, in another four or five years, I trust I will not have the stupid cruelty to tell my survivors: Thou wilt see my grave. As his monologue winds on in what will be perpetual cycle, Tithonus renders us grateful for his poetic power yet unable to accept his solipsistic agony. I have never understood the precise relation of this poem to Hallam's death or Tennyson's grief. Something vital is being repressed, and the force of that evasion gives the reader an uneasy splendor we experience simultaneously as pleasure and as pain. Though he went on to a reasonably happy marriage and fatherhood, Tennyson never loved anyone so much as Hallam, and I wonder whether that brilliant young critic understood how fierce Tennyson's passion truly was. It is certain that Tennyson himself never could apprehend how deep and turbulent the repressed drive had been.

# Alfred Tennyson,
## *Idylls of the King*

IN TENNYSON, as in tradition, the purest of Arthur's knights are Percivale and Galahad. Percivale's ruinous quest for the Holy Grail is Tennyson's equivalent of Browning's Childe Roland, whose search for the Dark Tower deforms and breaks everything he gazes upon. The difference allies Tennyson to T. S. Eliot in *The Waste Land:*

> Here is no water but only rock
> Rock and no water and the sandy road
> The road winding above among the mountains
> Which are mountains of rock without water
> If there were water we should stop and drink
> Amongst the rock one cannot stop or think
> Sweat is dry and feet are in the sand
> If there were only water amongst the rock
> Dead mountain mouth of carious teeth that cannot spit
> Here one can neither stand nor lie nor sit
> There is not even silence in the mountains
> But dry sterile thunder without rain
> There is not even solitude in the mountains
> But red sullen faces sneer and snarl
> From doors of mudcracked houses

Percivale, called "The Pure," before his death tells his story to a fellow monk and traces his own downward path to wisdom:

> 'And I was lifted up in heart, and thought
> Of all my late-shown prowess in the lists,

How my strong lance had beaten down the knights,
So many and famous names; and never yet
Had heaven appeared so blue, nor earth so green,
For all my blood danced in me, and I knew
That I should light upon the Holy Grail.

'Thereafter, the dark warning of our King,
That most of us would follow wandering fires,
Came like a driving gloom across my mind.
Then every evil word I had spoken once,
And every evil thought I had thought of old,
And every evil deed I ever did,
Awoke and cried, "This Quest is not for thee."
And lifting up mine eyes, I found myself
Alone, and in a land of sand and thorns,
And I was thirsty even unto death;
And I, too, cried, "This Quest is not for thee."

The pure quester, who does not seek only to fail, nevertheless reduces all things and persons to dust:

'And on I rode, and when I thought my thirst
Would slay me, saw deep lawns, and then a brook,
With one sharp rapid, where the crisping white
Played ever back upon the sloping wave,
And took both ear and eye; and o'er the brook
Were apple-trees, and apples by the brook
Fallen, and on the lawns. "I will rest here,"
I said, "I am not worthy of the Quest;"
But even while I drank the brook, and ate
The goodly apples, all these things at once
Fell into dust, and I was left alone,
And thirsting, in a land of sand and thorns.

'And then behold a woman at a door
Spinning; and fair the house whereby she sat,
And kind the woman's eyes and innocent,
And all her bearing gracious; and she rose

Opening her arms to meet me, as who should say,
"Rest here;" but when I touch'd her, lo! she, too,
Fell into dust and nothing, and the house
Became no better than a broken shed,
And in it a dead babe; and also this
Fell into dust, and I was left alone.

'And on I rode, and greater was my thirst.
Then flashed a yellow gleam across the world,
And where it smote the plowshare in the field,
The plowman left his plowing, and fell down
Before it; where it glittered on her pail,
The milkmaid left her milking, and fell down
Before it, and I knew not why, but thought
"The sun is rising," though the sun had risen.
Then was I ware of one that on me moved
In golden armour with a crown of gold
About a casque all jewels; and his horse
In golden armour jewelled everywhere:
And on the splendour came, flashing me blind;
And seemed to me the Lord of all the world,
Being so huge. But when I thought he meant
To crush me, moving on me, lo! he, too,
Opened his arms to embrace me as he came,
And up I went and touched him, and he, too,
Fell into dust, and I was left alone
And wearying in a land of sand and thorns.

Where Percivale's glance does not destroy, his touch devastates more
fully. Tennyson cannot define his own fierce vision and would not have
believed that he composed a parable of his own poetic consciousness
so dangerously thwarted by the loss of Hallam that it burns through
nature and through other selves. Like Browning's Childe Roland, Percivale descends directly from the remorseless Poet of Shelley's "Alas-
tor." Though Tennyson intended that Percivale represent an ascetic
Catholic consciousness, the poet's daemon usurped the quest and
instead gave us a burning desire to reduce everything that is not purely
a celebration of the self's sublimity:

'And I rode on and found a mighty hill,
And on the top, a city walled: the spires
Pricked with incredible pinnacles into heaven.
And by the gateway stirred a crowd; and these
Cried to me climbing, "Welcome, Percivale!
Thou mightiest and thou purest among men!"
And glad was I and clomb, but found at top
No man, nor any voice. And thence I past
Far through a ruinous city, and I saw
That man had once dwelt there; but there I found
Only one man of an exceeding age.
"Where is that goodly company," said I,
"That so cried out upon me?" and he had
Scarce any voice to answer, and yet gasped,
"Whence and what art thou?" and even as he spoke
Fell into dust, and disappeared, and I
Was left alone once more, and cried in grief,
"Lo, if I find the Holy Grail itself
And touch it, it will crumble into dust."

To say of the poetic spirit that its bright argosy sails only to obliterate by touching is a negative Romanticism carrying us back to the monitions of Shelley's *The Triumph of Life* and Keats's *The Fall of Hyperion*. Tennyson was at his strongest when not fully aware of what he was doing. Percivale gets away from him just as Ulysses does, but that was the Laureate's glory. Elsewhere in the *Idylls of the King*, the seductive Vivien, who will destroy Merlin, breaks through Tennyson's censor with a savage hymn to Eros:

But now the wholesome music of the wood
Was dumbed by one from out the hall of Mark,
A damsel-errant, warbling, as she rode
The woodland alleys, Vivien, with her Squire.

'The fire of Heaven has killed the barren cold,
And kindled all the plain and all the wold.
The new leaf ever pushes off the old.
The fire of Heaven is not the flame of Hell.

'Old priest, who mumble worship in your quire—
Old monk and nun, ye scorn the world's desire,
Yet in your frosty cells ye feel the fire!
The fire of Heaven is not the flame of Hell.

'The fire of Heaven is on the dusty ways.
The wayside blossoms open to the blaze.
The whole wood-world is one full peal of praise.
The fire of Heaven is not the flame of Hell.

'The fire of Heaven is lord of all things good,
And starve not thou this fire within thy blood,
But follow Vivien through the fiery flood!
The fire of Heaven is not the flame of Hell!'

Then turning to her Squire 'This fire of Heaven,
This old sun-worship, boy, will rise again,
And beat the cross to earth, and break the King
And all his Table.'

"The fire of Heaven is on the dusty ways." Sunlight of lust reverses
Percivale's pure touch that leaves dust and ashes. For him the light lies
dead in the dust. In Vivien's vision, that means love dies, lust remains.
Again the daemon fortunately has his way with Tennyson, whose
repressive force could not exclude the power of the sun.

# Alfred Tennyson, "Morte d'Arthur"

I WRITE THESE PARAGRAPHS on June 13, 2017, barely twenty-four hours back from six weeks' hospitalization and rehabilitation after two serious operations. I am so deeply exhausted that I scarcely speak. For comfort, I have returned to Tennyson and, for reasons not wholly evident to me, to "Morte d'Arthur."

The tradition is that this is a lament for Arthur Henry Hallam, but that seems to me misleading. Tennyson's greatness is frequently daemonic. Hallam understood Tennyson's conflict between a High Romantic sublime and a societal censor.

Had he lived, Hallam would have been a considerable literary critic. His passion was for Shelley and Keats rather than for Wordsworth. There are Keatsian echoes in "Morte d'Arthur," but the voice is very much Tennyson's own:

> So all day long the noise of battle roll'd
> Among the mountains by the winter sea;
> Until King Arthur's table, man by man,
> Had fallen in Lyonnesse about their Lord,
> King Arthur: then, because his wound was deep,
> The bold Sir Bedivere uplifted him,
> Sir Bedivere, the last of all his knights,
> And bore him to a chapel nigh the field,
> A broken chancel with a broken cross,
> That stood on a dark strait of barren land.
> On one side lay the ocean, and on one
> Lay a great water, and the moon was full.

Though there are Christian overtones, "Morte d'Arthur" might well be called a pagan religious poem: "A broken chancel with a broken cross." That powerful line juxtaposes to the poem's refrain: "Clothed in white samite, mystic, wonderful." The myth of Arthur constitutes a large portion of what is called the Matter of Britain. Its destructive legend of the Holy Grail relies upon the various traditions in which Joseph of Arimathea purchases the corpse of Jesus from Pilate and eventually brings it to Glastonbury in Britain. Tennyson's "Morte d'Arthur" does not directly invoke the Joseph of Arimathea stories, but they form a subtle under-song.

The dying Arthur commands Sir Bedivere to return the sword Excalibur to its mystic origins. Twice Bedivere disobeys, but then yields:

> Then quickly rose Sir Bedivere, and ran,
> And, leaping down the ridges lightly, plunged
> Among the bulrush-beds, and clutch'd the sword,
> And strongly wheel'd and threw it. The great brand
> Made lightnings in the splendour of the moon,
> And flashing round and round, and whirl'd in an arch,
> Shot like a streamer of the northern morn,
> Seen where the moving isles of winter shock
> By night, with noises of the northern sea.
> So flash'd and fell the brand Excalibur:
> But ere he dipt the surface, rose an arm
> Clothed in white samite, mystic, wonderful,
> And caught him by the hilt, and brandish'd him
> Three times, and drew him under in the mere.
> And lightly went the other to the King.

Tennyson's style rises to a crescendo when Bedivere bears the dying Arthur to his final voyage:

> But, as he walk'd, King Arthur panted hard,
> Like one that feels a nightmare on his bed
> When all the house is mute. So sigh'd the King
> Muttering and murmuring at his ear, 'Quick, quick!
> I fear it is too late, and I shall die.'
> But the other swiftly strode from ridge to ridge,

Clothed with his breath, and looking, as he walk'd
Larger than human on the frozen hills.
He heard the deep behind him, and a cry
Before. His own thought drove him like a goad.
Dry clash'd his harness in the icy caves
And barren chasms, and all to left and right
The bare black cliff clang'd round him, as he based
His feet on juts of slippery crag that rang
Sharp-smitten with the dint of armed heels—
And on a sudden, lo! the level lake,
And the long glories of the winter moon.

Tennyson once remarked that he knew the quantity of every English word except for "scissors." The splendor of this enhances his veracity. "Larger than human" is a fine touch and is exceeded by the dazzling symphony of sounds that bring together "clash'd," "clang'd," and "crag." Three Queens come in a dark barge to carry the wounded hero to the island-valley of Avilion.

Bedivere moves us intensely when he laments the solitude with which he must enter a new world:

And the days darken round me, and the years,
Among new men, strange faces, other minds.

Arthur's reply is poetry of the highest order:

The old order changeth, yielding place to new,
And God fulfils Himself in many ways,
Lest one good custom should corrupt the world.

I take what comfort I can from that eloquence. Certainly the final verse paragraph is more lament than celebration:

So said he, and the barge with oar and sail
Moved from the brink, like some full-breasted swan
That, fluting a wild carol ere her death,

Ruffles her pure cold plume, and takes the flood
With swarthy webs. Long stood Sir Bedivere
Revolving many memories, till the hull
Look'd one black dot against the verge of dawn,
And on the mere the wailing died away.

There are many glories in *Idylls of the King*, but nothing to match
"Morte d'Arthur." It shares the eminence of the great dramatic monologues "Ulysses," "Tithonus," and "Lucretius."

# Robert Browning,
## "A Toccata of Galuppi's"

A TOCCATA OF GALUPPI'S" uncannily invokes the eighteenth-century Venetian composer Baldassare Galuppi, famous in his own era for his light operas and his toccatas, or "touch pieces," for the clavichord. The fervent spirit and rapid movement of these toccatas challenges Browning's skill at mingling different voices with their rival tones. The speaker of this dramatic monologue is not Browning but an unnamed Victorian scientist or philosopher who seeks some natural information that can be reconciled with the Christian belief in the immortality of the soul:

I

Oh Galuppi, Baldassaro, this is very sad to find!
I can hardly misconceive you; it would prove me deaf and blind;
But although I take your meaning, 'tis with such a heavy mind!

II

Here you come with your old music, and here's all the good it
   brings.
What, they lived once thus at Venice where the merchants were
   the kings,
Where Saint Mark's is, where the Doges used to wed the sea
   with rings?

III

Ay, because the sea's the street there; and 'tis arched by . . . what
 you call
. . . Shylock's bridge with houses on it, where they kept the
 carnival:
I was never out of England—it's as if I saw it all.


IV

Did young people take their pleasure when the sea was warm in
 May?
Balls and masks begun at midnight, burning ever to mid-day,
When they made up fresh adventures for the morrow, do you
 say?

The lilt and mad energy of this carries us along, yet the speaker
is reluctant to accept the sophistication of Galuppi and of his audience. The useless good that Galuppi's music still brings saddens the
monologuist even as he performs the madcap piece, vainly resisting its
implications:


V

Was a lady such a lady, cheeks so round and lips so red,—
On her neck the small face buoyant, like a bell-flower on its bed,
O'er the breast's superb abundance where a man might base his
 head?


VI

Well, and it was graceful of them—they'd break talk off and
 afford
—She, to bite her mask's black velvet—he, to finger on his sword,
While you sat and played Toccatas, stately at the clavichord?

VII

What? Those lesser thirds so plaintive, sixths diminished, sigh
     on sigh,
Told them something? Those suspensions, those solutions—
     'Must we die?'
Those commiserating sevenths—'Life might last! we can but
     try!'


VIII

'Were you happy?'—'Yes.'—'And are you still as happy?'—'Yes.
     And you?'
—'Then, more kisses!'—'Did *I* stop them, when a million
     seemed so few?'
Hark, the dominant's persistence till it must be answered to!

Browning's charming devotion to the beauty of women animates and
estranges his speaker's sense of the gathering doom of the sweet life.
The kisses cannot reply to the dominant's persistence, and yet, even at
eighty-seven, one wants to share the illusion of more life, while knowing, like Galuppi's admirers, that time must have a stop:


IX

So, an octave struck the answer. Oh, they praised you, I dare say!
'Brave Galuppi! that was music! good alike at grave and gay!
I can always leave off talking when I hear a master play!'


X

Then they left you for their pleasure: till in due time, one by
     one,
Some with lives that came to nothing, some with deeds as well
     undone,

Death stepped tacitly and took them where they never see the
sun.


## XI

But when I sit down to reason, think to take my stand nor
swerve,
While I triumph o'er a secret wrung from nature's close reserve,
In you come with your cold music till I creep through every
nerve.


## XII

Yes, you, like a ghostly cricket, creaking where a house was
burned:
'Dust and ashes, dead and done with, Venice spent what Venice
earned.
The soul, doubtless, is immortal—where a soul can be
discerned.

The dance became a dance of death, with only two prospects: lives
coming to nothing, and deeds that should not have been. Seeking a
fixed point, the monologuist suffers his own illusive triumph but then
is overwhelmed by the cold splendor of the toccata. Sexually and finan-
cially, Venice spent what it earned, and Galuppi cricket-like sounds out
what Wallace Stevens, indebted to Browning's music poems, meant by
"The house will crumble and the books will burn" in "The Auroras of
Autumn":


## XIII

'Yours for instance: you know physics, something of geology,
Mathematics are your pastime; souls shall rise in their degree;
Butterflies may dread extinction,—you'll not die, it cannot be!

XIV

'As for Venice and her people, merely born to bloom and drop,
Here on earth they bore their fruitage, mirth and folly were the
    crop:
What of soul was left, I wonder, when the kissing had to stop?'


XV

'Dust and ashes!' So you creak it, and I want the heart to scold.
Dear dead women, with such hair, too—what's become of all the
    gold
Used to hang and brush their bosoms? I feel chilly and grown
    old.

The soul, mortal or immortal, can no longer be discerned when the
kissing has to stop. In the marvelous final tercet, to my ear and mind,
Browning, almost in spite of himself, fuses with his speaker. Several of
my remaining friends in my vanishing generation are given to quoting
the two final lines. I brood on women I loved who have departed forever and recall how beautifully they were attired on a particular day and
the glory of their tresses. I too feel chilly and grown old.

# Robert Browning, *Pauline*

"MEMORABILIA" was written by Browning in 1851. A friend recalled Browning saying "with characteristic vehemence: 'I was one day in the shop of Hodgson, the well-known London bookseller, when a stranger . . . spoke of something that Shelley had once said to him. Suddenly the stranger paused, and burst into laughter as he observed me staring at him with blanched face; and,' the poet continued, 'I still vividly remember how strangely the presence of a man who had seen and spoken with Shelley affected me.'"

Browning's sixteen-line tribute to things worth remembering has a simplicity beyond measure and yet condenses his lifelong obsession with Shelley, which began in 1826 when he was fourteen. He had been given a small pirated edition of Shelley's lyrics, and at once he renounced his mother's evangelical Christianity. His attachment to his mother was so close that he yielded to her and promised to abandon Shelley. That proved impossible, and all of his poetry, though it swerves from Shelleyan lyricism to dramatic monologues, in its essence was always Shelleyan:

I

Ah, did you once see Shelley plain,
  And did he stop and speak to you?
And did you speak to him again?
  How strange it seems and new!

II

But you were living before that,
    And you are living after;
And the memory I started at—
    My starting moves your laughter.


III

I crossed a moor, with a name of its own
    And a certain use in the world no doubt,
Yet a hand's-breadth of it shines alone
    'Mid the blank miles round about:


IV

For there I picked up on the heather
    And there I put inside my breast
A moulted feather, an eagle-feather!
    Well, I forget the rest.

Quatrains III and IV subtly translate Browning's wonder. Without any continuity, the poet crosses a moor, one brief stretch of which shines out of the blankness. He picks up a single moulted eagle-feather and places it inside his breast. And that is all. He shrugs and says, "I forget the rest." The aura of Shelley subdues any context. In the early poem *Pauline*, Browning had saluted Shelley as the Sun-treader:

Sun-treader, life and light be thine for ever!
Thou art gone from us; years go by and spring
Gladdens and the young earth is beautiful,
Yet thy songs come not, other bards arise,
But none like thee: they stand, thy majesties,
Like mighty works which tell some spirit there
Hath sat regardless of neglect and scorn,
Till, its long task completed, it hath risen

And left us, never to return, and all
Rush in to peer and praise when all in vain.
The air seems bright with thy past presence yet,
But thou art still for me as thou hast been
When I have stood with thee as on a throne
With all thy dim creations gathered round
Like mountains, and I felt of mould like them,
And with them creatures of my own were mixed,
Like things half-lived, catching and giving life.

This is the incarnation of the poetical character in 1826, very different from the birth of the poet in the odes of William Collins (1721–59). Dying at thirty-seven of alcoholism and derangement, Collins left only a slender body of work, but it included his wonderful "Ode on the Poetical Character." In our time, one thinks of the hilarious "Mrs. Alfred Uruguay" by Wallace Stevens, in which the youth with flashing eyes and floating hair of Collins and of Coleridge in "Kublai Khan" appears again as "A youth, a lover with phosphorescent hair," who rushes down the mountain to find "The ultimate elegance: the imagined land."

Browning beholds Shelley as the ultimate incarnation of the poet: "The air seems bright with thy past presence yet." Nothing could be more unlike "I feel chilly and grown old." Stevens saw the poet as being always in the sun, inheriting this from Shelley in part through the mediumship of Browning. The exceeding brightness of the Sun-treader makes his heirs conceive how dark they have become.

# The Condition of Fire
## at the Dark Tower

I CAN NO LONGER RECALL how many commentaries I have written upon "Childe Roland" (to call it that, since whether the poem has a title is questionable, as is all else in Browning's nightmare vision). The monologuist is nameless, and as a useful convention he can be called Roland. He is certainly not the hero of *The Song of Roland*, the battle epic that is the oldest poem in the French language.

Everyone who has been in a military situation, whether training troops or preparing for a particular mission, knows how dangerous over-preparing the event can be. Too long a focus on an expected action can lead to blindness when the actual site comes into view:

### XXIX

Yet half I seemed to recognize some trick
  Of mischief happened to me, God knows when—
  In a bad dream perhaps. Here ended, then,
Progress this way. When, in the very nick
Of giving up, one time more, came a click
  As when a trap shuts—you 're inside the den!

### XXX

Burningly it came on me all at once,
  This was the place! those two hills on the right,
  Couched like two bulls locked horn in horn in fight;

While to the left, a tall scalped mountain . . . Dunce,
Dotard, a-dozing at the very nonce,
   After a life spent training for the sight!

## XXXI

What in the midst lay but the Tower itself?
   The round squat turret, blind as the fool's heart,
   Built of brown stone, without a counterpart
In the whole world. The tempest's mocking elf
Points to the shipman thus the unseen shelf
   He strikes on, only when the timbers start.

"What in the midst lay but the Tower itself?" With that outcry, Roland's quest falls away into the iniquity of oblivion. Since he wants to fail, like the knights in "The Band" before him, his apparent defeat may also be victory:

## XXXII

Not see? because of night perhaps?—why, day
   Came back again for that! before it left,
   The dying sunset kindled through a cleft:
The hills, like giants at a hunting, lay,
Chin upon hand, to see the game at bay,—
   "Now stab and end the creature—to the heft!"

## XXXIII

Not hear? when noise was everywhere! it tolled
   Increasing like a bell. Names in my ears
   Of all the lost adventurers my peers,—
How such a one was strong, and such was bold,
And such was fortunate, yet each of old
   Lost, lost! one moment knelled the woe of years.

XXXIV

There they stood, ranged along the hill-sides, met
   To view the last of me, a living frame
   For one more picture! in a sheet of flame
I saw them and I knew them all. And yet
Dauntless the slug-horn to my lips I set,
   And blew. "Childe Roland to the Dark Tower came."

Browning said this astonishing monologue was the work of a single
day following a dream. The windowless tower suggests the imprisonment of the poet Torquato Tasso in the days of his madness and recalls
Shelley's "Julian and Maddalo":

I looked, and saw between us and the sun
A building on an island; such a one
As age to age might add, for uses vile,
A windowless, deformed and dreary pile;
And on the top an open tower, where hung
A bell, which in the radiance swayed and swung;
We could just hear its hoarse and iron tongue:
The broad sun sunk behind it, and it tolled
In strong and black relief.—'What we behold
Shall be the madhouse and its belfry tower,' . . .

Lines 98–107

Byron, in the guise of Count Maddalo, addresses Shelley, who
will enter Roland's monologue at the close: "Be through my lips to
unawakened earth / The trumpet of a prophecy!" Browning takes the
slug-horn from Thomas Chatterton, who poisoned himself at the age
of seventeen, when his forgery of the supposed Thomas Rowley was
uncovered and scorned. William Blake and William Wordsworth both
venerated Chatterton, seeing him as a harbinger of what we call High
Romanticism. "Slug-horn" was a Chattertonian corruption of "slogan"
and serves to bind Roland to the band of brothers that for Browning
embraced Shelley, Tasso, Chatterton, and all the other lost adventurers
who quested for the Dark Tower.

. . .

Roland, facing not an ogre but a sheet of flame constituted by his peers ringed round him, cries out:

> And yet
> Dauntless the slug-horn to my lips I set,
>     And blew. "Childe Roland to the Dark Tower came."

"Dauntless" is the word that the ruined quester has earned. Like Tennyson's Ulysses, Roland could also have chanted: "To strive, to seek, to find, and not to yield."

# Robert Browning,
## "Thamuris Marching"

R OBERT BROWNING, exuberant beyond belief, composed a palinode to his "Childe Roland to the Dark Tower Came" in a late, long
poem, *Aristophanes' Apology*. The poem I find barely readable except
for the chant of Thamuris as he marches pridefully and courageously
toward his doomed contest with the Muses. Here is Browning's source,
*Iliad* II, lines 594–600.

> . . . and Dorion, where the Muses
> encountering Thamyris the Thracian stopped him from singing
> as he came from Oichalia and Oichalian Eurytos;
> for he boasted that he would prevail, if the very Muses,
> daughters of Zeus who holds the aegis, were singing against
>   him,
> and these in their anger struck him maimed, and the voice of
>   wonder
> they took away, and made him a singer without memory. . . .
>                                   Translation by Richmond Lattimore

Shelley's ongoing influence on Browning emerges again in the
High Romanticism of a section of *Aristophanes' Apology* I have entitled
"Thamuris Marching":

> Thamuris marching,—lyre and song of Thrace—
> (Perpend the first, the worst of woes that were,
> Allotted lyre and song, ye poet-race!)

Thamuris from Oichalia, feasted there
By kingly Eurutos of late, now bound
For Dorion at the uprise broad and bare

Of Mount Pangaios (ore with earth enwound
Glittered beneath his footstep)—marching gay
And glad, Thessalia through, came, robed and crowned,

From triumph on to triumph, 'mid a ray
Of early morn,—came, saw and knew the spot
Assigned him for his worst of woes, that day.

Balura—happier while its name was not—
Met him, but nowise menaced; slipt aside,
Obsequious river, to pursue its lot

Of solacing the valley—say, some wide
Thick busy human cluster, house and home,
Embanked for peace, or thrift that thanks the tide.

The river Balyra, from the Greek for "cast away," was named because
Thamyris, after the Muses blinded him, threw his lyre into it. Robed
and crowned, glorified by the morning sunlight, Thamuris boldly
marches to disaster. But, in total antithesis to Childe Roland, this lost
adventurer rekindles the wasteland:

Thamuris, marching, laughed "Each flake of foam"
(As sparklingly the ripple raced him by)
"Mocks slower clouds adrift in the blue dome!"

For Autumn was the season: red the sky
Held morn's conclusive signet of the sun
To break the mists up, bid them blaze and die.

Morn had the mastery as, one by one,
All pomps produced themselves along the tract
From earth's far ending to near heaven begun.

Was there a ravaged tree? it laughed compact
With gold, a leaf-ball crisp, high-brandished now,
Tempting to onset frost which late attacked.

Was there a wizened shrub, a starveling bough,
A fleecy thistle filched from by the wind,
A weed, Pan's trampling hoof would disallow?

Each, with a glory and a rapture twined
About it, joined the rush of air and light
And force: the world was of one joyous mind.

Say not the birds flew! they forebore their right—
Swam, revelling onward in the roll of things.
Say not the beasts' mirth bounded! that was flight—

How could the creatures leap, no lift of wings?
Such earth's community of purpose, such
The ease of earth's fulfilled imaginings,—

So did the near and far appear to touch
I' the moment's transport,—that an interchange
Of function, far with near, seemed scarce too much;

And had the rooted plant aspired to range
With the snake's license, while the insect yearned
To glow fixed as the flower it were not strange. . . .

All of nature lives more blazingly in the sunlight of an autumn
morning. Rapturously, even ravaged trees, wizened shrubs, starveling
boughs, thistles, and weeds join the joyous rush of light and air. Birds
swim, beasts fly, as all of earth's imaginings are fulfilled. The transport
of each moment raises every dimension of being a step higher in the
scale. Singing as he marches, the poet Thamuris vaunts his lucid passion for the hopeless agon with the Muses:

No more than if the fluttery tree-top turned
To actual music, sang itself aloft;
Or if the wind, impassioned chantress, earned

The right to soar embodied in some soft
Fine form all fit for cloud-companionship,
And, blissful, once touch beauty chased so oft.

Thamuris, marching, let no fancy slip
Born of the fiery transport; lyre and song
Were his, to smite with hand and launch from lip—

Peerless recorded, since the list grew long
Of poets (saith Homeros) free to stand
Pedestalled 'mid the Muses' temple-throng,

A statued service, laurelled, lyre in hand,
(Ay, for we see them)—Thamuris of Thrace
Predominating foremost of the band.

Therefore the morn-ray that enriched his face,
If it gave lambent chill, took flame again
From flush of pride; he saw, he knew the place.

What wind arrived with all the rhythms from plain,
Hill, dale, and that rough wildwood interspersed?
Compounding these to one consummate strain,

It reached him, music; but his own outburst
Of victory concluded the account,
And that grew song which was mere music erst.

"Be my Parnassos, thou Pangaian mount!
And turn thee, river, nameless hitherto!
Famed shalt thou vie with famed Pieria's fount!

Here I await the end of this ado:
Which wins—Earth's poet or the Heavenly Muse."

Thamuris fuses with Percy Bysshe Shelley in this defiant lyric. The "Ode to the West Wind" hovers as the forest becomes a lyre and the wind companions the cloud. Childe Roland's band of brothers throng the pedestals of the temple of the Muses, and Thamuris, seeking to be foremost among them, reverses the outcry of: "Burningly it came on me all at once, / This was the place!" and takes flame: "he saw, he knew the place."

The Muses are cruel and blind him for his audacity. They destroy his possession by memory, and thus end his poetic gift. But when I chant his poem, to myself or to others, he seems among the victorious and not among the defeated. The terza rima adapted by Shelley from Dante makes me think of Brunetto Latini, whose instruction and whose poetry helped make Dante possible. Browning's Thamuris was his own final tribute to Shelley, without whom the master of dramatic lyrics and monologues might not have been able to begin.

# George Meredith,
## "A Ballad of Past Meridian"

G EORGE MEREDITH at fifty-five composed "A Ballad of Past Meridian" with an acute awareness of what Wallace Stevens at thirty-nine, in his "Le Monocle de Mon Oncle," ruefully confessed: "No spring can follow past meridian." Stevens was jocular, but Meredith was much darker:

I

Last night returning from my twilight walk
I met the grey mist Death, whose eyeless brow
Was bent on me, and from his hand of chalk
He reached me flowers as from a withered bough:
O Death, what bitter nosegays givest thou!

II

Death said, I gather, and pursued his way.
Another stood by me, a shape in stone,
Sword-hacked and iron-stained, with breasts of clay,
And metal veins that sometimes fiery shone:
O Life, how naked and how hard when known!

III

Life said, As thou hast carved me, such am I.
Then memory, like the nightjar on the pine,
And sightless hope, a woodlark in night sky,
Joined notes of Death and Life till night's decline
Of Death, of Life, those inwound notes are mine.

I chant this rather too frequently these March days, because the friends of my lifetime keep falling away. Death is rather less horrifying here than the stony shape of Life. Flowers, however bitter, are not bestowed by Life, whose shape is our creation. Perhaps Meredith recalls the withering of his first marriage, to the daughter of Thomas Love Peacock, who was a friend of Shelley's. Peacock is charmingly satirized by Shelley in *Nightmare Abbey* as Scythrop Glowry; Lord Byron appears as Mr. Cypress and Coleridge as Ferdinando Flosky. Readers of Meredith's masterpiece of a comic novel, *The Egoist*, will recognize Clara Middleton as a portrait of Mary Ellen Peacock, who ran off with the minor Pre-Raphaelite painter Henry Wallis after nine years of unhappy union with the poet-novelist, who surmounted this wound to his psyche only when he happily remarried in 1864.

Brilliantly, Meredith compares poetic memory to the nocturnal song of the nightjar or nighthawk, as it is named in North America, and blind hope to the woodlark in the night sky. The strains of Death and of Life are so wound in one another that only Meredith's ballad can fuse both dreadful entities. One hears in the far background an under-song of Keatsian tradition as modified by Dante Gabriel Rossetti. Meredith, during the unhappy interval between his two marriages, shared a single madhouse of a residence with Rosetti, Algernon Charles Swinburne, and a host of exotic animals.

I speculate sometimes as to what Keats would have thought had he survived to read "A Ballad of Past Meridian." As the most healthy-minded of any great poet since Shakespeare himself, he might have associated it with his magnificent "La Belle Dame sans Merci."

# Algernon Charles Swinburne, "August"

Algernon Charles Swinburne (1837–1909), like his master Shelley, was wholly daemonic and opposed to the theological traditions of the West. He admired Coleridge for the older poet's natural magic, yet demurred at any worship of the logos. Very few now read Swinburne, which is a great loss. In my long nights awake, I recite silently his exquisite "August" or, rather, chant it. The poet grew up on the Isle of Wight, where the demarcations between sea and beach constantly shift.

His cousin Mary Gordon was his constant playmate as they grew up together. Swinburne's sexual orientation became sadomasochistic, and by middle age he was a total alcoholic. His nostalgia for the familial love he had shared with his cousin never left him and triumphs in "August":

There were four apples on the bough,
Half gold half red, that one might know
The blood was ripe inside the core;
The colour of the leaves was more
Like stems of yellow corn that grow
Through all the gold June meadow's floor.

The warm smell of the fruit was good
To feed on, and the split green wood,
With all its bearded lips and stains
Of mosses in the cloven veins,
Most pleasant, if one lay or stood
In sunshine or in happy rains.

There were four apples on the tree,
Red stained through gold, that all might see
The sun went warm from core to rind;
The green leaves made the summer blind
In that soft place they kept for me
With golden apples shut behind.

This Keatsian ripeness matures into a sudden ecstasy:

The leaves caught gold across the sun,
And where the bluest air begun
Thirsted for song to help the heat;
As I to feel my lady's feet
Draw close before the day were done
Both lips grew dry with dreams of it.

In the mute August afternoon
They trembled to some undertune
Of music in the silver air;
Great pleasure was it to be there
Till green turned duskier and the moon
Coloured the corn-sheaves like gold hair.

That August time it was delight
To watch the red moons wane to white
'Twixt grey seamed stems of apple-trees;
A sense of heavy harmonies
Grew on the growth of patient night,
More sweet than shapen music is.

Dreams irradiate this poignant fantasy that catches the feeling-tone
of his unformed desire for his cousin. Moonlight colors corn-sheaves
as though they were Mary Gordon's golden tresses. Heavy harmonies,
however sweet, are hollowed out through unfulfillment:

But some three hours before the moon
The air, still eager from the noon,
Flagged after heat, not wholly dead;

Against the stem I leant my head;
The colour soothed me like a tune,
Green leaves all round the gold and red.

I lay there till the warm smell grew
More sharp, when flecks of yellow dew
Between the round ripe leaves that blurred
The rind with stain and wet; I heard
A wind that blew and breathed and blew,
Too weak to alter its one word.

The wet leaves next the gentle fruit
Felt smoother, and the brown tree-root
Felt the mould warmer: I too felt
(As water feels the slow gold melt
Right through it when the day burns mute)
The peace of time wherein love dwelt.

There were four apples on the tree,
Gold stained on red that all might see
That sweet blood filled them to the core:
The colour of her hair is more
Like stems of fair faint gold, that be
Mown from the harvest's middle floor.

When this is chanted aloud, its gathering force can be extraordinary. Those four apples in this Eden remain unbitten, and the Eve of Swinburne's paradise will never be the poet's bride. And yet "August" remains ecstatic though the implied narrative is one of loss. All fruit is filled with ripeness to the core, but this ripeness is scarcely all.

# Algernon Charles Swinburne, "Hertha"

S HELLEY'S INFLUENCE UPON Algernon Charles Swinburne was lifelong. A mythmaking poet who fused Shelley with other High Romantics—William Blake, Ralph Waldo Emerson, Walt Whitman, Victor Hugo, and that debased parody the Marquis de Sade—Swinburne wrote what he regarded as his central poem, "Hertha." This powerful stasis of a monologue is spoken by the Northern earth goddess who was the patroness of growth and fertility. With the touch of a Browning confession, she defines her own identity for us:

> I am that which began;
> > Out of me the years roll;
> > Out of me God and man;
> > > I am equal and whole;
> > God changes, and man, and the form of them bodily; I am the
> > > soul.

> > Before ever land was,
> > > Before ever the sea,
> > Or soft hair of the grass,
> > > Or fair limbs of the tree,
> > Or the fresh-coloured fruit of my branches, I was, and thy soul
> > > was in me.

> > First life on my sources
> > > First drifted and swam;
> > Out of me are the forces
> > > That save it or damn;

Out of me man and woman, and wild-beast and bird; before
    God was, I am.

    Beside or above me
        Nought is there to go;
    Love or unlove me,
        Unknow me or know,
I am that which unloves me and loves; I am stricken, and I am
    the blow.

.   .   .   .   .

    But what thing dost thou now,
        Looking Godward, to cry
    "I am I, thou art thou,
        I am low, thou art high"?
I am thou, whom thou seekest to find him; find thou but thyself,
    thou art I.

    I the grain and the furrow,
        The plough-cloven clod
    And the ploughshare drawn thorough,
        The germ and the sod,
The deed and the doer, the seed and the sower, the dust which is
    God.

That opening "I am" deliberately blasphemes Jesus in John 8:58, "Before Abraham was, I am," with its echo of Exodus 3:14: "And God said unto Moses 'I AM THAT I AM.'" A touch of the *Bhagavad-Gita* enters in "I am the blow," by way of Emerson's poem "Brahma":

If the red slayer think he slays,
    Or if the slain think he is slain,
They know not well the subtle ways
    I keep, and pass, and turn again.

Charmingly maintaining his blasphemy, Swinburne reduces God to the Adamic dust. His fixed hymn to surging growth continues with mounting urgency:

Hast thou known how I fashioned thee,
    Child, underground?
Fire that impassioned thee,
    Iron that bound,
Dim changes of water, what thing of all these hast thou known
    of or found?

Canst thou say in thine heart
    Thou hast seen with thine eyes
With what cunning of art
    Thou wast wrought in what wise,
By what force of what stuff thou wast shapen, and shown on my
    breast to the skies?

.  .  .  .  .

What is here, dost thou know it?
    What was, hast thou known?
Prophet nor poet
    Nor tripod nor throne
Nor spirit nor flesh can make answer, but only thy mother
    alone.

Mother, not maker,
    Born, and not made;
Though her children forsake her,
    Allured or afraid,
Praying prayers to the God of their fashion, she stirs not for all
    that have prayed.

The voice of God out of the whirlwind with its rhetorical questions
in Job 38–39 sets the pattern for Hertha's unanswerable queries. The
tripod, three-legged stool, sat upon by the Oracle's priestess at Delphi,
represents all of priesthood, and the evolving Mother of Nature rejects
any single act of Creation:

A creed is a rod,
    And a crown is of night;
But this thing is God,

To be man with thy might,
To grow straight in the strength of thy spirit, and live out thy
　　life as the light.

I am in thee to save thee,
　　　As my soul in thee saith;
Give thou as I gave thee,
　　　Thy life-blood and breath,
Green leaves of thy labour, white flowers of thy thought, and red
　　fruit of thy death.

．　．　．　．　．

I that saw where ye trod
　　　The dim paths of the night
Set the shadow called God
　　　In your skies to give light;
But the morning of manhood is risen, and the shadowless soul is
　　in sight.

The tree many-rooted
　　　That swells to the sky
With frondage red-fruited,
　　　The life-tree am I;
In the buds of your lives is the sap of my leaves: ye shall live and
　　not die.

But the Gods of your fashion
　　　That take and that give,
In their pity and passion
　　　That scourge and forgive,
They are worms that are bred in the bark that falls off; they shall
　　die and not live.

We fashion God and pray to him because we are afraid. With Sadean
gusto, the earth goddess tells us that creeds are whips and that our
darkness imposes kingship upon us. The true God emanates from
Blake's apocalyptic humanism, and Swinburne again echoes Shelley's
Promethean hope and Emerson's grand remark: "As men's prayers are

a disease of their will, so are their creeds a disease of the intellect."
Hertha, the goddess within, saves us from jingoism and religion. She
pays tribute to Swinburne's hero of Italian liberation, Mazzini, with the
green, white, and red colors of Italy's flag. Waning Christianities are
seen as lights that vanish as the sun rises. The God of Western mono-
theism is dismissed as a shadow, and instead the ash World-Tree of
Northern myth, Yggdrasil, mounts up to the sky from its myriad roots:

> My own blood is what stanches
>     The wounds in my bark;
> Stars caught in my branches
>     Make day of the dark,
> And are worshipped as suns till the sunrise shall tread out their
>     fires as a spark.

                    .   .   .   .   .

> That noise is of Time,
>     As his feathers are spread
> And his feet set to climb
>     Through the boughs overhead,
> And my foliage rings round him and rustles, and branches are
>     bent with his tread.

> The storm-winds of ages
>     Blow through me and cease,
> The war-wind that rages,
>     The spring-wind of peace,
> Ere the breath of them roughen my tresses, ere one of my
>     blossoms increase.

                    .   .   .   .   .

> All forms of all faces,
>     All works of all hands
> In unsearchable places
>     Of time-stricken lands,
> All death and all life, and all reigns and all ruins, drop through
>     me as sands.

Though sore be my burden
    And more than ye know,
And my growth have no guerdon
    But only to grow,
Yet I fail not of growing for lightnings above me or deathworms
    below.

These too have their part in me,
    As I too in these;
Such fire is at heart in me,
    Such sap is this tree's,
Which hath in it all sounds and all secrets of infinite lands and
    of seas.

Hertha might well be Krishna speaking to Arjuna in the *Bhagavad-Gita*, declaring that he contains everything and that liberation can be reached in every act and thought. But Swinburne's Hertha is a polemicist unceasingly battling against religiosity and tyranny. Also, she promises no Mary Gordon or reward for herself or for the reader. There is only growth. Echoing the high song of Shelley's "To a Skylark" throughout, her hymn is rather prolix; Swinburne envied but could not emulate Shelley's uncanny speed of cadence and precision of trope. Much as I have always been fascinated by Hertha, I could wish it shorter. Nevertheless, the poem raises itself to an eloquent drive beyond the pleasure principle in its closing strophes:

. . . . .

I bid you but be;
    I have need not of prayer;
I have need of you free
    As your mouths of mine air;
That my heart may be greater within me, beholding the fruits of
    me fair.

More fair than strange fruit is
    Of faiths ye espouse;
In me only the root is
    That blooms in your boughs;

Behold now your God that ye made you, to feed him with faith
  of your vows.

> In the darkening and whitening
>     Abysses adored,
> With dayspring and lightning
>     For lamp and for sword,
> God thunders in heaven, and his angels are red with the wrath
>   of the Lord.

.   .   .   .   .

> Lo, winged with world's wonders,
>     With miracles shod,
> With the fires of his thunders
>     For raiment and rod,
> God trembles in heaven, and his angels are white with the terror
>   of God.

> For his twilight is come on him,
>     His anguish is here;
> And his spirits gaze dumb on him,
>     Grown grey from his fear;
> And his hour taketh hold on him stricken, the last of his infinite
>   year.

> Thought made him and breaks him,
>     Truth slays and forgives;
> But to you, as time takes him,
>     This new thing it gives,
> Even love, the beloved Republic, that feeds upon freedom and
>   lives.

.   .   .   .   .

> One birth of my bosom;
>     One beam of mine eye;
> One topmost blossom

That scales the sky;
Man, equal and one with me, man that is made of me, man that
    is I.

Victor Hugo's sense of the Abyss in his posthumously published
mythopoeic brief epics, *The End of Satan* and *God*, is employed here
free-style, and Walt Whitman's "Song of Myself" hovers in the foreground. The Northern prophecy of the twilight of the gods will be
fulfilled by all the Christianities. Freedom will be Shelleyan: "love, the
beloved Republic," and we will be made one with a Nature different
indeed from Wordsworthian imaginings.

"Hertha," like most of Swinburne, has lost its audience, but that
is indeed an aesthetic sorrow. In his elegy for Baudelaire, "Ave Atque
Vale," the title taken from the final line of Catullus's lament for his
brother, Swinburne concludes nobly with the legend of Niobe, whose
children were slain by Apollo and Artemis, to satisfy their jealous
mother, Leto:

For thee, O now a silent soul, my brother,
    Take at my hands this garland, and farewell.
    Thin is the leaf, and chill the wintry smell,
And chill the solemn earth, a fatal mother,
    With sadder than the Niobean womb,
    And in the hollow of her breasts a tomb.
Content thee, howsoe'er, whose days are done;
    There lies not any troublous thing before,
    Nor sight nor sound to war against thee more,
For whom all winds are quiet as the sun,
    All waters as the shore.

Those last five lines never leave me. I lose old friends every month
or so now. Consolation is difficult to find, but elegiac poetry helps.
Swinburne praised Walt Whitman's "When Lilacs Last in the Dooryard Bloom'd" as "the most sonorous nocturne ever chanted in the
church of the world." Later, the mercurial and alcoholic disciple of
Sade recanted, but the eulogy stands. "Hertha" and a score of other
poems by Swinburne are permanent achievements and will survive
their current eclipse.

# Part Four

# The Imperfect Is Our Paradise:
## Walt Whitman
## and Twentieth-Century
## American Poetry

# The Psalms and Walt Whitman

I ONCE SPENT an afternoon with the late Richard Wilbur, admirable poet and translator. He began by reading to me his poem "A Black Birch in Winter," which had just appeared in the *Atlantic*, in January 1974. I requested a copy and wish to discuss it here in honor of his memory, since he died only two months ago, on October 14, 2017, at the age of ninety-six:

> You might not know this old tree by its bark,
> Which once was striate, smooth, and glossy-dark,
> So deep now are the rifts that separate
> Its roughened surface into flake and plate.
>
> Fancy might less remind you of a birch
> Than of mosaic columns in a church
> Like Ara Coeli or the Lateran
> Or the trenched features of an aged man.
>
> Still, do not be too much persuaded by
> These knotty furrows and these tesserae
> To think of patterns made from outside in
> Or finished wisdom in a shriveled skin.
> Old trees are doomed to annual rebirth,
> New wood, new life, new compass, greater girth,
> And this is all their wisdom and their art—
> To grow, stretch, crack, and not yet come apart.

Dick was only in his early fifties when he wrote this, yet it is an old man's poem, suitable for me at the age of eighty-seven. It is December 16, 2017, and New Haven is cold and icy. I wince a little at "flake and plate," nod at "Or the trenched features of an aged man," and hearten a little at being urged not to be too much persuaded to think I am unfinished wisdom in a shriveled skin. I wish I could believe fully in the final stanza, but would be content still "To grow, stretch, crack, and not yet come apart."

At Wilbur's suggestion, we alternated reading aloud to each other some of the Psalms, as well as passages from "Song of Myself." It was his idea that Whitman used the Psalms as his model. We know that Whitman's father and mother were followers of the radical Quaker circuit-riding Elias Hicks. In old age, Walt recalled hearing Hicks preach and continued to regard him as one of the prophets. The style of the Hicksite meetings encouraged participation and testimony and the singing of Psalms. It is important to have a clear conception of the Psalms before we fully encounter Whitman.

Biblical style in English carries on it the palpable impress of the Protestant martyr William Tyndale (1494–1536). Strangled and then burned, with the approval of Henry VIII, Tyndale did not have time to complete his translation of the Christian Old Testament, as he had the New. All English Bibles after Tyndale manifest his continued presence, and not only because he was the crucial forerunner. It is not excessive to judge that, after Shakespeare and Chaucer, Tyndale may be the greatest writer in the language. We go about daily—many of us—unknowingly repeating sentences, phrases, and words invented by Tyndale as by Shakespeare. The Geneva Bible (1560) was Shakespeare's resource, from Shylock and Falstaff in 1596 onward, and continued to be favored by John Milton. For most of the English, it yielded to the Authorized Version or King James Bible (1611), which maintains its hold on the English-speaking world, though that may be shifting. Both the Geneva and King James Bibles follow Tyndale wherever they can, so that he remains, with Shakespeare, a comprehensive influence upon us.

David Daniell, Tyndale's biographer, has written persuasively concerning the translator's effect upon Shakespeare's various styles in the later tragedies. Tyndale is the master, when he chooses to be, of a style of plain speaking: short pronouncements held together by parataxis, with no subordinate clauses. "Parataxis" is a word I employ reluctantly (it makes my students unhappy), but there is no good substitute for it, whether in discussing Tyndale and Shakespeare, or Walt Whitman and

Hemingway. It is from the Greek for "placing side by side" and emphasizes a way of juxtaposing phrases that is central to the style of Biblical Hebrew, with its parallel syntactic clauses, which tend also to possess a parallelism of meaning.

Shakespeare's grand gift, for phrasing so memorably that we find the language inevitable, is very nearly matched by Tyndale's outspoken directness of address, what Daniell calls his "everyday manner," and his aversion to Latinity. Getting Tyndale out of my head seems to me impossible: "Let there be light, and there was light"; "In him we live, and move, and have our being"; "Am I my brother's keeper?"; "The signs of the times"; "The spirit is willing, but the flesh is weak"; "Hast thou power wrestled with God and with men, and hast prevailed"; and scores of others. Whether I immerse myself in the Geneva or the King James Bible, Tyndale's genius (though not his Protestant zeal) enriches me.

The book of Psalms, particularly in the King James Version, is the best-known part of the Hebrew Bible (or Christian Old Testament, if you will). Psalm 23, in its King James text, indubitably is recognized even by people who have never read the Bible: "The Lord is my shepherd; I shall not want." Though ascribed to King David, whose historical existence is as uncertain as that of his supposed descendant Jesus, the Psalms are no more David's than the Song of Songs is Solomon's or the Five Books Moses's. There is not much in the Bible, whether Hebrew or Christian, that can withstand historical skepticism. The Exodus is as mythical as the Creation, or the Crucifixion. In the United States at this time, religion is politicized, and no one running for office dares to be other than outwardly pious. The abyss between the United States and Western Europe (barring Ireland) is now absolute, in this area.

Scholars agree that the Psalms are an anthology, or a bundle of anthologies, composed during six centuries. Many of the songs were written for use in the Jerusalem Temple, though later Psalms clearly tend to have been created for other purposes. We are likely to characterize all 150 Psalms as "religious poetry," but that is disputable. Six centuries of a poetic tradition, analogous to English poetry from Chaucer through Yeats, necessarily develop what we could now regard as aesthetic competition. Even with the esoteric tradition of Kabbalah, it helps to consider the literary motives of Kabbalistic authors, who frequently have an agonistic relation to one another.

Some of the early Psalms show a debt to Canaanite mythology, which was polytheistic. From 996 to 457 B.C.E. and beyond is an ocean of time. From Judges past the return from Babylon, ideas of God underwent many metamorphoses. The Authorized Version smooths out differences, but the God the Psalms address has varied guises that closeness to the Hebrew text is better able to reveal. Theologically, Tyndale and his progeny were Calvinists, and Yahweh is not a Presbyterian. But how refreshing it is to read the Psalms in their abrupt rhythms, cleared of irrelevant Protestant "salvation history." There is no Jewish theology before the Hellenistic Philo of Alexandria. Theology, a Greek idea and term, is alien to the Hebrew Bible. When I encounter discussions of "the theology of the Old Testament," I wander off, but I am held by its darkly economical texts.

Hebrew tradition always refers to the book of Psalms by a noun meaning "praises." On their surface, the Psalms praise Yahweh (under various names), and even the frequent appeals for his help abound with overtones of gratitude. From childhood through old age, I have been made uncomfortable by a God who demands sacrifices that are also thanksgivings. Post-Holocaust, this will not work for many among us, and I frequently retreat from the Psalms to the poetry of Paul Celan, which has a difficult rightness, and does not seek to praise what no longer can be praised.

The Psalms give us a Yahweh who himself is a living labyrinth of parallelisms and parataxis. Tradition affirms that Yahweh gave us Hebrew; did Hebrew syntax give us Yahweh? The Hebrew language, Yahweh, and his book, Tanakh, pragmatically are the same.

I wonder whether ancient Hebrew thinking is still available to us at all. Perhaps only Shakespeare rethought everything through for himself; the Psalms do not, though we can scarcely pick out what may once have been original in them. Was it a making of praise, gratitude, supplication, even despair into modes of *thinking*? Angus Fletcher and A. D. Nuttall, both in Wittgenstein's wake, gave us useful conjectures as to how Shakespeare thought. Biblical thinking is mostly opaque to our understanding, and the Psalms particularly puzzle me, since many of them are and yet are not prayers. The human analogues may aid in apprehending the Psalms. Anyone called upon too frequently to endorse books and students learns that praise can be both a subtle kind of thinking or rethinking, and also a treacherous one.

The God of the Psalms has comforted multitudes, whether in the valley of decision, or in the valley of the shadow of death. He does not comfort me, because I do not know how to think in a realm of gratitude. When I returned to life this late August, after nine days in a hospital recovering from a syncope, I went back to reading Shakespeare instead of the Bible. There is no separation between life and literature in Shakespeare. Because of American politics, and our crusading zeal abroad, one needs to keep the Bible apart from the way we live now.

The Psalms are a bolder and more problematic field for literary energies and knowledge to explore than either the Five Books or the David saga, because ancient Hebrew poetry seems untranslatable into contemporary American English. The King James Psalms are familiar, comforting or daunting, and almost continuously eloquent. Yet there is little that is Hebraic about them; they have become marvelous Christian prose poems. I prefer to be rougher about this two-thousand-year-old theft. The Old Testament is a captive work dragged along in the triumphal wake of Christianity. Tanakh, the Jewish Bible, is the Original Testament; the New Testament actually is the Belated Testament. I wince when my Jewish students speak of the Old Testament. Yet there are perhaps fourteen million self-identified Jews now alive, and some two billion, three hundred million ostensible Christians. The arithmetic is beyond me, but if God is with the big battalions, then he would seem to have forsaken his People of the Book.

Tyndale was a far stronger writer than Anthony Gilbey and his Geneva Bible colleagues, or than Gilbey's revisionists in King James. But Gilbey too was an extraordinary prose-poet—though, however good his Hebrew may have been, his intentions were doctrinal rather than aesthetic. The abruptness of the Hebrew, its powerful economy, is transferred to us, but the results sometimes are jagged. I start now with Tyndale, who rendered Psalm 18, embedded in 2 Samuel 22, and parts of Psalms 105, 96, and 106, included in 1 Chronicles 16. Here is the opening of Tyndale's Psalm 18:

And he said: The Lord is my rock, my castle and my deliverer.
 God is my strength, and in him will I trust: my shield and the
 horn that defendeth me: mine high hold and refuge: O my
 Saviour, save me from wrong.

I will praise and call on the Lord, and so shall be saved from
 mine enemies. For the waves of death have closed me about,
 and the floods of Belial have feared me. The cords of hell
 have compassed me about, and the snares of death have
 overtaken me. In my tribulation I called to the Lord, and
 cried to my God. And he heard my voice out of his temple,
 and my cry entered into his ears. And the earth trembled
 and quoke and the foundations of heaven moved and shook,
 because he was angry.
Smoke went up out of his nostrils, and consuming fire out of his
 mouth, that coals were kindled of him. And he bowed heaven
 and came down, and darkness underneath his feet. And he
 rode upon Cherub and flew: and appeared upon the wings
 of the wind. And he made darkness a tabernacle round about
 him, with water gathered together in thick clouds. Of the
 brightness, that was before him, coals were set on fire.
The Lord thundered from heaven, and the Most High put out
 his voice. And he shot arrows and scattered them, and hurled
 lightning and turmoiled them. And the bottom of the sea
 appeared, and the foundations of the world were seen, by the
 reason of the rebuking of the Lord, and through the blasting
 of the breath of his nostrils. He sent from on high and
 fetched me, and plucked me out of mighty waters.

With this Psalm, traditionally regarded as David's victory ode, Tyndale takes the Psalm, not of course for accuracy but for preternatural
force and eloquence. This may or may not be Yahweh, but certainly he
*is* John Calvin's ferocious God. Tyndale writes like a possessed man,
overcome by Jehovah's power. (I change God's name because "Jehovah" was Tyndale's own coinage, founded upon a spelling error.) King
James softens Tyndale's intensity in Psalm 18, wary of his burning
Calvinism.

The Psalms have drawn many verse translations, including poets
as gifted as Thomas Campion, Richard Crashaw, Thomas Carew, and
John Milton. But only scholars now read them, so I quote from the
King James Authorized Version of Psalm 137:

By the rivers of Babylon, there we sat down, yea, we wept, when
 we remembered Zion.

We hanged our harps upon the willows in the midst thereof.
For there they that carried us away captive required of us a song;
and they that wasted us required of us mirth, saying, Sing us
one of the songs of Zion.
How shall we sing the Lord's song in a strange land?
If I forget thee, O Jerusalem, let my right hand forget her
cunning.
If I do not remember thee, let my tongue cleave to the roof of
my mouth; if I prefer not Jerusalem above my chief joy.

The cadences of the Authorized Version are beyond argument. Who
would not choose "How shall we sing the Lord's song in a strange land?
If I forget thee, O Jerusalem"? The phrasing of 1611 is a miracle of
style, testifying to the Age of Shakespeare. The last word here belongs
to the poet-critic John Hollander:

The verse of the Hebrew Bible is strange; the meter in Psalms
and Proverbs perplexes.
It is not a matter of number, no counting of beats or syllables.
Its song is a music of matching, its rhythm a kind of paralleling.
One half-line makes an assertion; the other part paraphrases it;
sometimes a third part will vary it.
An abstract statement meets with its example, yes, the way a
wind runs through the trees moving leaves.
One river's water is heard on another's shore; so did this
Hebrew verse form carry across into English.

Walt Whitman made a rough start on what was to become *Leaves of
Grass* (1855) as early as 1850. But the notebook fragments that were
to become "Song of Myself," the principal poem of that volume, were
composed in 1853. After a career as a New York City journalist, Whitman returned to his parents and brothers and his native Long Island to
work as a carpenter and house builder:

I am your voice—It was tied in you—In me it begins to talk.
I celebrate myself to celebrate every man and woman alive;
I loosen the tongue that was tied in them,
It begins to talk out of my mouth.

I celebrate myself to celebrate you:
I say the same word for every man and woman alive.
And I say that the soul is not greater than the body,
And I say that the body is not greater than the soul.

This fragment commences the amazing immediacy of Whitman's poetic stance and style. He is our repressed voice, celebrating himself and all of us in the triple sense of acknowledging, performing, and honoring. Walt is a loosener, a liberator of the word, which is universal. He stands between soul and body, and urges them to become a unison. Yet the meeting of soul, fictive self, and the inward real me or me myself, is disruptive and overcome by the body's sexuality:

One touch of a tug of me has unhaltered all my senses but
    feeling
That pleases the rest so, they have given up to it in submission
They are all emulous to swap themselves off for what it can do
    to them.
Every one must be a touch
Or else she will abdicate and nibble only at the edges of the
    feeling.

They move caressingly up and down my body
They leave themselves and come with bribes to whatever part of
    me touches.—
To my lips, to the palms of my hand, and whatever my hands
    hold.
Each brings the best she has,
For each is in love with touch.
I do not wonder that one feeling now does so much for me,
He is free of all the rest,—and swiftly begets offspring of them,
    better than the dams.
A touch now reads me a library of knowledge in an instant.
It smells for me the fragrance of wine and lemon-blows.
It tastes for me ripe strawberries and mellons,—
It talks for me with a tongue of its own,
It finds an ear wherever it rests or taps.
It brings the rest around it, and they all stand on a headland and
    mock me

They have left me to touch, and taken their place on a headland.
The sentries have deserted every other part of me
They have left me helpless to the torrent of touch
They have all come to the headland to witness and assist against
    me.—
I roam about drunk and stagger
I am given up by traitors,
I talk wildly I am surely out of my head,
I am myself the greatest traitor.
I went myself first to the headland

Unloose me, touch, you are taking the breath from my throat!
Unbar your gates you are too much for me
Fierce Wrestler! do you keep your heaviest grip for last?
Will you sting me most even at parting?
Will you struggle even at the threshold with spasms more
    delicious than all before?
Does it make you to ache so to leave me?
Do you wish to show me that even what you did before was
    nothing to what you can do?
Or have you and all the rest combined to see how much I can
    endure?
Pass as you will; take drops of my life, if that is what you are
    after
Only pass to someone else, for I can contain you no longer
I held more than I thought
I did not think I was big enough for so much ecstasy
Or that a touch could take it all out of me.

This was the true starting point for "Song of Myself." The headland
is the first of what Whitman would call vistas or tallies, his prime images
of voice. When the incipient poet laments, "I am myself the greatest
traitor. I went myself first to the headland," then he acknowledges that
he went out too far on a precipice and could not unaided scramble back.
Materially, this refers to autoeroticism, but self-gratification is merely
an emblem of the actual adventure of achieving the incarnation of the
poetic character.

The adventure is hardly an easy achievement. At this fragmentary
stage, Whitman had no notion how to bring his scattered inward facul-

ties into a harmony. There is a contradictory range of affects assaulting him at once. His autoerotic climax mixes shame and pleasure. When he calls himself the greatest traitor, who or what has he betrayed? Who is the "I" who went first to the headland?

Contrary to his reputation, Walt Whitman is a very difficult poet. He may look easy, but that is a deception. His very original psychic cartography is still largely unmapped. And although his outrageous comedy has been studied, its full enormity requires further appreciation. Here is a wonderful early fragment:

> The crowds naked in the bath,
> Can your sight behold them as with oyster's eyes?
> Do you take the attraction of gravity for nothing?
> Does the negress bear no children?
> Are they never handsome? Do they not thrive?
> Will cabinet officers become blue or yellow from excessive gin?
> Shall I receive the great things of the spirit on easier terms than
>     I do a note of hand?
> Who examines the philosophies in the market less than a basket
>     of peaches or barrels of salt fish?
> Who accepts chemistry on tradition?
> The light picks out a bishop or pope no more than the rest.
> A mouse is a miracle enough to stagger billions of infidels.

Eight fierce questions are framed by the initial "The crowds naked in the bath" and then conclude with two lines juxtaposing a deprecation of the high clergy with the miracle of a mouse that somehow awes a vast horde of infidels. In between, the reader's sight yields to the defensive closing up of the oyster sensing danger. Then comes the nonsense of gravity set aside. The defiant celebration of the Negress bearing handsome and successful children meant more in the 1850s than it does now, even in Trump's America. Best of all is the speculation of whether the presidential Cabinet, after excessive indulgence in gin, will turn blue or yellow. The next three questions are rhetorical and thus self-answering.

Another Whitman, in his first appearance as the American Christ, daringly proclaims his Resurrection. Churches are dismissed as mere matter, and by implication the Bible is set aside by the human presence:

In vain were nails driven through my hands.
I remember my crucifixion and bloody coronation
I remember the mockers and the buffeting insults
The sepulchre and the white linen have yielded me up
I am alive in New York and San Francisco,
Again I tread the streets after two thousand years.
Not all the traditions can put vitality in churches
They are not alive, they are cold mortar and brick,
I can easily build as good, and so can you:—
Books are not men—

There is no word in any tongue,
No array, no form of symbol,
To tell his infatuation
Who would define the scope and purpose of God.

Mostly this we have of God; we have man.
Lo, the Sun;
Its glory floods the moon,
Which of a night shines in some turbid pool,
Shaken by soughing winds;
And there are sparkles mad and tossed and broken,
And their archetype is the sun.

Of God I know not;
But this I know;
I can comprehend no being more wonderful than man;
Man, before the rage of whose passions the storms of Heaven
    are but a breath;
Before whose caprices the lightning is slow and less fatal;
Man, microcosm of all Creation's wildness, terror, beauty and
    power,
And whose folly and wickedness are in nothing else existent.
O dirt, you corpse, I reckon you are good manure—but that I do
    not smell—
I smell your beautiful white roses—
I kiss your leafy lips—I slide my hands for the brown melons of
    your breasts.

To say that what we have of God is man establishes one of the affinities of Walt Whitman with William Blake, whom eventually he was to read. The worship of the sun, however, is not Blakean but more in the mode of D. H. Lawrence, whose later poetry was flooded by Whitman's. The description of man raging with passions and caprices, holding in wildness, terror, beauty, and power; folly will do very well for King Lear. Walt, making love to the earth, is like an Egyptian god pouring his semen into the ground as the act of creation.

The opening strophes of the 1855 *Leaves of Grass*, with the initial poem termed "Song of Myself," have become so familiar that we have to make an effort to read them with the shock of recognition that Ralph Waldo Emerson experienced when Walt Whitman sent him the strange-looking little book:

I celebrate myself,
And what I assume you shall assume,
For every atom belonging to me as good belongs to you.

I loafe and invite my soul,
I lean and loafe at my ease . . . . observing a spear of summer grass.

Houses and rooms are full of perfumes . . . . the shelves are
    crowded with perfumes,
I breathe the fragrance myself, and know it and like it,
The distillation would intoxicate me also, but I shall not let it.

The atmosphere is not a perfume . . . . it has no taste of the
    distillation . . . . it is odorless,
It is for my mouth forever . . . . I am in love with it,
I will go to the bank by the wood and become undisguised and
    naked,
I am mad for it to be in contact with me.
The smoke of my own breath,
Echoes, ripples, and buzzed whispers . . . . loveroot, silkthread,
    crotch and vine,
My respiration and inspiration . . . . the beating of my heart . . . .
    the passing of blood and air through my lungs,
The sniff of green leaves and dry leaves, and of the shore and
    dark-colored sea-rocks, and of hay in the barn,

The sound of the belched words of my voice . . . . words loosed
    to the eddies of the wind,
A few light kisses . . . . a few embraces . . . . a reaching around of
    arms,
The play of shine and shade on the trees as the supple boughs
    wag, fields and hillsides,
The delight alone or in the rush of the streets, or along the
    fields and hillsides,
The feeling of health . . . . the full-noon trill . . . . the song of me
    rising from bed and meeting the sun.


Have you reckoned a thousand acres much? Have you reckoned
    the earth much?
Have you practiced so long to learn to read?
Have you felt so proud to get at the meaning of poems?


Stop this day and night with me and you shall possess the origin
    of all poems,
You shall possess the good of the earth and sun . . . . there are
    millions of suns left,
You shall no longer take things at second or third hand . . . .
    nor look through the eyes of the dead . . . . nor feed on the
    spectres in books,
You shall not look through my eyes either, nor take things from
    me,
You shall listen to all sides and filter them from yourself.


This amazing declaration simultaneously offers us Walt Whitman
as mediator while telling us we do not need him. The crucial line of
the above excerpt is the final one: "You shall listen to all sides and filter
them from yourself."

Brilliantly anticipating the conclusion of "Song of Myself," Whitman offers us the rich trope of "filter." The penultimate tercet of the
epic illuminates this origin:


You will hardly know who I am or what I mean,
But I shall be good health to you nevertheless,
And filter and fibre your blood.

Try the experiment of reading this passage as though no one had ever read it before you. Though Harold Bloom has been a disciple of Emerson since 1965, he is well aware that he cannot *be* the sage of Concord. And Emerson, like the Hebraic sages, would remind him that his burden is to be Harold Bloom. Today is November 27, 2017, a Monday at 3:00. p.m. Weary from exercise and suffering pain in a highly arthritic left knee, the eighty-seven-year-old Bloom sits uncomfortably in his wheelchair, chants Whitman silently to himself, and dictates these sentences to a very helpful assistant.

The American epic, probably never to be matched, begins: "I celebrate myself." Whitman deliberately counterpoints that assertion against Homer's "Sing, goddess, the anger of Peleus' son Achilleus" *(Iliad)*; "Tell me, Muse, of the man of many ways, who was driven" *(Odyssey)*; and Virgil's "I sing of arms and of a man" *(Aeneid)*. Only Walt Whitman would dare to begin his central poem with self-celebration.

Attempt to imagine Emily Dickinson, Wallace Stevens, or T. S. Eliot starting a poem with "I celebrate myself." It is beyond belief. Hart Crane, obsessed with and inspired by Whitman, celebrates the Brooklyn Bridge as the myth of America, but when it comes to self, Crane destroys his own being as an Orphic sacrifice. But Walt Whitman has come to heal us.

Whitman was an admirer of Fanny (Frances) Wright (1795–1852) and had read her novel about Epicurus, *A Few Days in Athens* (1822). I have read it more than once and still find it useful, though aesthetic value is wanting. Wright employed the Epicurean philosophy as a noble materialism on behalf of labor, feminist, and abolitionist causes. Whitman first heard her lecture when he was seventeen, and retained a lifelong admiration for her. He read the greatest of Latin poets, Lucretius, in translation and absorbed a more refined version of the Epicurean philosophy. In *Democratic Vistas* (1871), Whitman boasted that he would go beyond Lucretius:

What the Roman Lucretius sought most nobly, yet all too blandly, negatively to do for his age and its successors, must be done positively by some great coming literatus, especially poet, who, while remaining fully poet, will absorb whatever science indicates, with spiritualism, and out of them, and out of his own genius, will compose the great poem of death.

To call Lucretius "bland" is absurd. Whitman's best poetry was written from 1855 to 1865, climaxing in his great poem of death, the "Lilacs" elegy for Abraham Lincoln. There is a sadness in Whitman's assertion. In his wonderful decade, he indeed had been the peer of Lucretius, like Shelley before him and Wallace Stevens in his wake.

Whitman loafs and invites his soul to behold a spear of summer grass. The remarkable trope, "leaves of grass," is endless to unpack. The leaves could be the pages of Whitman's book—or are they an emblem for Whitman's radically new poems? I invoke here a crucial phrase from Wallace Stevens: "the fiction of the leaves." That fiction comes down to Whitman and to Stevens from a long tradition that begins in the Bible and Homer and then goes through Virgil and Dante and then on through Milton to Coleridge and Shelley.

Here is the prophet Isaiah:

> And all the host of heaven shall be dissolved, and the heavens
> shall be rolled together as a scroll: and all their host shall fall
> down, as the leaf falleth off from the vine, and as a falling fig
> from the fig tree.
>
> Isaiah 34:4

And here is the great trope of human mortality from Homer:

> . . . why ask of my generation?
> As is the generation of leaves, so is that of humanity.
> The wind scatters the leaves on the ground, but the fine timber
> burgeons with leaves again in the season of spring returning.
> So one generation of men will grow while another
> dies. . . .
>
> *Iliad*, Book VI, lines 145–50, Lattimore translation

Virgil, imitating Homer as always, does not better him yet does something powerful:

> thick as the leaves that with the early frost
> of autumn drop and fall within the forest,

or as the birds that flock along the beaches,
in flight from frenzied seas when the chill season
drives them across the waves to lands of sun.
They stand; each pleads to be the first to cross
the stream; their hands reach out in longing for
the farther shore. But Charon, sullen boatman,
now takes these souls, now those; the rest he leaves;
thrusting them back, he keeps them from the beach.

Aeneid, Book VI, lines 310–19, Mandelbaum translation

Dante goes beyond his beloved Virgil and rivals Homer:

But those forlorn and naked souls changed color, their teeth chat-
tering, as soon as they heard the cruel words. They cursed God,
their parents, the human race, the place, the time, the seed of their
begetting and of their birth. Then, weeping loudly, all drew to the
evil shore that awaits every man who fears not God. The demon
Charon, his eyes like glowing coals, beckons to them and collects
them all, beating with his oar whoever lingers.

As the leaves fall away in autumn, one after another, till the
bough sees all its spoils upon the ground, so there the evil seed of
Adam: one by one they cast themselves from that shore at signals,
like a bird at its call. Thus they go over the dark water, and before
they have landed on the other shore, on this side a new throng
gathers.

Inferno, Canto III, lines 100–120, Singleton translation

I have juxtaposed these dark passages in a book I published many
years ago, *A Map of Misreading* (1975). But there I was concerned
with John Milton and his precursors, whereas here my interest is in
the Whitmanian difference. Begin again with the title *Leaves of Grass*.
Whitman, a Hicksite Quaker Bible reader, kept in mind an extraordinary trope from 2 Isaiah:

The voice said, Cry. And he said, What shall I cry? All flesh is
grass, and all the goodliness thereof is as the flower of the
field:
The grass withereth, the flower fadeth: because the spirit of the
Lord bloweth upon it: surely the people is grass.

The grass withereth, the flower fadeth: but the word of our God
shall stand for ever.

Isaiah 40: 6–8

Whitman is much more interested in the metaphor of the grass as
flesh than in leaves as comprising our individual mortality. He never
feared dying, a personal attribute, but also Epicurean and Lucretian
doctrine, which holds that dying is real and can be very painful but the
pain ends, and death is simply nonexistence. Whitman wavered on this,
yet seems to have finally settled on the vista that we survive only in our
works and in the loving memory of others. As the prophet of human
immediacy, Walt Whitman stresses the eternal *now*.

Walt as a healer can speak in the accent of the Christ who comes as
physician to cleanse us inside and out. An Epicurean Christ seems an
oxymoron and returns us to the complexity of Whitmanian metaphysi-
cal materialism striving against an Emersonian transcendentalism:

I have heard what the talkers were talking . . . . the talk of the
    beginning and the end,
But I do not talk of the beginning or the end.

There was never any more inception than there is now,
Nor any more youth or age than there is now;
And will never be any more perfection than there is now,
Nor any more heaven or hell than there is now.

Wallace Stevens interpreted this perceptively when he had his Whitman sing, "Nothing is final, he chants. No man shall see the end." As
a prophet, Whitman is interested in the here and now and not in the
last things.

Urge and urge and urge,
Always the procreant urge of the world.

Out of the dimness opposite equals advance . . . . Always
    substance and increase,
Always a knit of identity . . . . always distinction . . . . always a
    breed of life.

To elaborate is no avail . . . . Learned and unlearned feel that it
    is so.

Sure as the most certain sure . . . . plumb in the uprights, well
    entretied, braced in the beams,
Stout as a horse, affectionate, haughty, electrical,
I and this mystery here we stand.

"This mystery" is the real Me or Me myself:

Clear and sweet is my soul . . . . and clear and sweet is all that is
    not my soul.

Lack one lacks both . . . . and the unseen is proved by the seen,
Till that becomes unseen and receives proof in its turn.

Showing the best and dividing it from the worst, age vexes age,
Knowing the perfect fitness and equanimity of things, while they
    discuss I am silent, and go bathe and admire myself.

Welcome is every organ and attribute of me, and of any man
    hearty and clean,
Not an inch nor a particle of an inch is vile, and none shall be
    less familiar than the rest.

I am satisfied . . . . I see, dance, laugh, sing;
As God comes a loving bedfellow and sleeps at my side all night
    and close on the peep of the day,
And leaves for me baskets covered with white towels bulging the
    house with their plenty,
Shall I postpone my acceptation and realization and scream at
    my eyes,
That they turn from gazing after and down the road,
And forthwith cipher and show me to a cent,
Exactly the contents of one, and exactly the contents of two, and
    which is ahead?

Whitman chants that nothing is final and that no man shall see the
end. He and the moment share perfection, and he admires both. In

his ecstasy, he breaks into dance, laughter, and song and gives us a remarkable image of God, as much of a loving bedfellow as Ishmael was to Queequeg. I never cease my wonder at the startling image of God leaving behind him baskets of white towels to bulge Walt's house. But then the passage turns even wilder. Whitman turns upon himself and seems to chide some rift in his self-confidence. That fissure is then identified as the struggle between the three components of Walt Whitman's consciousness and being: his self, his real Me, or Me myself, and his unknown soul. There is a homely charm in God as Walt's lover who generously leaves for him those bulging baskets of white towels. Whitman and his siblings were living with their mother and father, and one gathers that clean towels were not in heavy supply:

> Trippers and askers surround me,
> People I meet . . . . the effect upon me of my early life . . . . of
>     the ward and city I live in . . . . of the nation,
> The latest news . . . . discoveries, inventions, societies . . . .
>     authors old and new,
> My dinner, dress, associates, looks, business, compliments, dues,
> The real or fancied indifference of some man or woman I love,
> The sickness of one of my folks—or of myself . . . . or ill-
>     doing . . . . or loss or lack of money . . . . or depressions or
>     exaltations,
> They come to me days and nights and go from me again,
> But they are not the Me myself.
>
> Apart from the pulling and hauling stands what I am,
> Stands amused, complacent, compassionating, idle, unitary,
> Looks down, is erect, bends an arm on an impalpable certain
>     rest,
> Looks with its sidecurved head curious what will come next,
> Both in and out of the game, and watching and wondering at it.

These last five lines, giving a vision of the Me myself, have an American magic in their stance and metric that prophesies our later poets, from T. S. Eliot on to John Ashbery. Unlike Walt Whitman—one of the roughs, an American, the outward self—this figure is androgynous. It awakens memories in me that go back seventy years, to an undergraduate attachment I had to a young lady from Kentucky who was a kind of female Huckleberry Finn. Myself very clumsy, then as now, I admired her grace of movement. She had a way of standing a little off balance and bending her arm on some rest that was not there. The side-curved head, charming in the aura of her long red hair, always seemed both detached and involved. Both of us had recently turned seventeen, and we were both content to maintain an affectionate friendship, seeking not to go further. I have a lovely memory of her taking me to the Cornell apple orchards, where we gathered fallen apples. Following her family tradition, she made a wicked applejack, which helped us get through the dreadful Ithaca winter. Twenty years later, I lectured on Whitman in Louisville. She was in the audience and invited me home to dinner with her husband and children. I like to think that Walt Whitman might have taken to this association with his marvelous lines about the Me myself.

> Backward I see in my own days where I sweated through fog
>     with linguists and contenders,
> I have no mockings or arguments . . . . I witness and wait.

> I believe in you my soul . . . . the other I am must not abase itself
>     to you,
> And you must not be abased to the other.

There is an intricate balance in this vexed relation between the soul and the real Me. It is as though the persona of the rough Walt or Me myself had the task of keeping soul and inner self from a master-slave conflict. Whitman's vision of a momentary reconciliation of his three psychic components is now frequently and rather weakly misread as a homoerotic encounter:

> Loafe with me on the grass . . . . loose the stop from your throat,
> Not words, not music or rhyme I want . . . . not custom or
>     lecture, not even the best,
> Only the lull I like, the hum of your valved voice.

> I mind how we lay in June, such a transparent summer morning;
> You settled your head athwart my hips and gently turned over
>     upon me,

And parted the shirt from my bosom-bone, and plunged your
    tongue to my barestript heart,
And reached till you felt my beard, and reached till you held my
    feet.

This is one of the oddest of embraces. Myself and the Me myself are
in a curious, rather Tantric entwining that defies our usual expectations.

Swiftly arose and spread around me the peace and joy and
    knowledge that pass all the art and argument of the earth;
And I know that the hand of God is the elderhand of my own,
And I know that the spirit of God is the eldest brother of my
    own,
And that all the men ever born are also my brothers . . . . and the
    women my sisters and lovers,
And that a kelson of the creation is love;
And limitless are leaves stiff or drooping in the fields,
And brown ants in the little wells beneath them,
And mossy scabs of the wormfence, and heaped stones, and
    elder and mullen and pokeweed.

Whitman is very precise at distinguishing the Me myself from the
ephemera of the everyday. His psychic cartography—my soul, my self,
the real Me or Me myself—remains one of the major difficulties that
our apprehension has been slow to assimilate. I once speculated that
Walt was driven to his triad of psychic entities as a reaction formation
to the influence of Emerson on most American conceptions of the soul.
That seems to me now too diffuse. There was of course an element
of the family romance in Whitman's sense of inner divisions. Walter
Whitman Sr. lay dying even as "Song of Myself" was being composed.
Less than a week after Walt published *Leaves of Grass*, his father died.

My self in *Leaves of Grass* is a fiction, Walt Whitman, one of the
roughs, an American. This outward, vital self is less consequential than
the homoerotic real Me/Me my self, but even that confessional reality
finally counts for less than Whitman's crucial trope, his fourfold soul,
comprising Night, Death, the Mother, and the Sea.

That has been a metaphor throughout the literary history of the
globe. Whitman captures it, to his peril, because he desired, like all

great poets, to assert his own power over the universe of death. Not even Dante, Shakespeare, or Milton could accomplish that. Outward sense will always triumph over the strongest imaginative wills. The Whitman of the second edition (1856) and of the third (1860) version of *Leaves of Grass* goes on battling in this war of poetry against the abyss. In *Drum-Taps* (1865), the warrior becomes the wound dresser and eloquently subsides.

After Lincoln's death, Whitman added a *Sequel* that included his magnificent "Lilacs" threnody. That sublime elegy both for the martyred President and for his own poetic self can be read as Whitman's yielding to the inexorable power of Night, Death, the Mother, and the Sea. But in "Song of Myself," we hear Walt Whitman in the glory of his strength:

> A child said, What is the grass? fetching it to me with full hands;
> How could I answer the child? . . . . I do not know what it is any
>     more than he.
>
> I guess it must be the flag of my disposition, out of hopeful
>     green stuff woven.
>
> Or I guess it is the handkerchief of the Lord,
> A scented gift and remembrancer designedly dropped,
> Bearing the owner's name someway in the corners, that we may
>     see and remark, and say Whose?
>
> Or I guess the grass is itself a child . . . . the produced babe of
>     the vegetation.
>
> Or I guess it is a uniform hieroglyphic,
> And it means, Sprouting alike in broad zones and narrow zones,
> Growing among black folks as among white,
> Kanuck, Tuckahoe, Congressman, Cuff, I give them the same, I
>     receive them the same.
>
> And now it seems to me the beautiful uncut hair of graves.
>
> Tenderly will I use you curling grass,
> It may be you transpire from the breasts of young men,

It may be if I had known them I would have loved them;
It may be you are from old people and from women, and from
    offspring taken soon out of their mothers' laps,
And here you are the mothers' laps.

This grass is very dark to be from the white heads of old
    mothers,
Darker than the colorless beards of old men,
Dark to come from under the faint red roofs of mouths.

O I perceive after all so many uttering tongues!
And I perceive they do not come from the roofs of mouths for
    nothing.

I wish I could translate the hints about the dead young men and
    women,
And the hints about old men and mothers, and the offspring
    taken soon out of their laps.

What do you think has become of the young and old men?
And what do you think has become of the women and children?

They are alive and well somewhere;
The smallest sprout shows there is really no death,
And if ever there was it led forward life, and does not wait at the
    end to arrest it,
And ceased the moment life appeared.

All goes onward and outward . . . . and nothing collapses,
And to die is different from what any one supposed, and luckier.

There is something magical and majestic in this gentle, gracious fantasia on the grass. Whitman begins by following the adage of Epicurus:
"The what is unknowable." But then he launches a cavalcade of brilliant tropes. The grass mutates from the optimistic green flag of Walt's
disposition to the flirtatious handkerchief of God. Since the question is
a child's, the grass itself becomes a child.

    The vista expands to a hieroglyphic, interpreted by Whitman as an
equalizing factor among races, nations, and social classes. At the next

line, which is a poem in itself, the speaker becomes like one of Yeats's denizens of Byzantium, a mouth that has no moisture and no breath, but that can summon breathless mouths: "And now it seems to me the beautiful uncut hair of graves." Homer has no such trope but might have envied it. Sparked by that superb line, Whitman mounts to a rhapsodic celebration of his own desires and of maternal mortality:

> This grass is very dark to be from the white heads of old
>     mothers,
> Darker than the colorless beards of old men,
> Dark to come from under the faint red roofs of mouths.

Walt Whitman is aware that he is following the Biblical style of parataxis, or employing brief statements and coordinating conjunctions, placed side by side so that there is no rhetorical subordination. There are thirty-three words in these wonderful lines, and only five are of more than one syllable. The monosyllabic effect suggests Hemingway, who, like Whitman, derives his style from the King James Bible.

I never quite get over the recitation of this tercet. Whitman can be the uncanniest of poets, and here he sounds at once estranged and at home. The vista should be grotesque but is somehow hallowed. At first encounter this can seem surrealistic. It is too strong for that, and too reverent. Our mothers and our fathers have gone to grass, and their mouths are too faint to be heard.

That is difficult and magnificent. But there are many Whitmans, and I cannot choose among them even in "Song of Myself":

> Shall I pray? Shall I venerate and be ceremonious?
> I have pried through the strata and analyzed to a hair,
> And counselled with doctors and calculated close and found no
>     sweeter fat than sticks to my own bones.

> In all people I see myself, none more and not one a barleycorn
>     less,
> And the good or bad I say of myself I say of them.

> And I know I am solid and sound,
> To me the converging objects of the universe perpetually flow,
> All are written to me, and I must get what the writing means.

And I know I am deathless,
I know this orbit of mine cannot be swept by a carpenter's
    compass,
I know I shall not pass like a child's carlacue cut with a burnt
    stick at night,

I know I am august,
I do not trouble my spirit to vindicate itself or be understood,
I see that the elementary laws never apologize,
I reckon I behave no prouder than the level I plant my house by
    after all.

I exist as I am, that is enough,
If no other in the world be aware I sit content,
And if each and all be aware I sit content.

One world is aware, and by far the largest to me, and that is
    myself,
And whether I come to my own today or in ten thousand or ten
    million years,
I can cheerfully take it now, or with equal cheerfulness I can
    wait.

My foothold is tenoned and mortised in granite,
I laugh at what you call dissolution,
And I know the amplitude of time.

I am the poet of the body,
And I am the poet of the soul.

The pleasures of heaven are with me, and the pains of hell are
    with me,
The first I graft and increase upon myself . . . . the latter I
    translate into a new tongue.

I am the poet of the woman the same as the man,
And I say it is as great to be a woman as to be a man,
And I say there is nothing greater than the mother of men.

I chant a new chant of dilation or pride,
We have had ducking and deprecating about enough,
I show that size is only development.

Have you outstript the rest? Are you the President?
It is a trifle . . . . they will more than arrive there every one, and
    still pass on.

I am he that walks with the tender and growing night;
I call to the earth and sea half-held by the night.

Press close barebosomed night! Press close magnetic nourishing
    night!
Night of south winds! Night of the large few stars!
Still nodding night! Mad naked summer night!

Smile O voluptuous coolbreathed earth!
Earth of the slumbering and liquid trees!
Earth of departed sunset! Earth of the mountains misty-topt!
Earth of the vitreous pour of the full moon just tinged with blue!
Earth of shine and dark mottling the tide of the river!
Earth of the limpid gray of clouds brighter and clearer for my
    sake!
Far-swooping elbowed earth! Rich apple-blossomed earth!
Smile, for your lover comes!

Prodigal! you have given me love! . . . . therefore I to you give
    love!
O unspeakable passionate love!

The poet who finds no sweeter fat than sticks to his own bones is
hardly going to venerate a gaseous vapor masquerading as the Holy
Spirit. As the poet both of the body and of the soul, of the woman as
of the man, Walt is the lover of the cosmos. Earth is his Prodigal who
returns to exchange passionate love with the American poet. When, in
"Voyages II," Hart Crane cries out, "O my Prodigal" to his lover, he
alludes to this rhapsodic passage.

Though Whitman may seem to be evading his Hicksite Quaker

heritage, it returns triumphantly as "Song of Myself" suddenly soars upward in a giant release of long-repressed human desire:

> Walt Whitman, an American, one of the roughs, a kosmos,
> Disorderly fleshy and sensual . . . . eating drinking and breeding,
> No sentimentalist . . . . no stander above men and women or
>     apart from them . . . . no more modest than immodest.

> Unscrew the locks from the doors!
> Unscrew the doors themselves from their jambs!

> Whoever degrades another degrades me . . . . and whatever is
>     done or said returns at last to me,
> And whatever I do or say I also return.

> Through me the afflatus surging and surging . . . . through me
>     the current and index.

> I speak the password primeval . . . . I give the sign of democracy;
> By God! I will accept nothing which all cannot have their
>     counterpart of on the same terms.

> Through me many long dumb voices,
> Voices of the interminable generations of slaves,
> Voices of prostitutes and of deformed persons,
> Voices of the diseased and despairing, and of thieves and dwarfs,
> Voices of cycles of preparation and accretion,
> And of the threads that connect the stars—and of wombs, and of
>     the fatherstuff,
> And of the rights of them the others are down upon,
> Of the trivial and flat and foolish and despised,
> Of fog in the air and beetles rolling balls of dung.

> Through me forbidden voices,
> Voices of sexes and lusts . . . . voices veiled, and I remove the
>     veil,
> Voices indecent by me clarified and transfigured.

I do not press my finger across my mouth,
I keep as delicate around the bowels as around the head and
    heart,
Copulation is no more rank to me than death is.

I believe in the flesh and the appetites,
Seeing hearing and feeling are miracles, and each part and tag of
    me is a miracle.

Divine am I inside and out, and I make holy whatever I touch or
    am touched from;
The scent of these arm-pits is aroma finer than prayer,
This head is more than churches or bibles or creeds.

If I worship any particular thing it shall be some of the spread of
    my body;
Translucent mould of me it shall be you,
Shaded ledges and rests, firm masculine coulter, it shall be you,
Whatever goes to the tilth of me it shall be you,
You my rich blood, your milky stream pale strippings of my life;
Breast that presses against other breasts it shall be you,
My brain it shall be your occult convolutions,
Root of washed sweet-flag, timorous pond-snipe, nest of
    guarded duplicate eggs, it shall be you,
Mixed tussled hay of head and beard and brawn it shall be you;
Trickling sap of maple, fibre of manly wheat, it shall be you;
Sun so generous it shall be you,
Vapors lighting and shading my face it shall be you,
You sweaty brooks and dews it shall be you,
Winds whose soft-tickling genitals rub against me it shall be
    you,
Broad muscular fields, branches of liveoak, loving lounger in my
    winding paths, it shall be you,
Hands I have taken, face I have kissed, mortal I have ever
    touched, it shall be you.

I dote on myself . . . . there is that lot of me, and all so luscious,
Each moment and whatever happens thrills me with joy.

There is a portion of this passage that bears repeating; it should have been burned on the American consciousness, though, alas, it never could be:

> Through me many long dumb voices,
> Voices of the interminable generations of slaves,
> Voices of prostitutes and of deformed persons,
> Voices of the diseased and despairing, and of thieves and
>     dwarfs,
> Voices of cycles of preparation and accretion,
> And of the threads that connect the stars—and of wombs, and of
>     the fatherstuff,
> And of the rights of them the others are down upon,
> Of the trivial and flat and foolish and despised,
> Of fog in the air and beetles rolling balls of dung.
>
> Through me forbidden voices,
> Voices of sexes and lusts . . . . voices veiled, and I remove the
>     veil,
> Voices indecent by me clarified and transfigured.

In his crippled old age, waning slowly in Camden, New Jersey, Whitman himself forgot these lines and talked nonsense about blacks and workers. But that was no longer Walt Whitman the poet and seer of his nation. How shall I convey the majesty and burning of this great chant? Part of the power is that it hardly seems that only one man is speaking. The hum of multitudes is there. This Whitman could be Micah, Amos, or the First Isaiah. The difference is Whitman's preternatural awareness of what nearly all of us would regard as unworthy of notice:

> Of the trivial and flat and foolish and despised,
> Of fog in the air and beetles rolling balls of dung.

No one but Whitman and Dickinson could have celebrated both fog and beetles. What for most of us is beyond the edge of being is for Walt a value. Fortified by his love of others and otherness, Whitman is able to face and overcome the challenge of nature:

To behold the daybreak!
The little light fades the immense and diaphanous shadows,
The air tastes good to my palate.

Hefts of the moving world at innocent gambols, silently rising,
    freshly exuding,
Scooting obliquely high and low.

Something I cannot see puts upward libidinous prongs,
Seas of bright juice suffuse heaven.

The earth by the sky staid with . . . . the daily close of their
    junction,
The heaved challenge from the east that moment over my head,
The mocking taunt, See then whether you shall be master!

Dazzling and tremendous how quick the sunrise would kill me,
If I could not now and always send sunrise out of me.

We also ascend dazzling and tremendous as the sun,
We found our own my soul in the calm and cool of the
    daybreak.

Captain Ahab in *Moby-Dick* cries out that he would strike the sun if
it insulted him. Walt, superbly balanced and confident, takes another
way. What other poet could greet the sunrise by sending forth sunrise
out of himself? Matching the sun, Whitman becomes Yahweh finding
his soul's comfort in the calm and cool daybreak.

My voice goes after what my eyes cannot reach,
With the twirl of my tongue I encompass worlds and volumes of
    worlds.

Speech is the twin of my vision . . . . it is unequal to measure
    itself.
It provokes me forever,
It says sarcastically, Walt, you understand enough . . . . why
    don't you let it out then?

Come now I will not be tantalized . . . . you conceive too much
    of articulation.

Do you not know how the buds beneath are folded?
Waiting in gloom protected by frost,
The dirt receding before my prophetical screams,
I underlying causes to balance them at last,
My knowledge my live parts . . . . it keeping tally with the
    meaning of things,
Happiness . . . . which whoever hears me let him or her set out
    in search of this day.

My final merit I refuse you . . . . I refuse putting from me the
    best I am.

Encompass worlds but never try to encompass me,
I crowd your noisiest talk by looking toward you.

Writing and talk do not prove me,
I carry the plenum of proof and every thing else in my face,
With the hush of my lips I confound the topmost skeptic.

This is Whitman at his strongest. The crucial line is "My knowledge
my live parts . . . . it keeping tally with the meaning of things."
The tally, whether verb or substantive, will become Whitman's
prime image of voice. His live parts or genitalia, through autoerotic
stimulation, will give us the best he has.

I hear the trained soprano . . . . she convulses me like the climax
    of my love-grip;
The orchestra whirls me wider than Uranus flies,
It wrenches unnamable ardors from my breast,
It throbs me to gulps of the farthest down horror,
It sails me . . . . I dab with bare feet . . . . they are licked by the
    indolent waves,
I am exposed . . . . cut by bitter and poisoned hail,
Steeped amid honeyed morphine . . . . my windpipe squeezed in
    the fakes of death,

Let up again to feel the puzzle of puzzles,
And that we call Being.

To be in any form, what is that?
If nothing lay more developed the quahaug and its callous shell
    were enough.

Mine is no callous shell,
I have instant conductors all over me whether I pass or stop,
They seize every object and lead it harmlessly through me.

I merely stir, press, feel with my fingers, and am happy,
To touch my person to some one else's is about as much as I can
    stand.

The onanistic frenzy ensues in rhapsody of whirling images. But
Whitman is moving toward crisis:

Is this then a touch? . . . . quivering me to a new identity,
Flames and ether making a rush for my veins,
Treacherous tip of me reaching and crowding to help them,
My flesh and blood playing out lightning, to strike what is
    hardly different from myself,
On all sides prurient provokers stiffening my limbs,
Straining the udder of my heart for its withheld drip,
Behaving licentious toward me, taking no denial,
Depriving me of my best as for a purpose,
Unbuttoning my clothes and holding me by the bare
    waist,
Deluding my confusion with the calm of the sunlight and
    pasture fields,
Immodestly sliding the fellow-sense away,
They bribed to swap off with touch, and go and graze at the
    edges of me,
No consideration, no regard for my draining strength or my
    anger,
Fetching the rest of the herd around to enjoy them awhile,
Then all uniting to stand on a headland and worry me.

The sentries desert every other part of me,
They have left me helpless . . . .

This returns us to the early fragment in which self-gratification is conveyed by the image of the headland.

I understand the large hearts of heroes,
The courage of present times and all times;
How the skipper saw the crowded and rudderless wreck of the
    steamship, and death chasing it up and down the storm,
How he knuckled tight and gave not back one inch, and was
    faithful of days and faithful of nights,
And chalked in large letters on a board, Be of good cheer, We
    will not desert you;
How he saved the drifting company at last,
How the lank loose-gowned women looked when boated from
    the side of their prepared graves,
How the silent old-faced infants, and the lifted sick, and the
    sharp-lipped unshaved men;
All this I swallow and it tastes good . . . . I like it well, and it
    becomes mine,
I am the man . . . . I suffered . . . . I was there.

The disdain and calmness of martyrs,
The mother condemned for a witch and burnt with dry wood,
    and her children gazing on;
The hounded slave that flags in the race and leans by the fence,
    blowing and covered with sweat,
The twinges that sting like needles his legs and necks,
The murderous buckshot and the bullets,
All these I feel or am.

I am the hounded slave . . . . I wince at the bite of the dogs,
Hell and despair are upon me . . . . crack and again crack the
    marksmen,
I clutch the rails of the fence . . . . my gore dribs thinned with
    the ooze of my skin,
I fall on the weeds and stones,

The riders spur their unwilling horses and haul close,
They taunt my dizzy ears . . . . they beat me violently over the
    head with their whip-stocks.


Agonies are one of my changes of garments;
I do not ask the wounded person how he feels . . . . I myself
    become the wounded person,
My hurt turns livid upon me as I lean on a cane and observe.


I am the mashed fireman with breastbone broken . . . . tumbling
    walls buried me in their debris,
Heat and smoke I inspired . . . . I heard the yelling shouts of my
    comrades,
I heard the distant click of their picks and shovels;
They have cleared the beams away . . . . they tenderly lift me
    forth.


I lie in the night air in my red shirt . . . . the pervading hush is
    for my sake,
Painless after all I lie, exhausted but not so unhappy,
White and beautiful are the faces around me . . . . the heads are
    bared of their firecaps,
The kneeling crowd fades with the light of the torches.


Distant and dead resuscitate,
They show as the dial or move as the hands of me . . . . and I am
    the clock myself.


The extraordinary image of Walt Whitman as the clock myself is
illuminated by the startling "Agonies are one of my changes of garments." Overidentification with victimized slaves and outcast women
is redeemed by another magnificent line of immediacy and humane
participation: "I am the man . . . . I suffered . . . . I was there."


I tramp a perpetual journey,
My signs are a rain-proof coat and good shoes and a staff cut
    from the woods;

No friend of mine takes his ease in my chair,
I have no chair, nor church nor philosophy;
I lead no man to a dinner-table or library or exchange,
But each man and each woman of you I lead upon a knoll,
My left hand hooks you round the waist,
My right hand points to landscapes of continents, and a plain
   public road.

Not I, not any one else can travel that road for you,
You must travel it for yourself.

It is not far . . . . it is within reach,
Perhaps you have been on it since you were born, and did not
   know,
Perhaps it is every where on water and on land.

Shoulder your duds, and I will mine, and let us hasten
   forth;
Wonderful cities and free nations we shall fetch as
   we go.

If you tire, give me both burdens, and rest the chuff of your
   hand on my hip,
And in due time you shall repay the same service to me;
For after we start we never lie by again.
This day before dawn I ascended a hill . . . .

This spirited declaration of American quest is unmatched. One hears
in it generations of American song and striving. Ascending the hill
returns to the imagery of a city on a hill, the American New Jerusalem.

The past and present wilt . . . . I have filled them and emptied
   them,
And proceed to fill my next fold of the future.

Listener up there! Here you . . . . what have you to confide
   to me?
Look in my face while I snuff the sidle of evening,

Talk honestly, for no one else hears you, and I stay only a minute
    longer.

Do I contradict myself?
Very well then . . . . I contradict myself;
I am large . . . . I contain multitudes.

I concentrate toward them that are nigh . . . . I wait on the
    door-slab.

Who has done his day's work and will soonest be through with
    his supper?
Who wishes to walk with me?

Will you speak before I am gone? Will you prove already too
    late?

The spotted hawk swoops by and accuses me . . . . he complains
    of my gab and my loitering.

I too am not a bit tamed . . . . I too am untranslatable,
I sound my barbaric yawp over the roofs of the world.

The last scud of day holds back for me,
It flings my likeness after the rest and true as any on the
    shadowed wilds,
It coaxes me to the vapor and the dusk.

I depart as air . . . . I shake my white locks at the runaway sun,
I effuse my flesh in eddies and drift it in lacy jags.

I bequeath myself to the dirt to grow from the grass I love,
If you want me again look for me under your bootsoles.

You will hardly know who I am or what I mean,
But I shall be good health to you nevertheless,
And filter and fibre your blood.

Failing to fetch me at first keep encouraged,
Missing me one place search another,
I stop some where waiting for you

Walt Whitman dissolves himself, flesh into air, identity into the grass. He will perpetually be up ahead of us, the American Christ waiting for his disciples to catch up with him. This has proved to be too accurate a prophecy.

# Fletcher, Whitman, and
# The American Sublime

$A$ NGUS FLETCHER was born June 23, 1930, in New York City. Eighteen days later, I was born in the East Bronx. We met as Yale graduate students in September 1951, and remained very close friends until Angus died, on November 28, 2016, in Albuquerque, New Mexico. Of all the literary critics in my own generation, I was always most allied to Angus. I cannot accept that he is gone. When I write, read, and teach, he is with me.

Angus published seven books, of which the first was the extraordinary *Allegory: The Theory of a Symbolic Mode* (1964, 2012). There followed *The Prophetic Moment: An Essay on Spenser* (1971), *The Transcendental Masque: An Essay on Milton's Comus* (1972), *Colors of the Mind: Conjectures on Thinking in Literature* (1991), *A New Theory for American Poetry: Democracy, the Environment, and the Future of Imagination* (2004), *Time, Space, and Motion in the Age of Shakespeare* (2007), and *The Topological Imagination: Spheres, Edges, and Islands* (2016). He left in manuscript an almost finished book relating the wave theories of physicists to the ebb and flow of Shakespearean and allied poetic imaginations.

Angus Fletcher's mind was endlessly speculative and original. When I consider the entire span of modern literary criticism, I think of Fletcher as the peer of William Empson, Kenneth Burke, Northrop Frye. Like them, he broke the vessels.

In the sixty-five years of our friendship, Angus and I shared a passion for the highest imaginative literature. Increasingly, we centered on Shakespeare and on Walt Whitman. We possessed many other holy books in common: Burton's *Anatomy of Melancholy*, the writings of Sir Thomas Browne, Spenser, Milton, the English Bible, and the entire Romantic tradition in English and American poetry, from Blake and

Wordsworth, Shelley and Keats, Browning and Tennyson, on to Wallace Stevens, Hart Crane, and John Ashbery.

Angus had a high regard for the poetry of John Clare, who represented for him a particular vision of the human horizon, as did the work of Walt Whitman and of John Ashbery. By "horizon," Fletcher meant actual horizons rather than the boundaries of thought. Horizon, as he studied it, is a guide to natural limitations, and not a gateway to aspirations.

Only now, after Angus's death, have I begun to understand a crucial difference between us. I have never been at home in the natural world. Angus, who spent his childhood and youth sailing around Long Island, was always alert to environmental splendors and the possibility that we would lose them.

For Angus, Walt Whitman broke with High Romanticism, and returned to something like the descriptive poetry of the eighteenth century. There is a lovely sentence in *A New Theory for American Poetry:* "The Americans are somehow troubled by the fact that Nature is simply bigger than we are, so that by artificial means we must acquire the same magnitude." I can recognize Walt Whitman in that, though Angus and I agreed that there was always more in Whitman than either he or his readers could comprehend. What I find in Whitman is his perpetually growing inner self. For Angus, that was held in balance by the Whitmanian concern for everyday experience. Fletcher's Whitman is not Homeric but is akin to Hesiod's *Works and Days*.

In the end, the loving agon between Angus and me turned on the nature of the American Sublime. We both agreed that it was daemonic, yet Angus urged caution lest all Enlightened measure and balance break. But that is what I had learned from the Hebrew Bible and from William Blake. You had to break measure and balance, in order to restore the image of the fully human. Emerson and Melville, Thoreau and Emily Dickinson, for all their differences, were as strenuous as Blake in longing for an unfallen American Adam and Eve. Walt Whitman, as Fletcher reminded me, was less dialectical, because he was large and contained multitudes.

As of this writing, it is more than seven months since Angus departed. Ten weeks ago, I suffered a dreadful accident and broke my hip. Major surgery had to be followed within a week by a second operation on my gastrointestinal system. Recuperating at home, I long for Angus.

I hope in this brief discussion to warm myself again with his marvelous presence. Beyond that, Fletcher is a constant challenge for me. For decades, we discussed Walt Whitman, and my reading of *Leaves of Grass* changed and is still changing under his stimulus.

In *Specimen Days,* Whitman recounts a train journey through the Rocky Mountains:

> "I have found the law of my own poems," was the unspoken but more-and-more decided feeling that came to me as I pass'd, hour after hour, amid all this grim yet joyous elemental abandon—this plenitude of material, entire absence of art, untrammel'd play of primitive Nature—the chasm, the gorge, the crystal mountain stream, repeated scores, hundreds of miles—the broad handling and absolute uncrampedness—the fantastic forms, bathed in transparent browns, faint reds and grays, towering sometimes a thousand, sometimes two or three thousand feet high—at their tops now and then huge masses pois'd, and mixing with the clouds, with only their outlines, hazed in misty lilac, visible.
>
> "An Egotistical 'Find' "

Angus granted that this was an experience of the American Sublime, akin to Shelley's "Mont Blanc" and to Wordsworth's epiphanies. He argued that Whitman's dream of America was to fuse ideas of nature's sublimity with the authentically wild forms of American imagination. The result would be the "environment-poem," of which "Song of Myself" is the masterpiece and some of the longer poems of A. R. Ammons and John Ashbery the worthy descendants.

Though Fletcher devotes much of his *A New Theory for American Poetry* to expounding what he calls the environment-poem, something in his conception evades me. Angus has a wonderful sentence: "Voice in Whitman is intended to surround us." That seems to me exactly right. Whitman's theater depends upon a curious effect of humming:

> Loafe with me on the grass . . . . loose the stop from your throat,
> Not words, not music or rhyme I want, not custom or lecture,
>    not even the best,
> Only the lull I like, the hum of your valved voice.
>
> "Song of Myself," Section 5

I think of Wallace Stevens in "Notes Toward a Supreme Fiction" speaking of "The hum of thoughts evaded in the mind." Fletcher's environment-poem is a kind of humming wave where boundaries, edges, and horizons abound and yet are endlessly metamorphic. It increases knowledge, but this is only secondarily a learning of fact:

> The environment-poem, by attending to nature's cyclical system, assures a place for the *animate* aspect of the life process. In antiquity a personification such as Iris—the rainbow—bridges thoughts of material and spiritual worlds, by voicing or imaging the messages her power enables her to carry between regions. Personifying figures generally prevent fact from having the last word, as if poets using them knew that no fact were sufficient without a spiritual and in that sense symbolic spin of some kind. As a Neoplatonist would claim, the poem and the scene mimetically encode the same phenomena as two modes of emanation, as of course all living creatures emanate from their own identities, as we now know, by virtue of a genetic code.

One problem with this is that the poem is always in a condition of waiting. Whitman is immensely gifted at persuading the reader that the poet is somewhere up ahead, waiting for the rest of us to catch up. Fletcher, like all great critics, was at work writing a defense of poetry. His purpose was to demonstrate what forms of thought and action came into being when we think in allegorical terms. In the afterword to his 2012 edition of *Allegory*, he brooded on what he called "the crisis of scale." He warned prophetically that any sense of sublime transcendence is going to vanish in our technological world. What is coming is the emptiness of allegory without ideas.

For Angus, the poet's point of departure was always the horizon. No one knows what lies beyond the horizon. Fletcher celebrated what he regarded as the great poems of natural limits, such as John Ashbery's "A Wave," or Whitman's "Crossing Brooklyn Ferry." I join my departed friend in such celebration, though I think that Ashbery and Whitman at their strongest verge on transcendence. The American Sublime survives, and with it the hope of moving beyond limits.

# The Freshness of Last Things:
## Wallace Stevens, "Tea at the Palaz of Hoon"

IN WHAT FOLLOWS, I will revisit a sequence of poems I have had to heart from late childhood on to this moment in old age. Some I have discussed in earlier books, but I trust the freshness of last things reveals new perspectives upon them. I will begin with the chant I repeat obsessively to myself, usually in a murmur:

> Not less because in purple I descended
> The western day through what you called
> The loneliest air, not less was I myself.
>
> What was the ointment sprinkled on my beard?
> What were the hymns that buzzed beside my ears?
> What was the sea whose tide swept through me there?
>
> Out of my mind the golden ointment rained,
> And my ears made the blowing hymns they heard.
> I was myself the compass of that sea:
>
> I was the world in which I walked, and what I saw
> Or heard or felt came not but from myself;
> And there I found myself more truly and more strange.

Stevens gave this the jocund title "Tea at the Palaz of Hoon." Writing to my colleague Norman Holmes Pearson, he said that "Hoon" was a cipher for the expanse of sky and space. I read that as a screen for Walt Whitman, a "kosmos," who speaks here with a sublime insouciance in the guise of the setting sun. It is what William Blake called the Idiot

Questioner in each of us that seeks to diminish this imperial descent
with the verbs sprinkled, buzzed, swept through. Walt/Hoon grandly
turns this to "rained," "blowing," and the wonderful "I was myself the
compass of that sea." The fourfold repetition of "myself" alludes to
"Song of Myself," whose singer defies the rising sun in section 25:

> Dazzling and tremendous how quick the sun-rise would kill me,
> If I could not now and always send sun-rise out of me.

Whenever I recite aloud or whisper Hoon's affirmation, I invariably
go on to Walt's magnificent epiphany in Stevens:

> In the far South the sun of autumn is passing
> Like Walt Whitman walking along a ruddy shore.
> He is singing and chanting the things that are part of him,
> The worlds that were and will be, death and day.
> Nothing is final, he chants. No man shall see the end.
> His beard is of fire and his staff is a leaping flame.
>
> Sigh for me, night-wind, in the noisy leaves of the oak.
> I am tired. Sleep for me, heaven over the hill.
> Shout for me, loudly and loudly, joyful sun, when you rise.

Those last three lines are yet another tribute to Whitman, since
deliberately they follow his verve and beat. What Louis Armstrong was
to jazz, Whitman was to his nation's poetry: a founder and preserver.
Possessing Hoon's poem and Stevens's tribute enhances and enlarges
my troubled midnights and the dead hours that linger afterward until a
surprisingly cold late-August dawn sweeps through that city of ordinary
evenings, New Haven.

# Wallace Stevens, "The Snow Man"

TWO-THIRDS OF A CENTURY ago, I had a solitary conversation with Wallace Stevens after he read a shorter version of "An Ordinary Evening in New Haven" to a small audience at Yale. An odd, awkward nineteen-year-old, I mostly listened but did ask a few questions about Shelley. It surprised me how many passages from "The Witch of Atlas" and *Prometheus Unbound* Stevens possessed by memory. If I could return to 1949, I would want to ask him if the leaves in the "Ode to the West Wind" cried out. Though he knew the poem by heart, I suspect he would have answered that they did.

At the age of seventy-one, Stevens composed "The Course of a Particular," a culmination of his lifelong obsession with the figure of the leaves:

Today the leaves cry, hanging on branches swept by wind,
Yet the nothingness of winter becomes a little less.
It is still full of icy shades and shapen snow.

The leaves cry . . . One holds off and merely hears the cry.
It is a busy cry, concerning someone else.
And though one says that one is part of everything,

There is a conflict, there is a resistance involved;
And being part is an exertion that declines:
One feels the life of that which gives life as it is.

The leaves cry. It is not a cry of divine attention,
Nor the smoke-drift of puffed-out heroes, nor human cry.
It is the cry of leaves that do not transcend themselves,

In the absence of fantasia, without meaning more
Than they are in the final finding of the ear, in the thing
Itself, until, at last, the cry concerns no one at all.

Now in my high eighties, I am disconcerted when I keep hearing
things, yet they are not there. When he was forty-two, Stevens wrote
"The Snow Man":

One must have a mind of winter
To regard the frost and the boughs
Of the pine-trees crusted with snow;

And have been cold a long time
To behold the junipers shagged with ice,
The spruces rough in the distant glitter

Of the January sun; and not to think
Of any misery in the sound of the wind,
In the sound of a few leaves,

Which is the sound of the land
Full of the same wind
That is blowing in the same bare place

For the listener, who listens in the snow,
And, nothing himself, beholds
Nothing that is not there and the nothing that is.

A single sentence sustained through fifteen lines, this initially
appears to be in agreement with John Ruskin's formulation of what
he called the "pathetic fallacy," in which a false life is attributed to the
object world. Ruskin must have known he contradicted himself, since
he defined a poet as a man to whom things speak. A natural Freudian
like Stevens wishes to live by the Reality Principle that accepts our need
to make friends with the necessity of dying. Yet there is always a conflict in Stevens, who was both a Keatsian poet and also Shelleyan and
Whitmanian. The glory of Keats is his heroic dismissal of all illusion:
death is absolute and imminent. Shelley's skepticism was tempered by
his idealism, and Whitman's epicureanism still allowed transcendental

yearnings. "The Snow Man" doubles back upon itself and concludes with a nihilism worthy of Hamlet.

Three times the leaves cry out in "The Course of the Particular." Stevens hears it and holds it off. At seventy-one, the exertion of being part of everything declines: "One feels the life of that which gives life as it is." That massive monosyllabic line should settle the uncanny cry, but it cannot. Neither we nor Stevens believe him when he insists this is not a human cry. Charmingly, he contradicts himself in the remarkable "It is the cry of leaves that do not transcend themselves." Leaves lacking transcendence cannot cry out. The course of this particular, the cry of the human, at last means the final finding each of us experiences as we die: "until, at last, the cry concerns no one at all."

Shelley's dead thoughts are driven like withered leaves by the pride of the poetic will. Promethean to his core, the revolutionary Shelley brings fire, sparks of prophecy. A Humean intellectual with a Promethean heart, he hears only reality and yet aspires to human renovation. Stevens, who echoes perpetually Shelley's "Defence of Poetry," defiantly joined his precursor when he proclaimed that the lights astral and Shelleyan would at last transform the world.

# Wallace Stevens, "Montrachet-le-Jardin"

WALLACE STEVENS evidently wrote "Montrachet-le-Jardin" early in 1942. He was a lover of French culture and Burgundy wine, and the Nazi occupation of France weighed upon his spirits. Deliberately declining to write war poetry, Stevens nevertheless profoundly catches both the moment and an eternal dimension in this subtle poem.

An oblique prelude culminates in the assertion "Man must become the hero of his world." Stevens then makes brilliant allusion to Shakespeare's song in *Cymbeline:*

Fear no more the heat o' th' sun,
Nor the furious winter's rages,
Thou thy worldly task has done,
Home art gone, and ta'en thy wages.
Golden lads and girls all must,
As chimney-sweepers, come to dust.

Fear no more the frown o' th' great,
Thou art past the tyrant's stroke;
Care no more to clothe and eat,
To thee the reed is as the oak:
The sceptre, learning, physic, must
All follow this and come to dust.

Fear no more the lightning-flash.
Nor th' all-dreaded thunder-stone.
Fear not slander, censure rash.
Thou hast finish'd joy and moan.

All lovers young, all lovers must
Consign to thee and come to dust.

No exerciser harm thee!
Nor no witchcraft charm thee!
Ghost unlaid forbear thee!
Nothing ill come near thee!
Quiet consummation have,
And renowned be thy grave!

Act 4, Scene 2

Fear never the brute clouds nor winter-stop
And let the water-belly of ocean roar,
Nor feel the x malisons of other men,

Since in the hero-land to which we go,
A little nearer by each multitude,
To which we come as into bezeled plain, . . .

This acute juxtaposition of Shakespeare and Stevens leads to a
moment of vision that haunts my painful nights as I struggle to recover:

A little while of Terra Paradise
I dreamed, of autumn rivers, silvas green,
Of sanctimonious mountains high in snow,

But in that dream a heavy difference
Kept waking and a mournful sense sought out,
In vain, life's season or death's element.

That "heavy difference" also stems from the song in *Cymbeline*. As
he does so frequently, Stevens turns to his muse, "the auroral creature
musing in the mind." It is again characteristic of Stevens that he closes
in the throwaway mode:

And yet what good were yesterday's devotions?
I affirm and then at midnight the great cat
Leaps quickly from the fireside and is gone.

It is not so much that Stevens negates his affirmation by qualifying it. The poem affirms. Like his true forerunner, Walt Whitman, Stevens is an affirmer and not an ironist. He could not always confront his own Whitmanian spirit. Yet it refuses to abandon him.

In "Waving Adieu, Adieu, Adieu," from the volume *Ideas of Order*, the opening is a negation:

> That would be waving and that would be crying,
> Crying and shouting and meaning farewell,
> Farewell in the eyes and farewell at the centre,
> Just to stand still without moving a hand.
>
> In a world without heaven to follow, the stops
> Would be endings more poignant than partings, profounder,
> And that would be saying farewell, repeating farewell,
> Just to be there and just to behold.

You can term this an acceptance of our mortality or a playful despair. The lilt goes against the somber realization. The Whitmanian spirit at the center of Wallace Stevens rises up:

> To be one's singular self, to despise
> The being that yielded so little, acquired
> So little, too little to care, to turn
> To the ever-jubilant weather, to sip

"The ever-jubilant weather" is the victor over both doctrine and hesitation:

> One likes to practice the thing. They practice,
> Enough, for heaven. Ever-jubilant,
> What is there here but weather, what spirit
> Have I except it comes from the sun?

Whitman and Stevens practiced their poetry for earth, not heaven. Envision "ever-jubilant" as a direct address to Walt Whitman. Weather is the movement of wind and the absence or presence of the sun. The poet in Stevens, as in Whitman, is always in the sun. There are poets like Shelley and Hart Crane for whom the rising of the wind is the crucial stimulus. Whitman and Stevens are elevated to vision by the jubilant sun.

Age has not diminished my delight in Stevens's "Extracts from Addresses to the Academy of Fine Ideas":

> What
> One believes is what matters. Ecstatic identities
> Between one's self and the weather and the things
> Of the weather are the belief in one's element,
> The casual reunions, the long-pondered
> Surrenders, the repeated sayings that
> There is nothing more and that it is enough
> To believe in the weather and in the things and men
> Of the weather and in one's self, as part of that
> And nothing more. So that if one went to the moon,
> Or anywhere beyond, to a different element,
> One would be drowned in the air of difference,
> Incapable of belief, in the difference.
> And then returning from the moon, if one breathed
> The cold evening, without any scent or the shade
> Of any woman, watched the thinnest light
> And the most distant, single color, about to change,
> And naked of any illusion, in poverty,
> In the exactest poverty, if then
> One breathed the cold evening, the deepest inhalation
> Would come from that return to the subtle centre.

"Poverty" in Stevens is imaginative need. The "subtle centre" is the self open to the weather. "Ecstatic identities" are the entire program of Whitman at his most exuberant. In Stevens we hear them as "The hum of thoughts evaded in the mind."

# Edwin Arlington Robinson,
## "Luke Havergal"

THE SHELLEYAN FICTION of the leaves achieved a triumph in Edwin Arlington Robinson's "Luke Havergal" (1896), though I will employ his revised text here. Robinson never married, because he was totally smitten with his sister-in-law and maintained a wholly honorable stance of reticence and reverence toward her throughout their lives. In 1914, he published his dark lyric "Eros Turannos," a chant devoted to the difficult marriage of his brother and his forbidden beloved:

> The falling leaf inaugurates
>     The reign of her confusion;
> The pounding wave reverberates
>     The dirge of her illusion;
> And home, where passion lived and died,
> Becomes a place where she can hide,
> While all the town and harbor side
>     Vibrate with her seclusion.

> We tell you, tapping on our brows,
>     The story as it should be,—
> As if the story of a house
>     Were told, or ever could be;
> We'll have no kindly veil between
> Her visions and those we have seen,—
> As if we guessed what hers have been,
>     Or what they are or would be.

Meanwhile we do no harm; for they
    That with a god have striven,
Not hearing much of what we say,
    Take what the god has given;
Though like waves breaking it may be,
Or like a changed familiar tree,
Or like a stairway to the sea
    Where down the blind are driven.

These are the three final octaves of a six-stanza poem. Amazingly dispassionate, "Eros Turannos" nevertheless conveys Robinson's endless despair and his stoic resolution. He mounts to a climactic intensity as he salutes the enclosed erotic struggle, first with a Wordsworthian "changed familiar tree," which recalls "But there's a tree, of many, one," from the "Intimations" ode. The final trope is Robinson's own invention and always makes me think of the dreadful scene in *The Battleship Potemkin* where the director, Sergei Eisenstein, portrays the slaughter on the Odessa Steps, down which victims are driven into the sea.

In "Luke Havergal," a poem I recite incessantly to myself, Robinson identifies with the lyric monologuist:

Go to the western gate, Luke Havergal,
There where the vines cling crimson on the wall,
And in the twilight wait for what will come.
The leaves will whisper there of her, and some,
Like flying words, will strike you as they fall;
But go, and if you listen she will call.
Go to the western gate, Luke Havergal—
Luke Havergal.

The western gate may be the threshold to the beyond. The "Ode to the West Wind" haunts Robinson, as the great trope of Shelley's dead thoughts drive like withered leaves to quicken a new birth. Darkly, Robinson imagines the death of his beloved, yet I always wonder who is speaking the poem.

No, there is not a dawn in eastern skies
To rift the fiery night that's in your eyes;

But there, where western glooms are gathering,
The dark will end the dark, if anything:
God slays Himself with every leaf that flies,
And hell is more than half of paradise.
No, there is not a dawn in eastern skies—
In eastern skies.

The unknown speaker urges Luke to turn his back on the east and accept instead a cosmos where "God slays Himself with every leaf that flies." With the next stanza, we receive the revelation that Luke's guide is among the dead:

Out of a grave I come to tell you this,
Out of a grave I come to quench the kiss
That flames upon your forehead with a glow
That blinds you to the way that you must go.
Yes, there is yet one way to where she is,
Bitter, but one that faith may never miss.
Out of a grave I come to tell you this—
To tell you this.

We are not told the motive of this admonisher. Robinson seems to have been fixated on a chaste kiss his sister-in-law once bestowed upon his forehead. I always wonder why that flame has to be quenched, and I distrust the speaker. And yet the final stanza achieves a cognitive music that verges upon the Sublime:

There is the western gate, Luke Havergal,
There are the crimson leaves upon the wall.
Go, for the winds are tearing them away,—
Nor think to riddle the dead words they say,
Nor any more to feel them as they fall;
But go, and if you trust her she will call.
There is the western gate, Luke Havergal—
Luke Havergal.

Shelley returns in that medley of crimson leaves, winds, dead words, and the image of falling. So strong is his presence that I entertain the fancy that the voice emanates from the Promethean bard himself, whose skepticism was allied to a visionary Platonism that consigned dust to the dust while hymning the pure spirit returning to the "burning fountain" or "unextinguished hearth" where dwelt forms more real than living man.

Riddling the dead words may be vain, yet the splendor of Robinson's poem transcends its unresolvable dilemma. The cumulative effect of the carefully crafted repetitions dwarfs the enigma of its plot and earns the belated poet something of the Shelleyan aura of victory despite the loss of eros. Yet Robinson was the bard of defeat, and the true epilogue of "Luke Havergal" is in "The Pity of the Leaves" (1897):

> Vengeful across the cold November moors,
> Loud with ancestral shame there came the bleak,
> Sad wind that shrieked, and answered with a shriek,
> Reverberant through lonely corridors.
> The old man heard it; and he heard, perforce,
> Words out of lips that were no more to speak—
> Words of the past that shook the old man's cheek
> Like dead, remembered footsteps on old floors.
> And then there were the leaves that plagued him so!
> The brown, thin leaves that on the stones outside
> Skipped with a freezing whisper. Now and then
> They stopped, and stayed there—just to let him know
> How dead they were; but if the old man cried,
> They fluttered off like withered souls of men.

Plangency is the mark of this exquisitely bleak sonnet, which anticipates Robert Frost, with whom Robinson shared mutual esteem. Shelley, as superb a reader as ever to appear among the major poets, might have winced urbanely at this diminution of his prophetic metaphor in which the withered leaves quicken a new birth.

# William Carlos Williams, "A Unison"

I REGRET THAT I HAD TO DECLINE Kenneth Burke's kind offer to bring William Carlos Williams to meet with me at Burke's home in Andover, New Jersey, in the early 1960s. Williams died in 1963, and I did not get down to Andover until the mid-1970s.

I came very late to a full appreciation of Williams. My conversion did not begin until I read the first volume of *Paterson* in 1951, five years after its publication. I went on to *Spring and All* (1923), which is one of the true American originals. Like most readers I was immediately enraptured by its superb opening lyric:

By the road to the contagious hospital
under the surge of the blue
mottled clouds driven from the
northeast—a cold wind. Beyond, the
waste of broad, muddy fields
brown with dried weeds, standing and fallen


. . . . . . . . . . . . . . . .

All along the road the reddish
purplish, forked, upstanding, twiggy
stuff of bushes and small trees
with dead, brown leaves under them
leafless vines—

Lifeless in appearance, sluggish
dazed spring approaches—

They enter the new world naked,
cold, uncertain of all
save that they enter. All about them
the cold, familiar wind—

Now the grass, tomorrow
the stiff curl of wildcarrot leaf

One by one objects are defined—
It quickens: clarity, outline of leaf

But now the stark dignity of
entrance—Still, the profound change
has come upon them: rooted, they
grip down and begin to awaken

This has a harsh intensity of inception, at once of infants, vegetation, and American poems. As an obstetrician and a pediatric physician, Williams delivered and cared for generations of babies, and one hears his love for that labor in the almost magical elegance of:

They enter the new world naked,
cold, uncertain of all
save that they enter.

In a prose passage of *Spring and All*, Williams cries out, "THE WORLD IS NEW." Walt Whitman is the fountainhead of this American proclamation:

I have heard what the talkers were talking . . . . the talk of the
    beginning and the end,
But I do not talk of the beginning or the end.

There was never any more inception than there is now
Nor any more youth or age than there is now;
And will never be any more perfection than there is now,
Nor any more heaven or hell than there is now.

"Song of Myself," Section 3

I turn to the shorter poem by Williams that most moves me, "A Unison," where the title brings together several of the meanings of "unison": the same words spoken at once by two or more speakers; an identity of pitch in music; a concord, agreement, harmony, or musical parts combined in octaves:

The grass is very green, my friend,
and tousled, like the head of—
your grandson, yes? And the mountain,
the mountain we climbed
twenty years since for the last
time (I write this thinking
of you) is saw-horned as then
upon the sky's edge—an old barn
is peaked there also, fatefully,
against the sky. And there it is
and we can't shift it or change
it or parse it or alter it
in any way. *Listen! Do you not hear*
*them? the singing?* There it is and
we'd better acknowledge it and
write it down that way, not otherwise.
Not twist the words to mean
what we should have said but to mean
—what cannot be escaped: the
mountain riding the afternoon as
it does, the grass matted green,
green underfoot and the air—
rotten wood. *Hear! Hear them!*
*the Undying.* The hill slopes away,
then rises in the middleground,
you remember, with a grove of gnarled
maples centering the bare pasture,
sacred, surely—for what reason?
I cannot say. Idyllic!
a shrine cinctured there by
the trees, a certainty of music!
a unison and a dance, joined
at this death's festival: Something

of a shed snake's skin, the beginning
goldenrod. Or, best, a white stone,
you have seen it: *Mathilda Maria*
*Fox*—and near the ground's lip,
all but undecipherable, *Aet Suae*
*Anno 9*—still there, the grass
dripping of last night's rain—and
welcome! The thin air, the near,
clear brook water!—and could not,
and died, unable; to escape
what the air and the wet grass—
through which, tomorrow, bejeweled,
the great sun will rise—the
unchanging mountains, forced on them—
and they received, willingly!
Stones, stones of a difference
joining the others, at pace. *Hear!*
*Hear the unison of their voices. . . .*

Williams from the start was divided by two prime precursors: John Keats and Walt Whitman. At first he kept his own poems that he derived from each in separate notebooks. As his work evolved, tentative fusions began to insinuate themselves. This long process culminates in "A Unison," where "Song of Myself" and the two *Hyperion* fragments cunningly come together. Asked by a child, "What is the grass?" Whitman chants a marvelous fantasia curiously prophetic of Hemingway's style:

This grass is very dark to be from the white heads of old
    mothers,
Darker than the colorless beards of old men,
Dark to come from under the faint red roofs of mouths.

"Leaves of Grass," Section 6

Williams borrows the metaphor, and his "very green" follows Whitman's suggestion that a "very green" becomes a "very dark" in the shadow of mortality. Keats, though, was even deeper in the consciousness of Williams, and "A Unison" returns us to the Saturnian shrine in the first *Hyperion*. "Sacred, surely—for what reason?" is perhaps unanswerable to Williams, and yet "a shrine cinctured there by/the trees, a certainty of music!" refers to Keats's characteristic mode of stationing, a sculpting at once natural and aesthetic. Keats pledges mortals and the dead poets, whereas Whitman insists, "The smallest sprout shows there is really no death." But Williams urges us to hear what he hears, the unison of their voices. Are we hearing enough more than the unison of the voices of John Keats and Walt Whitman?

So eloquent is "A Unison" that indeed we hear the true voice of William Carlos Williams himself. Though that voice has been endlessly imitated, its secret remains its own. The exegetes diminish him by their weirdly inflated assertions that his poems create a new reality. It is no service that they forget he is not Shakespeare or Dante. It is enough, and more than enough, to have been an American original. His poem "These" hurts and helps me in this cold spring of 2016, with so many of my friends recently dead or dying:

> houses of whose rooms
> the cold is greater than can be thought,
>
> the people gone that we loved,
> the beds lying empty, the couches
> damp, the chairs unused . . .

# Archie Randolph Ammons, *Sphere*

I N AUGUST 1968, my wife and I with our sons, six-year-old Daniel and three-year-old David, began to spend our afternoons in Stewart Park, at the foot of Lake Cayuga, in Ithaca, New York. It was there we first met Archie and Phyllis Ammons and their five-year-old son, John. I remember walking over to them to introduce myself and being instantly delighted. My knowledge of the poetry of Archie Randolph Ammons at that time consisted only of a recent reading of *Corsons Inlet* (1965).

We invited them to come back to the house in Cayuga Heights that we were renting for the year from Norman and Lee Malcolm. Phyllis was open and outgoing from the start, and the three little boys played together amiably then and throughout the year. Archie was very shy and said very little. At thirty-eight, I was rather talkative, and he was a good listener, but I was relieved when, after a few weeks together, he began to speak more freely. During that year, from August to August, I spent several hours in Archie's company virtually every day. When my wife and I returned to New Haven, our friendship deepened as we exchanged innumerable letters and frequent phone calls.

Archie gave several readings at Yale through the years and then chose to decline Yale's offer of a professorship as poet in residence in 1973. We remained close through the decades until his death on February 25, 2001. His presence lingers always, and is particularly strong when I reread and teach his poetry.

Like John Ashbery, with whom he shared a mutual admiration, Ammons was astonishingly prolific. I possess so many of his poems by memory that I hesitate where to begin these memorial remarks, but the dedicatory lines to the long poem *Sphere* have become part of my inmost being:

I went to the summit and stood in the high nakedness:
the wind tore about this
way and that in confusion and its speech could not
get through to me nor could I address it:
still I said as if to the alien in myself
    I do not speak to the wind now:
for having been brought this far by nature I have been
brought out of nature
and nothing here shows me the image of myself:
for the word *tree* I have been shown a tree
and for the word *rock* I have been shown a rock,
for stream, for cloud, for star
this place has provided firm implication and answering
    but where here is the image for *longing*:
so I touched the rocks, their interesting crusts:
I flaked the bark of the stunt-fir:
I looked into space and into the sun
and nothing answered my word *longing*:
    goodbye, I said, goodbye, nature so grand and
reticent, your tongues are healed up into their own
element
and as you have shut up you have shut me out: I am
as foreign here as if I had landed, a visitor:
so I went back down and gathered mud
and with my hands made an image for *longing*:
    I took the image to the summit: first
I set it here, on the top rock, but it completed
nothing: then I set it there among the tiny firs
but it would not fit:
so I returned to the city and built a house to set
the image in
and men came into my house and said
    that is an image for *longing*
and nothing will ever be the same again

My late friend John Hollander, an enthusiast for Ammons, termed this a poem of "restitution." It is not clear to me which of the meanings of "restitution" John intended. Is it the restoration of something lost? Is it compensation? Or is it a recoil to an originary shape? A university wit and formidable poet, Hollander probably meant all three. With a poem this sublime, even devoted exegetes must differ. As I read it, nothing is restored or can be. The wind, Virgilian guide to Ammons as Pilgrim of Eternity, no longer addresses him, nor can he speak to it. On the mount of vision, he stands out of nature and cannot find the Whitmanian image of himself. A yearning desire, not for self but for what William Blake called his Emanation, is the *longing* akin to Yahweh's Creation of Adam out of the Adamic red clay. I do not read this as parody but as lamentation. Ammons was not a Christian, yet he was Bible-soaked from his North Carolina boyhood on to his death.

There is no abode for the image of *longing*. Summit, tiny firs, the house or temple built in the city: nothing coheres. We read Ammons and confront only the shadow of yearning. I hear a kind of palinode when the poet ends with "and nothing will ever be the same again." A double alienation is the burden. We have been brought out of nature, yet only into an image. We desire firm implication and answering and cannot receive them in this place that is not our own.

Archie resisted his own transcendental impulses. He wanted to be steady in the everyday world. As a reader, I always wanted him to cut loose and give us the voice that was great within him. I see now this was bad advice. His true subject was poetic disincarnation, and his might addressed the alien in himself. Even his earliest poems listen to the wind, the ancient praxis of poets innumerable.

When I teach Ammons, I like to start with "Gravelly Run":

I don't know somehow it seems sufficient
to see and hear whatever coming and going is,
losing the self to the victory
    of stones and trees,
of bending sandpit lakes, crescent
round groves of dwarf pine:

for it is not so much to know the self
as to know it as it is known
    by galaxy and cedar cone,
as if birth had never found it
and death could never end it:

the swamp's slow water comes
down Gravelly Run fanning the long
   stone-held algal
hair and narrowing roils between
the shoulders of the highway bridge:

holly grows on the banks in the woods there,
and the cedars' gothic-clustered
   spires could make
green religion in winter bones:

so I look and reflect, but the air's glass
jail seals each thing in its entity:

no use to make any philosophies here:
   I see no
god in the holly, hear no song from
the snowbroken weeds: Hegel is not the winter
yellow in the pines: the sunlight has never
heard of trees: surrendered self among
   unwelcoming forms: stranger,
hoist your burdens, get on down the road.

At lunch one day with my friend Harry Ford, who died in 1999, I showed him this poem. Harry was a superb book designer and editor of poets as eminent as James Merrill, Richard Wilbur, W. S. Merwin, Mark Strand, Anthony Hecht, and Edgar Bowers. He winced as he read "Gravelly Run" and said, "Harold, every time I try to read Archie Ammons, I have the sensation that I am watching a sweater unravel." Eventually, I repeated this to Archie, who was not altogether amused. But I see what Harry, an exquisite formalist, was trying to protest. "Gravelly Run" is an astonishingly original poem. Walt Whitman almost always hovers in Ammons, but here he is exorcised. The cadences of "Gravelly Run" are ineluctable, as befits a poem essaying the impossible enterprise of knowing the self as it is known by the outer spaces and a natural particular. Ammons is true to what I have come to call the American Religion. The innermost self was unborn and so cannot know death. Should the self surrender, there are no forms to welcome it. From the time I first read it, "Gravelly Run" seemed uncanny in its music. It will not yield even to an Emersonian exegesis.

An even more powerful poem, "Guide" at first might seem capable of paraphrase, yet that is illusory. All of Ammons exalts the form of a motion and evades origin as best it can:

> You cannot come to unity and remain material:
> in that perception is no perceiver:
>     when you arrive
> you have gone too far:
>     at the Source you are in the mouth of Death:
>
> you cannot
>     turn around in
> the Absolute: there are no entrances or exits
>     no precipitations of forms
> to use like tongs against the formless:
>     no freedom to choose:
>
> to be
>     you have to stop not-being and break
> off from *is* to *flowing* and
>     this is the sin you weep and praise:
> origin is your original sin:
>     the return you long for will ease your guilt
> and you will have your longing:
>
>     the wind that is my guide said this: it
> should know having
>     given up everything to eternal being but
> direction:
>
> how I said can I be glad and sad: but a man goes
>     from one foot to the other:
> wisdom wisdom:
>     to be glad and sad at once is also unity
> and death:
>     wisdom wisdom: a peachblossom blooms on a particular

tree on a particular day:
    unity cannot do anything in particular:

are these the thoughts you want me to think I said but
    the wind was gone and there was no more knowledge then.

We long to return from the family romance of our origin, yet even
a major poet will not possess this longing. Hesitant to surrender to
eternal being, Ammons heartens me with his wistful quest for wisdom.
I wrote a book called *Where Shall Wisdom Be Found* and used "Guide" as
my epigraph. If wisdom blooms on a particular tree on a particular day,
it may be only an unwisdom. Thirsting after some knowledge, Ammons
receives none. The wind goes, and as a guide emulates Robert Frost in
"Directive":

. . . if you'll let a guide direct you
Who only has at heart your getting lost . . .

Frost is ironic; Ammons is not.

In so vast a panoply of poems, my mind turns back to a few that had
some part in shaping my own being. "The City Limits" is one of them:

When you consider the radiance, that it does not withhold
itself but pours its abundance without selection into every
nook and cranny not overhung or hidden; when you consider

that birds' bones make no awful noise against the light but
lie low in the light as in a high testimony; when you consider
the radiance, that it will look into the guiltiest

swervings of the weaving heart and bear itself upon them,
not flinching into disguise or darkening; when you consider
the abundance of such resource as illuminates the glow-blue

bodies and gold-skeined wings of flies swarming the dumped
guts of a natural slaughter or the coil of shit and in no
way winces from its storms of generosity; when you consider

that air or vacuum, snow or shale, squid or wolf, rose or lichen,
each is accepted into as much light as it will take, then
the heart moves roomier, the man stands and looks about, the

leaf does not increase itself above the grass, and the dark
work of the deepest cells is of a tune with May bushes
and fear lit by the breadth of such calmly turns to praise.

The word "consider" stems from the Latin *consideráre*, which means
literally to examine or contemplate the stars. The verb has a wide
range, but here means to take something into account when making
a judgment. "When you consider" is repeated five times as a prolepsis
foreboding radiance. The coming of this light is generous and profuse.
A secular grace descends without our deserving. I never get out of my
heart the astonishing:

that birds' bones make no awful noise against the light but
lie low in the light as in a high testimony . . .

I hunch over awkwardly, lest I make an awful noise against the light,
and accept that I cannot lie low in the light as in a high testimony. Our
swervings sustain and engender the radiance, and the storms of generosity fall down upon the lowest edge of being. I hear Walt Whitman in
the redemption of the minimal particulars:

that air or vacuum, snow or shale, squid or wolf, rose or lichen,
each is accepted into as much light as it will take . . .

The man is Archie Ammons, whose heart moves roomier as he stands
and looks about. Archie and I talked about the title *Leaves of Grass*, which
is multiform and turns upon that curious "of." Walt would have agreed
that the leaf does not increase itself above the grass. Ammons, master
of anxiety's prosody, transmutes his fear of mortality to praise. Of what?
There I touch my limits, which indeed are the city limits. Archie the
countryman is a pragmatic Emersonian and knows a new calm.

Today is Friday, December 22, 2017. I wrote those previous paragraphs
on Ammons some four years ago. In 2013, I received a book called *An*

*Image for Longing: Selected Letters and Journals of A. R. Ammons, 1951–
1974*, edited by Kevin McGuirk. Though Archie had died in February 2001 at the age of seventy-five, I was still grieving and was rather numb as I read through his letters and journals, many of them addressed to me, though not always sent. Four years later, my grief is still intense, but now almost all of my friends among the poets and critics of my generation have departed. Mourning for so many men and women does not diffuse an individual grief yet makes it seem less urgent.

Yesterday evening, I was happy to receive *The Complete Poems of A. R. Ammons*, edited by Robert M. West and with an introduction by my old friend Helen Vendler. Archie was prolific, and the two volumes contain nearly two thousand pages of poetry. I can think only of Victor Hugo as having composed so enormous a quantity of enduring verse.

As I read through the two volumes, I recognize most but not all of the poems. It is a kind of happy shock to confront my close friend as a ghostly companion on such a scale. I recall that in 1997 Archie sent me a poem called "Quibbling the Colossal":

I just had the funniest thought: it's the
singing of Wales and whales that I like so

much: you know, have you heard those men's
groups, those coal miners and church people in

Wales singing: to be deeply and sweetly undone,
listen in: and the scrawny rising and

screechings and deep bellowing of whales,
their arias personal (?) and predatory at

. love and prey—that makes up mind for us as
we study to make out mind in them: the reason

I can't attain world view or associational
complexity is that when I read I'm asleep by

the second paragraph: also, my poems come in
dislocated increments, because my spine between

the shoulderblades gets to hurting when I type:
also, my feet swell from sitting still: but

when the world tilts one way it rights another
which is to say that the disjunctiveness of my

recent verse cracks up the dark cloud and
covering shield of influence and lets fresh

light in, more than what little was left, a
sliver along the farthest horizon: room to

breathe and stretch and not give a shit, room
to turn my armies of words around in or camp

out and hide (bivouac): height to reach up
through the smoke and busted mirrors to clear

views of the beginnings high in the oldest
times: but seriously you know, this way of

seeing things is just a way of seeing things:
time is not crept up on by some accumulative

designer but percolates afresh every day like
a hot cup of coffee: and, Harold, if this is

an Evening Land, when within memory was it
otherwise, all of civilized time a second in

the all of time: good lord, we're all so
recent, we've hardly got our ears scrubbed,

hair unmatted, our teeth root-canaled: so,
shine on, shine on, harvest moon: the computers

are clicking, and the greatest dawn ever is
rosy in the skies.

CAST THE OVERCAST

I once wrote about this poem and got it wrong by identifying the colossal with Walt Whitman. Archie insisted that he meant me, an identification I evaded, though Whitman's first name was not Harold. Setting that aside, I love the stance of "Quibbling the Colossal." Ammons could be very charming, and here I suppose he was telling me that I had to let the light shine upon me, enabling me to breathe and stretch, a prophet of anxiety who should be more firmly grounded.

I write on Saturday, December 23, 2017, in dismal weather. I have never kept copies of letters I sent to friends, because they were all in longhand. At my age, I will not get up to Cornell to look at my letters in the Ammons Archive, or to Harvard to see my letters to John Ashbery. Indeed, I am too infirm to get over to Yale's Beinecke Rare Book and Manuscript Library to look at my myriad letters to Robert Penn Warren. I have their letters to me up in my attic, but will never have the time and energy to reread them. When Roger Gilbert's biography of Ammons appears, then I should achieve a better sense of my correspondence with Archie. Since I want to devote the rest of these memorial remarks to his long poem *Sphere*, I turn again to the volume *An Image for Longing*. I discussed the dedicatory poem to *Sphere* above but was a little shy of giving its title: "For Harold Bloom." It may be Archie's finest, though there are a score of other candidates. Here are excerpts from a letter he wrote me on January 25, 1974:

Thank you for your sweet words which I needed so much you wouldn't believe it. Anybody who needs as much as I do ought to be shot. It's a drain on the national energy level.

I made "I went to summit" your dedication poem so I hope you were telling the truth about liking it because you're stuck with it.

(Did you ever get the feeling that everything you're doing is delusional and doesn't mean a thing? I do.)

Believe it or not, we've had a day with sunshine but it's right back cosy cloudy now.

. . . .

I know you have some serious unvoiced reservations about Sphere but that you like some parts well enough to remain silent about the other parts. I can't change anything, now (maybe I could if I waited another year)—so it would be all right if you went ahead and told me the worst. I'm afraid it's a completely mad poem of separation, and I really don't like to offer bad products to the unsuspecting public that doesn't have enough sense to know whether something is good for it or not (and I don't either)—but, still, curiously enough, I never felt so connected to human reality as I have since finishing the poem. I wish I could be confident that the poem would have the same effect with others.

. . . .

I guess we will be [in] Ocean City again this summer. This time you must come down, and I will accept no declining gestures. I will look about and get you a good place. Then I will drive up and get you. Then, in due time, when you have a little sand on your bare feet and a little grit in your teeth, I will drive you back to New Haven. I have decided to give the orders from now on. But you may provide all the commentary you please.

I never did get to Ocean City, but then I have a lifelong horror of sandy beaches. I am like my late father: put me in the sun for an hour and I become a red lobster. Archie once joked to me that he could call his collected poems *The Influence of Anxiety*. I had not expressed any reservations to him about *Sphere*, since it seems to me the strongest of his long poems. But Ammons had a preternatural sensitivity to any critical qualms I might have felt in regard to his work, even when I was not aware of them.

Archie believed, as I do, that Whitman's "Song of Myself" was the greatest long poem of the last century and a half. *Sphere: The Form of a Motion* seems to me the most Whitmanian of all Ammons's poems. It is very much Archie's "Song of Myself" and moves with Whitmanian gusto. Ammons at the age of forty-eight had the self-confidence to take on the mantle of Whitman with verve and high humor:

122

.   .   .   .   .   .   .   .   .   .   .   .   .   .   .   .   .   .   .

. . . I can't understand my readers:
they complain of my abstractions as if the United States of
    America
were a form of vanity: they ask why I'm so big on the

one: many problem, they never saw one: my readers: what do
    they
expect from a man born and raised in a country whose motto
    is *E*
*pluribus unum:* I'm just, like Whitman, trying to keep things

half straight about my country: my readers say, what's all
this change and continuity: when we have a two-party system,
one party devoted to reform and the other to consolidation:


123


and both trying to grab a chunk out of the middle: either we
reconcile opposites or we suspend half the country into
disaffection and alienation: they want to know, what do I

mean *quadrants*, when we have a Southeast, Northeast,
    Southwest,
and Northwest and those cut into pairs by the splitting
Mississippi and the Mason-Dixon line: I figure I'm the
    exact

poet of the concrete *par excellence*, as Whitman might say:
they ask me, my readers, when I'm going to go politicized or
radicalized or public when I've sat here for years singing

unattended the off-songs of the territories and the midland
coordinates of Cleveland or Cincinnati: when I've prized
multeity and difference down to the mold under the leaf


124


on the one hand and swept up into the perfect composures of
nothingness on the other: my readers are baffling and
uncommunicative (if actual) and I don't know what to make of

or for them: I prize them, in a sense, for that: recalcitrance:
and for spreading out into a lot of canyons and high valleys
inaccessible to the common course or superhighway: though I

like superhighways, too, that tireless river system of streaming
unity: my country: my country: can't cease from its
sizzling rufflings to move into my "motions" and "stayings":

when I identify my self, my work, and my country, you may
think I've finally got the grandeurs: but to test the center
you have to go all the way both ways: from the littlest

to the biggest: I didn't mean to talk about my poem but
to tell others how to be poets: I'm interested in you, and
I want you to be a poet: I want, like Whitman, to found

a federation of loveship, not of queers but of poets, where
there's a difference: that is, come on and be a poet, queer
or straight, adman or cowboy, librarian or dope fiend,

housewife or hussy: (I see in one of the monthlies an astronaut
is writing poems—that's what I mean, guys): now, first of
all, the way to write poems is just to start: it's like

learning to walk or swim or ride the bicycle, you just go
after it: it is a matter of learning how to move with
balance among forces greater than your own, gravity, water's

126

buoyance, psychic tides: you lean in or with or against the
ongoing so as not to be drowned but to be swept effortlessly
up upon the universal possibilities: you can sit around

and talk about it all day but you will never walk the tightwire
till you start walking: once you walk, you'll find there's
no explaining it: do be afraid of falling off because it is

not falling off that's going to be splendid about you, making
you seem marvelous and unafraid: but don't be much afraid:
fall off a few times to see it won't kill you: O compatriotos,

sing your hangups and humiliations loose into song's
disengagements (which, by the way, connect, you know, when
they come back round the other way): O comrades! . . .

I remember the British poet-critic Donald Davie with affection and
respect. Some of his poems still linger in my memory, and his two marvelous studies of syntax and purity of diction in English poetry taught
me a great deal. We were only good acquaintances, yet I recall once
trying in vain to convert him to Ammons. I was all the more delighted
when *Sphere: The Form of a Motion* won him over:

I am way behind, getting to A. R. Ammons only now. And I know
why; everything I ever heard about him said that he wasn't my
cup of tea. (The Britishness of that idiom is much to the point.)
He was, I gathered, a poet who said "Ooh" and "Ah" to the universe, who had oceanic feelings about the multiplicity of things in
nature, and the ubiquity of nature's changes; a poet enamoured of
*flux*, therefore; and so, necessarily, a practitioner of "open form"—
which last comes uncomfortably close for my taste to being a contradiction in terms. In short, he was one whom Harold Bloom had
applauded as "a major visionary poet"; and if that doesn't raise my
hackles exactly, it certainly gives me goose-pimples.

And everything that I heard is true. Imagine! A poem 1,860
lines long, with only one full stop in it, at the end of the last line;
and put before *me*, who like to think of myself as Doctor Syntax, all for demarcations, a devotee of the sentence! Whatever
the opposite of an ideal reader is, I ought to have been that thing
so far as this poem is concerned. How could I be anything but
exasperated by it, profoundly distrustful, sure I was being bam-
boozled, sure I was being threatened? And how is it, then, that
I was on the contrary *enraptured*? Have I gone soft in the head?
Have I suffered a quasi-religious conversion? Shall I drag myself
on penitent knees to the feet of the saintly Bloom? No. I am as
suspicious as ever I was of Ammons's initial assumptions and gov-

erning pre-occupations. I still hunger for sentences and full stops, and for a colon that has precise grammatical and rhythmical work to do, instead of being the maid-of-all-work that Ammons makes it into. The cast of his temperament is as alien to me as I thought it would be. And yet I can't refuse the evidence of my senses and my feelings—there wasn't one page of his poem that didn't delight me.

*The New York Review of Books*, March 6, 1975

Donald Davie's authentic critical and poetical sensibility overcame his preconceptions in a manner I have tried to emulate as I age into more of an ability to set aside the polemics of a lifetime. Frequently at night, feeling my exhaustions, I recite T. S. Eliot's "Little Gidding" to myself, alternating it with "La Figlia Che Piange." At his strongest, Eliot comforts me, though I will never like him. With Ammons, as poet and as person, I was at home from the start. I read and teach *Sphere* in conjunction with "Song of Myself." I could not assert that Ammons equals Whitman, but among American poets only Emily Dickinson does.

Archie told me that what I called the anxiety of influence was what he termed hierarchy. The word "hierarchy" to the ancient Greeks meant "the rule of a priest." We tend by it to mean a group of individuals or entities graded by rank, by authority, or by capacity:

87

                     . . . the gods have come and gone
(or we have made them come and go) so long among us that
they have communicated something of the sky to us making us

feel that at the division of the roads our true way, too,
is to the sky where with unborn gods we may know no
further death and need no further visitations: what may have

changed is that in the future we can have the force to keep
the changes secular: the one:many problem, set theory, and
symbolic signifier: the pyramid, the pantheon (of gods and

men), the pecking order, baboon troop, old man of the tribe,
the hierarchy of family, hamlet, military, church, corporation,
civil service, of wealth, talent—everywhere the scramble for

place, power, privilege, safety, honor, the representative
notch above the undistinguished numbers: second is as good
as last: pyramidal hierarchies and solitary persons: the

hierarchies having to do with knowledge and law, the solitaries
with magic, conjuration, enchantment: the loser or apostate
turns on the structure and melts it with vision, with

summoning, clean, verbal burning: or the man at the top may
turn the hierarchy down and walk off in a private direction:
meanwhile, back at the hierarchy, the chippers and filers

hone rocks to skid together. . . .

"Hierarchy" is a metaphor for cognitive ordering, for those sharp
lines that do not exist in nature. Almost all of Ammons is a conflict
between the mind's assertion that it can take nature up into itself, and
the other vision, which knows nature will never be adequate to it. *Sphere*
gathers to a greatness in its final sequence, which again deliberately
evokes Whitman concluding his personal epic.

149

but the field, gone through, is open and in the woodburn
the jackpine cone flicks open and ejects seed: ferns rouse
subsoil curls: birds accept the brush margins of feeding

grounds and hawks police the new actions for waywardness:
the gods of care and economy of motion, the grass gods, the
god of the killdeer arrive, and the old god of the forest

begins to take everything away again: from other planets,
as with other planets from here, we rise and set, our presence,
reduced to light, noticeable in the dark when the sun is

away: reduced and distanced into light, our brotherhood
constituted into shining, our landforms, seas, colors
subsumed to bright announcement: we are alone in a sea that


150


shows itself nowhere in a falling surf but if it does not
go on forever folds back into a further motion of itself:
the plenitude of nothingness! planets seeds in a coronal

weaving so scant the fabric is the cloth of nakedness:
Pluto our very distant friend skims a gulf so fine and far
millions and thousands of millions of years mean little to—

how far lost we are, if saving is anywhere else: but light,
from any distance or point we've met it, shines with a similar
summation, margin affirmational, so we can see edges to the

black roils in the central radiances, galaxies colliding in
million-year meetings, others sprung loose into spiral
unwindings: fire, cold space, black concentration:


151


harmonies (in my magnum hokum) I would speak of, though
chiefly as calling attention to neglected aspects of fairly
common, at least overreaching, experience: with considerable

rasping along the edges, bulgings of boundaries, we made
and tamed into play each of these States: if the States
kept falling into lesser cluster about lesser points of

focus (and then the long division, so costly), still we
checked and balanced and, incorporating as much sin as grace
with each holding, kept the mobile afloat, together, each

dangle with good range to dip and rise and convey itself
roundly with windy happenstance, communicating, though, its
position throughout the network and receiving from the sums


152


of the network just adjustments: yes, we got it all together,
ocean to ocean, high temperate to low temperate, and took
in so much multiplicity that what we hold person to person

in common exists only in the high levels of constitution or
out to the neighbor's fence, an extreme, an extreme pity,
with little consolation in the middle after all: still,

it holds and moves within the established rigors: now, with
the same rasping and groaning, we try to put the nations and
communities of nations together and there, too, only by

joining tenuous extremes, asserting the dignity of the single
person above united nations: we pray this may succeed and
correct much evil in the dark edges of dislocation and


153


distraction: lately, we've left out the high ranges of music,
the planetary, from our response, though the one sin is here
as usual and the planets continue to obey holy roads: the

galaxy is here, nearly too much to speak of, sagely and
tremendously observing its rotation: we do have something to
tune in with and move toward: not homogenous pudding but

united differences, surface differences expressing the common,
underlying hope and fate of each person and people, a gathering
into one place of multiple dissimilarity, each culture to its

own cloth and style and tongue and gait, each culture, like
the earth itself with commonlode center and variable surface,
designed-out to the exact limit of ramification, to discrete


## 154

expression into the visible, specific congruence of form and
matter, energy moving into the clarification of each face, hand,
ear, mouth, eye, billions: still with the sense of continuous

running through and staying all the discretions, differences
diminished into the common tide of feelings, so that difference
cannot harden into aggression or hate fail to move with the

ongoing, the differences not submerged but resting clear at
the surface, as the surface, and not rising above the surface
so as to become more visible and edgy than the continuum:

a united, capable poem, a united, capable mind, a united capable
nation, and a united nation! capable, flexible, yielding,
accommodating, seeking the good of all in the good of each:


## 155

to float the orb or suggest the orb is floating: and, with the
mind thereto attached, to float free: the orb floats, a bluegreen
wonder: so to touch the structures as to free them into rafts

that reveal the tide: many rafts to ride and the tides make a
place to go: let's go and regard the structures, the six-starred
easter lily, the beans feeling up the stakes: we're gliding: we

*are* gliding: ask the astronomer, if you don't believe it: but
motion as summary of time and space is gliding us: for a while,
we may ride such forces: then, we must get off: but now this

beats any amusement park by the shore: our Ferris wheel, what a
wheel: our roller coaster, what mathematics of stoop and climb:
    sew
my name on my cap: we're clear: we're ourselves: we're sailing.

Walt Whitman, at the close of "Song of Myself," discards the past
and identifies himself with our future. The cost is the present moment.
Since Walt is somewhere up ahead of us and waiting, we need to catch
up and find him. Ammons preserves the present moment but has no
liberation to offer us. Archie is sailing *with* us. He floats along and is
going to lose his cap. Walt Whitman might say that it is not enough to
offer us an empty sublimity. In the earlier long poem "Hibernaculum,"
Ammons has an extraordinary passage that gives us both his greatest
strength and his ultimate vulnerability:

16

·   ·   ·   ·   ·   ·   ·   ·   ·   ·   ·   ·   ·

. . . to lean belief the lean word comes,
each scope adjusted to the plausible: to the heart
emptied of, by elimination, the world, comes the small

17

cry domesticating the night: if the night is to be
habitable, if dawn is to come out of it, if day is ever
to grow brilliant on delivered populations, the word

must have its way by the brook, lie out cold all night
along the snow limb, spell by yearning's wilted weed till
the wilted weed rises, know the patience and smallness

of stones: I address the empty place where the god
that has been deposed lived: it is the godhead: the
yearnings that have been addressed to it bear antiquity's

18

sanction: for the god is ever re-created as
emptiness, till force and ritual fill up and strangle
his life, and then he must be born empty again: I

accost the emptiness saying let all men turn their
eyes to the emptiness that allows adoration's life:
that is my whole saying, though I have no intention to

stop talking: our immediate staying's the rock but
the staying of the rock's motion: motion, that spirit!

The ancient religious discipline of theurgy, Neoplatonic and Kabbalistic, returns surprisingly in Ammons, who, like Whitman, is something of a shaman. In theurgy you draw down a god, maintain the god's
vitality, or strengthen a waning godhead. Confronting the empty place
where the god once lived, Ammons asks only for a divine rebirth that
will remain empty. I think of Hart Crane, the most intense of all American poets, who calls upon his Brooklyn Bridge to lend a myth to God.
Crane, an absolutist of the imagination, quested for the fullness while
lamenting emptiness. Ammons comes later, whereas Crane could not
accept his own belatedness. I do Archie little service by comparing him
to Walt Whitman and to Hart Crane, American demiurges. Ammons
was content to be a man of this world, despite the intimations of transcendence that never quite abandoned him.

# Hart Crane, "Possessions"

I N THE COURSE of a lifetime of reading, early possessions take on a particular aura. When I was twelve, I kept reciting to myself a poem by Hart Crane that I could not understand at all:

> Witness now this trust! the rain
> That steals softly direction
> And the key, ready to hand—sifting
> One moment in sacrifice (the direst)
> Through a thousand nights the flesh
> Assaults outright for bolts that linger
> Hidden,—O undirected as the sky
> That through its black foam has no eyes
> For this fixed stone of lust . . .
>
> Accumulate such moments to an hour:
> Account the total of this trembling tabulation.
> I know the screen, the distant flying taps
> And stabbing medley that sways—
> And the mercy, feminine, that stays
> As though prepared.
>
> And I, entering, take up the stone
> As quiet as you can make a man . . .
> In Bleecker Street, still trenchant in a void,
> Wounded by apprehensions out of speech,
> I hold it up against a disk of light—
> I, turning, turning on smoked forking spires,
> The city's stubborn lives, desires.

Tossed on these horns, who bleeding dies,
Lacks all but piteous admissions to be spilt
Upon the page whose blind sum finally burns
Record of rage and partial appetites.
The pure possession, the inclusive cloud
Whose heart is fire shall come,—the white wind rase
All but bright stones wherein our smiling plays.

As a child, I did not realize that the "bright stones" of the concluding line were an allusion to Revelation 2:17:

> He that hath an ear, let him hear what the Spirit saith unto the churches; To him that overcometh will I give to eat of the hidden manna, and will give him a white stone, and in the stone a new name written, which no man knoweth saving he that receiveth it.

I also did not know that "this fixed stone of lust" referred to the male genitalia. When Crane takes up the stone again, it implies the homoerotic desire that sends him out nightly to cruise the streets of Greenwich Village. So bitter is this poem "Possessions" that its ironies vacillate between a harshly reductive sexual realism and a phantasmagoria suggestive of Rimbaud. When Crane brings the fierce sufferings of this poem to a close, he plays upon his own name in the heart of fire that shall come when the bright stones of Revelation survive the white wind of erotic purgation.

As a poet consciously in Walt Whitman's tradition, Hart Crane takes up the "stone" as a tally or an image of voice. A preternaturally careful craftsman, Crane builds his poem on substantives and verbal forms of counting: "sifting," "a thousand nights," "accumulate," "account the total," "tabulation," "medley," "blind sum," "record." His drive is to wound the tally until it becomes only a faint echo of a voice.

Why does Crane call the poem "Possessions" rather than "Possession"? As I remarked earlier the root meaning of "possession" is potency. The poem's first possession is by lust: "undirected as the sky." The second is "the pure possession" that in Revelation is named as Jesus Christ. Hart Crane was not a Christian, but he had a severely Catholic sensibility and might have been better off if his questing temperament had allowed him to convert to Roman Catholicism. But he believed only in poetry and lived and died by it.

# Hart Crane, "To Brooklyn Bridge"

IN CONJUNCTION with Herman Melville's *Moby-Dick*, Walt Whitman is the American Sublime. We might speak either of the Passion of Captain Ahab or the Passion of Walt Whitman. Perhaps this could be extended. No one would want to chant the Passion of Wallace Stevens or William Carlos Williams. Yet it is possible to speak of the Passion of T. S. Eliot. Again above all others, we can affirm the Passion of Hart Crane.

Much of *White Buildings* (1926), a volume of darkly resonant lyrics and meditations, was given over to invocations of a God unknown. In his visionary epic *The Bridge* (1930), Crane stands in the shadow of Brooklyn Bridge at twilight and memorably calls down a God:

O harp and altar, of the fury fused,
(How could mere toil align thy choiring strings!)
Terrific threshold of the prophet's pledge,
Prayer of pariah, and the lover's cry,—

Again the traffic lights that skim thy swift
Unfractioned idiom, immaculate sigh of stars,
Beading thy path—condense eternity:
And we have seen night lifted in thine arms.

Under thy shadow by the piers I waited;
Only in darkness is thy shadow clear.
The City's fiery parcels all undone,
Already snow submerges an iron year . . .

O Sleepless as the river under thee,
Vaulting the sea, the prairies' dreaming sod,
Unto us lowliest sometime sweep, descend
And of the curveship lend a myth to God.

Brooklyn Bridge is both a vast aeolian harp and the altar of a new God. As a threshold, it stands between what the late Angus Fletcher termed labyrinth and temple. The labyrinth is inhabited by the lover's cry and the pariah's prayer, or the prophet pledging the way to the temple. There is a grand pietà in "And we have seen night lifted in thine arms."

Hart Crane had never read Saint John of the Cross, yet we are in his kind of version of the state of mysticism. There is an ultimate echo, mediated by the Whitman of the "Lilacs" elegy and of the Biblical Song of Songs. Hart Crane's spiritual canticle turns at last to the great leap of Brooklyn Bridge and prays that its curveship lend a myth to God, who so badly needs a new Word.

# Conrad Aiken, "Tetélestai"

S OMETIME IN 1963, I had dinner with Conrad Aiken and gave him the manuscript of what was to become *Preambles and Other Poems* by my friend Alvin Feinman, which was published in 1964. I had always been very moved by Aiken's poetry, and at my request we discussed it. Aiken died in 1973 at the age of eighty-four, having returned to live his final decade in his native Savannah. Thirty years later, in 2003, I wrote a foreword for a new edition of his *Selected Poems* in the hope of reviving his work. I would not say my effort was in vain, yet he is still very much a neglected master.

The firstborn child of transplanted New Englanders, Aiken suffered an awful childhood, because his father, a distinguished surgeon, during a paranoid seizure murdered his wife and then committed suicide. The eleven-year-old Conrad Aiken discovered the bodies and sustained a trauma. After the burial, Aiken and his siblings were taken north to be adopted by relatives. Separated from the others, the future poet became the ward of his uncle who was a librarian at Harvard University.

Entering Harvard in 1907, Aiken began to find himself as a poet. T. S. Eliot and Aiken formed what was to be a permanent friendship as Harvard undergraduates, but from the start a tension existed between them. Eventually, Eliot's neo-Christianity became intolerable to Aiken, who was always a Lucretian poet.

Aiken's best work was in his two sets of "preludes"—*Preludes for Memnon* (1931) and *Time in the Rock* (1936). The alternative title to the earlier sequence is *Preludes to Attitude*, where I take "attitude" to mean stance:

Winter for a moment takes the mind; the snow
Falls past the arclight; icicles guard a wall;
The wind moans through a crack in the window;
A keen sparkle of frost is on the sill.
Only for a moment; as spring too might engage it,
With a single crocus in the loam, or a pair of birds;
Or summer with hot grass; or autumn with a yellow leaf.
Winter is there, outside, is here in me:
Drapes the planets with snow, deepens the ice on the moon,
Darkens the darkness that was already darkness.
The mind too has its snows, its slippery paths,
Wall bayonetted with ice, leave ice-encased.
Here is the in-drawn room, to which you return
When the wind blows from Arcturus: here is the fire
At which you warm your hands and glaze your eyes;
The piano, on which you touch the cold treble;
Five notes like breaking icicles; and then silence.

This internalized winter is also celestial. Arcturus, brightest star in our Northern Hemisphere, blows the wind of space against the poet, and yet his own ears make the blowing wind they heard. As this initial prelude concludes, it heightens to a Lucretian severity:

Here is the tragic, the distorting mirror
In which your gesture becomes grandiose;
Tears form and fall from your magnificent eyes,
The brow is noble, and the mouth is God's.
Here is the God who seeks his mother, Chaos,—
Confusion seeking solution, and life seeking death.
Here is the rose that woos the icicle; the icicle
That woos the rose. Here is the silence of silences
Which dreams of becoming a sound, and the sound
Which will perfect itself in silence. And all
These things are only the uprush from the void,
The wings angelic and demonic, the sound of the abyss
Dedicated to death. And this is you.

Aiken had a lifelong obsession with silence, as did my late mentor Gershom Scholem, who shared Walter Benjamin's conviction that

silence was the mark of the unfallen. "You" and the Epicurean divinity
scarcely can be distinguished in Aiken's vision. The abyss, in the mode
of the late poems of Victor Hugo, returns in prelude XIV:

> —I saw myself and God.
> I saw the ruin in which godhead lives:
> Shapeless and vast: the strewn wreck of the world:
> Sadness unplumbed: misery without bound.
> Wailing I heard, but also I heard joy.
> Wreckage I saw, but also I saw flowers.
> Hatred I saw, but also I saw love . . .
> And thus, I saw myself.

> —And this alone?

> —And this alone awaits you, when you dare
> To that sheer verge where horror hangs, and tremble
> Against the falling rock; and, looking down,
> Search the dark kingdom. It is to self you come,—
> And that is God. It is the seed of seeds:
> Seeds for disastrous and immortal worlds.

> It is the answer that no question asked.

How much of ancient Gnosticism Aiken knew is unclear to me. Victor Hugo was versed in esoteric traditions, and I suspect Aiken was
also. In the Valentinian Speculation, the seed of seeds is both self and
God. Ghosts of change haunt Aiken and constitute his wavering self. In
prelude XXXIII, the poet again goes to the verge:

> Then came I to the shoreless shore of silence,
> Where never summer was nor shade of tree,
> Nor sound of water, nor sweet light of sun,
> But only nothing and the shore of nothing,
> Above, below, around, and in my heart:

> Where day was not, not night, nor space, nor time,
> Where no bird sang, save him of memory,
> Nor footstep marked upon the marl, to guide

My halting footstep; and I turned for terror,
Seeking in vain the Pole Star of my thought;

Where it was blown among the shapeless clouds,
And gone as soon as seen, and scarce recalled,
Its image lost and I directionless;
Alone upon the brown sad edge of chaos,
In the wan evening that was evening always;

Then closed my eyes upon the sea of nothing
While memory brought back a sea more bright,
With long, long waves of light, and the swift sun,
And the good trees that bowed upon the wind;
And stood until grown dizzy with that dream . . .

Silence and nothingness are the burden of this negative epiphany.
A vertigo possesses Aiken when he realizes the arbitrariness of: "Cal-
endars torn, appointments made and kept, / or made and broken . . ."
Approaching the conclusion of a hopeless quest, this version of Browning's "Childe Roland" subsides in a throwaway eloquence:

Thus systole addressed diastole,—
The heart contracting, with its grief of burden,
To the lax heart, with grief of burden gone.

Thus star to dead leaf speaks; thus cliff to sea;
And thus the spider, on a summer's day,
To the bright thistledown, trapped in the web.

No language leaps this chasm like a lightning:
Here is no message of assuagement, blown
From Ecuador to Greenland; here is only

A trumpet blast, that calls dead men to arms;
The granite's pity for the cloud; the whisper
Of time to space.

The Shelleyan trumpet of a prophecy echoed by Childe Roland—
"Dauntless the slug-horn to my lips I set / And blew"—now calls dead

men to arms, recalling Browning's vision of the band of failed questers and poets who stand around Roland in a sheet of flame. Aiken does not name his precursors, perhaps because they were so many: Shelley, Keats, Coleridge, Whitman, and Browning, among others. Associative rhetoric was both Aiken's mode and, sadly, his weakness. He did not try to make it new but to augment the foundations by relying upon the major poets of the Romantic tradition. Here is a vital instance of his mingled grandeur and limitation:

> It is morning, Senlin says, and in the morning
> When the light drips through the shutters like the dew,
> I arise, I face the sunrise,
> And do the things my fathers learned to do.
> Stars in the purple dusk above the rooftops
> Pale in a saffron mist and seem to die,
> And I myself on a swiftly tilting planet
> Stand before a glass and tie my tie.
>
> Vine leaves tap my window,
> Dew-drops sing to the garden stones,
> The robin chirps in the chinaberry tree
> Repeating three clear tones.
>
> It is morning. I stand by the mirror
> And tie my tie once more.
> While waves far off in a pale rose twilight
> Crash on a coral shore.
> I stand by a mirror and comb my hair:
> How small and white my face!—
> The green earth tilts through a sphere of air
> And bathes in a flame of space.
>
> There are houses hanging above the stars
> And stars hung under a sea.
> And a sun far off in a shell of silence
> Dapples my walls for me.
>
> It is morning, Senlin says, and in the morning
> Should I not pause in the light to remember God?

Upright and firm I stand on a star unstable,
He is immense and lonely as a cloud.
I will dedicate this moment before my mirror
To him alone, and for him I will comb my hair.
Accept these humble offerings, cloud of silence!
I will think of you as I descend the stair.

Vine leaves tap my window,
The snail-track shines on the stones,
Dew-drops flash from the chinaberry tree
Repeating two clear tones.

It is morning, I awake from a bed of silence,
Shining I rise from the starless waters of sleep.
The walls are about me still as in the evening,
I am the same, and the same name still I keep.
The earth revolves with me, yet makes no motion,
The stars pale silently in a coral sky.
In a whistling void I stand before my mirror,
Unconcerned, and tie my tie.

There are horses neighing on far-off hills
Tossing their long white manes,
And mountains flash in the rose-white dusk,
Their shoulders black with rains.

It is morning. I stand by the mirror
And surprise my soul once more;
The blue air rushes above my ceiling,
There are suns beneath my floor.

. . . It is morning, Senlin says, I ascend from darkness
And depart on the winds of space for I know not where,
My watch is wound, a key is in my pocket,
And the sky is darkened as I descend the stair.
There are shadows across the windows, clouds in heaven,
And a god among the stars; and I will go
Thinking of him as I might think of daybreak
And humming a tune I know.

Vine leaves tap at the window,
Dew-drops sing to the garden stones,
The robin chirps in the chinaberry tree
Repeating three clear tones.

This is the "Morning Song of Senlin" in the long sequence "Senlin: A Biography." Senlin is Aiken's alter ego, as Robinson was Weldon Kees's, but though Senlin's destiny is cloudy he is a far gentler daemon. His morning song haunts my current hard dawns as I study my countenance in the mirror, small and white, approaching eighty-eight. I cannot say that I pause in the dawn light to remember God, though uneasily mortality hovers.

Aiken never quite got over Edgar Allan Poe, whose cadences obtrude when I chant Senlin's morning song. Except at his very best, Aiken can be a kind of echo chamber. As his partisan, I turn to his grandeur in the five-part poem "Tetélestai," whose title refers to the final words of Jesus from the Cross: "It is finished." "Tetélestai" contrasts to T. S. Eliot's *The Waste Land*, also composed by 1922:

I

How shall we praise the magnificence of the dead,
The great man humbled, the haughty brought to dust?
Is there a horn we should not blow as proudly
For the meanest of us all, who creeps his days,
Guarding his heart from blows, to die obscurely?
I am no king, have laid no kingdoms waste,
Taken no princes captive, led no triumphs
Of weeping women through long walls of trumpets;
Say rather, I am no one, or an atom;
Say rather, two great gods, in a vault of starlight,
Play ponderingly at chess, and at the game's end
One of the pieces, shaken, falls to the floor
And runs to the darkest corner; and that piece
Forgotten there, left motionless, is I . . .
Say that I have no name, no gifts, no power,
Am only one of millions, mostly silent;
One who came with eyes and hands and a heart,

Looked on beauty, and loved it, and then left it.
Say that the fates of time and space obscured me,
Led me a thousand ways to pain, bemused me,
Wrapped me in ugliness; and like great spiders
Dispatched me at their leisure . . . Well, what then?
Should I not hear, as I lie down in dust,
The horns of glory blowing above my burial?

All of us confronting finality desire somehow trumpets of glory sounding above our funerals. Poets in particular want to be remembered by devoted readers. All his long career, Aiken labored vainly to find more than a small audience. At dinner he said to me, "They think I am already dead." He was seventy-four and died a decade later in relative obscurity. Eliot said that *The Waste Land* was a personal lament taken up by others as a vision of cultural decline. Powerful as its negations were and are, I long for the accent of the High Sublime, as here, in the second section of "Tetélestai":

II

Morning and evening opened and closed above me:
Houses were built above me; trees let fall
Yellowing leaves upon me, hands of ghosts;
Rain has showered its arrows of silver upon me
Seeking my heart; winds have roared and tossed me;
Music in long blue waves of sound has borne me
A helpless weed to shores of unthought silence;
Time, above me, within me, crashed its gongs
Of terrible warning, sifting the dust of death;
And here I lie. Blow now your horns of glory
Harshly over my flesh, you trees, you waters!
You stars and suns, Canopus, Deneb, Rigel,
Let me, as I lie down, here in this dust,
Hear, far off, your whispered salutation!
Roar now above my decaying flesh, you winds,
Whirl out your earth-scents over this body, tell me
Of ferns and stagnant pools, wild roses, hillsides!

Anoint me, rain, let crash your silver arrows
On this hard flesh! I am the one who named you,
I lived in you, and now I die in you.
I your son, your daughter, treader of music,
Lie broken, conquered . . . Let me not fall in silence.

Aiken remembers Robert Browning's salute to Shelley as the Sun-treader in *Pauline:*

Sun-treader—life and light be thine for ever;
Thou art gone from us. . . .

As another treader of music, Aiken scarcely hopes that life and light will be his forever, but however harsh the horns of glory blow over his flesh, he yearns at least for a whispered salutation. I myself have never written a poem, yet as an exegete I would hesitate to implore: Let me not fall in silence. The dark secret of self, which is universal, gives impetus to the third section:

III

I, the restless one; the circler of circles;
Herdsman and roper of stars, who could not capture
The secret of self; I who was tyrant to weaklings,
Striker of children; destroyer of women; corrupter
Of innocent dreamers, and laugher at beauty; I,
Too easily brought to tears and weakness by music,
Baffled and broken by love, the helpless beholder
Of the war in my heart of desire with desire, the struggle
Of hatred with love, terror with hunger; I
Who laughed without knowing the cause of my laughter, who
     grew
Without wishing to grow, a servant to my own body;
Loved without reason the laughter and flesh of a woman,
Enduring such torments to find her! I who at last
Grow weaker, struggle more feebly, relent in my purpose,
Choose for my triumph an easier end, look backward

At earlier conquests; or, caught in the web, cry out
In a sudden and empty despair, "Tetélestai!"
Pity me, now! I, who was arrogant, beg you!
Tell me, as I lie down, that I was courageous.
Blow horns of victory now, as I reel and am vanquished.
Shatter the sky with trumpets above my grave.

The trumpet of a prophecy cannot be sounded by Aiken. He is more
in the mode of Walt Whitman in "Elemental Drifts":

From the storm, the long calm, the darkness, the swell;
Musing, pondering, a breath, a briny tear, a dab of liquid or soil;
Up just as much out of fathomless workings fermented and
    thrown;
A limp blossom or two, torn, just as much over waves floating,
    drifted at random;
Just as much for us that sobbing dirge of Nature;
Just as much, whence we come, that blare of the
    cloud-trumpets . . .

To shatter the sky with trumpets is Shelleyan and Whitmanian but
hardly within the compass of Aiken. I chant section III of "Tetélestai"
to myself and think, of my life, that it is consumed. Some of us are
courageous, some are not. We look back and wonder if it was courage.
Aiken never went into the stupidity of battle, but few of my acquaintance came back from it enhanced. Summoning himself at the Chris-
tological age of thirty-three, Aiken is tempted to accept a total defeat:

IV

. . . Look! this flesh how it crumbles to dust and is blown!
These bones, how they grind in the granite of frost and are
    nothing!
This skull, how it yawns for a flicker of time in the darkness,
Yet laughs not and sees not! It is crushed by a hammer of
    sunlight,
And the hands are destroyed . . . Press down through the leaves
    of the jasmine,

Dig through the interlaced roots—nevermore will you find me;
I was no better than dust, yet you cannot replace me . . .
Take the soft dust in your hand—does it stir: does it sing?
Has it lips and a heart? Does it open its eyes to the sun?
Does it run, does it dream, does it burn with a secret, or tremble
In terror of death? Or ache with tremendous decisions? . . .
Listen! . . . It says: "I lean by the river. The willows
Are yellowed with bud. White clouds roar up from the south
And darken the ripples; but they cannot darken my heart,
Nor the face like a star in my heart . . . Rain falls on the water
And pelts it, and rings it with silver. The willow trees glisten,
The sparrows chirp under the eaves; but the face in my heart
Is a secret of music . . . I wait in the rain and am silent."
Listen again! . . . It says: "I have worked, I am tired,
The pencil dulls in my hand: I see through the window
Walls upon walls of windows with faces behind them,
Smoke floating up to the sky, an ascension of sea-gulls.
I am tired. I have struggled in vain, my decision was fruitless,
Why then do I wait? with darkness, so easy, at hand! . . .
But tomorrow, perhaps . . . I will wait and endure till
    tomorrow! . . ."
Or again: "It is dark. The decision is made. I am vanquished
By terror of life. The walls mount slowly about me
In coldness. I had not the courage. I was forsaken.
I cried out, was answered by silence . . . Tetélestai! . . ."

The terror of life can exceed the fear of dying. Silence, being
unfallen, cannot give answers we understand. Transported as I am by
"Tetélestai," I sorrow at its fifth and final section:

## V

Hear how it babbles!—Blow the dust out of your hand,
With its voices and visions, tread on it, forget it, turn homeward
With dreams in your brain . . . This, then, is the humble, the
    nameless,—
The lover, the husband and father, the struggler with shadows,
The one who went down under shoutings of chaos, the weakling

Who cried his "forsaken!" like Christ on the darkening
    hilltop! . . .
This, then, is the one who implores, as he dwindles to silence,
A fanfare of glory . . . And which of us dares to deny him?

Voices and visions, the high endowment of true poetry, blow away
into Adamic dust. Eliot in *The Waste Land* opens "What the Thunder
Said" with a very different evocation of the forsaken Christ:

After the torchlight red on sweaty faces
After the frosty silence in the gardens
After the agony in stony places
The shouting and the crying
Prison and palace and reverberation
Of thunder of spring over distant mountains
He who was living is now dead
We who were living are now dying
With a little patience

Though Eliot's formal conversion came five years later, in 1927 his
ethos was neo-Christian almost from the start. Aiken, always a skeptic, parodied Eliot's "Ash Wednesday" in section LXI of *Preludes for
Memnon:*

Shall we, then, play the sentimental stop,
And flute the soft nostalgic note, and pray
Dead men and women to remember us,
Imaginary gods to pity us?

Saying
We are unworthy, father, to be remembered,
We are unworthy to be remembered, mother,
Remember us, O clods from whom we come—

Shall we make altars of the grass and wind
Implore the evening:
Shall we make altars of water and sand
Invoke the changing:

Shall we desire the unknown to speak
Forget the knowing?

Aiken chose to die without spiritual hope. He did implore, as he dwindled to silence, a fanfare of glory, which, alas, he has not received. I would not assert that his eminence was that of Robert Frost and Wallace Stevens, Thomas Stearns Eliot and Hart Crane, yet to me at least he stands with William Carlos Williams and Marianne Moore, John Crowe Ransom and Robert Penn Warren, permanent poets in American tradition.

# Richard Eberhart, "If I Could Only Live at the Pitch That Is Near Madness"

I FIRST MET RICHARD EBERHART when I went to lecture at the University of Florida in Gainesville in the late 1960s. He was poet in residence, and I was there for a week's visit to lecture on Sigmund Freud. Eberhart, whose poetry I had long admired and still read with great pleasure, was a delightful personality. He was, if I remember accurately, in his middle sixties, and I was about thirty-nine. Eberhart had an aura of human warmth and rugged health. Indeed, he lived 101 years, and had a rich and fulfilling life. It saddens me that his poetry is now little read, but I cannot believe that several of the poems will not survive.

Eberhart served as a lieutenant commander with the Naval Reserve in World War II. That informed his splendid poem "The Fury of Aerial Bombardment":

> You would think the fury of aerial bombardment
> Would rouse God to relent; the infinite spaces
> Are still silent. He looks on shock-pried faces.
> History, even, does not know what is meant.

> . . . . . . . . . . . . .

> Was man made stupid to see his own stupidity?
> Is God by definition indifferent, beyond us all?
> Is the eternal truth man's fighting soul
> Wherein the Beast ravens in its own avidity?

> . . . . . . . . . . . . .

This is a considerable indictment of God and of man. An indifferent God presides over men who exult in their fighting soul. The last stanza has a poignance that haunts me.

Eberhart was a very original nature mystic. I always recall his poem:

If I could only live at the pitch that is near madness
When everything is as it was in my childhood
Violent, vivid, and of infinite possibility:
That the sun and the moon broke over my head.

Then I cast time out of the trees and fields,
Then I stood immaculate in the Ego;
Then I eyed the world with all delight,
Reality was the perfection of my sight.

There is a fusion of human kind and divinity in Eberhart's memories of his childhood. One of his two masterpieces is "The Groundhog":

In June, amid the golden fields,
I saw a groundhog lying dead.
Dead lay he; my senses shook,
And mind outshot our naked frailty.
There lowly in the vigorous summer
His form began its senseless change,
And made my senses waver dim
Seeing nature ferocious in him.
Inspecting close his maggots' might
And seething cauldron of his being,
Half with loathing, half with a strange love,
I poked him with an angry stick.
The fever arose, became a flame
And Vigour circumscribed the skies,
Immense energy in the sun,
And through my frame a sunless trembling.
My stick had done nor good nor harm.
Then stood I silent in the day
Watching the object, as before;
And kept my reverence for knowledge

Trying for control, to be still,
To quell the passion of the blood;
Until I had bent down on my knees
Praying for joy in the sight of decay.
And so I left; and I returned
In Autumn strict of eye, to see
The sap gone out of the groundhog,
But the bony sodden hulk remained.
But the year had lost its meaning,
And in intellectual chains
I lost both love and loathing,
Mured up in the wall of wisdom.
Another summer took the fields again
Massive and burning, full of life,
But when I chanced upon the spot
There was only a little hair left,
And bones bleaching in the sunlight
Beautiful as architecture;
I watched them like a geometer,
And cut a walking stick from a birch.
It has been three years, now.
There is no sign of the groundhog.
I stood there in the whirling summer,
My hand capped a withered heart,
And thought of China and of Greece,
Of Alexander in his tent;
Of Montaigne in his tower,
Of Saint Theresa in her wild lament.

This wild and persuasive rhapsody harks back to Thoreau and Emerson and also to the visionary poetry of William Blake. I still remember my happy shock at the sudden onset of a vitalistic epiphany:

The fever arose, became a flame
And Vigour circumscribed the skies,
Immense energy in the sun,
And through my frame a sunless trembling.

Eberhart achieves near greatness in his final return to the few remnants of the groundhog. His secular epiphany spans the ages and comprehends the diversity of Alexander the Great, the great skeptic Montaigne, and the Spanish mystic Saint Teresa. The pace and phrasing of these final lines have an inevitability that I associate with permanent poetry.

Eberhart's other masterwork is "The Soul Longs to Return Whence It Came." The poet revisits a graveyard that frightened him when he was a boy. On a brisk autumn day, he finds a new relationship to what had once appalled him:

I flung myself down on the earth
Full length on the great earth, full length,
I wept out the dark load of human love.
In pagan adoration I adored her.

He stands up again, and suddenly a fire like madness possesses him:

The mind will not accept the blood.
The sun and sky, the trees and grasses,
And the whispering leaves, took on
Their usual characters. I went away,
Slowly, tingling, elated, saying, saying
Mother, Great Being, O Source of Life
To whom in wisdom we return,
Accept this humble servant evermore.

After many years of elation, I find no abatement in my response to this vitalism. More even than in "The Groundhog," Eberhart has discovered the true posture of his spirit. I do not share his nature mysticism, yet I find it impossible to forget the wild eloquence that he achieves.

My clearest memory of the week I spent in Gainesville with Eberhart is comic. He insisted upon taking me down to look at the campus alligators. I found myself standing with him at the edge of a swampy marsh actually on the campus. After a few moments I said to him, "Dick, I don't see any alligator." He replied with high good humor: "Harold, you may not see him, but he is staring right at you." I stared again at what I'd taken to be a sodden log, and suddenly it had baleful eyes glaring at me. Never fleet of foot, I turned and ran back to Eberhart's car, and sat inside, breathing hard. Dick arrived, laughing, and when I said I did not appreciate the joke, he replied: "Harold, what a marvelous moment it would have been in the history of literary criticism! Critic devoured by alligator." Even now I shudder and do not find any of this merely humorous.

# Weldon Kees, "Aspects of Robinson"

WELDON KEES, born in 1914, an apparent suicide at the age of forty-one, was a contemporary of Elizabeth Bishop, May Swenson, John Berryman, Theodore Roethke, and Robert Lowell. Bishop stands apart: Kees is of the eminence of the others. I met Kees once, in 1951, at Minton's, a New York City jazz club in Harlem, where I think Norman Granz introduced us. We discussed Bud Powell, who was performing that evening with his trio, Curley Russell on bass and Max Roach on drums. It was not until I purchased and read his *Poems 1947–1954* that I began to appreciate that the jazz critic was also a unique poet.

I recall my first reading of "Aspects of Robinson" and my initial puzzlement:

> Robinson at cards at the Algonquin; a thin
> Blue light comes down once more outside the blinds.
> Gray men in overcoats are ghosts blown past the door.
> The taxis streak the avenues with yellow, orange, and red.
> This is Grand Central, Mr. Robinson.

> . . . . . . . . . . . . . . . . .

> Robinson afraid, drunk, sobbing Robinson
> In bed with a Mrs. Morse. Robinson at home;
> Decisions: Toynbee or luminol? Where the sun
> Shines, Robinson in flowered trunks, eyes toward
> The breakers. Where the night ends, Robinson in East Side
>     bars.

Robinson in Glen plaid jacket, Scotch-grain shoes,
Black four-in-hand and oxford button-down,
The jeweled and silent watch that winds itself, the brief-
Case, covert topcoat, clothes for spring, all covering
His sad and usual heart, dry as a winter leaf.

Robinson is Kees as Crusoe, the daemon of a solitary existence. A hovering presence, to my ear, is Conrad Aiken's Senlin rather than T. S. Eliot's Prufrock. Kees and Aiken corresponded on a very personal level, with the younger poet confessing the sorrows of his troubled marriage and his own nihilism. Aiken many years later told me at dinner that he had a fear Kees would die early: a fate shared with the English poet Malcolm Lowry, who died two years after Kees at the age of forty-seven. Alcohol and drugs killed Lowry, though it is unclear whether the death was suicide or perhaps murder by his distraught wife.

"Aspects of Robinson" yields to repeated readings as a vivid yet curiously dispassionate self-portrait of the poet drifting in a state of death-in-life. Kees cares and does not care. Whether at the literary haunt of the Algonquin, or at a party in Brooklyn Heights, or walking in solitude in the park, his alter ego mourns for the unlived life. In bed with a married woman, he is fearful, drunk, weeping. At home, it is equally flat, whether he reads or takes a drug. Swimming by day, drinking at night, Robinson is properly attired for a spring without renewal. The last line is a triumph of desolation: "His sad and usual heart, dry as a winter leaf." "Usual" is apt and hopeless. Acedia, the malady of monks, is the sin of being sullen in the sweet air, portrayed classically in canto VII of the *Inferno*.

There are three other Robinson poems. Here is the first:

The dog stops barking after Robinson has gone.
His act is over. The world is a gray world,
Not without violence, and he kicks under the grand piano,
The nightmare chase well under way.

The mirror from Mexico, stuck to the wall,
Reflects nothing at all. The glass is black.
Robinson alone provides the image Robinsonian.

.   .   .   .   .   .   .   .   .   .   .   .   .   .   .   .   .   .

The pages in the books are blank,
The books that Robinson has read. That is his favorite chair,
Or where the chair would be if Robinson were here.

All day the phone rings. It could be Robinson
Calling. It never rings when he is here.

Outside, white buildings yellow in the sun.
Outside, the birds circle continuously
Where trees are actual and take no holiday.

This is beyond acedia. The sun goes on; actual trees at their work
starkly contrast to Robinson, whose act, like his dog's, is over. With
nothing to reflect, the mirror blackens. Kees contrives a negation so
total that the poem scarcely can get written, and yet it does. Some
critics have called Kees a bitter poet, but that is accurate only with the
proviso that he is romancing the etonym. His bitterness is his bite. For
Hart Crane, white buildings gradually answer day. For Kees, they yellow silently. A kind of foreshadowing of Samuel Beckett is one of Kees's
saliences.

I hear that curious anticipation of Beckett's *Murphy* in the even more
acrid "Robinson at Home":

Curtains drawn back, the door ajar.
All winter long, it seemed, a darkening
Began. But now the moonlight and the odors of the street
Conspire and combine toward one community.

These are the rooms of Robinson.
Bleached, wan, and colorless this light, as though
All the blurred daybreaks of the spring
Found an asylum here, perhaps for Robinson alone,

Who sleeps. Were there more music sifted through the
    floors
And moonlight of a different kind,

He might awake to hear the news at ten,
Which will be shocking, moderately.

This sleep is from exhaustion, but his old desire
To die like this has known a lessening.
Now there is only this coldness that he has to wear.
But not in sleep.—Observant scholar, traveller,

. . . . . . . . . . . . . . .

All these are Robinson in sleep, who mumbles as he turns,
"There is something in this madhouse that I symbolize—
This city—nightmare—black—"
                                                    He wakes in sweat
To the terrible moonlight and what might be
Silence. It drones like wires far beyond the roofs,
And the long curtains blow into the room.

One might have thought Kees could not descend to a deeper negative, but for him there were only depths beneath depths. His moonlight
is terrible; his rooms are bleached, wan, colorless. The sleep of exhaustion yields nightmares of a mad city, and an ostensible silence is a wiry
drone and a wind blowing that might as well be a buzzing. I reread
"Robinson at Home" and I think of Stevens in "Esthétique du Mal,"
canto XV:

One might have thought of sight, but who could think
Of what it sees, for all the ill it sees?
Speech found the ear, for all the evil sound,
But the dark italics it could not propound. . . .

There is no one to speak or be spoken to and nothing to propound.
Robinson at home is Robinson in hell. Finally, in the fourth of the
series, "Relating to Robinson," the poet splits into equal components,
each refusing to be identified with the other:

Somewhere in Chelsea, early summer;
And, walking in the twilight toward the docks,
I thought I made out Robinson ahead of me.

From an uncurtained second-story room, a radio
Was playing *There's a Small Hotel;* a kite
Twisted above dark rooftops and slow drifting birds.
We were alone there, he and I,
Inhabiting the empty street.

Under a sign for Natural Bloom Cigars,
While lights clicked softly in the dusk from red to green,
He stopped and gazed into a window
Where a plaster Venus, modeling a truss,
Looked out at Eastbound traffic. (But Robinson,
I knew, was out of town: he summers at a place in Maine,
Sometimes on Fire Island, sometimes the Cape,
Leaves town in June and comes back after Labor Day.)
And yet, I almost called out, "Robinson!"

. . . . . . . . . . . . . . .

"I thought I saw the whirlpool opening.
Kicked all night at a bolted door.
You must have followed me from Astor Place.
An empty paper floats down at the last.
*And then a day as huge as yesterday in pairs*
*Unrolled its horror on my face*
*Until it blocked*—" Running in sweat
To reach the docks, I turned back
For a second glance. I had no certainty,
There in the dark, that it was Robinson
Or someone else.
          The block was bare. The Venus,
Bathed in blue fluorescent light,
Stared toward the river. As I hurried West,
The lights across the bay were coming on.
The boats moved silently and the low whistles blew.

One thinks of other doublings: Edgar Allan Poe's "William Wilson";
Henry James's "The Jolly Corner"; Philip Roth's *Operation Shylock*;
Jorge Luis Borges's "Death and the Compass"; Dostoevsky's *The Double*;
and above all E. T. A. Hoffmann's "The Sandman." Uncanny as these

are, they do not disturb me nearly as much as "Relating to Robinson." The singular and daemonic obsessiveness that floods Weldon Kees batters at the word "relating." It is consumed as he enters the whirlpool. Stages of his age and youth fail to pass before him. Death by water, an Eliotic mode derived from Shelley's life and work, haunted Kees, who contemplated Hart Crane's return to the waters of childhood.

Standing back from the four Robinson poems, I ask myself why they give pleasure though so painful. Nietzsche in *On the Genealogy of Morals* taught that pain is far more memorable than pleasure. Clarity when staring at the abyss is the gift of Weldon Kees. His optics cleanse to an essential slate. I come away from him wincing but a touch closer to the desolation of irreality.

# May Swenson, "Big-Hipped Nature"

I BEGAN READING MAY SWENSON in 1954, but intensively only from 1963 on. Our mutual friend John Hollander introduced us in 1965. After that, she and I occasionally would drink coffee together at Chumley's in Greenwich Village. We remained amiable acquaintances, as she seemed rather shy. Our conversations concerned friends in common but usually not her own work.

As a poet, May Swenson derives from Emily Dickinson, Gertrude Stein, Marianne Moore, and Elizabeth Bishop; she and Bishop formed a strong friendship. After her death in 1989, I made a number of attempts to stimulate the publication of her collected poems, but failed until my former student Langdon Hammer edited her for a Library of America edition (2013).

She is an authentic original whose genius is for surprise. Born in Logan, Utah, in 1913, she was the oldest of ten children of Swedish converts to the Latter-day Saints. Though she remained close to her family and respected their religion, her faith was in poetry alone. At twenty-three, she moved to Greenwich Village, and returned to Utah periodically for the rest of her days to see her family.

She realized early that her sexual orientation was lesbian, which remains unacceptable to the Mormon Church. But she would have left Utah in any case, as her passionate vocation was literary.

The first poem by May Swenson that I fiercely loved was her homage to her father, "Big-Hipped Nature":

Big-hipped nature bursts forth the head of god
from jungle clots of green
from pelvic heave of mountains

On swollen-breasted clouds he fattens and feeds
He is rocked in the crib of the sea


.   .   .   .   .   .   .   .   .   .   .   .


Swift and winding beasts with coats of flame
serpents in their languor black and blind
in the night of his dark mind express
his awe and anger his terror and magicness

Wherever we look his eye lies bottomless
fringed by fields and woods
and tragic moons
magnify his pupils with their tears

In fire he strides
Within the waterfall
he twines his limbs of light
Clothed in the wind and tall
he walks the roofs and towers
Rocks are all his faces
flowers the flesh of his flanks
His hair is tossed with the grasses everywhere
Stained by the rainbow every shell
roars his whispered spell

When sleep the enormous shadow of his hand descends
our tongues uncoil a prayer
to hush our ticking hearts our sparrow-like fear
and we lie naked within his lair
His cabalistic lightnings play upon us there

This is a firstborn child's vision of her father, returning May Swenson and her readers to the mythological memories earliest in our visions of paternal being. Though published when she was forty-one, it must have been written many years before.

Heraclean and benign, Dan Swenson is a kind of Adam Kadmon or Divine Man who contains in his limbs all things in heaven and earth.

In the child's eye, the father is magical, and all the sounds of nature emanate from him.

I recall discussing "Big-Hipped Nature" with May Swenson sometime in the later 1960s. It was the only one of her poems we ever talked about when we met. I particularly admire the final stanza, where the child May Swenson and her siblings fall asleep beneath the enormous shadow of Dan Swenson's hand. How much Kabbalah she knew I never inquired, yet the final image is true to the Jewish esoteric tradition. The protective father who is Adam Kadmon plays his emanations of light upon the sleeping children, who rest in the tragic moons of his tearful love as he broods over them.

# Delmore Schwartz,
## "The First Night of Fall and Falling Rain"

THE INFLUENCE OF William Butler Yeats on Delmore Schwartz was fairly constant, though mingled at times with traces of T. S. Eliot and of James Joyce, who was the god of Schwartz's idolatry. Schwartz died at the age of fifty-two, on July 11, 1966, which was my thirty-sixth birthday. I had listened to him hold forth at the White Horse Tavern in Greenwich Village five or six times in the late 1950s and early '60s. Though frequently intoxicated, he was outrageously eloquent, with a bitterness tempering his wonderful surge of language. I had read him only in literary magazines until I purchased his *Selected Poems: Summer Knowledge* in 1959, which I absorbed with delight and misgivings. There was from the start a trouble even in his most ebullient performances. I knew very little about his life until after his death, when I discussed him with Dwight Macdonald, Alfred Kazin, and Saul Bellow, whom I found invariably prickly and unpleasant. It may be that Schwartz is now best known as the model for Von Humboldt Fleisher in *Humboldt's Gift* (1975), but that seems to me an ungrateful travesty, since Bellow had begun as a kind of disciple to Delmore Schwartz.

In 1943, Schwartz had divorced his first wife after six years of marriage; he then repeated the pattern with the second. Both were literary, beautiful, and necessarily long-suffering, since the poet was increasingly paranoid. His decline ultimately resulted in a solitary death in a New York City hotel; it was three days before the body was found.

There are a score of poems by Delmore Schwartz that possess a kind of greatness. I am most haunted by one he composed in 1962, "The First Night of Fall and Falling Rain":

The common rain had come again
Slanting and colorless, pale and anonymous,

Fainting falling in the first evening
Of the first perception of the actual fall,
The long and late light had slowly gathered up
A sooty wood of clouded sky, dim and distant more and more
Until, as dusk, the very sense of selfhood waned,
A weakening nothing halted, diminished or denied or set aside
Neither tea, nor, after an hour, whiskey,
Ice and then a pleasant glow, a burning,
And the first leaping wood fire
Since a cold night in May, too long ago to be more than
Merely a cold and vivid memory.
Staring, empty, and without thought
Beyond the rising mists of the emotion of causeless sadness,
How suddenly all consciousness leaped in spontaneous gladness;
Knowing without thinking how the falling rain (outside, all over)
In slow sustained consistent vibration all over outside
Tapping window, streaking roof, running down runnel and drain
Waking a sense, once more, of all that lived outside of us,
Beyond emotion, for beyond the swollen distorted shadows and
    lights
Of the toy town and the vanity fair of waking consciousness!

If there is a voice here not wholly Schwartz's it would be Walt Whitman's more subdued moments of reflection and puzzlement. The repetitions are beautifully accomplished, and a keening of consonance is woven through the text, suggestive of Schwartz's Scripture, *Finnegans Wake*. Slanting, fainting falling, weakening, burning, leaping, staring, rising, knowing, thinking, failing, tapping, streaking, running down, waking: all concourse into a flow of consciousness at desperate impasse.

It is poignant that the falling rain is "common," and that the poem concludes with the recurrent sense of external selves beyond the poet's sorrow and his exhausted emotion. True that the "beyond" is a distortion, and that the life of New York City is a toy town and Bunyanesque vanity fair, a consciousness awake to no purpose. Nevertheless Schwartz has banished self-pity or any sense of persecution. Selfhood wanes, and memory of an earlier spring is frigid yet glowing. There is a nostalgia for the gladness of a poet's youth, but Schwartz holds off despondency and madness by the pleasure of his own extraordinary mastery of his medium.

A third of a century older than Delmore Schwartz at his death, I marvel at his use of memory for a Hamlet-like liberation without detachment. His august gift employs memory to transcend personal experience. Walter Pater defined the aesthetic as a seeing again more fully, a legacy brought to abundant harvest by James Joyce. There is a noble renunciation in "The First Night of Fall and Falling Rain." Schwartz of course could not emulate Joyce's clairvoyant sense of the end of the age, but, then, only Samuel Beckett accomplished that. It is more than enough that, at his best, Schwartz extended the American splendor of Walt Whitman, who was able to balance a lancing rapidity of self-awareness with a passion that could enable his "Whoever you are, now I place my hand upon you, that you be my poem." That too was a horizon Delmore Schwartz could not attain, but it is marvelous how much he risked in the quest.

# Alvin Feinman, "Pilgrim Heights"

I RECALL READING *I Wanted to Write a Poem: The Autobiography of the Works of a Poet* (1958) by William Carlos Williams sometime in the 1960s. Most of the poets to whom I was close have now departed: Robert Penn Warren, John Hollander, Archie Randolph Ammons, Mark Strand, Jay Macpherson, and John Ashbery among others. There were also such good acquaintances as Richard Eberhart, James Merrill, Anthony Hecht, May Swenson, Robert Fitzgerald, and many more. Like the living poets of distinction who are my friends—William Merwin, Jay Wright, Henri Cole, Rosanna Warren, Joseph Harrison, Peter Cole, Martha Serpas, and others—they all wanted to write poems. I think also of my close friends, the philosopher Richard Rorty, gone for a decade now, and of the literary critic Angus Fletcher, just departed. Like the poets, they wanted to write.

Before I fell, some years ago, the first in a long series of falls, I enjoyed writing in longhand with a pen in ledgers. My right hand, after a fall, no longer sustains that mode, so I have turned to dictating, which I still find strange. Yet the desire to go on exploring literature remains strong.

One of my closest friends was the poet Alvin Feinman (1929–2008), a superb though still largely unrecognized master. Alvin wrote his rather sparse lifework of poetry invariably against his own will. He did not want to write poems. His mind was so scrupulous that he despaired of conveying his scope and accuracy even in highly wrought poems. There was also his absolute veneration of John Milton and William Wordsworth, who to him represented poetry itself. That standard, of course, would be fatal for any poet in the twentieth century.

In what follows, I seek to revise my two earlier brief essays on Feinman, the first in *The Ringers in the Tower* (1971), and the other my foreword to *Corrupted into Song: The Complete Poems of Alvin Feinman* (2016).

I first met Alvin Feinman in September 1951, the day before I encountered another remarkable young man, who also became a life-long friend, Angus Fletcher. Alvin was twenty-two, a year older than we were, and a graduate student in philosophy at Yale, where Angus and I were students of literature. They are with me still. I think of them every day and try to go on learning from them.

Alvin at twenty-two was already a poet of astonishing individuation: the emergence of voice in him clarified as rapidly as it had in Rimbaud and Hart Crane. I recall reading the first of his three Relic poems sometime in October 1951:

> I will see her stand
> half a step back of the edge of some high place
> or at a leafless tree in some city park
> or seated with her knees toward me and her face turned toward
>     the window
>
> And always the tips of the fingers of both her hands
> will pull or twist at a handkerchief
> like lovely dead birds at a living thing
> trying to work apart something exquisitely, unreasonably joined.

A month later, I was introduced by Alvin to this beautiful, intense young woman in New York. Though lovers, she and my friend seemed remote from each other. I watched her hands in constant motion tugging at a handkerchief and wondered silently at the dispassionate tone of the eight-line lyric so precisely called "Relic."

Reciting the poem to myself these sixty years, I have come to see its relationship to Eliot's farewell to Emily Hale:

> Stand on the highest pavement of the stair—
> Lean on a garden urn—
> Weave, weave the sunlight in your hair—
> Clasp your flowers to you with a pained surprise—
> Fling them to the ground and turn

With a fugitive resentment in your eyes:
But weave, weave the sunlight in your hair.

"La Figlia Che Piange"

The dominant influences upon Feinman's poetry were Hart Crane, Wallace Stevens, T. S. Eliot, Paul Valéry, Rimbaud, Georg Trakl, and the earlier Rilke. I have listed them in the order of their importance in helping form his style and stance. Feinman's prime precursor was Hart Crane, and, like the poet of *White Buildings* and *The Bridge*, my friend began with a volume of difficult yet frequently radiant lyrics. Unlike Crane, Feinman was not able to go on to the larger form of a visionary romance, and his inability to continue doomed his remarkable volume to neglect.

Returning to *Preambles and Other Poems* floods me with memories. I had taken the little book to my editor at the Oxford University Press, the late Whitney Blake, and urged him to publish it, though not even a single poem had appeared in a magazine. Whitney discerned the high value of Alvin's poetry and agreed to publish it if I could provide endorsements by other poets and critics. Conrad Aiken, Allen Tate, R. W. B. Lewis, John Hollander, and Geoffrey Hartman joined me in support of the new poet. Hartman made a memorable comment:

> Thought thinks its ruin here without widening speculation. It finds what will not suffice. . . . Yet Feinman's poetry performs so total an époché on "discursions fated and inept" that only the stumble toward a preamble is left. For so rigorous a sensibility, writing verse must be like crossing a threshold guarded by demons. . . .

The Swiss critic Marcel Raymond characterized Paul Valéry's "The Young Fate" and "The Marine Cemetery" as a ceaseless agon between absolute consciousness and the acceptance of natural mutability:

> In them, a struggle takes place between two contrary attitudes: the pure (absolute) attitude, that of consciousness entrenching itself in its isolation, and the opposite, or impure attitude, that of the mind accepting life, change, action, giving up its dream of perfect

integrity and allowing itself to be beguiled by things and captivated by their changing forms.

These two attitudes can be defined as total detachment or total
involvement. In Valéry these contrary stances exist simultaneously.
Feinman's total detachment purchases its freedom at the expense of a
world of mutable splendors. The astonishing clarity of his best poems
makes them expensive torsos rather than comprehensive visions.

Alvin Feinman's difficult fusion makes it a strenuous act of readership to decide where the visual and the purely visionary part in him:

And the light, a wakened heyday of air
Tuned low and clear and wide,
A radiance now that would emblaze
And veil the most golden horn
Or any entering of a sudden clearing
To a standing, astonished, revealed . . .

That the actual streets I loitered in
Lay lit like fields, or narrow channels
About to open to a burning river;
All brick and window vivid and calm
As though composed in a rigid water
No random traffic would dispel . . .

As now through the park, and across
The chill nailed colors of the roofs,
And on near trees stripped bare,
Corrected in the scant remaining leaf
To their severe essential elegance,
Light is the all-exacting good,

That dry, forever virile stream
That wipes each thing to what it is,
The whole, collage and stone, cleansed
To its proper pastoral . . .
                                        I sit
And smoke, and linger out desire.

And know if I closed my eyes I'd hear
Again what held me awake all night
Beside her breathing: a rain falling
It seemed into a distant stillness,
On broad low leaves beside a pond
And drop upon drop into black waters.

"November Sunday Morning"

I cannot recall any other poem by Alvin that is this celebratory, though a cleansing light is the entire basis for rejoicing. When I first read "November Sunday Morning," actually handed to me by the poet on a Sunday morning just before Thanksgiving, it renewed memories of my youth, when I would wander round our neighborhood early in the day and experience instant clarification of streets grown too drearily familiar. I had no name then for these bursts of transcendence, nor did they move me to composition, since any desire to write poems was alien to me. Poetry was what I read incessantly, possessed by memory, and wanted to absorb gradually. The genesis of a literary critic, at least in me, was remote from any incarnation of the poetical character.

"November Sunday Morning" is a hymn to light and reminds me that Alvin enjoyed chanting aloud Milton's invocation to book III of *Paradise Lost*. I remarked once to my friend that he did not center upon the sun as did Walt Whitman and Wallace Stevens but only upon the light. It was as if his sense of natural light cut itself off from the solar trajectory, in defiance of Nietzsche's Zarathustra and of all poets who emerged from Nietzsche's shadow. What mattered about the light for Alvin was its cleansing effect upon everything open to perception. Plato would not have termed the light an all-exacting good, yet Feinman was no Platonist. Severe and rigorous, "November Sunday Morning" offers only a self-limiting transcendence. That so minimal a vision should become a poem of this extraordinary distinction continues to surprise me after so many decades of repeated recitations that I murmur to myself.

I remember Alvin's attachment to Pilgrim Heights on Cape Cod. When first he showed me this poem, I remarked it could take a Stevensian title: "I Was Myself the Compass of That Sea":

Something, something, the heart here
Misses, something it knows it needs

Unable to bless—the wind passes;
A swifter shadow sweeps the reeds,
The heart a colder contrast brushes.

So this fool, face-forward, belly
Pressed among the rushes, plays out
His pulse to the dune's long slant
Down from blue to bluer element,
The bold encompassing drink of air

And namelessness, a length compound
Of want and oneness the shore's mumbling
Distantly tells—something a wing's
Dry pivot stresses, carved
Through barrens of stillness and glare:

The naked close of light in light,
Light's spare embrace of blade and tremor
Stealing the generous eye's plunder
Like a breathing banished from the lung's
Fever, lost in parenthetic air.

Raiding these nude recesses, the hawk
Resumes his yielding balance, his shadow
Swims the field, the sands beyond,
The narrow edges fed out to light,
To the sea's eternal licking monochrome.

The foolish hip, the elbow bruise
Upright from the dampening mat,
The twisted grasses turn, unthatch,
Light-headed blood renews its stammer—
Apart, below, the dazed eye catches

A darkened figure abruptly measured
Where folding breakers lay their whites;
The heart from its height starts downward,

Swum in that perfect pleasure
It knows it needs, unable to bless.

"Pilgrim Heights"


Feinman's almost solipsistic rapture is partly inherited from Stevens's Whitmanian Hoon, who finds himself more truly and more strange by singing another "Song of Myself." When he gave me the poem, I initially felt wonder at what seemed Alvin's most distinguished performance up to that time. After more than sixty years, the sense of ecstasy that for him constituted the spirit of solitude has become more dialectical in my understanding. The darkened figure who breaks the poet's reverie restores the shadow of an external world. Feinman balances the perfect pleasure that the poetic heart requires against the cost of confirmation that is a stance excluding the power of blessing otherness, whether in persons or in the hawk's yielding balance. The poem labors to attain a generosity toward otherness and yet knowingly falls short of this accomplishment.

William Butler Yeats, another presence haunting Feinman's poetry, trusted that casting out remorse would give him a sense of being blessed by everything and then looking upon all otherness and blessing it. Feinman, who comes later, has a vision of the mind as a ceaseless activity, engaged in suffering a process of working apart all things that are joined by it. That rending allows no hope of being blessed even by the mind's power over a universe of death.

Alvin's major poem is "Preambles," a hard, driving gamble with the limits of discursiveness. Its opening never abandons my memory:


Vagrant, back, my scrutinies
The candid deformations as with use
A coat or trousers of one now dead
Or as habit smacks of certitude


Even cosmographies, broad orchards
The uncountable trees      Or a river
Seen along the green monotonies
Of its banks      And the talk

Of memorable ideals ending
In irrelevance      I would cite
Wind-twisted spaces, absence
Listing to a broken wall

Though it is a poem in three parts, each segment flows without break, a quality that adds to the difficulty of discussing individual passages. Thus the montage of "Wind-twisted spaces, absence / Listing to a broken wall" leads on to further wounded tropes:

And the cornered noons
Our lives played in, such things
As thwart beginnings, limit      Or
Juxtapose that longest vision

A bright bird winged to its idea
To the hand stripped
By a damaged resolution
Daily of its powers      *Archai*

Bruited through crumbling masteries
To hang like swollen apples
In the river, witnesses
Stilled to their clotted truth      All

Discursion fated and inept
So the superior reality
Of photographs      The soul's
Tragic abhorrence of detail.

I hear in the foreground of this the aura of Hart Crane's "Repose of Rivers" and a shadow of his "Sunday Morning Apples," a poem Alvin liked to recite to me. Yet Crane does not present us with the cognitive difficulties that are the matrix of "Preambles." Memory in Hart Crane transmembers the poet's sufferings into song, but in Feinman memory is always blocked. His scrutinies return to him damaged by their overreaching and yield him metaphors of deformation, twisting, absence, thwarting, limiting, stripping, and clotting. The image of working apart what has been inextricably and exquisitely joined is his central trope.

In the second preamble, an adagio intervenes, as if to lower the poem's intolerable tension, though the darkness gathers and does not fall:

> So
> Statues hold through every light
> The grave persuasive
>
> Candors of their stride      And so
> The mind in everything it joins
> And suffers to redeem apart
> Plays victim to its own intent

Wallace Stevens, in his "Saint John and the Back-Ache," has the Back-Ache, which I take to be the fallen history of each of us, complain to Saint John:

> The mind is the terriblest force in the world, father,
> Because, in chief, it, only, can defend
> Against itself. At its mercy, we depend
> Upon it.

I recall remarking to Alvin in 1955, while we toured Devon and Cornwall together, that Stevens had a premonition of the impasse "Preambles" was to constitute for the later poet. The final section of Feinman's major poem renders that impasse with an agile but self-undoing eloquence:

> These even love's rejoinder
> As of every severed thing
>
> The *ecce* only, only hands
> Or hardnesses, the gleam a water
> Or a light, a paused thing
> Clothes in vacua killed
>
> To a limbless beauty      Take
> These torn possessives there
> Where you plead the radiant
> Of your truth's gloom      Own

To your sleep, your waking
The tread that is walked
From the inner of its pace
The play of a leaf to an earth.

The image of severing always negates the gleams and radiances that
Feinman ultimately inherited from Wordsworth and from Stevens. For
Wordsworth, the light of common day at last subsumed the glory and
the freshness of his poetic dream. Stevens, who cried out jubilantly,
"What is there here but weather, what spirit/Have I except it come
from the sun," sustained his poetry in Whitman's mode of opening the
self to the wind and the weather and, above all, the sun. I sorrowed even
in the middle 1950s that Alvin was destroying his extraordinary gift by
an asceticism alien to poetic vision.

I do not find in any of his later poems anything equal to the best
work in *Preambles and Other Poems* (1964). The only one that moves me
greatly is "Matinal," initially titled "Morning-Hymn for the Breaker of
Horses." I have no idea when Alvin composed this, and at first reading
it seemed a kind of self-parody. Gradually, I have come to admire it,
but with some reservations, since its high style is rather hyperbolical.
Feinman must have been aware that W. B. Yeats is too strong a presence in "Matinal."

Where wild god-bridled terrors joy
My thundered pulse; not I,
Some lashed stone presence wakes
To wield, to quicken, buoy
This thrill galvanic gusto sky-
Ward where sun-slashed heavens break,

To chant the reins of spirit skilled
To bone, as is thy sling
Of brilliance turmoil bound,
Thy mounted salvos drilled
Past dare of conjuring
The paean of tempest deafness drowned . . .

Alvin was always happiest on or near rocky beaches, whether on
Cape Cod or in Cornwall. He particularly liked to watch dawn come

up, and exulted in the impact of wave on rock. His ascetic spirit was assuaged by the blast and vaulting of the wind's voice echoing cliffs and scattering the light of a new day. Nine years after his final vanishing, I continue to mourn both my friend and the gift he failed to nurture. I write this in the elegy season of September 2017 and wonder at the final quatrain of "Matinal":

> Wave shattering wave past sense,
> Past power commute the breath,
> O epic tempo of no birth or death
> Blastbind the blood thy reverence.

Something that is being released there had been long repressed by Feinman. It is as though his earlier avoidance of the high style in Yeats, Stevens, Hart Crane now takes a revenge upon him. His final poems and fragments are caught between his fundamental disjunctiveness and this belated desire to give expression to the voice that was great within him. I am strangely moved by one of them:

> The sun beating on his brain
> And a cat slouching on the woodpile
> And flies nauseous with heat
>
> He holds three eternal parameters
> The habit of his eye repeats
> The shapes he reifies
>
> Let the silence silence its own ache
>
> There is nothing but the plenum of a small red brain
>
> The flies fall suppurant among the sticks
> The cat prepares for life
>
> As though the moveable could move
> Even the impossible recedes
>
> As though within the clot of brain
> Were space or sun to make a world

> "Backyard, Hoboken, Summer"

I have no idea of the date of this rather Stevensian poem. It was not published in Alvin's lifetime. "Backyard, Hoboken, Summer" is hardly a poem one could love. Yet it could only have been written by Feinman. He had a unique power, stronger even than that of Elizabeth Bishop, to so order the visual and the visionary that the borders between them vanished. His consciousness was a plenum that could have created a heterocosm, where space and sun might have made another world.

As Alvin lay dying, his wife, Deborah Dorfman, read aloud his poem "Morning, Arraignment with Image":

> That wave that high turning that
> Once disresembled that
> Once disremembered a future—
> Now its wake broad conscripting suffices
> And leaves a roomful of years unmolested . . .
> Except for this short pre-morning of truck sounds,
> This barrack of seasons no longer embodied;
>
> You thought to have proffered an image of justice
> But the fall of that wave now
> But the scroll of that wave now
> Is heartbreak terror and boldness knowing
> That justice that hates you
> Your eyes its own eyes and our shame.

I have always found this dark and distinguished yet have never liked it. According to the writer James Geary, once Alvin's student, the dying Feinman asked his wife, "Who wrote that?" Deborah, once my student, took him to mean that the person who composed that poem was already gone. She said that his last words were "I'm past tense."

Love makes it difficult to render a full judgment upon a poet and his poems. A double handful of Feinman's poems will live. I could wish that he had been less of an ascetic of the spirit. But then he would not have been himself. To have written "November Sunday Morning," "Pilgrim Heights," and "Preambles" is a vindication of his rigor and integrity. For me they stand with Wallace Stevens and Hart Crane upon the heights.

# John Ashbery, "At North Farm"

I BEGAN TO READ John Ashbery's poetry in 1956, when I purchased *Some Trees* in a New Haven bookstore. Since I don't keep copies of my handwritten letters, I cannot precisely recall what I wrote the poet directly after I absorbed *Some Trees*. Doubtless my letters to John are preserved in his Harvard archive. His letters to me are up in my attic and will be transferred to Yale at my death.

Our friendship has been continuous these sixty years, and I have just phoned him at the Whittier Rehabilitation Center, where he was recovering rather slowly from double pneumonia. He and Archie Ammons saluted each other as peers and gave one joint reading somewhere on the Jersey Shore. Together with the late James Merrill, they seem to me the major poets of their generation.

Ashbery was very reticent concerning Frank O'Hara, who was his close friend from their days at Harvard until O'Hara's accidental death on Fire Island in 1966. Of Ashbery's companions in what was called the New York School, I knew Kenneth Koch mostly through introducing some of his readings both in New Haven and in New York City. James Schuyler, Barbara Guest, and O'Hara I knew only slightly. I enjoy rereading Frank O'Hara, but he falls away from me, as does Guest. Schuyler, a very considerable poet, sustains study.

Ashbery stands apart. I begin with "Evening in the Country," a poem in his beautiful fourth volume, *The Double Dream of Spring*:

I am still completely happy.
My resolve to win further I have
Thrown out, and am charged by the thrill
Of the sun coming up. Birds and trees, houses,

These are but the stations for the new sign of being
In me that is to close late, long
After the sun has set and darkness come
To the surrounding fields and hills.
But if breath could kill, then there would not be
Such an easy time of it, with men locked back there
In the smokestacks and corruption of the city.
Now as my questioning but admiring gaze expands
To magnificent outposts, I am not so much at home
With these memorabilia of vision as on a tour
Of my remotest properties, and the eidolon
Sinks into the effective "being" of each thing,
Stump or shrub, and they carry me inside
On motionless explorations of how dense a thing can be,
How light, and these are finished before they have begun
Leaving me refreshed and somehow younger.
Night has deployed rather awesome forces
Against this state of affairs: ten thousand helmeted footsoldiers,
A Spanish armada stretching to the horizon, all
Absolutely motionless until the hour to strike
But I think there is not too much to be said or be done
And that these things eventually take care of themselves
With rest and fresh air and the outdoors, and a good view of
    things.
So we might pass over this to the real
Subject of our concern, and that is
Have you begun to be in the context you feel
Now that the danger has been removed?
Light falls on your shoulders, as is its way,
And the process of purification continues happily,
Unimpeded, but has the motion started
That is to quiver your head, send anxious beams
Into the dusty corners of the rooms
Eventually shoot out over the landscape
In stars and bursts? For other than this we know nothing
And space is a coffin, and the sky will put out the light.
I see you eager in your wishing it the way
We may join it, if it passes close enough:

This sets the seal of distinction on the success or failure of your
    attempt.
There is growing in that knowledge
We may perhaps remain here, cautious yet free
On the edge, as it rolls its unblinking chariot
Into the vast open, the incredible violence and yielding
Turmoil that is to be our route.

I could not persuade Ashbery to include this poem in any of the
many readings at which I introduced him. Like the famous "Soonest
Mended," it seems to be an aftereffect of O'Hara's death. It is an epilogue to a dark passage in "Soonest Mended":

These then were some hazards of the course,
Yet though we knew the course *was* hazards and nothing else
It was still a shock when, almost a quarter of a century later,
The clarity of the rules dawned on you for the first time.
*They* were the players, and we who had struggled at the game
Were merely spectators, though subject to its vicissitudes
And moving with it out of the tearful stadium, borne on
    shoulders, at last.

There is ambiguity in that last line: is a slain agonist or a victor carried out?
"Evening in the Country" is a poem of rehabilitation that commences in the tonal flatness of trauma:

I am still completely happy.
My resolve to win further I have
Thrown out, and am charged by the thrill
Of the sun coming up.

Ashbery gently wants to read the vista as a new signature of being,
yet the menace abides. On an edge between traumatic event and turmoil to come, the poem tropes that edge as an "unblinking chariot."
The image fuses a Yeatsian pitiless blankness and what one might call
the vehicular form of divinity. I think of John currently rehabilitat-
ing from severe illness and my own congenital struggle each morning

with the consequences of heart failure. Ashbery with his acute clairvoy-
ance, his noble far-seeing, catches the anxious expectation of trauma to
come.

*Houseboat Days* (1977) was Ashbery's seventh major volume and one
of the three or four best. I introduced him in 1976 at a Yale reading and was startled by first encountering "Wet Casements." I asked
him for a copy after the reading and absorbed it during the next few
days:

> When Eduard Raban, coming along the passage, walked
> into the open doorway, he saw that it was raining. It was
> not raining much.
>
> Kafka, *Wedding Preparations in the Country*


The concept is interesting: to see, as though reflected
In streaming windowpanes, the look of others through
Their own eyes. A digest of their correct impressions of
Their self-analytical attitudes overlaid by your
Ghostly transparent face. You in falbalas
Of some distant but not too distant era, the cosmetics,
The shoes perfectly pointed, drifting (how long you
Have been drifting; how long I have too for that matter)
Like a bottle-imp toward a surface which can never be
    approached,
Never pierced through into the timeless energy of a present
Which would have its own opinions on these matters,
Are an epistemological snapshot of the processes
That first mentioned your name at some crowded cocktail
Party long ago, and someone (not the person addressed)
Overheard it and carried that name around in his wallet
For years as the wallet crumbled and bills slid in
And out of it. I want that information very much today,

Can't have it, and this makes me angry.
I shall use my anger to build a bridge like that
Of Avignon, on which people may dance for the feeling
Of dancing on a bridge. I shall at last see my complete face

Reflected not in the water but in the worn stone floor of my
    bridge.

I shall keep to myself.
I shall not repeat others' comments about me.

The poem itself is an epistemological snapshot of its poet. Ashbery
seems haunted by Shakespeare's dark comedy *Troilus and Cressida* and
by one exchange between Achilles and the dog-fox Ulysses:

ACHILLES:  . . . what, are my deeds forgot?
ULYSSES:  Time hath, my lord, a wallet at his back
    Wherein he puts alms for oblivion . . .

Reflections, streaming, ghostly transparency, drifting, prepare processes crumbling and sliding until the poet's name threatens to be lost.
Time the overhearer has a wallet at his back wherein he puts bills for
oblivion. In my frequent phone conversations with John Ashbery, both
of us knowing we would not meet again, I sometimes concluded by
quoting to him the direct credo of the closing lines of "Wet Casements":

I want that information very much today,

Can't have it, and this makes me angry.
I shall use my anger to build a bridge like that
Of Avignon, on which people may dance for the feeling
Of dancing on a bridge. I shall at last see my complete face
Reflected not in the water but in the worn stone floor of my
    bridge.

I shall keep to myself.
I shall not repeat others' comments about me.

For me this is haunting. A few nights back, I had a singular nightmare in which I had walked too far and hailed a taxi to take me back to
the Greenwich Village loft I am now forsaking. I had only a few coins
for payment and was penalized by a grotesque incarceration. In the
dream, I recited this closing passage of Ashbery's poem to placate the

irate driver, to no avail. I awoke bleakly and wondered whether I feared
I never would see my complete face reflected in anything I could build.
Ashbery's glory is to have built an escape from narcissism into the haven
of his constant readers.

*Houseboat Days* is rich and various. One of its splendors is the Orphic
elegy with a difference, "Syringa." "Syrinx," by way of Latin, stems
from the Greek for "channel" or "pipe" and can mean a set of panpipes.
In relaxed mode and almost limpid, the poem opens with the myth
rendered as a throwaway:

Orpheus liked the glad personal quality
Of the things beneath the sky. Of course, Eurydice was a
    part
Of this. Then one day, everything changed. He rends
Rocks into fissures with lament. Gullies, hummocks
Can't withstand it. The sky shudders from one horizon
To the other, almost ready to give up wholeness.
Then Apollo quietly told him: "Leave it all on earth.
Your lute, what point? Why pick at a dull pavan few care to
Follow, except a few birds of dusty feather,
Not vivid performances of the past." But why not?
All other things must change too.
The seasons are no longer what they once were,
But it is the nature of things to be seen only once,
As they happen along, bumping into other things, getting along
Somehow. That's where Orpheus made his mistake.
Of course Eurydice vanished into the shade;
She would have even if he hadn't turned around.
No use standing there like a gray stone toga as the whole wheel
Of recorded history flashes past, struck dumb, unable to utter an
    intelligent
Comment on the most thought-provoking element in its train.
Only love stays on the brain, and something these people,
These other ones, call life. Singing accurately
So that the notes mount straight up out of the well of
Dim noon and rival the tiny, sparkling yellow flowers
Growing around the brink of the quarry, encapsulates
The different weights of the things.

Ashbery's Apollo is unique. Current readers, a few birds of dusty feather, seem archaic, and even an Orphic agon hardly competes with the vivid performances of the past. Insouciantly, Ashbery asks, "Why not?," embracing the Heraclitian flux. Orpheus and Apollo are mistaken. Ashbery places his faith in singing accurately, thus following Wallace Stevens in "Notes Toward a Supreme Fiction":

IT MUST BE ABSTRACT

IX

. . . . . . . . . . . . .

         . . . But apotheosis is not
The origin of the major man. He comes,

Compact in invincible foils, from reason,
Lighted at midnight by the studious eye,
Swaddled in revery, the object of

The hum of thoughts evaded in the mind,
Hidden from other thoughts, he that reposes
On a breast forever precious for that touch,

For whom the good of April falls tenderly,
Falls down, the cock-birds calling at the time.
My dame, sing for this person accurate songs.

Gentler than Stevens, Ashbery is slyly content to trace the origin of the minor man who steps aside knowing it must change:

But it isn't enough
To just go on singing. Orpheus realized this
And didn't mind so much about his reward being in heaven
After the Bacchantes had torn him apart, driven
Half out of their minds by his music, what it was doing to them.
Some say it was for his treatment of Eurydice.
But probably the music had more to do with it, and

The way music passes, emblematic
Of life and how you cannot isolate a note of it
And say it is good or bad. You must
Wait till it's over. "The end crowns all,"
Meaning also that the "tableau"
Is wrong. For although memories, of a season, for example,
Melt into a single snapshot, one cannot guard, treasure
That stalled moment. It too is flowing, fleeting;
It is a picture of flowing, scenery, though living, mortal,
Over which an abstract action is laid out in blunt,
Harsh strokes. And to ask more than this
Is to become the tossing reeds of that slow,
Powerful stream, the trailing grasses
Playfully tugged at, but to participate in the action
No more than this. Then in the lowering gentian sky
Electric twitches are faintly apparent first, then burst forth
Into a shower of fixed, cream-colored flares. The horses
Have each seen a share of the truth, though each thinks,
"I'm a maverick. Nothing of this is happening to me,
Though I can understand the language of birds, and
The itinerary of the lights caught in the storm is fully apparent
    to me.
Their jousting ends in music much
As trees move more easily in the wind after a summer storm
And is happening in lacy shadows of shore-trees, now, day after
    day."

Again Ashbery remembers Shakespeare's *Troilus and Cressida*:

ULYSSES:  Sir, I foretold you then what would ensue:
    My prophecy is but half his journey yet;
    For yonder walls, that pertly front your town,
    Yon towers, whose wanton tops do buss the clouds,
    Must kiss their own feet.

HECTOR:  I must not believe you.
    There they stand yet, and modestly I think
    The fall of every Phrygian stone will cost

A drop of Grecian blood: the end crowns all,
And that old common arbitrator, Time,
Will one day end it.

Orpheus and Ashbery alike are chastened by the flowing and fleeting. With an eloquent shrug, each disavows finalities and subsides in
acquiescence. Time renders regret otiose:

But how late to be regretting all this, even
Bearing in mind that regrets are always late, too late!
To which Orpheus, a bluish cloud with white contours,
Replies that these are of course not regrets at all,
Merely a careful, scholarly setting down of
Unquestioned facts, a record of pebbles along the way.
And no matter how all this disappeared,
Or got where it was going, it is no longer
Material for a poem. Its subject
Matters too much, and not enough, standing there
    helplessly
While the poem streaked by, its tail afire, a bad
Comet screaming hate and disaster, but so turned inward
That the meaning, good or other, can never
Become known. The singer thinks
Constructively, builds up his chant in progressive stages
Like a skyscraper, but at the last minute turns away.
The song is engulfed in an instant in blackness
Which must in turn flood the whole continent
With blackness, for it cannot see. The singer
Must then pass out of sight, not even relieved
Of the evil burthen of the words. Stellification
Is for the few, and comes about much later
When all record of these people and their lives
Has disappeared into libraries, onto microfilm.
A few are still interested in them. "But what about
So-and-so?" is still asked on occasion. But they lie
Frozen and out of touch until an arbitrary chorus
Speaks of a totally different incident with a similar name
In whose tale are hidden syllables

Of what happened so long before that
In some small town, one indifferent summer.

Earlier in the poem, Ashbery plays on another meaning of "syringe" when accurate singing mounts notes that rival the tiny, sparkling yellow lilacs. Orpheus, transmuted into a lilac-like cloud, casts aside regrets and with Ashbery embraces a Whitmanian tally that may not be materia poetica. Whitman would have been appalled by Ashbery's vision of a poem afire, a bad comet turned so inward that meaning is lost. Song and singer pass into blackness.

The Orphic poet that Emerson prophesied and Whitman fulfilled, like almost all poets, vanishes into libraries. I recall attending the last of a series of lectures given by Robert Graves at Cambridge University in 1954 that took the angry title "These Be Your Gods, O Israel!" in reference to the molten calf in Exodus 32:8. I winced as Graves denounced Yeats, Eliot, and other idols. Questions were invited. I had some acquaintance with Graves and felt free to ask, "What about Wallace Stevens?" Graves looked puzzled and then said, "Ah yes, Walker Stevens, I heard he was getting on." I allowed myself to comment: "One would hope so. He is now seventy-five." Graves confused the major American poet of our era with an advertising agency. Over a drink at the Anchor Pub afterward, the prophet of the White Goddess granted that some early Wallace Stevens gave him pleasure.

I cite this because I had told Ashbery this anecdote, since "But what about / So-and-so?" always reminded me of that Gravesian moment. The sadness of poetic demise is in the bleakness of lying frozen and out of touch until a mistake renews memory. When I think of John Ashbery's style and ethos, I find them encapsulated in the hidden syllables:

Of what happened so long before that
In some small town, one indifferent summer.

That American closure leads me on to Ashbery's tenth volume, *A Wave* (1984), which opens with the condensed menace of "At North Farm":

Somewhere someone is traveling furiously toward you,
At incredible speed, traveling day and night,

Through blizzards and desert heat, across torrents, through
    narrow passes.
But will he know where to find you,
Recognize you when he sees you,
Give you the thing he has for you?

Hardly anything grows here,
Yet the granaries are bursting with meal,
The sacks of meal piled to the rafters.
The streams run with sweetness, fattening fish;
Birds darken the sky. Is it enough
That the dish of milk is set out at night,
That we think of him sometimes,
Sometimes and always, with mixed feelings?

The Finnish epic *Kalevala* has had a singular effect upon Ashbery.
North Farm is on the border of hell. Heroes go there to win their
brides, who resist since they are witches. John told me once that his
farm upbringing gave him no pleasure. "At North Farm" opens with
a courier who is somewhat Kafkan and unlikely to find you. There is
an ironic allusion to the account in Herodotus of the Persian system of
mounted postal carriers:

It is said that as many days as there are in the whole journey, so
many are the men and horses that stand along the road, each horse
and man at the interval of a day's journey; and these are stayed neither by snow nor rain nor heat nor darkness from accomplishing
their appointed course with all speed.

All of us recognize this as the origin of the motto of the American
postal system, which is now a travesty.

This sestet has no immediate reference to North Farm. But we worry
about the thing the messenger intends to give us. Can it be our death?
The octave enhances the quiet terror of our waiting. Almost nothing
grows, yet meal, fish, and birds are abundant. An open question doubles
itself when we propitiate the impending with the apotropaic dish of
milk. Will it suffice to hold off what is coming?

Sestet and octave abide as open questions. I have loved John Ashbery's poetry and the poet himself for sixty years and wonder if that openness is the subtlest clue to his very American negative sublimity.

Those paragraphs were written while Ashbery was still alive. He died at the age of ninety. I had known him since 1956. In the sixty years of our friendship, we stayed in touch mostly by phone calls and letters, though I introduced him frequently at his poetry readings in New Haven and New York City. We also spent time together in Portugal and once or twice in Paris.

John abroad seemed very different from John in America. He was quietly joyous, and anxious only about hotels and schedules. When I think of him and Archie together, I realize that Archie, who looked serene, suffered considerably from anxious expectations at certain times. John on the surface might seem troubled, but generally was more at home in the world. I loved them both as poets and as persons, yet I was closer to Archie and more in awe of John. Both were major poets and central to American tradition. Now, in early January 2018, I realize that the Age of Ashbery has just ended, even as the Stevens era reached conclusion in early August 1955, a month before I started my ongoing teaching career at Yale.

# John Wheelwright, "Fish Food"

I N AN EARLY POEM composed only three years after Hart Crane's suicide, John Berryman elegized his precursor with fervor:

O mourn the legend left here in the first
Full sun, fragments of light to tell the day.
Tread slowly, softly silence while the dust
Whirls up the sky and walls the sound away.

Cantlets of speech: beyond reach of light
Beyond all architecture, the last ledge,
He is obscure in ocean in the night—
Monstrous and still, brooding above the bridge.

These closing lines by a twenty-one-year-old ephebe catch something of Hart Crane's metric. The fragments of light are matched by the cantlets or fragments of speech. Crane has become a kind of god, brooding upon the face of the waters and above the bridge he celebrated.

Elegies for Crane are numerous and very varied. There is a peculiarly nasty one by Geoffrey Hill that nevertheless beholds something of lasting value:

Publish his name, exile's remittancer,
prodigal who reclaimed us brought to book.

Yvor Winters, once Crane's friend, indulged himself by inverting the High Romantic visionary's Orphic identification:

Yet the fingers on the lyre
Spread like an avenging fire.
Crying loud, the immortal tongue,
From the empty body wrung,
Broken in a bloody dream,
Sang unmeaning down the stream.

"Unmeaning" is too absurd to be argued. Better to look at the elegies
for Crane that have some poetic value.

He jumped, seeing an island like a hand,
And where he lived, the hands were all unfriendly.
The island rose to take him: at the end
He saw all things unclearly.

This is a tribute from 1942 by the minor British poet Julian Symons.
Malcolm Cowley, Crane's friend, saluted him in the poem "The Flower
in the Sea," alluding to the marvelous trope in "Voyages II": "Close
round one instant in one floating flower." Except for "Fish Food: An
Obituary to Hart Crane" by John Brooks Wheelwright, which I intend
to appreciate more fully, the crown of laments is held by Robert Lowell's "Words for Hart Crane" in *Life Studies:*

"When the Pulitzers showered on some dope
or screw who flushed our dry mouths out with soap,
few people would consider why I took
to stalking sailors, and scattered Uncle Sam's
phoney gold-plated laurels to the birds.
Because I knew my Whitman like a book,
stranger in America, tell my country: I,
*Catullus redivivus,* once the rage
of the Village and Paris, used to play my role
of homosexual, wolfing the stray lambs
who hungered by the Place de la Concorde.
My profit was a pocket with a hole.
Who asks for me, the Shelley of my age,
must lay his heart out for my bed and board."

This irregular sonnet acutely names Hart Crane as both a reborn Catullus and the Shelley of our time. The contrast with Geoffrey Hill's later squib is instructive. Reluctantly, I acknowledge, as always, that Hill is the major English poet since Thomas Hardy and D. H. Lawrence, whereas Lowell began superbly, in my judgment fell off, yet rallied again and again. I could well believe that Crane speaks Lowell's poem, although its discursiveness is counter to the poetics of metaphor sublimely evident in almost all that characterizes the true heir of Walt Whitman and Herman Melville.

John Wheelwright also descended from Emerson and Whitman and befriended Crane. He died eight years after Hart Crane, struck down by a drunken driver in Boston at the age of forty-three. A patrician Trotskyite, Wheelwright helped to found the Socialists Workers Party after he was expelled by the Socialists. Probably bisexual, though evidently ascetic, he was the center of Boston literary culture in his lifetime, frequently clashing with his cousin, the formidable Amy Lowell, yet on amiable terms with Robert Fitzgerald, Austin Warren, his brother-in-law the noted Blake scholar S. Foster Damon, Quincy Howe, John Peale Bishop, Malcolm Cowley, Horace Gregory, and other literary luminaries.

Wheelwright is mostly forgotten, but I agree with John Ashbery that the Boston revolutionary was a major poet. Flamboyant and outrageous in life as in literature, he sported an archaic raccoon coat in all kinds of weather and mounted soapboxes to preach the Gospel of Leon Trotsky to the workers of Boston. Wheelwright was proud of his descent from the Reverend John Wheelwright, who was banished from the theocratic Massachusetts Bay Colony when he endorsed the antinomian doctrines of his sister-in-law Anne Hutchinson. Austin Warren, whom I knew and revered in my far-off youth, called John Brooks Wheelwright a New England saint. In religion the poet became an Anglo-Catholic, though of a sect of one, deeply influenced by the Kabbalah and other esoteric traditions.

His elegy for Hart Crane relies upon the Old Norse fable of Thor draining a flagon and thus lowering the level of the ocean. Thor then lifted a peculiar cat and in doing so dislodged the tortoise who held up the earth, which then slipped from its accustomed place:

As you drank deep as Thor, did you think of milk or wine?
Did you drink blood, while you drank the salt deep?
Or see through the film of light, that sharpened your rage with
    its stare,
a shark, dolphin, turtle? Did you not see the Cat
who, when Thor lifted her, unbased the cubic ground?
You would drain fathomless flagons to be slaked with vacuum—
The sea's teats have suckled you, and you are sunk far
in bubble-dreams, under swaying translucent vines
of thundering interior wonder. Eagles can never now
carry parts of your body, over cupped mountains
as emblems of their anger, embers to fire self-hate
to other wonders, unfolding white, flaming vistas.

Fishes now look upon you, with eyes which do not gossip.
Fishes are never shocked. Fishes will kiss you, each
fish tweak you; every kiss take bits of you away,
till your bones alone will roll, with the Gulf Stream's swell.
So has it been already, so have the carpers and puffers
nibbled your carcass of fame, each to his liking. Now
in tides of noon, the bones of your thought-suspended structures
gleam as you intended. Noon pulled your eyes with small
magnetic headaches; the will seeped from your blood. Seeds
of meaning popped from the pods of thought. And you fall. And
    the unseen
churn of Time changes the pearl-hued ocean;
like a pearl-shaped drop, in a huge water-clock
falling; from *came* to *go*, from *come* to *went*. And you fell.

Waters received you. Waters of our Birth in Death dissolve you.
Now you have willed it, may the Great Wash take you.
As the Mother-Lover takes your woe away, and cleansing
grief and you away, you sleep, you do not snore.
Lie still. Your rage is gone on a bright flood
away; as, when a bad friend held out his hand
you said, "Do not talk any more. I know you meant no harm."
What was the soil whence your anger sprang, who are deaf
as the stones to the whispering flight of the Mississippi's rivers?

What did you see as you fell? What did you hear as you sank?
Did it make you drunken with hearing?
I will not ask any more. You saw or heard no evil.

Wheelwright favored long lines, here a hexameter and sometimes
the Blakean fourteener. "Fish Food" belies its throwaway title by its
weight and prophetic gravity. The poem has fascinated me since I
first read it in my childhood, but in old age it becomes something of
a puzzle. Hart Crane, when sober, was gentle and remarkably sweet-
natured. His searing poem "Possessions" calls itself "Record of rage
and partial appetites," but even that Inferno of a lyric concludes with
"All but bright stones wherein our smiling plays." Why does Wheelwright speak of Crane's sharpening of his rage? Later, Wheelwright
remarks on the departure of Crane's rage when he forgave the elegist's
blunder. And yet Crane's anger is invoked again in the closing lines in
an allusion to "The River," a canto of *The Bridge:*

You will not hear it as the sea; even stone
Is not more hushed by gravity . . . But slow,
As loth to take more tribute—sliding prone
Like one whose eyes were buried long ago

John Ashbery, an intense admirer both of Wheelwright and of
Crane, concludes his wonderful "Wet Casements" with lines always in
my memory:

Can't have it, and this makes me angry.
I shall use my anger to build a bridge like that
Of Avignon, on which people may dance for the feeling
Of dancing on a bridge. I shall at last see my complete face
Reflected not in the water but in the worn stone floor of my
    bridge.

I shall keep to myself.
I shall not repeat others' comments about me.

In a conversation with Ashbery, I recall telling him that for me this
links with Hart Crane's "Brooklyn Bridge" and Wheelwright's vision

of Crane. Ashbery's anger ensues in bridge building for our aesthetic pleasure, as the fury of creation is rightly ascribed by Wheelwright to Crane, the visionary of bridge building. I think also of T. S. Eliot's tribute to Hart Crane in the opening lines of "The Dry Salvages":

> I do not know much about gods; but I think that the river
> Is a strong brown god—sullen, untamed and intractable,
> Patient to some degree, at first recognised as a frontier;
> Useful, untrustworthy, as a conveyor of commerce;
> Then only a problem confronting the builder of bridges.

Ashbery, rejecting the role of Narcissus, at last will see his complete face reflected in the worn stone floor of his bridge, since we his dancers and readers have made it a mirror of the self. Wheelwright's Crane has a more august fate, since the structures of his bridge gleam in his afterlife. "Fish Food" rises to something of Hart Crane's own preternatural eloquence as it asks the open questions:

> What did you see as you fell? What did you hear as you sank?
> Did it make you drunken with hearing?
> I will not ask any more. You saw or heard no evil.

Neither we nor Wheelwright know what Crane saw or heard as he fell into the Caribbean. It is enough that the most gifted of all American poets, at least since Walt Whitman and Emily Dickinson, returned to natal power without a sense of foreboding:

> The sea raised up a campanile . . . The wind I heard
> Of brine partaking, whirling into shower
> Of column that breakers sheared in shower
> Back into bosom,—me—her, into natal power . . .

That is a fragment written by Crane in 1926–27. Wheelwright could not have read it, but he did not need to. Myself a reader of Crane for more than three-quarters of a century, I learn more about his unique daemon by reading Wheelwright than by all but a few of my fellow exegetes.

# James Merrill, *The Book of Ephraim*

I FIRST MET JAMES MERRILL in 1959 and began reading him soon after. Though we corresponded and talked on the phone until sometime in the early 1990s, our friendship was more literary than personal. He was gentle, kind, and charmingly courteous, but we had very different temperaments, and our bafflement was mutual.

Until I read and reviewed *Divine Comedies* in 1976, I had mostly a qualified admiration for his poetry. There were exceptions: "Mirror," "For Proust," and "Days of 1964." These found me. All that changed with *Divine Comedies*, which I reviewed upon its appearance in 1976. I was charged by "Lost in Translation" and *The Book of Ephraim*.

In response, Merrill dazzled with a note in which he impishly suggested he was Ganymede to my Zeus. A year later, he began regularly mailing me the developing *Mirabell: Books of Number* and, a touch later, *Scripts for the Pageant*. When I pled for more J.M. and less of the long passages in capital letters, he properly reproved me with a plaintive note saying that the cupbearer to the gods had been cast away. I repented, yet have never been as happy with *Mirabell* and *Scripts for the Pageant* as I go on being enchanted by *Ephraim*.

From 1976 to 1978, Merrill and I had an ongoing conversation, sometimes face-to-face, more often by phone, in which we explored W. B. Yeats's *A Vision*, the Gnostic religion, and the relation of Yeats to Shelley and to Blake. We abstained from contrasting our rival views of poetic influence. I grinned cheerfully at the palpable hit in *Scripts*: HIDEOUS BLOOMS TO STIR UP RIVALRY AT HIGH LEVELS.

James Merrill experienced a long day's dying culminating February 6, 1995, one month before what would have been his sixty-ninth birthday. Some of the final poems are extraordinary, including "Days of 1994" with its celebration of "The knowing glance from star to star, / The laughter of old friends."

*The Book of Ephraim* loses too much when excerpted, so I will center here upon "Mirror," "Lost in Translation," the miraculous version of Paul Valéry's "Palme," and the canzone "Samos," which for me is the high point of *Scripts for the Pageant*.

Though relatively early in Merrill's development, "Mirror" is the apologia for his poetic mind:

I grow old under an intensity
Of questioning looks. *Nonsense,*
I try to say, *I cannot teach you children
How to live.—If not you, who will?*
Cries one of them aloud, grasping my gilded
Frame till the world sways. *If not you, who will?*
Between their visits the table, its arrangement
Of Bible, fern and Paisley, all past change,
Does very nicely. If ever I feel curious
As to what others endure,
Across the parlor *you* provide examples,
Wide open, sunny, of everything I am
Not. You embrace a whole world without once caring
To set it in order. That takes thought. Out there
Something is being picked. The red-and-white bandannas
Go to my heart. A fine young man
Rides by on horseback. Now the door shuts. Hester
Confides in me her first unhappiness.
This much, you see, would never have been fitted
Together, but for me. Why then is it
They more and more neglect me? Late one sleepless
Midsummer night I strained to keep
Five tapers from your breathing. *No,* the widowed
Cousin said, *let them go out.* I did.
The room brimmed with gray sound, all the instreaming
Muslin of your dream . . .
Years later now, two of the grown grandchildren
Sit with novels face-down on the sill,
Content to muse upon your tall transparence,
Your clouds, brown fields, persimmon far

And cypress near. One speaks. *How superficial*
*Appearances are!* Since then, as if a fish
Had broken the perfect silver of my reflectiveness,
I have lapses. I suspect
Looks from behind, where nothing is, cool gazes
Through the blind flaws of my mind. As days,
As decades lengthen, this vision
Spreads and blackens. I do not know whose it is,
But I think it watches for my last silver
To blister, flake, float leaf by life, each milling-
Downward dumb conceit, to a standstill
From which not even you strike any brilliant
Chord in me, and to a faceless will,
Echo of mine, I am amenable.

A dramatic monologue uttered by a mirror is not unique, and yet I cannot recall any reflecting glass so eloquent as this self-portrait of a decaying aesthetic sensibility fixed in place and opposing a window open to experience. Aging augmented by neglect, Mirror's pride diminishes even as its function dwindles. Crisis arrives in Merrill's stroke when two grown grandchildren muse upon Window's tall transparence and one of them breaks the vessels of Mirror's consciousness:

> One speaks. *How superficial*
> *Appearances are!* Since then, as if a fish
> Had broken the perfect silver of my reflectiveness,
> I have lapses. I suspect
> Looks from behind, where nothing is, cool gazes
> Through the blind flaws of my mind. As days,
> As decades lengthen, this vision
> Spreads and blackens.

Merrill sublimely fetches a fish from superficial, and every sense of reflectiveness breaks. A paranoia enters Mirror's lapses. Nothing is got for nothing, and poetic mind flaws blindly in a play on the etymon of "flaw" as a windblown flake. With masterly tact, Merrill associates proleptically the milling-downward of poetic conceit gone silent with the blistering, flaking, floating leaf of Mirror's vital silver. There is a Yeatsian touch in the faceless will that echoes Mirror's decline. The poem ends marvelously with "I am amenable," where that rich word comprehends its full range of meanings. Mirror-Merrill is submissive, tractable, leadable, above all open to testing or to judgment.

I did not read "Lost in Translation" until *Divine Comedies* appeared, though it had been printed two years earlier in *The New Yorker*. The poem transported me with rare immediacy, particularly its conclusion:

I've spent the last days, furthermore,
Ransacking Athens for that translation of "Palme."
Neither the Goethehaus nor the National Library
Seems able to unearth it. Yet I can't
Just be imagining. I've seen it. Know
How much of the sun-ripe original
Felicity Rilke made himself forego
(Who loved French words—verger, mûr, parfumer)
In order to render its underlying sense.
Know already in that tongue of his
What Pains, what monolithic Truths
Shadow stanza to stanza's symmetrical
Rhyme-rutted pavement. Know that ground plan left
Sublime and barren, where the warm Romance
Stone by stone faded, cooled; the fluted nouns
Made taller, lonelier than life
By leaf-carved capitals in the afterglow.
The owlet umlaut peeps and hoots
Above the open vowel. And after rain
A deep reverberation fills with stars.

Lost, is it, buried? One more missing piece?

But nothing's lost. Or else: all is translation
And every bit of us is lost in it
(Or found—I wander through the ruin of S
Now and then, wondering at the peacefulness)
And in that loss a self-effacing tree,
Color of context, imperceptibly
Rustling with its angel, turns the waste
To shade and fiber, milk and memory.

The epigraph to "Lost in Translation" is from Rilke's version of Valéry's "Palme," the first four lines of the poem's seventh stanza. Merrill translated these with a supple elegance:

These days which, like yourself,
Seem empty and effaced
Have avid roots that delve
To work deep in the waste.

The search for the Rilke translation informs one meaning of "lost in translation," yet that is only one strand in Merrill's vision of loss. If all is translation and we are lost in it, then Yeats sustains us by his lament in "Nineteen Hundred and Nineteen":

But is there any comfort to be found?
Man is in love and loves what vanishes,
What more is there to say?

Merrill, Yeats-haunted, turns to Valéry for a different comfort:

And in that loss a self-effacing tree,
Color of context, imperceptibly
Rustling with its angel, turns the waste
To shade and fiber, milk and memory.

The tree is the palm. Valéry and Wallace Stevens may have known the Shiite Sufi myth that after the creation of Adam there was a remnant of the *adamah*, or red clay. From that remnant Allah fashioned the palm tree as Adam's sister. I do not think Merrill knew this until I told him in the early 1990s, and yet that scarcely matters, since he evidenced no surprise.

Like Yeats, Marcel Proust, and C. P. Cavafy, Merrill is the poet of our lost paradises of eros. I can hear him cheerfully intoning, in his tribute to Proust, "The loved one always leaves." I suspect that Yeats might not have taken to James Merrill's poetry but that Proust and Cavafy might have cherished it.

As *The Book of Ephraim* approaches conclusion, Merrill achieves something close to the High Sublime:

Shall I come lighter-hearted to that Spring-tide
Knowing it must be fathomed without a guide?
With no one, nothing along those lines—or these
Whose writing, if not justifies, so mirrors,
So embodies up to now some guiding force,
It can't simply be written off. In neither
The world's poem nor the poem's world have I
Learned to think for myself, much. The twinklings of
Insight hurt or elude the naked eye, no
Metrical lens to focus them, no kismet
Veiled as a stern rhyme sound, to obey whose wink
Floods with rapture its galaxy of sisters.
Muse and maker, each at a loss . . .

The texture, marvelously interwoven, reveals no interstice for pause. Like the early Mirror, this is an epitome. Wit, dangerously intense, is carried to the edge of parody and then withdrawn. A lightness fiercely knowing suggests the lineage of Alexander Pope and Lord Byron.

It may be that Merrill's strongest lyric is the canzone "Samos." I chant it frequently and wonder if anything else in *Scripts for the Pageant* can survive:

And still, at sea all night, we had a sense
Of sunrise, golden oil poured upon water,
Soothing its heave, letting the sleeper sense
What inborn, amniotic homing sense
Was ferrying him—now through the dream-fire
In which (it has been felt) each human sense
Burns, now through ship's radar's cool sixth sense,
Or mere unerring starlight—to an island.
Here we were. The twins of Sea and Land,
Up and about for hours—hues, cries, scents—
Had placed at eye level a single light
Croissant: the harbor glazed with warm pink light.

Fire-wisps were weaving a string bag of light
For sea stones. Their astounding color sense!
Porphyry, alabaster, chrysolite
Translucences that go dead in daylight

Asked only the quick dip in holy water
For the saint of cell on cell to come alight—
Illuminated crystals thinking light,
Refracting it, the gray prismatic fire
Or yellow-gray of sea's dilute sapphire . . .
Wavelengths daily deeply score the leit-
Motifs of Loom and Wheel upon this land.
To those who listen, it's the Promised Land.

A little spin today? Dirt roads inland
Jounce and revolve in a nerve-jangling light,
Doing the ancient dances of the land
Where, gnarled as olive trees that shag the land
With silver, old men—their two-bladed sense
Of spendthrift poverty, the very land
Being, if not loaf, tomb—superbly land
Upright on the downbeat. We who water
The local wine, which "drinks itself" like water,
Clap for more, cry out to *be* this island
Licked all over by a white, salt fire,
*Be* noon's pulsing ember raked by fire,

Know nothing, now, but Earth, Air, Water, Fire!
For once out of the frying pan to land
Within their timeless, everlasting fire!
Blood's least red monocle, O magnifier
Of the great Eye that sees by its own light
More pictures in "the world's enchanted fire"
Than come and go in any shrewd crossfire
Upon the page, of syllable and sense,
We want unwilled excursions and ascents,
Crave the upward-rippling rungs of fire,
The outward-rippling rings (enough!) of water . . .
(Now some details—how else will this hold water?)

Our room's three flights above the whitewashed water-
front where Pythagoras was born. A fire
Escape of sky-blue iron leads down to water.

Yachts creak on mirror berths, and over water
Voices from Sweden or Somaliland
Tell how this or that one crossed the water
To Ephesus, came back with toilet water
And a two kilo box of Turkish delight
—Trifles. Yet they shine with such pure light
In memory, even they, that the eyes water.
As with the setting sun, or innocence,
Do things that fade especially make sense?

Samos. We keep trying to make sense
Of what we can. Not souls of the first water—
Although we've put on airs, and taken fire—
We shall be dust of quite another land
Before the seeds here planted come to light.

A canzone, which we associate with Dante, Petrarch, Boccaccio, began in Provence in the eleventh century and was prevalent first in Italy and then in Spain. Frequently in five stanzas and a coda, it employs, in place of a refrain, a scheme of five rhyme words. Merrill triumphs with the interplay: "sense," "water," "fire," "land," and "light." Samos is an island in the eastern Aegean, famous as the birthplace of Pythagoras and of Epicurus. Samian wine was treasured in antiquity and is still quite drinkable.

For Merrill, Samos is the Promised Land. The Byzantium of William Butler Yeats hovers and is deftly evaded. The evasion wavers when Merrill cries out to be Samos, much in the mode of Yeatsian flames begotten by flame. The coda is apotheosis:

Samos. We keep trying to make sense
Of what we can. Not souls of the first water—
Although we've put on airs, and taken fire—
We shall be dust of quite another land
Before the seeds here planted come to light.

Praise is redundant. James Merrill's countenance had a curious poignance, a spindrift gaze toward lost paradise. I recite the coda and rue his departure.

# Jay Macpherson, "Ark Parting"

T HE CANADIAN POET AND SCHOLAR Jay Macpherson became a
dear friend during my many visits as a lecturer to the University of
Toronto. Jay was a year younger than I was, and though she was shy, we
took to each other very quickly. I had always been a lover of her poetry,
and I am proud that I insisted that her superb *The Spirit of Solitude:
Conventions and Continuity in Late Romance* (1982) be published. The
last time I went to Toronto to give a lecture series, I stayed as a guest
at Jay's home. Her death in 2012 desolated me. She was so rare a spirit
that I simply cannot compare her to anyone else I have ever known.

Jay was a direct descendant of James Macpherson, who asserted
he had translated the ancient Scottish bard Ossian from manuscripts.
These have never been discovered, and Ossian was James Macpherson.
Jay dedicated *The Spirit of Solitude* to her father, also James Macpherson, who never gave up his faith in the authenticity of Ossian.

Jay's poetry is unlike anyone else's. It is deceptively childlike yet is
immensely sophisticated. One of my favorites is "Mermaid":

The fish-tailed lady offering her breast
Has nothing else to give.
She'll render only brine, if pressed,
That none can drink and live.

She has a magic glass, whose spell
Makes bone look wondrous white.
By day she sings, though, travellers like to tell,
She weeps at night.

The chill of this epiphany stays with me. A tone this uncanny is characteristic of Jay Macpherson. It becomes heightened to a kind of sublime in what I take to be her masterpiece, "The Beauty of Job's Daughters":

The old, the mad, the blind have fairest daughters.
Take Job: the beasts the accuser sends at evening
Shoulder his house and shake it; he's not there,
Attained in age to inwardness of daughters,
In all the land no women found so fair.

Angels and sons of God are nearest neighbours,
And even the accuser may repair
To walk with Job in pleasures of his daughters:
Wide shining rooms more warmly lit at evening,
Gardens beyond whose secrets scent the air.

Not wiles of men nor envy of the neighbours,
Riches of earth, nor what heaven holds more rare,
Can take from Job the beauty of his daughters,
The gardens in the rock, music at evening,
And cup so full that all who come must share.

Perhaps we passed them? it was late, or evening,
And surely those were desert stumps, not daughters,
In fact we doubt that they were ever there.
The old, the mad, the blind have fairest daughters.
In all the land no women found so fair.

The book of Job enchants and devastates me. When Jay first gave me a copy of this poem, I recall both my instant admiration and my bewilderment. Job's daughters and his sons are all slaughtered by the accuser, who is sanctioned by Yahweh. In the pious nonsense interpolated into the end of Job's book, we are told that he acquires an entirely new set of sons and daughters, as good as the murdered ones. Jay Macpherson has a Job entirely her own, though there is a touch of William Blake in it. "Inwardness of daughters" is a gentle irony that yet may be more than that.

After three stanzas of mysterious splendor, Macpherson undoes her poem. The beautiful daughters were desert stumps or never existed. The lingering refrain "In all the land no women found so fair" subdues the rest of the poem to Jay Macpherson's whimsical transformation of a supposed theodicy, that justifies nothing, into her own version of late Romance. Jay's vision of late Romance emphasized pastoral and elegiac currents, from Comus to Thomas Mann's *Death in Venice*. I enjoyed reciting, in her company, her own variations on Milton's Eve:

Painful and brief the act. Eve on the barren shore
Sees every cherished feature, plumed tree, bright grass,
Fresh spring, the beasts as placid as before
Beneath the inviolable glass.

There the lost girl gone under sea
Tends her undying grove, never raising her eyes
To where on the salt shell beach in reverie
The mother of all living lies.

The beloved face is lost from sight,
Marred in a whelming tide of blood:
And Adam walks in the cold night
Wilderness, waste wood.

"Eve in Reflection"

The Fall, as in Milton, becomes a narcissistic reverie in which Eve beholds herself and falls in love with what she sees. Jay's title plays upon both senses of reflection, meditation and the mirror of Narcissus. Nature becomes an "inviolable glass," and the lost Eve submerged by ocean continues to tend her garden, more than ironically never gazing to her own reverie on the salt shell beach.

Eve's self-reflection vanishes, damaged by the tide of blood that goes from Cain to our present moment. An estranged Adam walks in a wasteland, a cold darkness replacing the warmth of Eden. Jay Macpherson pursued that darkness in her poem "The Land of Nod":

Cain since first he fled
Is endless bound to run

Under a scorching sun
That burns a baneful red,

Or hunt among cold rocks
And stiffened marble streams.
Only in Abel's dreams
The crushing wheel unlocks.

For Abel's sake, the dead
Shepherd dear to God,
Cain in the Land of Nod
Covers his dreadful head.

Where Abel, cheek on hand,
Sleeps his silver night,
An arky moon makes bright
Calm sheepfolds, quiet land;

And while his brother's keeper
Lies so near God's heart,
There shall no judgment fall to part
Sleeper from sleeper.

Jay's teacher was Northrop Frye, and the prime influence upon her poetry is William Blake. She inherits from Blake a subtly antinomian stance and an ironic mode of presenting it. The burden of the final quatrain of "The Land of Nod" is a Blakean equivocation. The God who favored Abel over Cain is incapable of judging one sleeper from another. Blake remarked that in equivocal worlds, up and down are equivocal.

Jay Macpherson had a great preference for Noah's Ark over Noah himself. She began with a singular lyric, "The Ark":

Cock-robin and the jenny-wren,
The eagle and the lark,
The cuckoo and the broody-hen,
The heavens did remark
Consorting in the Ark:

The pelican in her piety,
The peacock in his pride,
Cormorant insatiety,
The feather-breasted bride,
All bedded down inside.

There sat upon the hatch-lid
The turtle and the crow.
One I've heard the Flood did,
One the Fire shall, o'erthrow
—Not in our lifetime, though.

A sexual revel is transferred from Noah, his wife, and Ham to all the birds in the ark. The turtledove, sacred to Venus, is different after the Flood. The crow will be destroyed only in the final Fire. Laconically, Macpherson concludes, "Not in our lifetime, though."

Noah haunts Macpherson. In her first volume, *The Boatman and Other Poems*, the title poem, "The Boatman," intricately turns inside out the story of the Flood:

You might suppose it easy
For a maker not too lazy
To convert the gentle reader to an Ark:
But it takes a willing pupil
To admit both gnat and camel
—Quite an eyeful, all the crew that must embark.

After me when comes the deluge
And you're looking round for refuge
From God's anger pouring down in gush and spout,
Then you take the tender creature
—You remember, that's the reader—
And you pull him through his navel inside out.

That's to get his beasts outside him,
For they've got to come aboard him,
As the best directions have it, two by two.
When you've taken all their tickets

And you've marched them through his sockets,
Let the tempest bust Creation: heed not you.

For you're riding high and mighty
In a gale that's pushing ninety
With a solid bottom under you—that's his.
Fellow flesh affords a rampart,
And you've got along for comfort
All the world there ever shall be, was, and is.

The verve and rapidity of this is a total delight. Macpherson's metric
has the buoyancy of Gilbert and Sullivan and of the nonsense verse of
Lewis Carroll and Edward Lear. We are to become her Ark. The wonderful play on "pupil" returns us to a parable of Jesus.

Macpherson will save us from the Flood by pulling each of us inside
out through the navel. Our beasts will then be able to come aboard us,
and the jaunty pararhyme of "tickets" and "sockets" augments the rush
and splendor. Our beasts externalized come aboard us, and we and they
are safe from the tempest. The reader's solid bottom becomes a rampart. All of existence—past, present, future—depends upon ourselves,
as readers, taking on the role of Noah.

Eight tiny lyrics are then uttered by the Ark. The best of them is the
last, "Ark Parting":

You dreamed it. From my ground
You raised that flood, these fears.
The creatures all but drowned
Fled your well of tears.

Outward the fresh shores gleam
Clear in new-washed eyes.
Fare well. From your dream
I only shall not rise.

The plangency of this is exquisite. I hear in it a voice unlike any
other, and one that will survive.

# Amy Clampitt, "A Hermit Thrush"

I KNEW AMY CLAMPITT ONLY SLIGHTLY, though her life's companion, the legal scholar Harold Korn, had been my close undergraduate
friend at Cornell University. In 1983, when *The Kingfisher* appeared, I
instantly admired her poetry, in part because she was a master of what
Paul Fussell had named as the American Shore Ode. "Beach Glass"
took its place for me with the procession from Walt Whitman's "Sea-
Drift" elegies through Wallace Stevens, T. S. Eliot, and Hart Crane on
to Elizabeth Bishop, May Swenson, A. R. Ammons, and James Wright.
I have written about "Beach Glass" in my book *The Anatomy of Influence* and will not revisit it here. Amy Clampitt's strongest books were
*Westward* (1990) and the finality of *A Silence Opens* (1994). Her most
moving poem remains "A Hermit Thrush" from the volume *Archaic
Figure* (1987):

> Nothing's certain. Crossing, on this longest day,
> the low-tide-uncovered isthmus, scrambling up
> the scree-slope of what at high tide
> will be again an island,
>
> to where, a decade since well-being staked
> the slender, unpremeditated claim that brings us
> back, year after year, lugging the
> makings of another picnic—
>
> the cucumber sandwiches, the sea-air-sanctified
> fig newtons—there's no knowing what the slamming
> seas, the gales of yet another winter
> may have done. Still there,

. . . . . . . . . . . . . .

but, like our own prolonged attachment, holding.
Whatever moral lesson might commend itself,
there's no use drawing one,
there's nothing here

to seize on as exemplifying any so-called virtue
(holding on despite adversity, perhaps) or
any no-more-than-human tendency—
stubborn adherence, say,

to a wholly wrongheaded tenet. Though to
hold on in any case means taking less and less
for granted, some few things seem nearly
certain, as that the longest day

will come again, will seem to hold its breath,
the months-long exhalation of diminishment
again begin. Last night you woke me
for a look at Jupiter,

that vast cinder wheeled unblinking
in a bath of galaxies. Watching, we traveled
toward an apprehension all but impossible
to be held onto—

that no point is fixed, that there's no foothold
but roams untethered save by such snells,
such sailor's knots, such stays
and guy wires as are

mainly of our own devising. From such an
empyrean, aloof seraphic mentors urge us
to look down on all attachment,
on any bonding, as

in the end untenable. Base as it is, from
year to year the earth's sore surface

mends and rebinds itself, however
and as best it can, with

.    .    .    .    .    .    .    .

and what can't finally be mended, the salt air
proceeds to buff and rarefy: the lopped carnage
of the seaward spruce clump weathers
lustrous, to wood-silver.

Little is certain, other than the tide that
circumscribes us that still sets its term
to every picnic—today we stayed too long
again, and got our feet wet—

and all attachment may prove at best, perhaps,
a broken, a much-mended thing. Watching
the longest day take cover under
a monk's-cowl overcast,

with thunder, rain and wind, then waiting,
we drop everything to listen as a
hermit thrush distills its fragmentary,
hesitant, in the end

unbroken music. From what source (beyond us, or
the wells within?) such links perceived arrive—
diminished sequences so uninsistingly
not even human—there's

hardly a vocabulary left to wonder, uncertain
as we are of so much in this existence, this
botched, cumbersome, much-mended,
not unsatisfactory thing.

Amy Clampitt is well aware of the hermit thrush in "When Lilacs
Last in the Dooryard Bloom'd" and in *The Waste Land*. She glides past
these formidable precursors by stationing the unbroken music of her
thrush at the close of this infinitely gentle testament to an attachment

never to end. Fragmentary and hesitant, the thrush's song contrasts with the holding-on, rebinding, breaking, much-mending, mutual existence of Harold Korn and Amy Clampitt.

A student remarked to me that seventy-six lines might seem excessive for hymning even a lifelong attachment. I do not remember replying, but since I was already well past eighty, I probably reflected that in sixty years my student might no longer agree with herself. Even had Hal Korn not been a close friend of my youth, I still believe "A Hermit Thrush" would retain its poignance for me.

I turn to "Voyages," the eighth lyric in the sequence of that title, which is an homage to John Keats:

> On April twenty-seventh, 1932, Hart Crane
> walked to the taffrail of the *Orizaba*,
> took off his coat, and leaped. At seventeen,
> a changeling from among the tire-and-rubber
>
> factories, steel mills, cornfields of the Ohio
> flatland that had absent-mindedly produced him,
> on an enthralled first voyage he'd looked into
> the troughed Caribbean, and called it home.
>
> Back where he'd never been at home, he'd once
> watched the early-morning shift pour down South Main—
> immigrant Greeks eager to be Americans—
> and then tried to imagine Porphyro in Akron
>
> (Greek for "high place"); the casement, the arras,
> the fabricated love nest, the actual sleet storm,
> the owl, the limping hare, the frozen grass,
> Keats's own recurring dream of being warm—
>
> who'd been so often cold he looked with yearning even
> into blacksmiths' fires: "How glorious," he wrote
> of them, shivering (with Stevens) to see the stars put on
> their glittering belts: of what disaster was that
>
> chill, was that salt wind the imminence? The cold—
> a-long-time, lifetime snow man did not know.

Beside the Neva, Osip Mandelstam wrote of the cold,
the December fog-blurs of Leningrad. O to throw

open (he wrote) a window on the Adriatic!—a window
for the deprived of audience, for the unfree
to breathe, to breathe even the bad air of Moscow.
Yet on the freezing pane of perpetuity,

.   .   .   .   .   .   .   .   .   .   .   .   .

The dream of being warm, tattered cargo
brought too late to Italy, a mere dire fistful
of blood (*the sea had soaked his heart through*):
the voyage, every voyage at the end is cruel.

In February 1937, from exile to flatland
Voronezh, a kind of twin of Akron, Mandelstam
wrote, in an almost posthumous whisper, of round
blue bays, of sails descried—scenes parted from

as now his voyage to the bottom of a crueler
obscurity began, whose end only the false-haired
seaweed of an inland shipwreck would register.
Untaken voyages, Lethean cold, O all but unendured

arrivals! Keats's starved stare before the actual,
so long imagined Bay of Naples. The mind's extinction.
Nightlong, sleepless beside the Spanish Steps, the prattle
of poured water. Letters no one will ever open.

It astonishes me that Amy Clampitt intricately weaves together Hart
Crane, John Keats, Wallace Stevens, and Osip Mandelstam in a dozen
quatrains. Keats's dream of being warm becomes Mandelstam's and
links to Hart Crane's sense at seventeen of coming home to the Medi-
terranean, and to Wallace Stevens's vision of the auroras transmuted
into stellar splendor. "The sea had soaked his heart through," George
Chapman's powerful rendering from *Odyssey* V of the death of a ship-

mate of Ulysses, kindled Keats to his own incarnation of the poetical character.

Amy Clampitt found her warmth in poetry and in life. "Voyages," both the sequence and the concluding lyric, charts her own odyssey back to her forerunners. She entitled her book of essays *Predecessors, Et Cetera*. A deep reader and admirer of her work, I am nevertheless aware, as she was, that Keats, Hart Crane, Stevens, Mandelstam constituted a galaxy she could not join. Her persistence and permanence are of another order. She loved Gerard Manley Hopkins, himself a superb amalgam of Keats and Walt Whitman, and did not presume to share his eminence. Yet I go on returning to her poems.

[ *Coda* ]


# In Search of Lost Time

[ *Coda* ]

# IN SEARCH OF LOST TIME

Though I have been reading Proust since I was nineteen and have written about him thrice before, I turn to him now because I have just understood, six years after I began *Possessed by Memory*, that he is more central to my project than anyone else, except for Shakespeare and Dr. Samuel Johnson. What matters most in Proust are the privileged moments, sudden ecstasies of revelation. You can count these many different ways, but they seem to me innumerable.

The great original for most of our theories of time and memory remains Saint Augustine. For Augustine, cognition and love both depend upon the workings of memory. You can see Augustine as the greatest of Christian Platonists, but largely because he identified Christ as the Wisdom of God. Peter Brown, in his great biography *Augustine of Hippo* (1967), demonstrates that the Christ of Augustine's boyhood was very different from our expectations. There were no crucifixes in the fourth century. Christ was the Wisdom of God.

Brian Stock, in his *Augustine the Reader* (1996), argues persuasively that Augustine invented reading, precisely in his conviction that only God was the true reader. That meant that reading well was to imitate God and the angels.

For Augustine, reading was the road for conversion to Christ. That made him skeptical of the reader's ability to interpret correctly. And yet, by inventing autobiographical memory, Augustine was the first to say that only the book could nourish memory and thought.

Wisdom and faith are very different from wisdom and literature. If they are brought together in Augustine, it is in one great outcry, in section 154 of Erich Przywara's *An Augustine Synthesis* (1958):

These days have no true being; they are gone almost before they arrive; and when they come they cannot continue; they press upon one another, they follow the one the other, and cannot check themselves in their course. Of the past nothing is called back again; what is yet to be expected is something which will pass away again; it is not yet possessed, whilst as yet it is not arrived; it cannot be kept when once it is arrived. The Psalmist therefore asks, 'what is the number of my days' (Ps. xxxviii, 5), what *is*, not what is *not*; and (for this confounds me by a still greater and more perplexing difficulty) both *is* and *is not*. For we can neither say that that *is*, which does not continue, nor that it is *not* when it is come and is passing. It is that absolute IS, that true IS, that IS in the strict sense of the word, that I long for, that IS which is in the Jerusalem which is the bride of my Lord, where . . . the day shall not pass away but shall endure, a day which no yesterday precedes nor a morrow ousts. This number of my days, which *is*, I say, make Thou known to me.

When Proust meditates in this mode, he puts his faith in art. Augustine, a lifelong reader and lover of Virgil, nevertheless chooses Jerusalem, the bride of God. In his *Confessions*, composed in Latin from 397 to 400 C.E., he inaugurated the Western tradition of the autobiographical inner life. The book is addressed directly to God. Its material is memory. Augustine distinguishes between his two wills, old carnal and new spiritual.

Augustine pioneers the search for lost time. He seeks for the fact in memory yet is highly aware that the remembering self always disrupts the past. Augustine has a vision of the labyrinth of memory. He speaks of it as a place that is no place. We are given a very difficult distinction among three times: things past that are yet present, things present, future things already present. What is most crucial for literary tradition is what Augustine calls returning moments of spiritual enlightenment, which arrive, as he says, "in a thrust of a trembling glance." We confront here the birth of a major trope, variously termed an epiphany, or a good or privileged moment.

At one time, Augustine and his mother, Monica, spoke to each other about God's eternal Light. In a rapid cognitive illumination, they suddenly were dazzled by the flash of the eternal Wisdom. It departed. And yet it performed a work not only for them but for a myriad of writers, secular and sacred, on to almost our era.

Jean-Jacques Rousseau (1712–78), in his unfinished work *Reveries of a Solitary Walker* (1776–78), perhaps inaugurated the secular epiphany. He was followed by a cascade of German Romantic poets and philosophers, including Schelling, Goethe, and, most powerfully, Hölderlin. What Augustine had called *momentum* (the moment) was termed by Hölderlin and the others *der Augenblick*, a moment of freedom in which the soul returned to ecstasy.

William Blake wrote of what he called the "Moment in each Day that Satan cannot find" that "renovates every Moment of the Day if rightly placed"; or the epiphany "Within a Moment: a Pulsation of the Artery when the Poet's Work is Done" (*Milton* 35.42–45, 29.1–3).

William Wordsworth, who inaugurated modern poetry, is also the pivotal figure in the secularization of the epiphany. He did this by his myth of memory, which turned upon what he called "spots of time." These are flashes of radiance against a darkened background. They give evidences of the power of the poet's mind over a universe of death. For certain moments, they imply that the mind is lord and master, outward sense the servant of its will.

My friend and former student, the late Thomas Weiskel, emphasized the surprising proximity of the "spots of time" to images and memories of death and dying. There is a kind of visionary dreariness in these benign manifestations. Visionary power rises out of the darkness of human mortality. The Romantic Sublime, secular even when the poet professed Christianity, cannot rely upon the Incarnation and the Resurrection.

A humanistic privileged moment has no sanction except its own eloquence and reverberation. Wordsworth had an extraordinary gift for memorable phrasing, the most powerful in the language since Shakespeare and Milton. Though he owed much to both of them, he consciously endeavored to use words that he regarded as being brought down to the earth and that would speak of us as we are. This was something of a self-deluded idealism, since Wordsworth remained more Miltonic than Shakespearean. Many great poets have insisted that they would use a fresh language, available to all women and men. More often than not, this is a noble fantasy. Walt Whitman, strongest of American poets, asserted that he wished to be read by common, uneducated persons. And yet he remains an elitist poet, subtle, evasive, and difficult.

Shakespeare is always the exception, but, then, he remains an inexplicable miracle. The Good Moment was then transformed by John Ruskin and Robert Browning, who then bequeathed it to Walter Pater, whose Privileged Moments deeply affected all of what we used to call Modernism. Among Pater's progeny were Oscar Wilde, William Butler Yeats, James Joyce, Virginia Woolf, and, despite himself, T. S. Eliot. In the United States, there is a strong element of Pater in Wallace Stevens and Hart Crane.

Samuel Beckett's monograph on Proust is haunted by his master Joyce, but also by the invisible line that goes from Wordsworth to Ruskin, and then from Ruskin to the novelist of *In Search of Lost Time*. Rather mordantly, Beckett terms Proust's privileged moments "fetishes." He lists eleven, but admits incompletion. My friend Roger Shattuck, who died in 2005 at the age of eighty-two, was a more accurate guide to Proust's epiphanies than the magnificent Samuel Beckett. In Shattuck's book *Proust's Binoculars* (1963), he makes a superb observation:

It might be possible now to define *A la recherche* as the dramatization of a set of moral and epistemological truths; but the weakest part of that description is the word "dramatization." Marcel's drama is so slow-paced, so extended and even attenuated between beginning and end, that we can use the word only in a restricted, nearly Oriental sense of an inward drama expressed in a few highly ritualized gestures. And the Oriental aspect of *A la recherche* goes very deep. A multiplicity of images, laws, and fleeting illuminations lie along the course of our existence, but only sustained and disciplined pursuit of ourselves inwardly, only life truly lived leads to wisdom. One of the greatest achievements in the Western tradition of the novel, *A la recherche* also joins the Oriental tradition of works of meditation and initiation into the mysteries of life. We can read as far into it as our age and understanding allow. A dedicated *mondain* in Paris for half his life, Proust went on to probe far beyond the culture that reared him, and far beyond Catholicism, Judaism, and idealist philosophy.

Like Shattuck, I would not suggest that Marcel Proust had ever read the *Bhagavad-Gita*. I cannot read Sanskrit and have to rely upon translations and commentaries. R. C. Zaehner, in his translation (1969), gives an elaborate commentary based upon the original sources. I have a fondness for the version by Barbara Stoler Miller (1986). Brooding on the little I can apprehend in the *Bhagavad-Gita*, I tend to remember the three categories: lucidity, passion, dark inertia. The *Gita* defines memory as an intuition of the past transcending individual experience. It is not the recall of past happenings but the revival of latent impressions abandoned by earlier perceptions. Time in the *Gita* also means death.

Proust, as his novel ends, has moved from dark inertia through passion into a sublime lucidity. His search for lost time is very close to the *Gita*. And for him also, time is both liberation and death. The most remarkable of the Good Moments has to be quoted in full:

Upheavel of my entire being. On the first night, as I was suffering from cardiac fatigue, I bent down slowly and cautiously to take off my boots, trying to master my pain. But scarcely had I touched the topmost button than my chest swelled, filled with an unknown, a divine presence, I was shaken with sobs, tears streamed from my eyes. The being who had come to my rescue, saving me from barrenness of spirit, was the same who, years before, in a moment of identical distress and loneliness, in a moment when I had nothing left of myself, had come in and had restored me to myself, for that being was myself and something more than me (the container that is greater than the contained and was bringing it to me). I had just perceived, in my memory, stooping over my fatigue, the tender, preoccupied, disappointed face of my grandmother, as she had been on that first evening of our arrival, the face not of that grandmother whom I had been astonished and remorseful at having so little missed, and who I had nothing in common with save her name, but of my real grandmother, of whom, for the first time since the afternoon of her stroke in the Champs-Elysees, I now recaptured the living reality in a complete and involuntary recollection. This reality does not exist for us so long as it has not been recreated by our thought (otherwise men who have been engaged in a titanic struggle would all of them be great epic poets); and thus, in my wild desire to fling myself into her arms, it was only at that moment—more than a year after her burial, because of the anachronism which so often prevents the calendar of facts from corresponding to the calendar of feelings—that I became conscious that she was dead. I had often spoken about her since then, and thought of her also, but behind my words and thoughts, those of an ungrateful, selfish, cruel young man, there had never been anything that resembled my grandmother, because, in my frivolity, my love of pleasure, my familiarity with the spectacle of her ill health, I retained within me only in a potential state the memory of what she had been. No matter at what moment we consider it, our total soul has only a more or less fictitious value, in spite of the rich inventory of its assets, for now some, now others are unrealizable, whether they are real riches or those of the imagination—in my own case, for example, not only of the ancient name of Guermantes but those, immeasurably graver, of the true memory of my grandmother. For with the perturbations of memory are linked the intermittencies of the heart. It is, no doubt, the existence of our body, which we may compare to a vase enclosing our spiritual nature, that induces us to suppose that all our inner wealth, our past joys, all our sorrows, are perpetually in our possession. Perhaps it is equally inexact to suppose that they escape or return. In any case if they remain within us, for most of the time it is in an unknown region where they are of no use to us, and where even the most ordinary are crowded out by memories of a different kind, which preclude any simultaneous occurrence of them in our consciousness. But if the context of sensations in which they are preserved is recaptured, they acquire in turn the same power of expelling everything that is incompatible with them, of installing alone in us the self that originally lived them. Now, inasmuch as the self that I had just suddenly become once again had not existed since that evening long ago when my grandmother had undressed me after my arrival at Balbec, it was quite naturally, not at the end of the day that had just passed, of which that self knew nothing, but—as though Time were to consist of a series of different and parallel lines—without any solution of continuity, immediately after that first evening at Balbec long ago, that I clung to the minute in which my grandmother had stooped over me. The self that I then was, that had disappeared for so long, was once again so close to me that I seemed still to hear the words that had just been spoken, although they were now no more than a phantasm, as a man who is half awake thinks he can still make, out close, by the sound of his receding dream. I was now solely the person who had sought a refuge in his grandmother's arms, had sought to obliterate the traces of his sorrows by smothering her with kisses, that person whom I should have had as much difficulty in imagining when I was one or other of those that for some time past I had successively been as now I should have had in making the sterile effort to experience the desires and joys of one of those that for a time at least I no longer was. I remembered how, an hour before the moment when my grandmother had stooped in her dressing-gown to unfasten my boots, as I wandered along the stiflingly hot street, past the pastry-cook's, I had felt that I could never, in my need to feel her arms round me, live through the hour that I had to spend without her. And now that this same need had reawakened, I knew that I might wait hour after hour, that she would never again be by my side. I had only just discovered this because I had only just, on feeling her for the first time alive, real, making my heart swell to breaking-point, on finding her at last, learned that I had lost her forever. Lost forever; I could not understand, and I struggled to endure the anguish of this contradiction: on the one hand an existence, a tenderness, surviving in me as I had known them, that is to say created for me, a love which found in me so totally its complement, its goal, its constant lodestar, that the genius of great men, all the genius that might have existed from the beginning of the world, would have been less precious to my grandmother than a single one of my defects; and on the other hand, as soon as I had relived that bliss, as though it were present, feeling it shot through by the certainty, throbbing like a recurrent pain, of an annihilation that had effaced my image of that tenderness, had destroyed that existence, retrospectively abolished our mutual predestination, made of my grandmother, at the moment when I had found her again as in a mirror, a mere stranger whom chance had allowed to spend a few years with me, as she might have done with anyone else, but to whom, before and after those years, I was and would be nothing.

"The Intermittencies of the Heart," between chapters 1 and 2
in *Sodom and Gomorrah*, Part Two

I wrote about this passage fifteen years ago and confessed how it hurt me. The deaths of those we love bring an immediate grief, and yet mourning, unless it continues into a condition of melancholia, frequently heals itself over time. Proust is far subtler than that. He deals with the guilt of having forgotten and the mingled shock and joy of suddenly remembering a love that nurtured him. I recall how baffled I was that something so universal was given voice almost uniquely by Proust.

At seventy-two I had experienced many losses, but at eighty-seven I feel abandoned by virtually everyone I loved in my own generation. They are all gone, perhaps into a world of light, or a final darkness. In the last month, a great poet and a magnificent critic have departed, both of them friends for more than sixty years.

I love Proust but cannot incarnate his wisdom. He was the lucidity of his city and should be the joy of his nation. Sometimes at night my parents enter my dreams. It is two-thirds of a century since they died. Reading Proust, I try to realize an intermittence of the heart, yet it is still beyond me. Dante believed that the perfect age was eighty-one, nine nines. He died at fifty-six. At eighty-one he expected to realize everything, but it was not to be. I remember that at eighty-one I was four months in a hospital, having broken my back. At eighty-seven I struggle to recover from recent operations. Sometimes I play with the idea that if I reach ninety I will begin to understand much that is veiled from me. But I am a reader and a teacher, and not a creator. Vico said that we only know what we ourselves have made.

Proust's knowledge is *In Search of Lost Time.* Even seventy years of rereading have not given me a complete grasp of that creation. Returning to Proust is like again experiencing Dante, Cervantes, Montaigne, Shakespeare, Tolstoy, Joyce. The Proustian difference is that his principal characters—Charlus, Morel, Albertine, Swann, the Duchesse de Guermantes, Saint-Loup, Françoise, Odette, Gilberte, Bloch, Marcel's mother, most of all the unnamed narrator finally revealed as Marcel—change more radically for me than even the great Shakespearean figures. *In Search of Lost Time* is a whirligig of shifting perspectives. We see and hear Charlus, a cultured noble of high rank, decline into a pathetic victim of his masochistic fantasies. At moments he seems grotesque. At other times there are touches of his ebbing grandeur. Rereading now, I wince where once I felt a deep sympathy.

. . .

I sense that I am still in my own alternations of passion and dark inertia. When the narrator and Marcel fuse, at the end of *Time Regained*, the authorial voice achieves lucidity:

> I understood now why it was that the Duc de Guermantes, who to my surprise, when I had seen him sitting on a chair, had seemed to me so little aged although he had so many more years beneath him than I had, had presently, when he rose to his feet and tried to stand firm upon them, swayed backwards and forwards upon legs as tottery as those of some old archbishop with nothing solid about his person but his metal crucifix, to whose support there rushes a mob of sturdy young seminarists, and had advanced with difficulty, trembling like a leaf, upon the almost unmanageable summit of his eighty-three years, as though men spend their lives perched upon living stilts which never cease to grow until sometimes they become taller than church steeples, making it in the end both difficult and perilous for them to walk and raising them to an eminence from which suddenly they fall. And I was terrified by the thought that the stilts beneath my own feet might already have reached that height; it seemed to me that quite soon now I might be too weak to maintain my hold upon a past which already went down so far. So, if I were given long enough to accomplish my work, I should not fail, even if the effect were to make them resemble monsters, to describe men as occupying so considerable a place, compared with the restricted place which is reserved for them in space, a place on the contrary prolonged past measure, for simultaneously, like giants plunged into the years, they touch the distant epochs through which they have lived, between which so many days have come to range themselves—in Time.

Like so many other people my age, I dread falling every time I get up to walk. I have lost several friends to falling and experienced four terrible falls myself. This final passage in Proust moves me on several levels. Aside from the merely personal, it makes me reflect on my desire to go on teaching and writing as a lesser instance of Proust's drive toward searching for lost time. Though Proust had a Jewish mother, he seems to me neither Christian nor Jewish. His wisdom is his own, and though it has an analogue in Shakespeare's detachment, I think it is indeed closer to Hindu philosophy. There is a curious difficulty here. All of Proust turns upon erotic relationships, yet in time all of these are renounced or abandoned. And yet, without them, *In Search of Lost Time* could not have been composed. Marcel observes that Albertine fertilized him through unhappiness.

After many readings, one learns that Proust essentially is a great comic writer. He defines friendship as being "halfway between physical exhaustion and mental boredom." Again, he remarks that being in love is "a striking example of how little reality means to us." He exalted "the perfect lie" as our only chance for the revelation of surprise. I treasure his reflection that death cures us of the desire for immortality.

Krishna's final teaching in the *Bhagavad-Gita* instructs the warrior Arjuna in the natural qualities of all humans and gods:

Arjuna, now hear about joy,
the three ways of finding delight
through practice
that brings an end to suffering.

The joy of lucidity
at first seems like poison
but is in the end like ambrosia,
from the calm of self-understanding.

The joy that is passionate
at first seems like ambrosia
when sense encounter sense objects,
but in the end it is like poison.

The joy arising from sleep,
laziness, and negligence,
self-deluding from beginning to end,
is said to be darkly inert.

There is no being on earth
or among the gods in heaven

free from the triad of qualities
that are born of nature.

Translated by Barbara Stoler Miller

Palpably, this is Proustian to the core. And yet it darkens as much as illuminates if we interpret Marcel's development as being from dark inertia in interplay with passion, to the sublimation of both in indubitable lucidity. The vast cavalcade of his characters does not follow so clear a pattern. Marcel eventually will become Proust, yet we never see precisely how he emerges from the labyrinth of his self.

Frequently, in teaching Shakespeare, which I have done for more than sixty years, I have the realization or fantasy that simultaneously I know both everything and nothing about Hamlet, Falstaff, Cleopatra, Lear, Iago, Macbeth, and the other major characters. I have never taught Proust, but I read him and meditate upon him endlessly. How much do I know about the narrator, Charlus, Swann, Odette, Gilberte, Albertine, Saint-Loup, Marcel's mother and grandmother, Françoise, Bloch, Bergotte, Cottard, Elstir, Oriane Guermantes, Basin Guermantes, Norpois, Morel, Madame Verdurin, the Marquise de Villeparisis? More than nothing, but rather less than everything that matters most.

Proust's scholars rightly tend to agree that psychological reduction is useless in apprehending his characters. That is one of his prime Shakespearean aspects. A Proustian reading of Freud is more productive than any psychoanalytical investigation of Charlus or Albertine. I have never found a word to describe Shakespeare's stance toward his characters. You can call him detached or impartial, but that is very limited. Proust loves his characters, even Charlus. There is an eloquent passage in Part One of *Sodom and Gomorrah:*

Their honour precarious, their liberty provisional, lasting only until the discovery of their crime; their position unstable, like that of the poet one day fêted in every drawing-room and applauded in every theater in London, and the next driven from every lodging, unable to find a pillow upon which to lay his head, turning the mill like Samson and saying like him: "The two sexes shall die, each in a place apart!"; excluded even, except on the days of general misfortune when the majority rally round the victim as the Jews round Dreyfus, from the sympathy—at times from the

society—of their fellows, in whom they inspire only disgust at seeing themselves as they are, portrayed in a mirror which, ceasing
to flatter them, accentuates every blemish that they have refused
to observe in themselves, and makes them understand that what
they have been calling their love (and to which, playing upon the
word, they have by association annexed all that poetry, painting,
music, chivalry, asceticism have contrived to add to love) springs
not from an ideal of beauty which they have chosen but from an
incurable disease; like the Jews again (save some who will associate only with those of their race and have always on their lips the
ritual words and the accepted pleasantries), shunning one another,
seeking out those who are most directly their opposite, who do
not want their company, forgiving their rebuffs, enraptured by
their condescensions; but also brought into the company of their
own kind by the ostracism to which they are subjected, the opprobrium into which they have fallen, having finally been invested, by
a persecution similar to that of Israel, with the physical and moral
characteristic of race, sometimes beautiful, often hideous, finding
(in spite of all the mockery with one who, more closely integrated
with, better assimilated to the opposing race, is in appearance
relatively less inverted, heaps upon one who has remained more
so) a relief in frequenting the society of their kind, and even some
support in their existence, so much so that, while steadfastly deny-
ing that they are a race (the name of which is vilest of insults), they
readily unmask those who succeed in concealing the fact that they
belong to it, with a view less to injuring them, though they have
no scruple about that, than to excusing themselves, and seeking
out (as a doctor seeks out cases of appendicitis) cases of inversion
in history, taking pleasure in recalling that Socrates was one of
themselves, as the Jews claim that Jesus was one of them, without reflecting that there were no abnormal people when homo-
sexuality was the norm, no anti-Christians before Christ, that the
opprobrium alone makes the crime because it has allowed to survive only those who remained obdurate to every warning, to every
example, to every punishment, by virtue of an innate disposition
so peculiar that it is more repugnant to other men (even though it
may be accompanied by high moral qualities) than certain other
vices which exclude those qualities, such as theft, cruelty, breach

of faith, vices better understood and so more readily excused by the generality of men; less suspected than that of the Lodges, for it rests upon an identity of taste, needs, habits, dangers, apprenticeship, knowledge, traffic, vocabulary, and one in which even members who do not wish to know one another recognize one another immediately by natural or conventional, involuntary or deliberate signs. . . .

This extraordinary passage is a hymn to the two lost legions, homosexuals and Jews. The poet of the first sentence is Oscar Wilde, sublime genius and eternal martyr. The vision of Wilde as Samson turning the mill at Gaza quotes from Alfred de Vigny's "La Colère de Samson": "Les deux sexes mourront chacun de son côté" ("The two sexes shall die, each in a place apart!"). For Proust, the two sexes are one, even if they die in diverse regions.

Proust came to believe that in the double aspect of time, destruction and creation, he had found his quest for meaning fulfilled. To understand death was to understand his calling as a novelist. At once he beheld the spirit realized in the fusion of love and pain. Like Schopenhauer, Proust avoids mere concepts. Wittgenstein, in the mode of Schopenhauer, observed, "What the solipsist *says* is wrong but what the solipsist *means* is right." Proust is a solipsist only in that sense. He pursues the world as will and idea and creates a new world as his Representation.

Samuel Beckett related Proust's art to Schopenhauer's remark that the artist contemplates the world independently of the rules of reason. On that basis, Beckett concluded that in Proust there is no collapse of the will. There is a subtle element in Proust's will that refuses power over the interpretation of his own novel.

Meditating upon Albertine, long after her death, Marcel says of himself, "I was not one man only, but as it were the march-past of a composite army in which there were passionate men—jealous men not one of whom was jealous of the same woman." There is no cure for jealousy in Proust or in our lives. What saves Marcel from his dark inertia and useless passion is the lucidity that comes in his privileged moments:

But it is sometimes just at the moment when we think that every-thing is lost that the intimation arrives which may save us; one has knocked at all the doors which lead nowhere, and then one stumbles without knowing it on the only door through which one can enter—which one might have sought in vain for a hun-dred years—and it opens of its own accord.

Revolving the gloomy thoughts which I have just recorded, I had entered the courtyard of the Guermantes mansion and in my absent-minded state I had failed to see a car which was coming towards me; the chauffeur gave a shout and I just had time to step out of the way, but as I moved sharply backwards I tripped against the uneven paving-stones in front of the coach-house. And at the moment when, recovering my balance, I put my foot on a stone which was slightly lower than its neighbour, all my discourage-ment vanished and in its place was that same happiness which at various epochs of my life had been given to me by the sight of trees which I had thought that I recognised in the course of a drive near Balbec, by the sight of the twin steeples of Martinville, by the flavor of a madeleine dipped in tea, and by all those other sensations of which I have spoken and of which the last works of Vinteuil had seemed to me to combine the quintessential charac-ter. Just as, at the moment when I tasted the madeleine, all anxiety about the future, all intellectual doubts had disappeared, so now those that a few seconds ago had assailed me on the subject of the reality of my literary gifts, the reality even of literature, were removed as if by magic.

I had followed no new train of reasoning, discovered no deci-sive argument, but the difficulties which had seemed insoluble a moment ago had lost all importance. The happiness which I had just felt was unquestionably the same as that which I had felt when I tasted the madeleine soaked in tea. But if on that occasion I had put off the task of searching for the profounder causes of my emo-tion, this time I was determined not to resign myself to a failure to understand them. The emotion was the same; the difference, purely material, lay in the images evoked: a profound azure intoxi-cated my eyes, impressions of coolness, of dazzling light, swirled round me and in my desire to seize them—as afraid to move as I had been on the earlier occasion when I had continued to savour

the taste of the madeleine while I tried to draw into my consciousness whatever it was that it recalled to me—I continued, ignoring
the evident amusement of the great crowd of chauffeurs, to stagger as I had staggered a few seconds ago, with one foot on the
higher paving-stone and the other on the lower. Every time that I
merely repeated this physical movement, I achieved nothing; but
if I succeeded, forgetting the Guermantes party, in recapturing
what I had felt when I first placed my feet on the ground in this
way, again the dazzling and indistinct vision fluttered near me, as
if to say: "Seize me as I pass if you can, and try to solve the riddle
of happiness which I set you." And almost at once I recognised
the vision: it was Venice, of which my efforts to describe it and
the supposed snapshot taken by my memory had never told me
anything, but which the sensation which I had once experienced
as I stood upon two uneven stones in the baptistery of St. Mark's
had, recurring a moment ago, restored to me complete with all
the other sensations linked on that day to that particular sensation, all of which had been waiting in their place—from which
with imperious suddenness a chance happening had caused them
to emerge—in the series of forgotten days. In the same way the
taste of the little madeleine had recalled Combray to me. But why
had the images of Combray and of Venice, at these two different
moments, given me a joy which was like a certainty and which
sufficed, without any other proof, to make death a matter of indif-
ference to me?

Still asking myself this question, and determined today to find
the answer to it, I entered the Guermantes mansion, because
always we give precedence over the inner task that we have to
perform to the outward role which we are playing, which was, for
me at this moment, that of guest. But when I had gone upstairs,
a butler requested me to wait for a few minutes in a little sitting-
room, next to the room used as a library, next to the room where
the refreshments were being served, until the end of the piece of
music which was being played, the Princess having given orders
for the doors to be kept shut during its performance. And at that
very moment a second intimation came to reinforce the one
which had been given to me by the two uneven paving-stones
and to exhort me to persevere in my task. A servant, trying unsuc-

cessfully not to make a noise, chanced to knock a spoon against a plate and again that same species of happiness which had come to me from the uneven paving-stones poured into me; the sensation was again of great heat, but entirely different: heat combined with a whiff of smoke and relieved by the cool smell of a forest background; and I recognised that what seemed to me now so delightful was that same row of trees which I had found tedious both to observe and to describe but which I had found just now for a moment, in a sort of daze—I seemed to be in the railway carriage again, opening a bottle of beer—supposed to be before my eyes, so forcibly had the identical noise of the spoon knocking against the plate given me, until I had had time to remember where I was, the illusion of the noise of the hammer with which a railway man had done something to a wheel of the train while we stopped near the little wood. And then it seemed as though the signs which were to bring me, on this day of all days, out of my disheartened state and restore to me faith in literature, were thronging eagerly about me, for, a butler who had long been in the service of the Prince de Guermantes having recognised me and brought me in the library where I was waiting, so that I might not have to go to the buffet, a selection of petits fours and a glass of orangeade, I wiped my mouth with the napkin which he had given me; and instantly, as though I had been the character in the *Arabian Nights* who unwittingly accomplishes the very rite which can cause to appear, visible to him alone, a docile genie ready to convey him to a great distance, a new vision of azure passed before my eyes, but an azure that this time was pure and saline and swelled into blue and bosomy undulations, and so strong was this impression that the moment to which I was transported seemed to me to be the present moment: more bemused than on the day when I had wondered whether I was really going to be received by the Princess de Guermantes or whether everything round me would collapse, I thought that the servant had just opened the window on the beach and that all things invited me to go down and stroll along the promenade while the tide was high, for the napkin which I had used to wipe my mouth had precisely the same degree of stiffness and starchedness as the towel with which I had found it so awkward to dry my face as I stood in front of

the window on the first day of arrival at Balbec, and this napkin
now, in the library of the Prince de Guermantes's house, unfolded
for me—concealed within its smooth surfaces and its folds—the
plumage of an ocean green and blue like the tail of a peacock. And
what I found myself enjoying was not merely these colours but a
whole instant of my life on whose summit they rested, an instant
which had been no doubt an aspiration towards them and which
some feeling of fatigue or sadness had perhaps prevented me from
enjoying Balbec but which now, freed from what is necessarily
imperfect in external perception, pure and disembodied, caused
me to swell with happiness.

*Time Regained*

Proust's epiphanies, unlike everything before them except for Shakespeare, are tragicomic. From Marcel's perspective, they are a kind of
grace, but Marcel is not yet Proust. What would Saint Augustine,
Goethe, Wordsworth, Ruskin, Walter Pater have made of degrees of
stiffness and starchedness in a towel? Joyce, Beckett, and Kafka are
perhaps closer to Proust's good moments, since they too are tragico-
medians of the awakened spirit.

In my long life I can recall only two or three moments from early youth
in which I was caught up in a sudden radiance. They seem now to be
heretical intimations of a lost gnosis. Proust's crucial stimulus was John
Ruskin's gift for experiencing intimations of immortality.

Why did Proust find his earlier self in Ruskin? John Ruskin died
in 1900. His beautiful and fragmentary autobiography *Præterita* was
published posthumously in 1908. Proust read it, for his command of
Ruskin was absolute, extending even to the extravagant *The Queen of
the Air. Præterita* is the most Proustian of Ruskin's works. It also tells us
that the only paradises are the ones we have lost.

Proust's reaction to Ruskin's death was to say, "When I see how
mightily this dead man lives . . . I know how slight a thing death is."
Proust had translated two of Ruskin's books, and he argued with friends
that Ruskin far outshone Walter Pater. His worship of Ruskin never
ended; he made the charming remark that he did not claim to know
English but that he did claim to know Ruskin.

The last words that Ruskin wrote for publication form the passage that concludes *Præterita:*

86. How things bind and blend themselves together! The last time I saw the Fountain of Trevi, it was from Arthur's father's room—Joseph Severn's, where we both took Joanie to see him in 1872, and the old man made a sweet drawing of his pretty daughter-in-law, now in her schoolroom; he himself then eager in finishing his last picture of Marriage in Cana, which he had caused to take place under a vine trellis, and delighted himself by painting the crystal and ruby glittering of the changing rivulet of water out of the Greek vase, glowing into wine. Fonte Branda I last saw with Charles Norton, under the same arches where Dante saw it. We drank of it together, and walked together that evening on the hills above, where the fireflies among the scented thickets shone fitfully in the still undarkened air. *How* they shone! moving like fine-broken starlight through the purple leaves. How they shone! through the sunset that faded into thunderous night as I entered Siena three days before, the white edges of the mountainous clouds still lighted from the west, and the openly golden sky calm behind the Gate of Siena's heart, with its still golden words, "Cor magis tibi Sena pandit," and the fireflies everywhere in sky and cloud rising and falling, mixed with the lightning, and more intense than the stars.

Brantwood,
June 19th, 1889.

My friend William Arrowsmith, who died twenty-five years ago at the age of sixty-seven, wrote an eloquent essay "Ruskin's Fireflies" (1982). Arrowsmith emphasized that fireflies, an obsessive trope in Ruskin, were emblems both of joy and of menace. Increasingly, Ruskin's thwarted love for Rose La Touche assimilated the fireflies to Dante's *Inferno*, where in canto 17, the usurers are burned by flakes of fire. I cannot recall fireflies anywhere in Proust's vast novel, and, unlike Ruskin, he was not haunted by Dante. If any precursor made him anxious, it would have been Baudelaire. Proust, in a late essay, ranked Baudelaire with Alfred de Vigny as the strongest poets of the nineteenth century. Baudelaire's vision of Paris may have inspired the swerve by which Proust chose the aristocracy as his milieu, in contrast. Both men were inescapably bound to their mothers, but Proust was able to enjoy his mother's undivided love.

Proust spiritually concludes *In Search of Lost Time* with a glorious passage beyond anxiety:

> And I observed in passing that for the work of art which I now, though I had not yet reached a conscious resolution, felt myself ready to undertake, this distinctness of different events would entail very considerable difficulties. For I should have to execute the successive parts of my work in a succession of different materials; what would be suitable for mornings beside the sea or afternoons in Venice would be quite wrong if I wanted to depict those evenings at Rivebelle when, in the dining-room that opened on to the garden, the heat began to resolve into fragments and sink back into the ground, while a sunset glimmer still illumined the roses on the walls of the restaurant and the last water-colours of the day were still visible in the sky—this would be a new and distinct material, of a transparency and a sonority that were special, compact, cool after warmth, rose-pink.
>
> Over all these thoughts I skimmed rapidly, for another inquiry demanded my attention more imperiously, the inquiry, which on previous occasions I had postponed, into the cause of this felicity which I had just experienced, into the character of the certitude with which it imposed itself. And this cause I began to divine as I compared these diverse happy impressions, diverse yet with this in common, that I experienced them at the present moment and at the same time in the context of a distant moment, so that the past was made to encroach upon the present and I was made to doubt whether I was in the one or the other. The truth surely was that the being within me which had enjoyed these impressions had enjoyed them because they had in them something that was common to a day long past and to the present, because in some way they were extra-temporal, and this being made its appearance only when, through one of these identifications of the present with the past, it was likely to find itself in the one and only medium in which it could exist and enjoy the essence of things,

that is to say: outside time. This explained why it was that my anxiety on the subject of my death had ceased at the moment when I had unconsciously recognised the taste of the little madeleine, since the being which at that moment I had been was an extra-temporal being and therefore unalarmed by the vicissitudes of the future. This being had only come to me, only manifested itself outside of activity and immediate enjoyment, on those rare occasions when the miracle of an analogy had made me escape from the present. And only this being had the power to perform that task which had always defeated the efforts of my memory and my intellect, the power to make me rediscover days that were long past, the Time that was Lost.

*Time Regained*

When I stand back and contemplate Proust in relation to such diverse peers as Tolstoy and Walt Whitman, the immediate difference is that he is all flow, no ebb. *In Search of Lost Time* begins to seem an ocean-river relentless and without events. The book moves from perspective to perspective and renders us rapt with the wonder of its optics:

It is one of the faculties of jealousy to reveal to us the extent to which the reality of external facts and the sentiments of the heart are an unknown element which lends itself to endless suppositions. We imagine that we know exactly what things are and what people think, for the simple reason that we do not care about them. But as soon as we have a desire to know, as the jealous man has, then it becomes a dizzy kaleidoscope in which we can no longer distinguish anything. Had Albertine been unfaithful to me? With whom? In what house? On what day? On the day when she had said this or that to me, when I remembered that I had in the course of it said this or that? I could not tell. Nor did I know what her feelings were for me, whether they were inspired by self-interest or by affection. And all of a sudden I remembered some trivial incident, for instance that Albertine had wished to go to Saint-Mars-le-Vêtu, saying that the name interested her, and perhaps simply because she had made the acquaintance of some peasant-girl who lived there. But it was useless that Aimé should have informed me of what he had learned from the woman at the baths, since Albertine must remain eternally unaware that he had informed me, the need to know having always been exceeded, in my love for Albertine, by the need to show her that I knew; for this broke down the partition of different illusions that stood between us, without having ever had the result of making her love me more, far from it. And now, since she was dead, the second of these needs had been amalgamated with the effect of the first: the need to picture to myself the conversation in which I would have informed her of what I had learned, as vividly as the conversation in which I would have asked her to tell me what I did not know; that is to say, to see her cheeks become plump again, her eyes shed their malice and assume an air of melancholy; that is to say, to love her still and to forget the fury of my jealousy in the despair of my loneliness. The painful mystery of this impossibility of ever making known to her what I had learned and of establishing our relations upon the truth of what I had only just discovered (and would not have been able, perhaps, to discover but for her death) substituted its sadness for the more painful mystery for her conduct. What? To have so desperately desired that Albertine—who no longer existed—should know that I had heard the story of the baths! This again was one of the consequences of our inability, when we have to consider the fact of death, to picture ourselves the person who had concealed from me that she had assignations with women at Balbec, who imagined that she had succeeded in keeping me in ignorance of them. When we try to consider what will happen to us after our own death, is it not still our living self which we mistakenly project at that moment? And is it much more absurd, when all is said, to regret that a woman who no longer exists is unaware that we have learned what she was doing six years ago than to desire that of ourselves, who will be dead, the public shall still speak with approval a century hence? If there is more real foundation in the latter than in the former case, the regrets of my retrospective jealousy proceeded none the less from the same optical error as in other men the desire for posthumous fame. And yet, if this impression of the solemn finality of my separation from Albertine had momentarily supplanted my idea of her misdeeds, it only succeeded in aggravating them by bestowing upon them an irremediable character. I saw myself astray in life as on an endless beach where I was alone and where, in whatever direction I might turn, I would never meet her.

*The Fugitive*

The Proustian question is: did he ever meet her in the first place? Germaine Bree, who died in 2001 at the age of ninety-three, wisely remarked that Proust divests his characters of everything explicable, so that we have to confront their inner essence, an act that can be performed only by aesthetic vision. The narrator does not achieve that summit until the closing segment of *Time Regained.*

As a lifelong admirer of Proust, I like to compare his capacity for the creation of character with Shakespeare's overwhelming invention of personality. Shakespeare is richer. He does not close off his characters as Proust does. In his cosmos, friendship, love, rivalry, remorse, and self-destruction are abundant. We learn from him that each of us is her or his own worst enemy. Deliberately, Proust excludes all of that. Shakespeare is not in search of lost time.

All of Proust is a sacrifice upon the altar of time. He worships an unknown God who yet is knowable. Curiously, Proust seems a more Biblical writer than Shakespeare or even Tolstoy. That may be partly because he is haunted by the fate of Sodom and Gomorrah. He chronicles the jealousies of the exiles from the Cities of the Plains and intimates that these are more turbulent and creative than the erotic envies of heterosexuals. This becomes yet more complex when he deals with a bisexual figure like Saint-Loup:

> In homosexuals like Saint-Loup the ideal of virility is not the same, but it is just as conventional and just as false. The falsehood consists for them in the fact that they do not want to admit to themselves that physical desire lies at the root of the sentiments to which they ascribe another origin. M. de Charlus had detested effeminacy. Saint-Loup admired the courage of young men, the intoxication of cavalry charges, the intellectual and moral nobility of friendships between man and man, entirely pure friendships, in which each is prepared to sacrifice his life for the other. War, which turns capital cities, where only women remain, into an abomination for homosexuals, is at the same time a story of pas-

sionate adventure for homosexuals if they are intelligent enough
to concoct dream figures, and not enough to see through them,
to recognise their origin, to pass judgment on themselves. So that
while some young men were enlisting simply in order to join in
the latest sport—in the spirit in which one year everybody plays
diabolo—for Saint-Loup, on the other hand, war was the very
ideal which he imagined himself to be pursuing in his desires
(which were in fact much more concrete but were clouded by
ideology), an ideal which he could serve in common with those
whom he preferred to all others, in a purely masculine order of
chivalry, far from women, where he would be able to risk life to
save his orderly and die inspiring a fanatical love in his men. And
this, though there were many elements in his courage, the fact
that he was a great nobleman was one of them, and another, in an
unrecognisable and idealized form, was M. de Charlus's dogma
that it was of the essence of a man to have nothing effeminate
about him. But just as in philosophy and in art ideas acquire their
value only from the manner in which they are developed, and two
analogous ones may differ greatly according to whether they have
been expounded by Xenophon or by Plato, so, while I recognise
how much, in his behaviour, the one has in common with the
other, I admire Saint-Loup, for asking to be sent to the point of
greatest danger, infinitely more than I do M. de Charlus for refusing to wear brightly coloured cravats.

*Time Regained*

I wonder why Proust, who detested public violence, allows the Narrator to admire the courage of a warrior in preference to an aesthetic
sensibility, however depraved? Part of the answer must be that Proust
is both a classical moralist, in the mode of Montaigne, and a wisdom
writer, in the normative tradition of Koheleth. He values courage of any
kind even though his own life and work are founded upon an audacity
peculiar to his own life history. His attachment to his Jewish mother
was absolute. She worried always how he could survive her, so great
was his dependence.

Anyone going on eighty-eight is likely to have lost both parents. My
father died at seventy-three, my mother at eighty-nine. Something in

me became numb after both losses. A kind of exuberance departed and has never returned. Proust died at only fifty-one of pneumonia, after suffering from asthma all his life. The last third of his life took place after his mother's death, and was marked by the heroic creation of *In Search of Lost Time*, from 1909 to the end in 1922. It has to be called valiant, since he labored in exhaustion and illness and endless mourning for his mother. Here is a salient passage from the superb biography *Marcel Proust: A Life* by William C. Carter:

On September 2, Marcel wrote to Anna de Noailles and described his mother in death: "She has died at fifty-six, looking no more than thirty since her illness made her so much thinner and especially since death restored to her the youthfulness of the day before her sorrows; she hadn't a single white hair. She takes away my life with her, as Papa had taken away hers." Marcel explained that because his mother had not given up "her Jewish religion on marrying Papa, because she regarded it as a token of respect for her parents, there will be no church, simply at the house tomorrow Thursday at 12 o'clock . . . and the cemetery. . . . Today I have her still, dead but still receiving my caresses. And then I shall never have her again." Reynaldo Hahn, whose memoirs are strangely reticent about his famous friend, recorded this scene of Marcel grieving by his mother's body: "I still see him by Mme Proust's bed, weeping and smiling through his tears at her body."

Sometimes I interpolate reading Proust with going back to Freud's grand essay "Mourning and Melancholia." A kind of dialogue commences between the two until it becomes a dialogue of one. *In Search of Lost Time* is ultimately tragicomic, and yet, in a more immediate sense, it performs the work of mourning. This is more than the mourning for Marcel's mother. It is a celebratory lamentation for the look of things:

Certain people, whose minds are prone to mystery, like to believe that objects retain something of the eyes which have looked at them, that old buildings and pictures appear to us not as they originally were but beneath a perceptible veil woven for them over the centuries by the love and contemplation of millions of admirers. This fantasy, if you transpose it into the domain of what

is for each one of us the sole reality, the domain of his own sensibility, becomes the truth. In that sense and in that sense alone (but
it is a far more important one than the other), a thing which we
have looked at in the past brings back to us, if we see it again, not
only the eyes with which we looked at it but all the images with
which at the time those eyes were filled. For things—and among
them a book in a red binding—as soon as we have perceived them
are transformed within us into something immaterial, something
of the same nature as all our preoccupations and sensations of
that particular time, with which, indissolubly, they blend. A name
read long ago in a book contains within its syllables the strong
wind and brilliant sunshine that prevailed while we were reading it. And this is why the kind of literature which contents itself
with "describing things," with giving of them merely a miserable
abstract of lines and surfaces, is in fact, though it calls itself realist,
the furthest removed from reality and has more than any other
the effect of saddening and impoverishing us, since it abruptly
severs all communication of our present self both with the past,
the essence of which is preserved in things, and with the future,
in which things incite us to enjoy the essence of the past a second
time. Yet it is precisely this essence that an art worthy of the name
must seek to express; then at least, if it fails, there is a lesson to be
drawn from its impotence (whereas from the successes of realism
there is nothing to be learnt), the lesson that this essence is, in
part, subjective and incommunicable.

*Time Regained*

"Essence" here conveys the transformation of impressionism into
knowledge. Proust's Ruskinian heritage is affirmed and transcended by
a memory that will not yield to time. The Narrator's authentic respect
for old age is a direct consequence:

And now I began to understand what old age was—old age, which
perhaps of all the realities is the one of which we preserve for
longest in our life a purely abstract conception, looking at calen-
dars, dating our letters, seeing our friends marry and then in their
turn the children of our friends, and yet, either from fear or from
sloth, not understanding what all this means, until the day when

we behold an unknown silhouette, like that of M. d'Argencourt, which teaches us that we are living in a new world; until the day when a grandson of a woman we once knew, a young man whom instinctively we treat as a contemporary of ours, smiles as though we were making fun of him because to him it seems that we are old enough to be his grandfather—and I began to understand too what death meant and love and the joys of the spiritual life, the usefulness of suffering, a vocation, etc. For if names had lost most of their individuality for me, words on the other hand now began to reveal their full significance. The beauty of images is situated in front of things, that of ideas behind them. So that the first sort of beauty ceases to astonish us as soon as we have reached the things themselves, but the second is something that we understand only when we have passed beyond them.

The cruel discovery which I had just made could not fail to be of service to me so far as the actual material of my book was concerned. For I had decided that this could not consist uniquely of the full and plenary impressions that were outside time, and amongst those other truths in which I intended to set, like jewels, those of the first order, the ones relating to Time, to Time in which, as in some transforming fluid, men and societies and nations are immersed, would play an important part. I should pay particular attention to those changes which the aspect of living things undergoes, of which every minute I had fresh examples before me, for, whilst all the while thinking of my work, which I now felt to be launched with such momentum that no passing distractions could check its advance, I continued to greet old acquaintances and to enter into conversation with them.

*Time Regained*

Of all the novels I have read, I now find, in my own old age, the two most eminent to be Samuel Richardson's *Clarissa* (1748) and *In Search of Lost Time*. They are about equal in their profound apprehension of human nature. If I had to choose between them, it would be Richardson, but only because Clarissa Harlowe and Lovelace, who rapes her and finally dies in a duel with her kinsman, are both more vital beings than even the Narrator (or Marcel) and Swann, Charlus, Albertine, and the other marvelous characters of *In Search of Lost Time*.

Proust had no anxieties in regard to the French tradition of the novel. He admired Stendhal, Balzac, and Flaubert, but owed much less to them than he did to Ruskin. Proust's truth is compounded of perception, involuntary memory, impressionism, a search for spiritual meaning, and a kind of atheistic mysticism:

And then, after I had dwelt for some little time upon these resurrections of the memory, the thought came to me that in another fashion certain obscure impressions, already even at Combray on the Guermantes way, had solicited my attention in a fashion somewhat similar to these reminiscences, except that they concealed within them not a sensation dating from an earlier time, but a new truth, a precious image which I had sought to uncover by efforts of the same kind as those that we make to recall something that we have forgotten as if our finest ideas were like tunes which, as it were, come back to us although we have never heard them before and which we have to make an effort to hear and to transcribe. I remembered—with pleasure because it showed me that already in those days I had been the same and that this type of experience sprang from a fundamental trait in my character, but with sadness also when I thought that since that time I had never progressed— that already at Combray I used to fix before my mind for its attention some image which had compelled me to look at it, a cloud, a triangle, a church spire, a flower, a stone, because I had the feeling that perhaps beneath these signs there lay something of a quite different kind which I must try to discover, some thought which they translated after the fashion of those hieroglyphic characters which at first one might suppose to represent only material objects. No doubt the process of decipherment was difficult, but only by accomplishing it could one arrive at whatever truth there was to read. For the truths which the intellect apprehends directly in the world of full and unimpeded light have something less profound, less necessary than those which life communicates to us against our will in an impression which is material because it enters us through the senses but yet has a spiritual meaning which it is possible for us to extract. In fact, both in the one case and in the other, whether I was concerned with impressions like the one which I had received from the sight of the steeples of Martinville or with reminiscences like that of the unevenness of the two steps or the taste of the madeleine, the task was to interpret the given sensations as signs of so many laws and ideas, by trying to think—that is to say, to draw forth from the shadow—what I had merely felt, by trying to convert it into its spiritual equivalent. And this method, which seemed to me the sole method, what was it but the creation of a work of art? Already the consequences came flooding into my mind: first, whether I considered reminiscences of the kind evoked by the noise of the spoon or the taste of the madeleine, or those truths written with the aid of shapes for whose meaning I searched in my brain, where—church steeples or wild grass growing in a wall—they composed a magical scrawl, complex and elaborate, their essential character was that I was not free to choose them, that such as they were they were given to me. And I realised that this must be the mark of their authenticity. I had not gone in search of the two uneven paving-stones of the courtyard upon which I had stumbled. But it was precisely the fortuitous and inevitable fashion in which this and the other sensations had been encountered that proved the trueness of the past which they brought back to life, of the images which they released, since we feel, with these sensations, the effort that they make to climb back towards the light, feel in ourselves the joy of rediscovering what is real. And here too was the proof of the trueness of the whole picture formed out of those contemporaneous impressions which the first sensation brings back in its train, with those unerring proportions of light and shade, emphasis and omission, memory and forgetfulness to which conscious recollection and conscious observation will never know how to attain.

*Time Regained*

Proust did not come easily to this lucid stance: "For the truths which the intellect apprehends directly in the world of full and unimpeded light have something less profound, less necessary than those which life communicates to us against our will in an impression which is material because it enters us through the senses but yet has a spiritual meaning which it is possible for us to extract." That sentence could exemplify Western and also Eastern wisdom. It adheres to the tradition of Augustinian epiphany, yet is also in consonance with Hindu scriptures.

· · ·

Here is another instance of Proustian epiphany, this one from *Swann's Way:*

> But it was in vain that I lingered beside the hawthorns—breathing
> their invisible and unchanging odour, trying to fix it in my mind
> (which did not know what to do with it), losing it, recapturing it,
> absorbing myself in the rhythm which disposed the flowers here
> and there with a youthful light-heartedness and at intervals as
> unexpected as certain intervals in music—they went on offering
> me the same charm in inexhaustible profusion, but without let-
> ting me delve any more deeply, like those melodies which one can
> play a hundred times in succession without coming any nearer
> to their secret. I turned away from them for a moment so as to
> be able to return to them afresh. My eyes travelled up the bank
> which rose steeply to the fields beyond the hedge, alighting on
> a stray poppy or a few laggard cornflowers which decorated the
> slope here and there like the border of a tapestry whereon may
> be glimpsed sporadically the rustic theme which will emerge tri-
> umphant in the panel itself; infrequent still, spaced out like the
> scattered houses which herald the approach of a village, they
> betokened to me the vast expanse of waving corn beneath the
> fleecy clouds, and the sight of a single poppy hoisting upon its
> slender rigging and holding against the breeze its scarlet ensign,
> over the buoy of rich black earth from which it sprang, made my
> heart beat like that of a traveller who glimpses on some low-lying
> ground a stranded boat which is being caulked and made sea-
> worthy, and cries out, although he has not yet caught sight of it,
> "The Sea!"
>
> And then I returned to the hawthorns, and stood before them
> as one stands before those masterpieces which, one imagines, one
> will be better able to "take in" when one has looked away for a
> moment at something else; but in vain did I make a screen with
> my hands, the better to concentrate upon the flowers, the feeling
> they aroused in me remained obscure and vague, struggling and
> failing to free itself, to float across and become one with them.
> They themselves offered me no enlightenment, and I could not

call upon any other flowers to satisfy this mysterious longing. And then, inspiring me with that rapture which we feel on seeing a work by our favourite painter quite different from those we already know, or, better still, when we are shown a painting of which we have hitherto seen no more than a pencilled sketch, or when a piece of music which we have heard only on the piano appears to us later clothed in all the colours of the orchestra, my grandfather called me to him, and, pointing to the Tansonville hedge, said to me: "You're fond of hawthorns; just look at this pink one—isn't it lovely?"

And it was indeed a hawthorn, but one whose blossom was pink, and lovelier even than the white. It, too, was in holiday attire—for one of those days which are the only true holidays, the holy days of religion, because they are not assigned by some arbitrary caprice, as secular holidays are, to days which are not specially ordained for them, which have nothing about them that is essentially festal—but it was attired even more richly than the rest, for the flowers which clung to its branches, one above another, so thickly as to leave no part of the tree undecorated, like the tassels wreathed about the crook of a rococo shepherdess, were every one of them "in colour," and consequently of a superior quality, by the aesthetic standards of Combray, if one was to judge by the scale of prices at the "stores" in the Square, or at Camus's, where the most expensive biscuits were those whose sugar was pink. For my own part, I set a higher value on cream cheese when it was pink, when I had been allowed to tinge it with crushed strawberries. And these flowers had chosen precisely one of those colours of some edible and delicious thing, or of some fond embellishment of a costume for a major feast, which, inasmuch as they make plain the reason for their superiority, are those whose beauty is most evident to the eyes of children, and for that reason must always seem more vivid and more natural than any other tints, even after the child's mind has realised that they offer no gratification to the appetite and have not been selected by the dressmaker. And indeed I had felt at once, as I had felt with the white blossom, but with even greater wonderment, that it was in no artificial manner, by no device of human fabrication, that the festal intention of these flowers was revealed, but that it was Nature herself who had spontaneously expressed it, with the simplicity of a woman from a village shop labouring at the decoration of a street altar for some procession, by overloading the bush with these little rosettes, almost too ravishing in colour, this rustic pompadour.

Though he died in middle age, Proust never abandoned the eyes of childhood and would have maintained that vision into old age, had he not committed slow suicide through incredible habits, forsaking common sense, of absurd self-medication, outrageous refusals to sleep, and a diet frequently consisting of ice cream and iced beer and nothing more. In his final days, he raced to complete his vast book and essentially accomplished his life's enterprise. I think of Balzac, dead at fifty-one, who killed himself by overwork, lack of sleep, and an ocean of strong coffee, yet who left us his *Human Comedy*. Proust is most himself as he contemplates the beauty of flowers with eyes of a child:

And these flowers had chosen precisely one of those colours of some edible and delicious thing, or of some fond embellishment of a costume for a major feast, which, inasmuch as they make plain the reason for their superiority, are those whose beauty is most evident to the eyes of children, and for that reason must always seem more vivid and more natural than any other tints, even after the child's mind has realised that they offer no gratification to the appetite and have not been selected by the dressmaker.

Childlike vision in Proust is allied to phantasmagoria and to the world of dreams, as in this comic account of Swann's modified delirium:

He was mistaken. He was destined to see her once again, a few weeks later. It was while he was asleep, in the twilight of a dream. He was walking with Mme Verdurin, Dr. Cottard, a young man in a fez whom he failed to identify, the painter, Odette, Napoleon III and my grandfather, along a path which followed the line of the coast, and overhung the sea, now at a great height, now by a few feet only, so that they were continually going up and down. Those of the party who had reached the downward slope were no longer visible to those who were still climbing; what little daylight yet remained was failing, and it seemed as though they were about to be shrouded in darkness. From time to time the waves dashed against the edge, and Swann could feel on his cheek a shower of freezing spray. Odette told him to wipe it off, but he could not, and felt confused and helpless in her company, as well as because he was in his nightshirt. He hoped that, in the darkness, this might pass unnoticed: Mme Verdurin, however, fixed her astonished gaze upon him for an endless moment, during which he saw her face change shape, her nose grow longer, while beneath it there sprouted a heavy moustache. He turned round to look at Odette; her cheeks were pale, with little red spots, her features drawn and ringed with shadows; but she looked back at him with eyes welling with affection, ready to detach themselves like tears and to fall upon his face, and he felt that he loved her so much that he would have liked to carry her off with him at once. Suddenly Odette turned her wrist, glanced at a tiny watch, and said: "I must go." She took leave of everyone in the same formal manner, without taking Swann aside, without telling him where they were to meet that evening, or next day. He dared not ask; he would have liked to follow her, but he was obliged, without turning back in her direction, to answer with a smile some question from Mme Verdurin; but his heart was frantically beating, he felt that he now hated Odette, he would gladly have gouged out those eyes which a moment ago he had loved so much, have crushed those flaccid cheeks. He continued to climb with Mme Verdurin, that is to say to draw further away with each step from Odette, who was going downhill in the other direction. A second passed and it was many hours since she had left them. The painter remarked to Swann that Napoleon III had slipped away immediately after Odette. "They had obviously arranged it between them," he added. "They must have met at the foot of the cliff, but they didn't want to say good-bye together because of appearances. She is his mistress." The strange young man burst into tears. Swann tried to console him. "After all, she's quite right," he said to the young man, drying his eyes for him and taking off the fez to make him feel more at ease. "I've advised her to do it dozens of times. Why be so distressed? He was obviously the man to understand her." So Swann reasoned with himself, for the young man whom he had failed at first to identify was himself too; like certain novelists, he had distributed his own personality between two characters, the one

who was dreaming the dream, and another whom he saw in front
of him sporting a fez.

*Swann's Way*

Napoleon III and Odette form a couple worthy of meditation,
but even that charms me less than the younger Swann sporting a fez
and being advised by the mature Swann that the dubious emperor is
uniquely fitted to comprehend Odette. One can see again that Proust
was a comedian of the spirit.

Yet he was also a deep spirit who could associate the survival of the
inner self with a world founded upon benignity. Here is the death of
the novelist Bergotte in *The Captive:*

The circumstances of his death were as follows. A fairly mild
attack of uraemia had led to his being ordered to rest. But, an art
critic having written somewhere that in Vermeer's *View of Delft*
(lent by the Gallery at The Hague for an exhibition of Dutch
painting), a picture which he adored and imagined that he knew
by heart, a little patch of yellow wall (which he could not remember) was so well painted that it was, if one looked at it by itself,
like some priceless specimen of Chinese art, of a beauty that was
sufficient in itself, Bergotte ate a few potatoes, left the house, and
went to the exhibition. At the first few steps he had to climb, he
was overcome by an attack of dizziness. He walked past several
pictures and was struck by the aridity and pointlessness of such
an artificial kind of art, which was greatly inferior to the sunshine
of a windswept Venetian palazzo, or of an ordinary house by the
sea. At last he came to the Vermeer which he remembered as
more striking, more different from anything else he knew, but in
which, thanks to the critic's article, he noticed for the first time
some small figures in blue, that the sand was pink, and, finally, the
precious substance of the tiny patch of yellow wall. His dizziness
increased; he fixed his gaze, like a child upon a yellow butterfly
that it wants to catch, on the precious little patch of wall. "That's
how I ought to have written," he said. "My last books are too dry,
I ought to have gone over them with a few layers of colour, made
my language precious in itself, like this little patch of yellow wall."
Meanwhile he was not unconscious of the gravity of his condition.

In a celestial pair of scales there appeared to him, weighing down one of the pans, his own life, while the other contained the little patch of wall so beautifully painted in yellow. He felt that he had rashly sacrificed the former for the latter. "All the same," he said to himself, "I shouldn't like to be the headline news of this exhibition for the evening papers."

He repeated to himself: "Little patch of yellow wall, with a sloping roof, little patch of yellow wall." Meanwhile he sank down on to a circular settee; whereupon he suddenly ceased to think that his life was in jeopardy and, reverting to his natural optimism, told himself: "It's nothing, merely a touch of indigestion from those potatoes, which were under-cooked." A fresh attack struck him down; he rolled from the settee to the floor, as visitors and attendants came hurrying to his assistance. He was dead. Dead for ever? Who can say? Certainly, experiments in spiritualism offer us no more proof than the dogmas of religion that the soul survives death. All that we can say is that everything is arranged in this life as though we entered it carrying a burden of obligations contracted in a former life; there is no reason inherent in the conditions of life on this earth that can make us consider ourselves obliged to do good, to be kind and thoughtful, even to be polite, nor for an atheist artist to consider himself obliged to begin over again a score of times a piece of work the admiration aroused by which will matter little to his worm-eaten body, like the patch of yellow wall painted with so much skill and refinement by an artist destined to be for ever unknown and barely identified under the name Vermeer. All these obligations, which have no sanction in our present life, seem to belong to a different world, a world based on kindness, scrupulousness, self-sacrifice, a world entirely different from this one and which we leave in order to be born on this earth, before perhaps returning there to live once again beneath the sway of those unknown laws which we obeyed because we bore their precepts in our hearts, not knowing whose hand had traced them there—those laws to which every profound work of the intellect brings us nearer and which are invisible only—if then!—to fools. So that the idea that Bergotte was not dead for ever is by no means improbable.

They buried him, but all through that night of mourning, in

the lighted shop-windows, his books, arranged three by three, kept vigil like angels with outspread wings and seemed, for him who was no more, the symbol of his resurrection.

Proust was a fierce admirer of Vermeer and implicitly identifies with Bergotte in this beautiful reverie. At this moment in my own old age, this is my favorite passage in Proust. So large was Marcel Proust that he could be at once an atheist and a mystic. Here he writes an elegy for himself. It is *In Search of Lost Time* that burns on in the lighted shop-windows, the intimation of Proust's resurrection.

Is there a relation between a writer's immortality and a reader's search for consolation in regard to the death of friends or family and intimations of the reader's own impending mortality? I cite Samuel Johnson as the best guide I know here:

> Nothing is more evident than that the decays of age must terminate in death; yet there is no man, says Tully, who does not believe that he may yet live another year; and there is none who does not, upon the same principle, hope another year for his parent or his friend; but the fallacy will be in time detected; the last year, the last day must come. It has come and is past. The life which made my own life pleasant is at an end, and the gates of death are shut upon my prospects.
>
> The loss of a friend upon whom the heart was fixed, to whom every wish and endeavour tended, is a state of dreary desolation in which the mind looks abroad impatient of itself, and finds nothing but emptiness and horror. The blameless life, the artless tenderness, the pious simplicity, the modest resignation, the patient sickness, and the quiet death, are remembered only to add value to the loss, to aggravate regret for what cannot be amended, to deepen sorrow for what cannot be recalled.
>
> These are calamities by which Providence gradually disengages us from the love of life. Other evils fortitude may repel, or hope may mitigate; but irreparable privation leaves nothing to exercise resolution or flatter expectation. The dead cannot return, and nothing is left us here but languishment and grief.

Yet such is the course of nature, that whoever lives long must outlive those whom he loves and honours. Such is the condition of our present existence, that life must one time lose its associations, and every inhabitant of the earth must walk downward to the grave alone and unregarded, without any partner of his joy or grief, without any interested witness of his misfortunes or success.

Misfortune, indeed, he may yet feel, for where is the bottom of the misery of man? But what is success to him that has none to enjoy it. Happiness is not found in self-contemplation; it is perceived only when it is reflected from another.

We know little of the state of departed souls, because such knowledge is not necessary to a good life. Reason deserts us at the brink of the grave, and can give no further intelligence. Revelation is not wholly silent. "There is joy in the Angels of Heaven over one Sinner that repenteth," and surely this joy is not incommunicable to souls disentangled from the body, and made like Angels.

Let hope therefore dictate, what revelation does not confute, that the union of souls may still remain; and that we who are struggling with sin, sorrow, and infirmities, may have our part in the attention and kindness of those Who have finished their course, and are now receiving their reward.

*The Idler*, Number 41

I possess this Johnsonian dirge by memory but do not often recite it to myself. Though I revere him, we part company, and not just because he was a believing Christian. For me, survival is a mode akin to the work of mourning. Our beloved dead live only as long as we absorb them into our daily thoughts and feelings. When we die, our own survival will be the extent to which we have changed the lives of those who come after us.

Yesterday I was visited by two recent students, a young woman and a young man, both of whom had been a great comfort to me because they were brilliant, hardworking, and independent in spirit. They brought little presents from their days abroad, and I gave each of them the first three volumes of a series, *Shakespeare's Personalities*, that I finished writing last year. I am still in a wheelchair, recuperating from two serious operations, and I tire easily. But I went to bed last night cheered by their return.

Today has been a nightmare of a day, comic only in retrospect. As I was leaving my house this morning with my wife and a care provider, in order to have a CT scan of my painfully arthritic left knee, the care provider prematurely closed the back door of our house. We were locked out. After getting through the medical procedure, we came home, but I had to huddle three-quarters of an hour in the car while we waited for a locksmith to arrive. By the time I staggered back to my wheelchair, I was more than exhausted. It is now three hours later, and I have returned to the composition of this book. Nearing eighty-eight, I have to consider how little I know of time to come.

Doubtless it is better that way. Foretelling can be destructive. At this moment Proust is rather more of a comfort than my lifetime hero Dr. Samuel Johnson. Proust, like Shakespeare, teaches patience and the deliberate pace of an aesthetic awakening. Johnson's need is more urgent. His perilous balance is always in danger. Melancholia lurks, and Johnson fights idleness and dark inertia. You can hardly be more lucid than Johnson, but who has the strength to emulate him? Here he is bidding farewell to essay writing:

> Though the Idler and his reader have contracted no close friendship, they are, perhaps, both unwilling to part. There are few things not purely evil, of which we can say, without some emotion of uneasiness, "this is the last." Those who never could agree together, shed tears when mutual discontent has determined them to final separation; of a place which has been frequently visited, tho' without pleasure, the last look is taken with heaviness of heart; and the Idler, with all his chillness of tranquillity, is not wholly unaffected by the thought that his last essay is now before him.
>
> This secret horrour of the last is inseparable from a thinking being whose life is limited, and to whom death is dreadful. We always make a secret comparison between a part and the whole; the termination of any period of life reminds us that life itself has likewise its termination; when we have done any thing for the last time, we involuntarily reflect that a part of the days allotted us is past, and that as more is past there is less remaining.
>
> It is very happily and kindly provided, that in every life there are certain pauses and interruptions, which force consideration upon the careless, and seriousness upon the light; points of time

where one course of action ends, and another begins; and by vicissitudes of fortune or alteration of employment, by change of place or loss of friendship, we are forced to say of something, "this is the last."

An even and unvaried tenour of life always hides from apprehension the approach of its end. Succession is not perceived but by variation; he that lives to-day as he lived yesterday, and expects that, as the present day is, such will be the morrow, easily conceives time as running in a circle and returning to itself. The uncertainty of our duration is impressed commonly by dissimilitude of condition; it is only by finding life changeable that we are reminded of its shortness.

This conviction, however forcible at every new impression, is every moment fading from the mind; and partly by the inevitable incursion of new images, and partly by voluntary exclusion of unwelcome thoughts, we are again exposed to the universal fallacy; and we must do another thing for the last time, before we consider that the time is nigh when we shall do no more.

*The Idler,* Number 103

I find these paragraphs to be almost painful in their lucidity. If a pause or an interruption is a dangerous accident or illness, it would take Johnson's strength to call that a kind of fortunate fall. Mutability is double-edged. Though indubitably we are alerted by it, that awareness, as Johnson emphasizes, presages conclusion. Doing anything for the last time can resemble seeing a loved one depart. The time when we shall see, hear, and do no more is nigh in one's later eighties.

A NOTE ABOUT THE AUTHOR

Harold Bloom is a Sterling Professor of Humanities at Yale University and a former Charles Eliot Norton Professor at Harvard. His more than forty books include *The Anxiety of Influence, Shakespeare: The Invention of the Human, The Western Canon, The American Religion,* and *The Daemon Knows: Literary Greatness and the American Sublime.* He is a MacArthur Fellow, a member of the American Academy of Arts and Letters, and the recipient of many awards and honorary degrees, including the American Academy of Arts and Letters' Gold Medal for Belles Lettres and Criticism, the Catalonia International Prize, and Mexico's Alfonso Reyes International Prize. He lives in New Haven, Connecticut.

A NOTE ON THE TYPE

This book was set in Janson, a typeface long thought to have been made by the Dutchman Anton Janson, who was a practicing typefounder in Leipzig during the years 1668–1687. However, it has been conclusively demonstrated that these types are actually the work of Nicholas Kis (1650–1702), a Hungarian, who most probably learned his trade from the master Dutch typefounder Dirk Voskens. The type is an excellent example of the influential and sturdy Dutch types that prevailed in England up to the time William Caslon (1692–1766) developed his own incomparable designs from them.

*Composed by North Market Street Graphics, Lancaster, Pennsylvania*

*Printed and bound by Berryville Graphics, Berryville, Virginia*

*Designed by Maggie Hinders*